This book is an invaluable guide to one of the most singularly original contributions to social thought in the last 50 years. McHugh *et al.*'s *On The Beginning of Social Inquiry* began something genuinely new: radical reflexive analysis as a method of theorizing. Analysis begins from ethnomethodology's insight that social theory cannot uncover an objective 'reality', but rather than treating this as a limit, Analysis chooses instead to take it up as an invitation to discourse. Embracing ideas from Continental philosophy – Heidegger, Gadamer, Wittgenstein, Foucault, Derrida, Lacan are just some of the people who are folded into their ken – leading us backwards and forwards through the dialectic – Hegel, and always the Greeks, especially Socrates – the members of the Analysis community whose work is collected here bring us with them on a journey, soaring over broad vistas of social thought; taking us down into the capillaries of social life, revealing structures and processes in lucid and astonishing detail; leading us into illuminated clearings, taking us to the edge of vertiginous aporias, showing us radiant epiphanies; so that by the time one leaves the pages of this book you know as never before what Hegel means when he says that 'the path towards truth coincides with the truth itself'. The contributors of this book show Analysis is still fresh and powerful today, while other currents of theory have flooded and ebbed. Simultaneously an intellectual genealogy and a display of the art of Analysis in practice, Blum's own chapter is a virtuoso performance.

Kieran Keohane, *School of Sociology and Philosophy, University College Cork,*
Ireland

This is a profound book, dealing with nothing less than the problems of the grounds for reflexive speech, radical self-reflection and encountering indebtedness. It is a timely collection of reflexive dialogic inquiries; particularly germane in the present climate of new positivistic empiricisms associated with the dataverse. It will be of great interest to anyone concerned with the future of sociological theorizing and its ethical and ontological dimensions.

Martin Hand, *Department of Sociology, Queen's University, Canada*

The Reflexive Initiative

The Reflexive Initiative is an authoritative intervention in the practice and tradition of reflexive social theory. It demonstrates the importance of the reflexive imperative, not only in the investigation of everyday life but across a wide range of human sciences and philosophical perspectives. Forty years after the publication of *On the Beginning of Social Inquiry*, the chapters in this collection range from re-appraisals of earlier essays on topics such as 'reunions', 'rethinking art' and 'expats' to contributions emphasizing the opening of radical dialogues with other reflexive traditions and perspectives. These include psychoanalysis, Lacan, Hegel, René Girard, *Daseinanalysis*, dialectical method, critical feminism, and the dialogical tradition.

In this dialogical spirit, the book contributes to the continuing project of analytic theorizing associated with the work of Alan Blum and Peter McHugh, and the recent turn to more 'existential' topics and politically engaged forms of reflexive research. It will be of particular use to students working in interpretive traditions of sociology, Critical theory, Postmodern thought and debates associated with reflexivity and dialectics in other disciplines and research programmes.

Stanley Raffel is Honorary Fellow in the Department of Sociology at the University of Edinburgh, UK.

Barry Sandywell is Honorary Fellow in Social Theory in the Department of Sociology at the University of York, UK.

Routledge Advances in Sociology

The Reflexive Initiative

On the grounds and prospects of analytic theorizing

Edited by Stanley Raffel and Barry Sandywell

Routledge
Taylor & Francis Group

LONDON AND NEW YORK

First published 2016 by Routledge

2 Park Square, Milton Park, Abingdon, Oxfordshire OX14 4RN
52 Vanderbilt Avenue, New York, NY 10017

Routledge is an imprint of the Taylor & Francis Group, an informa business

First issued in paperback 2019

British Library Cataloguing in Publication Data
A catalogue record for this book is available from the British Library

Library of Congress Cataloging in Publication Data
Names: Raffel, Stanley, editor. | Sandywell, Barry, editor.
Title: The reflexive initiative : on the grounds and prospects of analytic
theorizing / edited by Stanley Raffel and Barry Sandywell.
Description: New York : Routledge, 2016. | Series: Routledge advances in
sociology
Identifiers: LCCN 2015041854| ISBN 9781138911468 (hardback) |
ISBN 9781315692654 (e-book)
Subjects: LCSH: Sociology.
Classification: LCC HM585 .R44 2016 | DDC 301–dc23
LC record available at http://lccn.loc.gov/2015041854

ISBN: 978-1-138-91146-8 (hbk)
ISBN: 978-0-367-87342-4 (pbk)

Typeset in Times New Roman
by Wearset Ltd, Boldon, Tyne and Wear

For Isabel Sandywell and Elaine Samuel

Contents

Contributors

Steve Bailey is Associate Professor in the Department of Humanities and Department of Science and Technology Studies York University, Toronto, and Researcher in the Culture of Cities Centre, Toronto, Canada.

Alan Blum is Executive Director of the Culture of Cities Centre Toronto and Senior Scholar in the Departments of Sociology, Social and Political Thought, and Communication and Culture at York University, Toronto, Canada.

Kieran Bonner is Professor, Chair of Sociology and Legal Studies and Director of Human Sciences at St. Jerome's University in the University of Waterloo, Ontario, Canada.

Patrick Colfer is an Independent Scholar at Whitehorse, Yukon, Canada.

Richard Feesey is an Independent Scholar at Maentwrog, North Wales.

Saeed Hydaralli is Assistant Professor in the Department of Anthropology and Sociology at Roger Williams University, Bristol, Rhode Island.

Stephen Kemp is Senior Lecturer in the Department of Sociology at the University of Edinburgh, UK.

Eric Laurier is Senior Lecturer in Geography and Interaction in the Department of Geography at the University of Edinburgh, UK.

David A. Lynes is Associate Professor in the Department of Sociology at St. Frances Xavier University in Antigonish, Nova Scotia, Canada.

Andriani Papadopoulou is Instructor at the Institute of Training of The National Centre of Public Administration & Local Government (EKDDA) and Senior Investigator at the Human Rights Department of the Greek Ombudsman, Athens, Greece.

Stanley Raffel is Honorary Fellow in the Department of Sociology at the University of Edinburgh, UK.

Barry Sandywell is Honorary Fellow in Social Theory in the Department of Sociology at the University of York, UK.

Gregor Schnuer is Research Associate in History at the University of Luxembourg in Luxembourg City, Luxembourg.

Part I
Editors' introduction

1 The origins and prospects of analytic theorizing

Stanley Raffel and Barry Sandywell

The papers collected in this book were originally presented at a conference held at Edinburgh University in June 2014 to celebrate the 40th anniversary of the publication of *On the Beginning of Social Inquiry* (McHugh *et al.*, 1974). Here we seek to provide some sense of what the 1974 book represented and why it seemed right both to celebrate it and now to publish, in considerably revised form, many of the papers from the conference.

Origins and beginnings

In the second half of the 1960s, Alan Blum and Peter McHugh, two young sociology professors who were then at Columbia University in New York, began to teach and work together. Their intellectual collaboration, aided by a small group of committed students, resulted in an initiative that amounted to creating nothing less than a new method for doing sociology, called Analysis. The complex range of sources and resources, both classic and contemporary, that influenced Blum and McHugh during this period are depicted in the chapter by Sandywell in Part II of this volume. Undoubtedly, however, the key conscious influence was another new sociological method becoming well known at the time, the Ethnomethodology of Harold Garfinkel (Garfinkel, 1967). Ethnomethodology cast doubt on the claim to objectivity of any and all accounts, not least the supposedly scientific accounts offered by certain traditions of sociology, by pointing to their reflexive nature and how they are inevitably produced in and by members' situated work rather than being merely neutral *observations* or *representations* of the 'real world'.

Blum and McHugh thoroughly endorsed Ethnomethodology's radical critique as a provocation for more principled reflection on the motivation and rationales of sociological work. For them the irreducible reflexivity of all sociological work and research, in both its theories and its supposed 'findings', means that whatever its conclusions amount to, they can no longer be considered things in the world that one can claim to have discovered. While Analysis accepted Ethnomethodology's critique of conventional or normative sociology, it did not accept the consequences that Garfinkel and his students derived from this critique. To retain the empirical credentials and programmatic momentum of his new method Garfinkel had concluded that it was necessary to avoid reflexivity entirely and, in an attempt to do so, recommended that all researchers could do was to describe others' (including sociologists') methods for producing what they (naively) thought of as their findings. Contesting this conclusion, Blum and McHugh argued that this kind of positivist indifference to self-reflection resulted in an extremely narrow and limited role for the sociologist and, more generally, for creative sociological work. According to Garfinkel, not just conventional empirical findings, but also the entire enterprise of theorizing, could be set aside or even abandoned altogether. 'Theory' had become 'mere theory'. All received talk of critical reason, philosophical tradition and dialectical transgression was to be treated as merely theorists' versions of everyday life on par with members' accounts of similar phenomenal objects. Against this attitude, Analysis suggested that as long as one could propose a mode of theorizing that, far from denying, embraced reflexivity and self-reflection, abandoning theorizing, besides being undesirable, was not actually necessary or, perhaps, even possible. As a consequence of this commitment the meaning of the art of theorizing and the significance of past efforts to live and think theoretically became much more consequential.

The path beyond ethnomethodological indifference was first tentatively displayed in the jointly authored paper, 'The Social Ascription of Motives' (Blum and McHugh, 1971), and then, in much more fully articulated form, in two books published in 1974: the book that is the subject of this conference, *On the Beginning of Social Inquiry*, and Alan Blum's *Theorizing* (Blum, 1974). In keeping with the content of this current book, we focus on how the method is developed in *On the Beginning of Social Inquiry* (*OBSI*). Several, on the face of it, peculiar features of this work become comprehensible given the task the authors faced.

Like other theoretical works, *OBSI* offers formulations of real-life phenomena such as bias, evaluation, snubs, art, and travel. However, it insists that the reader pay equal or even more attention, not to the formulations, but to how the formulations are being produced. This insistence provides ways in which the theorist can recover the methodic character of her own reflexivity and research as situated practices. Furthermore, it is admitted that, even though the formulations begin by attending to how 'members' would understand the topics addressed, what eventually ensues are violations of members' understanding. This theorists' 'violence' is designed to show that without the methodic commitments that the authors are consciously utilizing to produce their work, their productions, however desirable, would not be possible. This principle of displaying the artful, rhetorical, and moral grounds of practices – whether lay or professional – would become a recognizable feature of Analytic work.

OBSI is distinctive amongst collectively authored books in the claim that multiple authorship is, for the Analytic perspective, a matter of principle. Second authors, tasked to work out the method of production of first authors, are essential as another way in which there can be at once a product and yet an attentiveness to how the product was both concretely and theoretically produced, that is, to its reflexive nature as a mediated formulation.

Still another apparent oddity is the authors' refusal to claim that their completed book is finished and, furthermore, that this incompleteness should not be regarded as a defect or limitation. The way in which the work is unfinished is that, *qua* product, how it too was produced itself needs to be grasped for the book to be intelligible. In this case, the reflexive nature of the work is further sustained by asking readers to reflect on how the authors could have produced their work and, thereby, to 'finish' what the book had only started. The papers in the 1974 work were in every sense both initiatives for and provocations to further reflexive thought and research.

Collaboration as an analytic topic and resource

On the Beginning of Social Inquiry was aptly named because what the work proposed was indeed the beginning of something quite different from conventional forms of sociology and social theory. We do not propose here to offer a full history of what happened next, among other reasons this not being possible because the story is by no means over. We confine ourselves to aspects of the subsequent history necessary to provide contexts for the current book. Blum and McHugh were determined to sustain their collaboration after leaving Columbia. After a few years of temporary posts, both managed to secure positions at York University in Toronto where they remained for their entire teaching careers. At York, the method of Analysis was developed not just in their writing but also in the distinctive way in which both theorists innovated in teaching and relating to their students.

For the most part, they avoided, as much as possible, and especially with advanced students who had grasped and were committed to the rudiments of Analysis, traditional academic lectures in favour of a form of teaching in keeping with their commitment to reflexivity. Students were encouraged, indeed required, to express opinions about the topics at hand and these were treated, like the papers in *On the Beginning of Social Inquiry*, as reflexive accomplishments whose mode of production needed to be formulated. This recurrent work of formulation and reformulation constituted the concerted task of contributors to these seminars.

While the seminar format is an accepted form of good university practice, what Blum and McHugh were doing was actually as different from the conventional seminar as it was from conventional lectures. In the typical seminar, the focus is on the exchange of opinions, students being encouraged to have as many of them as possible. In their seminars, what was meant to be attended to – dwelt upon – was the possibility of any one opinion. When, being accustomed to the more typical procedure, a student tried merely to offer another opinion, that act was discouraged as constituting a distraction and deferring the engagement with analytic *work*.

As a result, the classes could be disconcerting, with students realizing that whatever they said would be taken seriously, producing the consequence that there were long periods of silence, with the teacher declining to fill the void just for the sake of it. While some students failed to appreciate this new experience that was being offered to them, a growing group of them came to identify themselves with the project of Analysis and this identification continues to this day. The present text, *The Reflexive Initiative*, has been designed to demonstrate the work of current practitioners of Analysis. While working out a new method for social theorizing, because of its explicit commitment to self-reflection, what was emerging as a collectivity, indeed even a kind of community, came to see that what it was doing was not so new after all. The community came to see its activities as having deep resonances with a classic tradition of theorizing, originating in the dialectical tradition of ancient Greek thought, and 'perhaps best encapsulated in the complex figure of Socrates' (Blum and McHugh, 1979: 1; cf. Blum and McHugh, 1980: 1–2).

As such, whereas in common with other academic movements, the Analysis community held conferences, it is fair to say that its conferences were different, more intense, affairs because any and all presented material was, again in keeping with the principle of dialogue and self-reflexivity, grist for extended collective reformulation. Many of the papers in *The Reflexive Initiative* stress the fundamental importance of this 'dialogical turn' in contemporary social and philosophical theory (see, in particular, the chapters by Sandywell, Bonner, and Lynes). These collective events were where what was attempted in the classroom was freed from the inevitable limitations generated by institutional constraints and so was allowed freely to flourish. What ensued was a far cry from the conventional and, it has to be said, reified format of an author presenting a paper followed by a limited and ritualistic few minutes of 'discussion'. Collective reformulation, when it worked, served the purpose, not of either leaving papers intact or robbing authors of their selves but of giving them a voice in something like Jean-Luc Nancy's sense that we are best seen not as 'individuals' but as 'multiple … existences, which nonetheless only make sense by existing in common' (Nancy, 1991: xl). Participating in such conferences, like doing Analytic research or writing Analytic sociology, became a fully collaborative enterprise. The outcomes of this kind of dialogical collaboration were singular texts that exemplified this kind of collectively distributed creativity. The lengths to which Analysis went to pursue its interest in developing a viable form of reflexive dialogue should not be underestimated. Even the idea of a normal length conference in an academic setting was seen as too constricting. What eventually became the norm was Analysts meeting every summer for three full weeks. These events were described by Blum and McHugh as follows:

> The international summer institute convenes every year in Perugia, Italy, under our direction it is intended to invigorate and sustain the intellectual interests of its participants by encouraging their collaboration for the purpose of developing, deepening and discussing their work, and to re-fertilize communal interest in self-reflection through the conversation of its members.
>
> (Blum and McHugh, 1980: 4)

The main reason for having such extended events in a congenial setting was to overcome the limitations imposed on self-reflective dialogue by the classroom and its institutional constraints. But an interesting, if largely unanticipated, consequence of this format should also be noted. Some young Analysts were becoming *so* committed to self-reflection that they were losing a sense of how it could and should be integrated with the rest of their lives and with the non-Analytic community.

There was the danger that, as they were becoming adept at the work, they were losing the ability to be, in ordinary ways, sociable. Besides enabling practitioners to develop their skills at engaging in self-reflection, working and living together in this extended way also helped Analysts to see where, when, and how they could integrate normal life with their developing commitment.

As these scenarios gave the community a unique opportunity to 'do Analysis' in a more dynamic and extended way than was possible in the traditional classroom setting, its conferences were considered an essential activity of the community and tradition of reflexive sociology. They were, for some years, held annually and were a major communal event. However, for various practical reasons, not least life exigencies and competing academic and even financial demands upon ex-students who were now academics in their own right, they ceased to happen with the last one in fact being way back in 1984.

Revisiting *On the Beginning of Social Inquiry*

In 2014, Alan Blum, mindful of the fact that many of the core group of Analysts were not getting any younger and perhaps, above all, of the fact that his collaborator, Peter McHugh, had sadly recently passed away, suggested that the time was ripe to have again what we had not had for so long, another Analysis conference. He also suggested, as the topic, revisiting the book that had started it all, the occasion being the 40th anniversary of the original publication of *On the Beginning of Social Inquiry* in 1974.

Some twenty participants gathered in Edinburgh in June 2014. Edinburgh University's geography department kindly provided the venue and its sociology department generously offered some financial assistance. The event was organized by Stanley Raffel and Eric Laurier, two lecturers at Edinburgh University. Participants were unified by their interest in and knowledge of Analysis, yet despite being unified in this way it was at the same time a surprisingly diverse group, including ex-students of Blum and McHugh of various ages, much younger students of their students, and persons who knew the work only through its publications. There were participants who still worked together on a daily basis, some who knew each other well but had not met for many years, and others who, on a personal level at least, were total strangers.

We have suggested that conferences occupy a special, arguably more important, place for Analysis than for other academic disciplines or groups because its meetings are conceived as concerted conversational opportunities. They are not just where the work is reported. They are a place where the work – and process of working – is actually done. As such, each conference amounts to an event. Things, often surprising things, happen. The conference itself therefore presents itself as another subject for self-reflection on the life and processes of communality.

A sense of the actual process of the Edinburgh conference is not, of course, accessible just by reading this volume (interested readers are directed to the Edinburgh University web site at www.sedit.org.uk/Events/Beginnings/ where the presentations are available as video and audio files). However, something of its flavour can be conveyed by comparing it to Blum and McHugh's retro-spective remarks on the collective's very first conference, held just a few years after the two books that launched Analysis were published. That first conference, held at Goldsmith's College in London, brought together a large number of Blum and McHugh students from York University, Toronto with other students and young lecturers, also interested in Analysis, either based at Goldsmith's or Edinburgh University. Given the intensely polemical context of social theory during this decade, the event proved not to be completely harmonious. It gener-ated tensions which are described by Blum and McHugh as follows.

The conference:

> made an issue of what it is to be familiar and of how to reconcile the viol-ence of theorizing with the humane and nurturant roots of familiarity.... The conference permitted many to see that they had wanted familiarity at the price of criticalness and often these many left disappointed. It also per-mitted others to appreciate how criticism could turn into contempt unless it respected its unity with those whom it sought to engage and some of these others left a little wiser.
>
> (Blum and McHugh, 1979: 17)

The two concrete phenomena to which they are referring are the challenges that the composition of the participants produced both for relations among familiars and for those with mutual strangers. Those familiar with one another had to face the fact, with varying degrees of eventual acceptance, that sheer familiarity did not exempt anyone from criticism. At the same time, strangers had to face the fact, again with varying degrees of acceptance, that the inevitable differences between them could too easily obscure a fundamental unity that could be developed if only they could resist the temptation of contempt with the aid of the considerable resources that the constructive engagement that is conversation could provide.

The issues faced at this first conference became some of the topics for Ana-lysis in subsequent years. In teaching and further conferences, there was a greater awareness of the danger of becoming insular and that the expression of differences and, not least, the activity of self-criticism were therefore to be encouraged. As for the problem of the stranger, it was continually stressed that speaking to those who appear strange, far from being an occasion for contempt, is a prime way in which Analysis can practice its principle.

In applying this principle of engaged self-reflective conversation with strangers, both sides of the coin need to be remembered. While newcomers – non-familiars – may well appear strange to veteran analysts, equally these Analysts must realize that, due to the fact that their method is neither natural nor even in keeping with common sense, they will inevitably appear strange even to the most receptive of newcomers. Here, learning that sociability is not inconsistent with self-reflection, as Perugia tried to teach in practice, was a critical resource.

In that its composition was very similar to the Goldsmith's conference since it too included both individuals who were already familiar with one another (though in many cases long separated by time and place) and also many who did not know each other personally but had a shared interest in Analysis, largely through having read *On the Beginning of Social Inquiry*, the Edinburgh event amounted to a test of whether the community had changed in these desirable ways over the years. We think it is fair to say that the event did not suffer from the same problems as its predecessor. Instead of familiars expecting to be exempted from criticism, some of the strongest criticism was among those well acquainted with one another. And instead of contempt for those among whom unity of purpose was not immediately apparent, the mutual respect developed in the course of the conference among those meeting for the first time was very striking. We think the differences suggest that the collective is now both less dogmatic and less insular. At the same time it is in keeping with the self-reflective principle of Analysis that we at least consider whether some of this new-found openness to the outside and relative harmony within might be at the cost of some weakening of the work's originary violence, which is to say the way the work displays its difference from the practices of 'members'.

Themes from *The Reflexive Initiative*

As the conference was deemed a success, we proposed publishing a volume of selected papers presented and discussed by participants. In keeping with Analysis' principles, each of the authors represented here has been asked to revise his or her paper in the aftermath of and in the light of the conversation as it developed at the Edinburgh event. The studies in this volume, then, should be thought of as the results of the collective engagement with their papers that each of our authors experienced as they presented their paper and listened to the other papers presented to the group as a whole. We think their worth is best seen if they are thought of as still separate voices that manage, albeit in very different ways, to further develop and even deepen what was produced at the beginning.

In line with Analysis' core principles, we now offer our own, but certainly not anything like an exhaustive, reflection on what we, as editors, make of what both unifies and distinguishes the papers that follow.

Both Bailey and Kemp try to show how it is misleading merely to assess the work as an offshoot of Ethnomethodology. Bailey concentrates on its relation to a continental interpretive tradition. He also emphasizes its playful, even poetic, qualities that belie any sense that it is best seen as a form of science, the status that Ethnomethodology claims for itself. In a similar spirit Kemp identifies Analysis' affinities with Feminist Constructionism rooted in an interest in the situated nature of speech and a resistance to neutrality that the two approaches share in common.

Colfer and Papadopoulou both address the fact that the 1974 book was a work of collaboration. Colfer worries whether, at least in this early work, the authors have achieved their self-confessed ideal of a method that is, among other things, enjoyable, since he sees the form of collaboration articulated as more in the tragic than comic mode. Papadopoulou suggests that a stronger version of collaboration than the authors envision would necessitate that one pay more explicit attention to the inevitability of resistance whenever and wherever collaboration is attempted. Lynes, too, addresses the book's dialectical method but in his case the issue that concerns him is further developing how Analysis can at once orient to the concrete-and-everyday and yet differentiate and sustain its own activity of being an Analytic exploration of mundane phenomena and the quotidian world.

Several authors follow the earlier book in analysing specific topics, often by reflecting further on aspects of the topics covered in that book. Taking his bearings from the book's analyses of snubs and bias, Schnuer explores how sincerity could be an Analytic version of honesty. If we accept his conclusion, we see that even avowedly anti-positivist work can have an interest in a kind of truth. Laurier is also stimulated by the *Snubs* paper, but in his case by imagining a different ending for the usage where instead of a snub, the opposite happens. He and we learn that the opposite would not be, as the *Snubs* paper would assume, just a greeting but instead what Laurier depicts as a reunion, with, as his analysis shows, everything entailed by that particular form of social interaction.

Raffel returns to the terrain occupied by the *Art* paper by examining ambiguities not yet touched on or at least fully addressed there concerning the nature of art. He also suggests, contrary to a possible impression created by the earlier book, how some art forms may be quite revealing of the material out of which they are produced. Feesey, taking his initial orientation from the depiction of travel in the 1974 book, analyses persons who cease merely to travel by becoming expats. He develops the ironies that cannot be avoided by a group who he interprets as seeking to have nothing more than an instrumental relation to their place of residence. Hydaralli, while recognizably using Analysis as his method, applies the method to a topic for which there is no precedent in the earlier book, the social activity of complaining. Whereas, as he points out, complainers are normally maligned, his idea is that there is a need for complaints to be artful and, insofar as they are, their social worth should not be underestimated.

The most wide-ranging papers in the volume discussing, in various ways, Analysis as a whole, are those by Bonner, Sandywell, and Blum. What is perhaps most striking in Bonner's paper is the demonstration of Analysis' willingness to face what other forms of theorizing ignore, either unintentionally or even wilfully. As he brings to the surface the original authors' struggle with seemingly contradictory demands, we see both the inventiveness and even a kind of courage that the development of the method required.

Sandywell shows how the 1974 book which all the papers and the conference were revisiting was, in so many ways, an *eventful*, game-changing text within larger theoretical frameworks and philosophical debates. He suggests how the work was at once singular and yet not (despite numerous claims to the contrary by mainstream sociologists and other critics) eccentric. He shows it to be quite other than eccentric both because it can be seen as a dialectical product of its time and yet, not being confined to its initial context, it retains its status as a significant contribution to an enduring tradition, the beginning of a new beginning for social thought.

Blum helps us to realize that, for a self-reflective theorist, the benefit of hindsight is no vice. He draws out implications and resonances of *On the Beginning of Social Inquiry* that were not apparent at the time, not just to his co-authors but even to Blum himself. What emerges is a book whose revealed architectural structure makes it seem more coherent today than it did on first publication. He is also prepared, as others and especially Sandywell do in places, to suggest reservations about how Analysis originally presented itself. In particular, he finds the way the work first announced itself as too polemical. We can say, therefore, that a clear sign that the work has progressed would be if the papers in this volume that do engage at length with notions and theories other than their own manage to do so in a way that cannot be dismissed as adversarial.

Analysis and its relevance for contemporary social thought

Another issue that a volume of this nature, returning to a work published so long ago, must address is, of course, the question of its continuing relevance. We suggest that the clearest answer to this question can be found in the papers that follow and the exposition of existential and theoretical principles that lies at their core. Many of these contributions are explicitly concerned with developing themes that are of enduring concern to any kind of social analysis. Indeed, several of the papers, notably Blum's and Sandywell's, show how what Analysis proposes and implements – what we have called *the reflexive initiative* – continues to exercise current theorists and researchers, including the most cutting-edge developments in contemporary social thought. Our fundamental claim is that Analytic theorizing retains its significance as a radical intervention within the major discourses of social theory and the human sciences.

To introduce readers to these issues we can briefly sketch a number of themes and problems that remain central to both Analysis and the wider project of modern social thought.

The first is the question of the attitude that contemporary radical inquiry should adopt in coming to terms with what might be called the 'postmodern turn' in social thought. Poststructuralist thought in particular – exemplified in the texts of Jacques Derrida, Roland Barthes, Julia Kristeva, Michel Foucault, Jean-François Lyotard, Gilles Deleuze, Alain Badiou, among others – had also discovered that every form of analysis is only possible through the discourses and practices provided by the wider symbolic order – these being typically identified by an intensive concern with the work of language, discourse and the symbolic constitution of the subject, and gendered subjectivity. This also interfaced with the so-called 'cultural turn' in Cultural Studies and Literary Theory (or what has simply been called 'Theory' (Culler, 1997)). Both currents converged in making language, cultural signification, and the unrepresentable horizon of desire and alterity – what Jacques Lacan would call 'the Other' (1977, 1978) – central to any kind of human identity and self-understanding. The most influential proposals for a critical alternative to orthodox inquiry over the past two or three decades – Deconstruction, Poststructuralist Feminism, Critical Theory, Genealogy, Critical Hermeneutics, Critical Narratology, New Historicism, Postcolonial Theory, Social Constructivism, Discourse Analysis, among these – have in practice defined their programmes by challenging and revising earlier forms of knowledge and theory. But these frameworks rarely make their status as language or their own implicit sense of critique and methodic commitments thematic as fundamental concerns. In many cases they efficiently analyse the aftermath of what Max Weber called 'the disenchantment of the world' but offer no alternatives or ethical critique of the social world after the demise of grand narratives (Lyotard, 1984). In this sense they remain complicit with the object of their critiques. This lack of self-reflection impacted upon sociology (and the social sciences) in multiple ways. One was the shared reception of poststructural thought as merely another variation of cultural relativism. Another was to view all these alternatives as a kind of pick-and-mix resource for constructing 'research-as-usual'. A third was to mistake the concern for the power of language and self-reflection as a diversion from the 'serious' work of doing sociology, social research, philosophy and other academic pursuits. For example, methodology after the 'cultural turn' to language and signification could no longer settle for the 'either/or' that divides inquiry into qualitative description and narrative or quantitative algorithms. But it also could not question its own 'over-determination' in being socially and historically located within many of the problems and paradoxes of postmodern culture. Exponents of new methodological breakthroughs and conceptual innovations refused to engage in more radical reflection on their own discursive possibility and moral status. In other words, the 'limits of disenchantment' were neither fully understood nor transcended (Dews, 1995). Even the most radical of 'alternatives' such as the grammatology of Derrida (1976, 1978) or the fusion of Hegelian dialectics and Lacanian psychoanalysis (Žižek, 1993, 2007), arguably, were unable to develop a convincing alternative to the metaphysics of presence and the inherited model of language as reflection, neutral reference, and representation. For example, the very idea of dividing method into either descriptive representation or mathematical modelling proved to be another variation of the received ontology of subjectivity and objectivity. Even the practices of Deconstruction remain vulnerable to one of the radical claims of Analysis, that a theory must provide for its own possibility rather than just interpret, however 'playful' or 'active', rather than objective, it claims its interpretations to be. In this respect Analysis was even more decisive in rejecting positivist, correspondence-based ways of thinking about language and reality. Once every form of methodic procedure – whether classical, modernist or postmodernist – is grasped as a particular *rhetoric* or discursive formation, the processes and outcomes of these methodological procedures appear as *topics* that invite reflexive interrogation and critical reformulation.

What can contemporary sociology and social theory learn from Analysis? The answer is already implicit in Blum and McHugh's editorial introduction to their journal *Maieutics*:

> The difference between our community … and other communities resides in our continuous desire to formulate the moral character of the authority which centres and animates discourse as a way of conducting our own self-reflection upon the limits of community. Yet that difference will remain covert or merely external until the reader collaborates in the work of recollecting the ways in which our studies reflect and embody this desire, and this is our invitation to the reader.
>
> (1980: 2–3)

The reflexive imperative requires every form of inquiry – indeed every way of making the world meaningful – to answer the question, How is your own form of speech, narrative, and algorithmic reason possible as a moral commitment and form of life? What are the existential problems for which *these* ways of speaking are solutions? Here reflexive sociology was already acutely aware that epistemological and ontological self-critique is only the first phase of a much more radical ethical interrogation of discourse formations and ways of life. In this context the reformulations of tradition and history undertaken by theorists like Derrida, Lyotard, Foucault, and Deleuze were insufficiently self-reflexive and critical toward their own ways of conducting inquiry and pursuing self-reflective work. Or, expressed, more analytically, the metaphoric image of tradition as a linear conversation of critical discourse and of history as an unproblematic resource were left unquestioned. How their own discourses 'constituted' viable alternative ways of thinking and critiques were thus left unexplicated. Analysis argued that this kind of blindness was in fact a *generic* problem for all unreflective conceptions of social science and philosophical analysis. And even more consequentially, the multiple possibilities and intermittency of past forms of life and their disruptive heterogeneity with respect to received versions of language and historical reason were occluded (cf. Gibson, 2012).

Second, one of the key initiatives of the 1974 work was not merely a critique of objectivism and the general climate of positivism that characterized the social science methodologies of the day, but an indication of the nature of the kind of radicalism that would not only be capable of uncovering the ontological and ethical premises of every type of scientism, but of formulating the parameters for an alternative way of speaking and theorizing that might replace every form of unreflective social science. As the papers by Bonner, Blum, and Sandywell suggest, the continued relevance of this argument points towards a much more radical idea of collaborative dialogue underwritten by a conception of dialectical thought and writing that invites self-transformation and extension to whole domains of contemporary phenomena and problematics. As we have noted above, Analysis presupposes a radically different attitude to academic teaching and writing as *productive sites of moral life*. It follows from the principle of continuous dialogue that education as self-formulation and transformation necessarily requires basic changes in pedagogic formats and learning procedures. Besides the evidence of the work itself, it perhaps suffices to say that Analysis has passed the test of time in at least two ways, both that what it is arguing against still needs the vigorous opposition it initiated and that what it proposes continues to be the most constructive way forward beyond the impasse of Critical Theory and Postmodern thought.

One particular example of this regression to the discredited methodologies of traditional sociology is the renewal of a 'global' empiricism linked to the development of 'big data' analytics. It is true that the digital revolution and the expansion of new social media and the Internet of Things have made the collection, archiving, and algorithmic analysis of vast amounts of 'social data' a routine feature of both private and public agencies. But far from making the concerns of classical and critical theorizing redundant, the politics of data archiving and their corporate and administrative application in shaping what passes for collective choice and democratic life makes reflexive social inquiry even more imperative. In this respect the critique of administrative thinking and the commitment to the universality of self-reflexive work remains as an enduring legacy of Analysis and its particular exemplification in *On the Beginning of Social Inquiry*. In the present climate of neo-liberalism and revisionary empiricisms the need for the theory and practice of self-reflection is even more imperative.

Third, the continuing relevance of questions of meaning, interpretation and significance in social analysis. The perspective Analysis exemplifies is one of the most explicit ways in which questions of meaning and language in everyday life – and more particularly how we are always-already related to one another – can be made analysable and accessible. We refer here to the recognition, shared for example with Phenomenology, Deconstruction and Discourse Analysis, intellectual movements that are certainly not going away, that the work of addressing questions of meaning and understanding requires a willingness and, indeed, eagerness to undertake the adventure and risks of engaged interpretation. The *Experience-World correlation* of these earlier traditions appears in Analytic work as the *Language-Being nexus* that informs the deep structure of everyday life activities. This revaluation of engaged speech as a form of communal experience is a consequence of the principled rejection of conceptions of sense as merely effects of either passive looking and seeing or the application of pre-formed concepts and discourse. Both extensionalist and intentionalist conceptions of meaning elide the irreducible contingency and the situated creativity of figural language, metaphor and meaningful interpretation as this unfolds in everyday life, the arts, and analytic work (Raffel, 2013).

The historical arc of Analysis has moved from relatively traditional and 'bounded' debates within the human sciences – initially motivated by concerns with self-reflection that arose in relation to debates within phenomenological thought and ethnomethodological studies – to broader questions concerned with the very meaning, significance, and survival of inquiry in the Information Age, the cultural functions of dialogue and traditions of dialectical thought as ways of interrogating the technological transformation of everyday life, and the question of the ethical grounds of reflection in the sciences, arts, and philosophy. All of these questions indicate problems for future Analytic work.

Finally, what Analysis has defended for more than four decades retains its investigative and political relevance. The core idea of the art of theorizing 'expresses our desire to re-collect the centre of discourse, to address in various ways the question of how discourse is morally centred. In turn, our interest in centring the art of theorizing is expressed through the creation of different ways of articulating our commitment to the problem of morally centred inquiry' (Blum and McHugh, 1980: 2). Taken together these emergent issues and problematics lead to a more radical attitude toward hermeneutic interpretation and collective work that we hope will restore the sense of collective engagement, humour, and jouissance that we suggest are essential features of all creative dialogue.

Bibliography

Blum, Alan (1974) *Theorizing*. London: Heinemann.

Blum, Alan and McHugh, Peter (1971) 'The Social Ascription of Motives' *American Sociological Review*, Vol. 36, No. 1, pp. 98–109.

Blum, Alan and McHugh, Peter (1979) 'Introduction', in *Friends, Enemies, and Strangers*. Norwood, New Jersey: Ablex.

Blum, Alan and McHugh, Peter (1980) 'Editors' Introduction' *Maieutics*, Vol. 1, No. 1, pp. 1–4.

Culler, Jonathan (1997) *Literary Theory. A Very Short Introduction*. Oxford: Oxford University Press.

Derrida, Jacques (1976) *Of Grammatology*. trans. Gayatri Chaktavorty Spivak. Baltimore: Johns Hopkins University Press.

Derrida, Jacques (1978) *Writing and Difference*. trans. A. Bass, Chicago: University of Chicago Press.

Dews, Peter (1995) *The Limits of Disenchantment: Essays on Contemporary European Philosophy*. London and New York: Verso.

Garfinkel, Harold (1967) *Studies in Ethnomethodology*. Englewood Cliffs, New Jersey: Prentice Hall.

Gibson, Andrew (2012) *Intermittency: The Concept of Historical Reason in Recent French Philosophy*. Edinburgh: Edinburgh University Press.

Lacan, Jacques (1977) *Écrits: A Selection*. trans. A. Sheridan. London: Routledge, New York: W.W. Norton.

Lacan, Jacques (1978) *The Four Fundamental Concepts of Psycho-Analysis*. trans. A. Sheridan. New York: W.W. Norton.

Lyotard, Jean-François (1984) *The Postmodern Condition: A Report on Knowledge*. trans. G. Bennington and B. Massumi. Manchester: University of Manchester Press.

McHugh, Peter, Raffel, Stanley, Foss, Daniel C., and Blum, Alan (1974) *On the Beginning of Social Inquiry*. London: Routledge and Kegan Paul.

Nancy, Jean-Luc (1991) *The Inoperative Community* trans. P. Connor, L. Garbus, M. Holland and S. Sawhney. Minneapolis: University of Minnesota Press.

Raffel, Stanley (2013) *The Method of Metaphor*. Bristol: Intellect.

Žižek, Slavoj (1993) *Tarrying with the Negative: Kant, Hegel and the Critique of Ideology*. Durham, North Carolina: Duke University Press.

Žižek, Slavoj (2007) *How to Read Lacan*. New York: W.W. Norton.

Part II

History and contexts of analytic theory

2 Dialectic, indebtedness, ambivalence, and the pursuit of analytic speech

Revisiting *On the Beginning of Social Inquiry*

Barry Sandywell

The following essay has been developed from analyses, questions, and responses occasioned by an invitation from Stanley Raffel and Eric Laurier to re-visit and re-read On the Beginning of Social Inquiry *(OBSI in the text). Given its particular context these responses are necessarily incomplete, originating from commentary and marginalia made in my original copy of the 1974 publication, from memories of my own participation in seminars with Alan Blum and Peter McHugh during the early 1970s (c.1971–1974), and from creative – and continuing – questions that the papers in the book, and the project of Analytical theorizing more generally, still provoke and inspire. Modifications to the original text were helped by lectures and discussions held at the Edinburgh Conference on OBSI from June 10th to June 11th 2014.*

I have organized these marginalia into topics that are, of course, in no way independent, complete or definitive of the possibilities disclosed by the Analytic studies assembled in OBSI. My hope is that these are not simply an observer's 'nomenclature of headings' (OBSI: 105) that disguise and defer my own historical involvement with the kind of reflexive issues raised by Analytic sociology. I would, rather, commend these headings as dialectical images (in the sense of Walter Benjamin's reflexive 'constellations') and provocations for further thought and theorizing. Needless to say quotes and citations in these notes are first tributes and only then incentives for future work. My aim is to move from speaking about the book to speaking to and continuing the work of reflexive analysis.

   Organization

1 *Revisiting as dialogue and dialectic*
2 *Reflexive problematics in 1960s and 1970s Sociology and Philosophy*
3 *The project of Analytic sociology*
4 *The genealogy of grounds and auspices*
5 *Multiple voices in 'On the Beginning of Social Inquiry'*
6 *Reflexive sociology as collaborative dialectics*
7 *Concrete and analytic community*
8 *The politics of Analysis*

1 Revisiting as dialogue and dialectic

> For they give justice and pay retribution to each other for their mutual injustice according to the ordered process of time.
>
>   (Anaximander, Fragment 1, in Diels-Kranz (DK 12 B 1))

What is it to *revisit*? How do we – and how should we – make sense of such a commonplace notion? Of course the image and metaphor of revisiting (*re-visiting*) can be understood in a number of different ways from the most concrete to the most analytic. In the multiple contexts of everyday life the sense of returning is announced in the prefix '*re*': *re*-reading, *re*-membering, *re*-enacting, *re*-iterating, *re*-marking, *re*-locating, *re*-covering, *re*-cuperation, *re*-telling, *re*-novating, *re*-naissance, *re*-newal, *re*-union, and so on. And, not least among this open collection, the idea of thought as *re*-thinking (with all the implications of *re*-forming, thinking-again, thinking differently, reconfiguring the self or, as ordinary usage has it, 'changing one's mind').

1.1 Looking back

Taken literally, the desire of revisiting as *recherche du temps perdu* suggests a journey *back* to a previously known place, locale, or *milieu*; for example, our desire to nostalgically recover a past event, object, relationship, or self – the action of an 'interested' traveller intent on retrieving the memories of some past place, a lover returning to the meeting point of his or her first love, a student reunited with his old school (the popular slogan of 'friends reunited'). Each of these retroactive movements is implicitly driven by a *question*. And all such questions posit a *self* (or *version of self* to be recalled and recovered) and thus involve some form of *memory work* or 'knowing-again' that we might call *recollective consciousness*. In this sense every form of memory work is already grounded in a metaphysics of retrospection, as witnessed by the fact that every variant of this desire to 'return', 'look back', and 'remember' converges around the anticipated experience of recovering an enduring *past-in-the-present* and, perhaps by exploiting that regained *sense of place and time*, the possibility that we might *think differently* and even disturb and change the present. It is both disarming and inspiring to learn that every act that returns to the vast ocean of recollection is somehow already implicated in metaphysics. Consider, however, the political differences between revolutionary uses of the past and nostalgic confirmations of pastness that reconcile us to the present. Such possibilities already entail and introduce the idea of *self-reflection* or *reflexivity*.

Approached as symbolic interaction or, in its widest sense, as a form of *social communication*, revisiting can be viewed less as a movement in space and more as a reflexive journey in personal and historical time, a process of *remembering* and *rekindling* a prior relationship, a motivated journey of recovery occasioned by a sense of indebtedness, of unfinished business and the promise of renewed communication, dialogue, and collaborative work. This version of memory as *Erinnerung* comes close to the notion of reappraisal as a way of making sense of earlier episodes in a personal history or revaluating past efforts to speak thoughtfully and responsibly about important concerns and preoccupations. It also evidences the utopic moment of *transcendence* – the principle of *hope* – implicit in many forms of human experience but most emphatically exemplified in what our tradition calls 'theorizing' as the philosophic site of a desire to 'look again' at experience and see differences and possibilities of renewal in what were previously accepted as stable identities and closed episodes.

The image of travelling beyond the confines of the self – of *transcendence* – as a *principled* repetition of consciousness already moves in the vicinity of the ancient philosophical project of *self-reflection* as both an instrument of self-inquiry and as a distinctive way of life. Understood as a hopeful project of self-recovery every form of thoughtful reflection necessarily appears as an *ecstatic* effort to re-experience a lost 'object' and is itself exemplary evidence of the will to resist the manifold threats of personal and collective amnesia. The shock occasioned by this nexus of transcendence, memory, and freedom, perhaps, is the only way in which we can radically recover the intangible objects correlated with the layered experiences we insist on calling the *self*. Here 'thinking' – in one of its many senses – acquires the meaning of recollective desire that aspires to speak *about* speech and what shadows speech. In this way we have an intimation of an even older desire that seeds the unquiet at the root of every act of significant self-recovery: we stumble upon the idea of *narrative desire*, of recollection as a struggle to come to terms with trauma, the incitement to live an examined life, to communicate about the past, to unravel the muddle we call the *self*, to recover and retell our story. This in its most emphatic sense is the dream of being re-*membered*.

Both of these constellations entail an encounter with real or virtual sites of origin. When understood as social action such projects implicate complex processes of deliberation, acknowledgement, self-description, and judgement animated by the task of resolving some enduring question or unresolved problem. The experience of trauma plays a central role in such journeys. Traumas are the cicatrices of the past that endure in the present. The impulse of every form of retrospective consciousness – from the transient flicker of everyday curiosity to the most sustained pursuit of autobiographic and philosophic memory work – is to 'unearth' the sedimented strata of lost meaning formations, to trace the contours of a former self through the darkness of the other and what has become 'other-than-self'. In this context, psychoanalytic therapy – with its utopian image of the ideal listener as a perfect 'archaeologist of the unconscious' – may be viewed as one exemplary instance of the dangerous *arts* of revisiting traumatic, contradictory experiences undertaken by the self in search of a lost *other*, insistent *absence* or *enigmatic alterity*. Similar considerations apply *mutatis mutandis* to the founding impulse of transcendental phenomenology as a genealogy of pre-reflective strata of occluded intentional formations. Indeed, as motivated projects of thoughtful recollection, *every* 'talking' therapy – whether psychoanalytic, phenomenological, hermeneutic, literary, philological or genealogical – implicitly presupposes and tacitly exemplifies the *anamnetic* work of reflection – and by implication, a faith in the liberating powers of memory and the possible adventure of *alethic* dialogue – as the concrete provocation and medium of its practice. When experienced with full awareness of these reflexive entailments, psychoanalytic dialogue might be cited as a paradigm case of a transformational encounter where both *analyst* and *analysand* are transfigured (ironically, with the exception of the ambivalent gesture of 'transference' and 'countertransference', we still know very little of the impact of therapeutic narrative upon Freud's own work and changing sense of identity). In classical psychoanalysis – and in all subsequent logotherapies – the journey into the darkness of the past is motivated by the promise of a cure or, more realistically, of redirecting a damaged self toward a *process* of healing, a *making whole*. In so-called 'higher' spheres of human praxis reflexive *anamnesis* is oriented to the lost 'objects' of affective, personal, sociocultural, and spiritual life. Here the surface topicalities of everyday life appear as occasions that conceal their occluded historical genesis and traumatic conditions of possibility.

In its own way Analytic sociology is also concerned with the *psyche* and its forgotten communal and historical horizons. Given Analysis' preoccupation with theorizing as the dialectical recovery of occluded sites and the silent auspices of ostensibly mundane phenomena we will return to the motifs of *amnesia* and *transcendence* and their *logological* complexities throughout this chapter.

This sense overlaps with a further set of meanings clustering around the idea that the incentive to recollect and re-learn involved in living reflectively flows from our *being-gifted* through language, being unwittingly responsible to congealed legacies of thought and, ultimately, to the enigma of our *life-in-the-world* as members of ongoing communities of thoughtful speech and action responding to the violence and vicissitudes of living and social relationships.

We can readily revisit places and times that have been woven into our life-world and even venture into the occluded operations of pre-reflective horizons and the unconscious, but what are we to make of the idea of recovering the horizon of our *conversational life* itself – of our own *identities* as particular symbolic formations? We wonder and theorize about myriads of concrete problems and concerns but can we imagine a 'theory of life' or, as phenomenology desired, a theory of the *life-world* (*Lebenswelt*), the world we experience and live prior to all reflection? Even more dramatically, can we imagine recovering the life-worlds of victims, of subjects subject to violence and terror? Vernacular conventions treat such a notion as nonsense or, at best, as a misuse of the word 'life' (for example, in such banal claims as 'you can never "get outside" *life*' or 'you cannot live someone else's *life*'). Life – manifested in the countless spheres and rhythms of human existence – is not a *theme* or *object* for abstract theorizing. At best it is what is *sublimated* under the aegis of compulsive political forms and violent translation practices. Does this mean that we can never fully recover the lives of others? That there can be no 'science of life' just as there is no 'science of death' (if we ignore the regional object domains of the physiological, biological and medical sciences that define life and death in technical and causal terms). Indeed, the poets relate that the grey cast of reflection reifies the golden stream of life. Life is to be lived: abandon the *bios theoretikos* and *act*. However, we might legitimately respond: 'To act and live creatively we somehow need to think through the nexus of life/death, we need to situate the self in a more reflective relationship to others and the organizing principles of our activities and their *modus operandi*; and perhaps above all, we need to use the limit-terms *life* and *death* to motivate a more thoughtful and imaginative life, to return to the lost communality and historicity of our lived experience, to act differently, to change the way we live'.

We might respond to our sceptical interlocutor: *What if what you call 'life' (and 'death') actively occasions and precipitates reflection?* Life's infinite occasions – the endless appearances and phantasms of *erôs* and *thanatos* – elicit wonder and reflection: how does this single 'part' (of life) relate to the 'whole' (of life)? How does this singular moment of being relate to the dark horizon of Being? How is the Many somehow gathered within the One? How can we distinguish the unreflective artfulness of living (loving, making, doing, inventing, imagining, thinking, acting, suffering, dying, etc.) from the multiple forms of reflection that formulate these activities as 'arts' (*technai*) and trace their origins and development? How are the multiple meanings of *life* (*erôs*) and *death* (*thanatos*) – as *communal images* and *versions* of living and dying – implicated in the language of reflection itself and inscribed in the fabric of our lives and culture? Life simply *is* the capacity to return and recuperate; but there is no recovery from the trauma of death (death – passing on – being conventionally troped as a kind of journey).

What if reflection and recollection are themselves material powers with the potential to change our relationship to the past? One of the oldest philosophical intuitions is that 'life' and 'reflection' – Being and Thinking – share a common, if incomprehensible, ground 'for thinking and being are the same thing' (Parmenides, DK 28B3). Perhaps what we reify as 'life' is the sum total of ways of forgetting the demand contained in this ancient equation: how to relate to *this* absent ground is the first imperative – the primary vocation – of all self-reflective practice. Above all we need to remember that human beings can only live 'in the world' by exploiting their extraordinary linguistic capacity to think what is absent, to witness past acts and by shaping thought into images and metaphors imagine other ways of being, other ways of *going on*, other images of *social existence*, other *forms of life*. Memory, imagination, and thinking are all modes of recollection and forms of life. Perhaps what remains to be thought is the concealed reference to *erôs* and its libidinal economies in our expressions 'life' and 'forms of life'. Knowing what we do of our recent personal and collective pasts how are we to 'live on'? How should we *imagine* living-on?

Being always-already embedded in a sustaining *life-world* we remain open to the idea that what a given community frames as *life* – the manifold occasions of mundane *living*, practice, ordinary consciousness, *everyday* life – appears in end-lessly variable narrative editions and is actualized in manifold permutations of embodied *social praxis*. Here differentiation and variation in lived experience is the universal norm. And acts of difference in human experience are profoundly linked to the desire to experience and form new integrations and identities. Even austere practices like science and philosophy inevitably have existential and libidinal resonances embedded in prior forms of life. Reflecting upon the structure and dynamics of such practices is not an either/or matter, but a gradient of concern unique to the spirit of human experience and self-consciousness. In this sense every struggle to recall and articulate death – as an icon of *life-lost, disappearance*, and *lack of sense* – is occasioned by the irreducible ambiguities of living and dying. Yet without this darkness there would be no illumination. As Jacques Lacan would teach, the unconscious being structured like a language remains the other of consciousness, the unsayable horizon implicit in every act of positing, saying, and identification (Lacan, 1978). What could be closer to us than life and death?

We are enveloped by icons of disappearance. Perhaps all creative praxis, every adventure of the spirit, has its genesis in questions of ontological need and lack: *How to acknowledge and repay the gift of life (and death)?* How to remember and work through the traumatic sources of our own lives and the past lives we call traditions? Perhaps this irreducible 'gap' between our individual existence and the horizon of Being – between existence and nonexistence – is why both consciousness and the unconscious can only be structured symbolically. Being *worldly* and *social* creatures we are gifted with a life capable of reflecting upon itself and the manifold forms of value and desire that constitute human selves. But 'life itself' eludes reflection. All we have are *forms* of life. What philosophers have posited as 'the self', 'subject', 'consciousness', 'self-consciousness', 'reason' or, simply *subjectivity* – now appears as evidence of an ontological 'fold' or reticular axiological formation that can never be closed. Being aware of and having to deal with the process of dying, human beings are from the beginning value-oriented ethical creatures, beings whose existence is mediated by desire, forms of life that flourish by recognizing others and desire recognition by others (the root form of 'the Law of the Father' but also the grammatical core of what Hegel calls 'spirit' (*Geist*), Simmel calls 'life' (*Leben*), and Gadamer calls 'tradition'). To *become reflexive* is first of all to recognize our deep ethical complicity with anonymous others.

What layers of injustice are already implicated in the *givenness* of our *being* present, in our *being* alive, in *living an identity* accepted as a gift without a giver, in being born of the flesh of another, in having experienced a childhood, in understanding that other lives have been lost and destroyed? In whatever idiom we choose we already have an intimation of our most primordial debts: we are beholden to the anonymous gift of life, to objects of desire encoded in the community we share with others, to the lives of unknown and unknowable strangers, and ultimately to the strange facticity of loss and the absence of being itself (expressed in the universal egalitarianism of life's fatal contract that demands that 'every creature must pay for a life with a death'). The stream of experience that seems to lie beyond description, explanation, and representation turns out to encircle the most important occasions of our life and thought.

1.2 On re-visiting as indebtedness

We are simply the kind of opaque beings that acquire a fragile sense of identity or *wholeness* through a multiplicity of unconsidered historical acts of recollection and acknowledgment, each of these acts symbolizing iconic occasions of desire, emotional attachment, communal remembrance, and creative sociality. In this sense we are *always-about-to-enter* the 'symbolic order'. Yet another aspect of re-visiting is the interactional moment of paying *homage* and expressing gratitude to the work of teachers who have provided essential orientations and shaped paths along our own intellectual itineraries. We travel back to sites of valued instruction; we struggle *not* to forget, to recognize and acknowledge the other. We struggle against *disappearance*.

The mundane activity of *reading* or *interpretation* provides a concrete image of these sense-making ventures, where particular texts are said to empower readers to travel in space and time, to recover 'lost times and places', to uncover 'other worlds', to learn to see the world differently. Overlooking their roots as *metaphor* we innocently say we have been *translated* or *transported* to other worlds. We have been *instructed*, our minds *enlarged*; we have *witnessed* others and otherness. Opening a book is an invitation to an adventure. This suggests that our imaginative faculty is beholden to the generosity of words and the vanishing mediators called *language, society*, and *tradition*. A work of visual or verbal art discloses the world as a multiverse and the self as *le sujet de la jouissance* that we recognize as instances of *self-conscious life*. The dialectic of mediation and disappearance – the logic of translation – appears in the experience of involuntary memory. One of the fundamental pleasures of literacy (and recollection) is the discovery that what was understood to be 'given', 'ordinary', and 'past' – the constraints dictated by our particular *milieu* – secrete other possibilities, extraordinary worlds of meaning and invitations to re-read, re-think, and productively re-write. Even what passes for *history* and *social reality* can be, and perhaps needs to be, rewritten. The remembered past is our only way forward to a more humane future.

The gifts of reading, interpretation, and translation provide the reader with an *ersatz* encounter with life and death (in this sense the narrative of crime and punishment is the archetypal literary form). While fascinated by its symbolic content the child also learns that both Word and World are indeterminate and enigmatic, perhaps irredeemably incomplete, and in *this* recognition of hermeneutic openness begins the crafting of a provisional self with a reading future, a speaking subject drawn into the future by the lures of *imaginative desire*. We meet, in other words, the curious possibility of a sense of selfhood that desires to refashion, remake, and rewrite itself. Conventional usage diminishes this miracle of irresolution in the modest word 'education'.

As far back as Plato's *Meno*, education has been metaphorically configured as both *travel* and *anamnesis*, as *movement* and *recollection*, as *reflection and self-reflection* troped as a journey of self-development. Such metaphors are not arbitrary signs, but iconic images revealing an unavoidable dialectic of mutual recognition that is native to human experience. In the dialogue *Meno*, for example, Socrates appears as the ideal theorist leading his interlocutor from everyday commonplaces and mundane forms of reasoning to more existentially challenging places and problematics, a journey from the world-as-taken-for-granted to a more resonant sense of self and life as responsible self-fashioning praxis. Socrates is both translator and mediator, a figure touched by the gods Apollo and Hermes. In this process the child is taught to remember and begin again (to *re*-commence). The message of educability is that whoever would learn must enter the symbolic order again as a child. In this respect Socrates is also the teacher of self-reflection, of the living *techné* of how to question clichés and platitudes to recuperate and redirect the education of the soul.

Travel might also be envisioned as a pathway of transformational dialogue understood as the struggle or odyssey of the opaque self as it traces the painful dialectical movement from inchoate consciousness to articulate self-consciousness. If we can accept the Hegelian image of self-education (*Bildung*), the experiences generated by such disjunctions would form the core provocations of educability and the self-transfiguration of existence that education promises. Education (or more precisely, *educability*) begins with an acknowledgement of the *need* or *desire* to understand the self through the person of the other (the process of self-recognition as the need to desire the desire of the other that Hegelian exegetes call *meta-desire*). For Hegel – and indeed for Vico, Herder, Nietzsche, Dilthey, Freud, Simmel, and many other educators – *Bildung* is structured like a conversation in search of a lost spiritual language (Hegel, 1977). Educability is to this extent closely bound up with a renewal of the 'tragic sense of life' and the vocation of recovering our own individual and collective sense of identity (ignited by the *kairos* or decisive moment that initiates the long transformation from consciousness '*in-itself*' to consciousness '*in-and-for-itself*').

Aspiring students must, in some sense, already recognize themselves as incomplete and needy (the common sense version of which is 'ignorance' or, further along the path of self-inquiry, the sceptical consciousness that insists on 'bracketing' operative rules and taken-for-granted procedures), but as in some sense already having taken the first steps of a journey, projecting themselves in the figure of a future self, a *dialogical collaborator*, that is 'on the way to language' and the disturbing experiences that language shelters and enfolds. The moment of genuine *experience* – and hence genuine understanding and self-translation – begins with the tension between *chronos* and *kairos* marked by the appearance of reflective desire or what common usage calls 'the love of learning' (expressed in another register as the *anxiety of influence* or even *neurosis*).

This image of desire (*erôs*) – like the ambivalent movement of the opportune moment – prompts the founding question of all learning: Can the desire to inquire, to live a meaningful life, be taught? Can students be taught the virtue of reflection and critical inquiry? Can this particular species of virtue – *arête* – be transmitted from teacher to student? More generically, how can another person acquire the moral commitment, indeed the *habitus*, to question the difference between the ordinary and the extraordinary, between thoughtless activity and thoughtful speech? The pursuit of *alethic* dialogue we know as dialectical reasoning already presupposes a critical, if ironic, distinction between closed and open souls. The enigmatic tension of this pre-reflective orientation toward the *logos* then becomes both the motivation and the topic of self-understanding.

As an attempt to renew the Socratic tradition, one of the seminal preoccupations of *On the Beginning of Social Inquiry* was/is the issue of *educability* and *self-transformation*. How can the endemic closure of the soul be cured? How, more locally, can the soul of sociology, philosophy, and other putative 'human sciences' be rescued from their alienated and reified forms? How, as the texts of *OBSI* recurrently ask their readers, can we transcend usage (opinion), recollect lost grounds, and begin to speak responsibly and historically in the full sense of these terms? Analysis had grasped the fact that 'educability' designates the faculty of self-consciously assuming a history, bracketing what passes for objective reality and striving to live a life as a life ruled by the reflexive imperative with its principled sense of historicity and openness to the past.

The question of 'history' as a *conversational* return-to-self that operates as a sub-text throughout the studies assembled in *OBSI* and the emerging notion of the *historicity* of self and community that weaves throughout the 'Introduction' to *OBSI* are as difficult to articulate as the elemental question of how we might learn to *ask questions* or activate the nascent commitment to think, speak, and write thoughtfully. The insistent question of tradition and our relation to the past returns: How in the face of *irresolution* and *uncertainty* can the love of truth be acquired and nurtured? How can we, inhabitants of the twenty-first century, recover the therapeutic idea of theorizing and the *bios theoretikos*? How can an image of the good society be forged from the traumas and ghosts that inhabit the past?

1.3 On revisiting as 'history' and 'lived experience': the obligation of the gift, the debt, and being-indebted

Living in a hegemonic present that has 'abolished' the dark past, how can we loosen the grip of everyday language and common sense to see differently, how can we honour the difference that makes all seeing and thinking possible? In conventional interpretations of learning and understanding, acquiring a fluency in ideas, thinking differently, beginning to write, and acquiring an 'education' in its original etymological sense (*e-ducare*, to lead) inevitably begins in a relationship of unequal or asymmetrical exchange. This is the conventional pedagogic model of *apprenticeship*: *I learn from those who already know*. As a novitiate (someone who has not mastered the relevant rules, procedures, and skills) I am taught by one who possesses this mastery. I learn to manipulate and use a tradition. No doubt genuine apprenticeship – as opposed to the mechanical transmission of techniques and information – presupposes a strong version of reciprocity, but to enter fully into the intersubjective space of thought requires the gentle authority of the other (not necessarily another person). Alterity might be language or some transgressive episode of language, an extraordinary personal experience, or even, perhaps, the vaguest intimation of the absent-presence of what philosophers have problematically called *Being, World, Language, Experience, Spirit* or *Life*.

The teacher may no longer be alive. We are also apprentices in the necropolis of dead speakers and writers who 'live-on' in the ghostly circuitry of written texts, audiovisual recordings, and other traces. As one vital mode of living-on, dialogue is also, and perhaps primarily, a dialogue with the dead. It is often the insistent voices of the dead who ask the living: *What makes a debt a debt?* By assuming the *ethical* demands of the reciprocal life of dialogue the other is posited as a possible self, a transfigured 'medium' in which novitiates can 'think for themselves', sustain independent development, and flourish as autonomous 'other selves' (*alter egos*). This is the gift of existence the dead grant to the living. This is the *mortgage* animating language, learning and art when understood as *inheritances*. But, given the vagaries of memory and circumstances, we are never certain where different forms of speech have led us or what kinds of selves are placed in question by the ghosts of earlier modes of speech and action.

What dialectical learning teaches, however, is that self-awareness can never be a one-dimensional assimilation of the past given that what we call the past has an indeterminate and heteroglossial structure. In reality the past cannot be recovered without the mediation of *courageous* speech and language. And here our only guides are cultural *prostheses*: painful testimony, exemplary lives, pedagogic images, forms, heuristics, methods, textual legacies, inscriptions, traces, ghosts.

Whatever else they may be, methods are also programmatic ways of travelling, heuristics, provocations and incentives to continue thinking and, more especially, to think and speak *differently*. The novitiate must negotiate the fragile balance between playful openness – and necessary vulnerability – and the seriousness of resolute application and sustained analytic work. The novice must be prepared to work upon themselves, to change their way of doing things, adopt different methods, and exercise judgement themselves.

In such reflections we are continually drawn to the question of the value – the 'good' – of learning itself. Why *inquire*?, Why *judge*?, Why *resist* silence?, Why *create*?, Why struggle to think at all? We are, of course, aware that the *reflexive imperative* – the desire to speak and think – was occasioned and animated in the ancient Greek world by the idea of the Good as an iconic image (*eidos*) 'beyond Being and Not-Being'. How can the transcendence of the Good – the enigma of transcendence – enter into the prosaic modern world of everyday learning and instrumental education? How can the vocation of intellectual activity – of philosophy as *therapeia* – flourish in the modern political climate of cynicism and nihilism (Carlisle and Ganeri, 2010)? These questions already point to the implicit politics of Analysis: what kind of 'self-transformation' and 'political experience' is implicit in the institutional implementation of forms of radical self-reflection? Or even more radically, how can analytic speech resist the nihilistic drift of the age and restore the spirit of reflection?

In the course of our everyday activities – living within the world of everyday praxis and pragmatic concerns – we routinely find our way around these dilemmas and exigencies by tracking the paths of absent others – no doubt the first gesture of moral learning has its roots in such pre-predicative meaning practices. I learn to speak, to feel and express within the horizon of *received* languages and by engaging with the hybrid worlds articulated by other souls. But others are never innocent. Even the *forms* of the questions I ask are drawn from a collective archive of ghosts (where occasionally asking *different kinds* of question is regarded as a threat to the dominant normative order). But here, of course, we meet the danger of merely functioning as a conduit of earlier modes of thought and habituated praxis. We acquiesce in the silences of others. Yet we never lose the feeling that extant language-games prove inadequate to capture what we experience, that translation is a traduction. We suffer the pain that the failure of inherited forms inflict on our own thought and experience. We become locked into a process of mechanical repetition. To interrupt this repetition the student needs to learn that the vital experience of learning and thinking is never granted without struggle or, if the phrase can be used analytically, without *a measure of violence*. Another term for this struggle is *dialectic*. In general every 'loosening' of discourse and language – every attempt to *think dialectically* and *do analysis* – will involve the disruption of conventions and what currently passes for speech and thought. The fundamental *dialectical* impulse of radical reflection already signals a decisive break with the Word and World as already-given and taken-for-granted. In trying to locate the grounds of the possibility of description it is no use offering another description.

In my everyday life I am indebted to others for their patience and guidance when learning a craft or acquiring a skill. Yet as a presupposition of any kind of learning I must first discover myself – *re*-cognize myself – as an apprentice and commit to the task of learning by *persisting*: enduring, imitating, pursuing common lines of inquiry, making creative mistakes, asking 'similar' questions, cooperating, interpreting together, *working-with-others*, but above all *interrupting* and *disagreeing*. To enter the ethical space of *language-as-discourse* as a participant I must be able to excise pride and the vanity of intellectual *hubris*; I must surrender to the provocation of 'what goes unsaid', 'bracketing' what is commonplace and established in order to listen to the other; eventually I must 'forget' others and perform the skill as though I had never been taught. I may then learn to 'stand on my own feet', use my own judgement, and speak for myself. Judgement, however, still needs the words of others (and other words). Critical judgement promises a different sense of self and new possibilities of self-understanding. Theorizing is such a translation practice. Theorizing is essentially the promise of a new kind of *voice*, of speaking in another idiom and for other-than-conventional reasons. Through theorizing we may become another person or, more precisely, another *kind* of person. Here the existential turmoil that draws the self to theorizing results in a new form of praxis governed by the hope that we can lead another way of life.

We might exemplify this kind of spirited learning by comparing education to the craft of learning to play a musical instrument, acquiring the grace and cadence that animate the lines of a play, learning to apply an investigative method, training the heart to sing a complex piece of music, learning another language. Paradoxically, the competent acquisition of a craft – say an ability to play a Chopin polonaise, perform a Shakespeare soliloquy, or solve a quadratic equation – is one in which the slow processes of step-by-step acquisition are forgotten and, so to speak, lost in the performance as the spirit of the music enters the body of the performer. In the process we learn to see, play, and act differently. By engaging with a particular tradition we modify its meaning. Occasionally the acquisition of a skill opens up a new way of being-in-the-world. At base, however, it is the speaking other – here the musical, dramatic, or mathematical other – who, in teaching a new skill, encourages the novitiate to see again, to review previous ways of seeing/playing/acting/being, to change routines and customary habits, granting the self other ways of speaking, acting, and performing. Moreover, every such activity of integrated transgression is also the embodiment of grace, *jouissance*, and practice-shaped pleasures. We affectively perform what a tradition gifts.

More profoundly, to revisit is to re-listen and re-learn, to gain 'perspective' and a different context through which we might recover the meaning of events that now belong to a lost domain. The more 'resonant' the original event, the more difficult it is to re-listen and re-learn. Reflection itself precipitates the questions: What *was* this event?, What *is* an event?, and How can the eventfulness of the past and possible futures be gathered into a new unity, transmuted into another kind of event? This is where the authentic 'politics of education' and the *therapeutic* distinction between rote-learning and spirited knowledge, customary rule-base 'morality' and 'ethicality', the life of the intellect, and the wisdom of the heart are to be found. Revisiting might offer another chance to learn, to become other to the same, to recollect and recover the same in the other. Where the infant (the *infans*) originally 'learned' by actively participating in a form of life with its local conventions, obligations, and demands, re-learning is a return to those sites as vital occasions in an interminable cycle of ethical self-*othering* (and other-*selfing*). If, as Rimbaud claimed, the 'I is an other', recovering past forms of life, like recovering *from* past forms of life, whether personal or collective, grants the self a kind of second chance, perhaps a second *life*.

In learning the art of self-reflection I need to distinguish between the *moral* order and *ethical* life, to experience the difference between the conservative *principles of teaching/learning* (the transmission grammars of traditional pedagogies) and the transgressive grammars of *principled teaching/learning/judgement* (the imperative of reflexive pedagogy that goes by the Greek name *paideia* or the German word *Bildung*). By *living* this difference, selves acquire the hard lesson of how to be other than the norm or conventional standard, to deviate from a normative order in order to take *responsibility for their own education*;

the self must learn how to learn, how to creatively relate to language and its polyphonic traditions.

1.4 Loyalty as acknowledgement

This notion of belonging and the bond of loyalty it presupposes – for example, being committed to the adventure of dialectical thought as simultaneously an *ethical* and *political* ideal – is where the notion of 'incurring a debt' or 'owing the other' enters the picture. By returning to and rethinking the remarkable collaborative venture of *On the Beginning of Social Inquiry* we may recover notions of 'repaying' and 'cancelling' debts as intrinsic to the work of dialectical thought (we know in an abstract way that *aufgehoben* in the Hegelian sense of *Aufheben* involves both the negation and the 'preservation' and 'elevation' of interrelated moments of an ongoing project of thought).

Those fortunate enough to have read *OBSI* on its first appearance remain aware of gifts acknowledged and unacknowledged. In retrospect (and, of course, this visual image is to some extent systematically misleading) we also need to think about – to conceptualize and reflect upon – the process of being-gifted and, with this, such difficult but necessary concepts as 'bequeathal', 'legacy', 'inheritance', and 'tradition'. With the insistence of the question of *obligation* – or, if you like, of the dialectical idea of the social bond as a profoundly *ethical* relationship – we are faced with the question of how to acknowledge the agonistic work of teachers, how to 're-pay' or 'recompense' the work of principled teaching – certainly not how to *cancel* the debt (to take the pecuniary image to its absurd limit), but how to recognize by being loyal to and continuing the work embodied in the original gift?

Above all we need to learn to listen, to remain open toward and graciously accept the work of significant others. This moral sense of obligation is also part of the 'givenness' or goodness inherent in language as the living medium of all education. 'We do not merely speak *the* language', as Heidegger observes, 'we speak *by way* of it. We can do so solely because we always have already listened to the language. What do we hear there? We hear language speaking.... Language speaks by saying, that is, by showing' (Heidegger, 1971b: 124).

1.5 Ambivalence

Revisiting – or what narratology calls *analepsis* – cannot be free from its own horizons of ambiguity and ambivalence. Despite the cinema's misleading artifice of flashbacks the past will never completely shed its aura of being an alien landscape. Yet the estrangement that pervades the experience of ambivalence also bestows the gift of dissonance and remediation. The fact that no identity or unity – no *homecoming* whether verbal or non-verbal – can escape mediation does not negate the legitimate demands of retrospection, recuperation, and integration (indeed definition-resistant notions like *mediation, remediation, particularity, circumstantiality, singularity, undecidability* still remain categorial unities).

Even the manifold ways in which 'experience' and 'integration' can fail in the arts of life still stand witness to the interminable desire for unity. Every act of recuperation, of 'time recovered', risks distorting and falsifying the achieved integrity of past events, mis-identifying and mis-interpreting the gift of the other in acts of false-recollection and pseudo-historicizing. The verbal tense of the living past collapses into the preterite tense of fictional narrative.

What I believed to be the pleasures of retrospective self-revelation turn out to involve dissimulation and self-deception. Being shot-through with desire, retro-spection – perhaps like every act of memory – readily defaults to self-protective distortion and its ideological equivalents that historians gather under the cat-egories of *revisionism* and *false consciousness*. Given the existential risks and vicissitudes that accompany any reactivation of times past, we are continuously faced with the disjunction between earlier and later meaning contexts, the experi-ence of irresolution in discovering that things 'look different' (in both senses of this phrase), that the past is a foreign country, that the course of subsequent life and the promise of theorizing have irreparably fallen apart. We then feel some sympathy with Groucho Marx's sentiment: '*I wouldn't join a club that would have me as a member*' (or the ironic words of an earlier Marx: '*Je ne suis pas un Marxiste*'). Given space this would be the place to explore the antinomies and conflicts of self-deception, dissimulation, bad faith, and transference that are woven through the languages and the memory-mediated practices of everyday life.

Perhaps even more disturbing, we return and find 'nothing has changed': we become *simulacra* of ourselves frozen in a reified museum of artefacts gazing out upon objects. What was once a living *situation* is now moribund. As Marx writes in the *18th Brumaire of Louis Bonaparte*, we learn that the traditions of dead generations weigh like a nightmare on the minds of the living. The original enchantment, attachments, and passions have vanished into a thanatonic vault that only abstract narration can unlock. The past has become a deathly archive of objects without context, things that no longer 'speak' and move us to thought and reflection. The self I imagined in the past has become alien and unrecogniz-able. Ageing has stolen my image of the past. The anticipated *fusion of horizons* – the noble promise of Gadamerian hermeneutics – has regressed into contextual *fission* – not a more holistic *sense* or *deepening* of self-understanding, but the abjection and fragmentation of insight. Faced with the morbidities of closure we stop thinking, drift into resignation and abandon the reflexive imperative for what currently passes for common sense, practicality and reasonableness. The 'shock of the old' no longer functions to disturb and transform the self and world of the present (Sandywell, 1998). We can no longer convey a message from the past to those future selves who might listen in unknowable times and places. We can only relate to the past through the self-mortifying acid of regret, guilt, self-reproach, shame, and vengeance. We become, in other words, *jaded* and *indifferent*.

The collective parallel to this alienation occurs in the omnipresent tempta-tions of quietism, cynicism, and nihilism; these responses, in turn, raise the question of what it is to understand and misunderstand a gift (and with this also question the issue of the politics of memory, dialogue, and recollection – in both its most concrete and most analytic senses as personal and collective forms of *re*-gathering). How can we overcome indifference?

We also need to ask: What is it to look a gift horse in the mouth, to *refuse a gift*, to resist the learning experience, to deprecate *conversation* and *logos*, and withdraw from the promise of community implicit in the pursuit of radical reflection? Here again the monadic temptation of monologue, solipsism, and relativism (in their endless historical variants) represents a constant threat to the life of dialogue. Failure here is not only a self-destructive withdrawal from questioning and conversation, but something like an illness of the sprit, a disease that can erode the grounds of language and, indeed, of a whole society and culture.

In struggling to recover the concrete encounters (conversations, dialogues, writing experiences, affectivities, friendships, lived experiences, spirited possibilities of education) of earlier texts and teachers we risk misunderstanding the demands of collaborative work and dialogical writing by framing these lessons in the templates of disembodied, non-dialectical metaphors. Confronted by disturbing difference we settle for comfortable identities. We continue speaking *to* the other, but fail to speak *with* the other. In this way, perhaps unintentionally, we violate the reflexive imperative by reducing the singularity of the other (and the other's experience and language) to the terms of an existing role, frame of reference, established method or borrowed language. Intentionally or unwittingly we disrespect the spirit of language.

Needless to say, the immediate 'reception' and subsequent 'history' of *OBSI* would predictably illustrate the literal procedures of reductive commentary and thoughtless exegesis that police the world of academic social science and philosophy.

2 Reflexive problematics in 1960s and 1970s sociology and philosophy

To provide some background for readers who were not personally involved with the development of Analytic sociology we might situate the many distortions and misunderstandings of the studies assembled in *OBSI* (and later with respect to Blum and McHugh's *Self-Reflection in the Arts and Sciences* and the collection *Friends, Enemies and Strangers*) by considering some of the 'theoretical vectors' struggling for a place in the force-field of candidate Reflexive sociologies from around 1960 to the mid-1970s. We also need to bear in mind that the larger part of what passes for sociological theory today still remain notational variations of these 'perspectives' and their underlying versions of reflection and community. In this respect Analytic sociology retains its power to interrupt and reconfigure what passes for sociological inquiry and social thought. It also remains a potent source of rethinking and reconfiguration for possible future forms of social theory.

2.1 Historical, political, and academic contexts

First the *historical* context. While not wishing to indulge in nostalgia or irony about 1960s counter-culture, the youth-movement, sex-drugs-and-rock'n'roll, and the like, it *is* important to recall the remarkable concentration of creative work that appeared over the period from roughly 1960 to the mid-1970s. The *cultural revolution* of the 1960s is certainly more than a figure of speech. While this is generally recognized for the worlds of art, music, film, politics, and popular culture, it is less often noted for innovative work in social theory and philosophy. Yet the 'Theory Wars' that would both energize and split university departments of Sociology, Literature, and Cultural Studies in the 1970s and 1980s all have their roots in this period of intense social and intellectual change.

This is the decade when Anglo-American students first heard of the existence of Phenomenology, Hermeneutics, Structuralism, Semiotics, Critical Theory, Feminism, post-Freudian Psychoanalysis, and other heterodox language-games. The same decade also saw the first intimations of Post-Structuralism, Decon-struction, Genealogy, Discourse Analysis, Post-colonialism, Post-feminism, among other more exotic counter-discourses and theoretical frameworks. What is now generally referred to as the global age of *postmodern culture* and the *postmodernization* of society were prefigured in widely different attempts to cri-tique reductive, positivist, and administrative conceptions of language, thought, and culture. The rejection of one-dimensional 'naturalism' as a deeply conser-vative epistemology and self-serving politics is also where the contemporary preoccupation with power and knowledge, the social construction of subject-ivity, identity politics, the historical conditions of discursive productivity, and the politics of disciplinary knowledge acquired their contemporary articulation and resonance.

Critics, radicals, and dreamers of all stripes converged on the same *onto-logical irony* that the very things that are closest to human activities – the grounds and material conditions that made such activities possible – had been left concealed and unspoken. To many young intellectuals it became evident that the orthodox discourses of the day could not even account for their own discur-sive possibility and limited rationality let alone provide a critical theory of mind, self, and society. What passed for 'theory' and 'analysis' was diagnosed as radically deficient in both experiential, literary, and ethicopolitical relevance ('theory' had been uncoupled from its historical problematics and communal origins and repackaged for its abstract instrumental applications in the various academic and research industries). A whole generation had seen that the thought-less celebration of this deficit of critical self-reflection and political self-consciousness had become the brand of identity of mainstream 'value-free' social science (with its image of scientific inquiry completely detached from all existential concerns and normative values). By the 1970s the idolatry of decon-textualized 'science' seemed securely embodied and institutionalized in both mainstream social science and in the mechanical reductionism of most of its structuralist and Marxist 'alternatives'.

In this polemical context the phrase 'the failure of positivism' became a rallying cry for a number of intellectual constituencies searching for alternative post-empiricist and post-positivist futures for social inquiry. The existential vacuity of the positivist tradition would lead many intellectuals to turn to occluded and marginalized traditions of thought – to the Greek classics of Plato and Aristotle, Spinoza's *Ethics*, Vico's *New Science*, Hegel's *Phenomenology of Spirit*, Marx's *Economic and Philosophical Mansucripts*, Nietzsche's posthumous *Will to Power*, Simmel's *Philosophy of Money*, Weber's *Wirtschaft und Gesellschaft*, and Benjamin's *Arcades Project (1927–1940)* – as more vital sources of theoretical and political imagination. At root 'the failure of positivism' came to be viewed as a metonym for the deleterious moral and political consequences of uncritical science *per se* and its dominant empiricist justifications and metaphysical applications. The revolt against these orthodoxies represented, in hindsight, a radical rejection of both technocratic discourse and the technocratic version of modernity that had replaced the experimental modernism of the first half of the twentieth century. The ensuing ideological and theoretical cacophony would eventually be framed as a dialectical consequence of the failed attempts to 'liquidate' and 'close' the Western metaphysical tradition.

The immediate *academic* context to *On the Beginning of Social Inquiry* was the transition from the expansion of social science and humanities programmes in American higher education in the late 1940s and 1950s to the crisis and radicalization of universities in the late 1960s and 1970s (Lodge, 2014: 183; cf. Sica and Turner, 2005). The wider political scene, of course, was America's position as a world power, the post-Cold War climate of nuclear fear and collective paranoia (the Cuban missile crisis, Bay of Pigs, mutually-assured-destruction, etc.), counter-cultural movements for sexual liberation (the women's movement, movements for gay rights, ethnic identity, environmentalism, and single-issue politics), recurrent political crisis and dissent (dramatized by the Watergate crisis, the resignation of Richard Nixon on 9 August 1974, and the cold economic reality of 'business as usual'), the Civil Rights Movement, the protracted violence of the war in Vietnam and Cambodia, the long-term impact of the 1970s OPEC-led oil crisis, the relentless erosion of lived experience and democratic civil institutions, great cities in meltdown, the student revolt symbolized by 'Paris May 1968', the Prague Spring of 1968, the Situationist movement, the music of Bob Dylan, The Doors, The Velvet Underground, The Ramones, Jimi Hendrix, and so on. This many-layered polemical constellation of overdetermined events and social activism led many not only to reject what passed for political realism and the capitalist version of work and life ('the American dream', 'the Affluent Society', 'Consumerism'), but to question the authoritarian and technocratic functions of the university and the educational establishment as a whole, to criticize the logic of expertise, specialization and determinism justified by the dominant interpretation of naturalistic science, to argue that the boundaries between the practices of everyday life, the sciences, humanities, literary studies, and philosophy were permeable, and to suggest that other theoretical sites and creative discourses were both possible and necessary. Many came to the somewhat shocking idea that social inquiry should approach people as if they were human beings. Here it was not merely the vitality of the human sciences and humanities that was at issue, but the very survival of humane forms of life and, at the peak of Cold War exterminism and possible nuclear holocaust, the survival of the human species itself.

Three such polemical sites proved to be consequential:

1   The first site clustered around the discovery of the complexity of 'the ordinary' or the material practices of 'everyday life' and the 'problematizations' of embodiment, consciousness, affectivity and practical knowledge as both the unrecognized horizon of human activities and the vital source of resistance to dominant institutions and organized power, exemplified, for example, by anti-capitalist accounts of the reification of a 'world in fragments' (Theodor Adorno, Walter Benjamin, Jürgen Habermas, and others), the alienation of social life resulting from the rationalized processes of an increasingly bureaucratized modernity (from Henri Lefebvre and Georges Bataille to the Situationist International of Guy Debord and on to the academic research of Alain Touraine, Michel Foucault, Pierre Bourdieu, Cornelius Castoriadis, and related thinkers), and the turn to the quotidian world of lived experience (the *Lebenswelt*) and the phenomenology of everydayness as the sustaining matrix for meaningful human practices, community and symbolic forms (Smith, 1987). Many of these currents intersected and converged to promote more dialectical metanarratives of constitutive social practices and imaginary institutions (for example Harvey, 1973; Bourdieu, 1993; Castoriadis, 1987, 1997b; Said, 1978; Touraine, 1981). The 'discovery' of the intersubjective life-world as a 'layered world' of symbolic practices resonated with theorizations of post-Enlightenment modernity (and (post)modernities) viewed as an emerging order of reflexive institutions intensively questioning their own founding logics and political rationales. This postmodern turn also facilitated more critical readings of the canonical texts of *modernism* and *late modernity* as attempts to explore and institutionalize experimental practices of self-reflection and 'new social movements' across every sphere of social life (Sandywell, 1996, volume 1).

2   The second site flowed from a series of 'linguistic/discursive/cultural turns' characterized by a principled preoccupation with the material, temporal, social and ideological processes of language and culture. Not language approached as objective representation, disembodied argumentative reason or a Cartesian mirror-like medium, but language as *world-constituting praxis*, as textual productivity and interactive work, as a polemical zone of *cultural* interaction, selfhood, and tradition – what would eventually be called the *symbolic order* or simply *culture*, anticipating the turn toward the intractable problematics of conflict, power, domination and 'cultural capital' in subsequent critiques of late modern societies. While difficult to date, we could say that by 1970 the turn toward 'popular culture' and the broader conception of cultural materialism had become a common focus for a wide

range of different analytic concerns. Recall, for example, the many different 'linguistic turns' associated with the names Nietzsche, Saussure, Wittgenstein, Austin, Heidegger, Gramsci, Benjamin, Bakhtin and the 'Bakhtin Circle', Chomsky, Habermas, Barthes, Gadamer, Ricoeur, Lacan, Derrida, Foucault, Kristeva, Cixous, Iragaray, among many others (a development that came to public notice in the 1966 Johns Hopkins University Conference centred on 'the structuralist controversy' in literary criticism and 'the sciences of man' (Macksey and Donato, 1972)). With this renewed emphasis upon social action, the relative autonomy and 'undecidability' of semiotic structuration and the ambivalence and complexity of the symbolic order came an awareness of the diversity of language-games, the indexical character of all communication and the irreducible ambiguities and conflicts of representation and cultural interpretation, reading practices and cultural resistance across every sphere of social and cultural life. Paradoxically, what is closest to the ethical and political life of human experience – embodiment, meaning-making, signification, desire, responsibility, commitment, conversation, everyday lived culture, and so on – is also the source of what is alien, ambiguous and *other-than-human*. To many it appeared that it was this concrete dialectics of violence, interpretive repertoires and symbolic creativity that abstract theory and the metaphysical tradition more generally had systematically concealed. Positivist social theory had simply ignored the fact that individuals lead conversational lives by discursively negotiating their actions and activities within pre-given traditions and forms of life.

3   A third decisive context and source of innovation was the appearance of self-referentiality or self-reflexivity as both a mundane feature of human being-in-the-world and as a subversive problem for orthodox conceptions of epistemology and metaphysics – what became known as the *tu quoque* principle of 'you too' or 'you also' – that is, that one's own speech stands in need of justification, that all theoretical speech needs to respond to the criticism that turns the charge back on the accuser: *tua res agitur*, 'it is your concern/ cause'. The ubiquitous and paradoxical self-referentiality of speaking and writing occasioned the wider question as to how investigative disciplines like psychology, sociology, political theory, literary scholarship, and philosophy should incorporate (or, more commonly) repress 'subjective' and 'intersubjective' phenomena such as symbolic mediation, situated meanings (essential indexicality), self-referential beliefs, points-of-view, *qualia*, and so on). What steps would such disciplines need to take to comprehend their own concepts and research outcomes as particular historical and social constellations, as particular ways of being-in-the-world that routinely occluded gender, class, ethnicity, and so on from their models of the social world? Here the practices of postmodern fiction and narrative strategies (the metafiction of Donald Barthelme, B.S. Johnson, John Fowles, Thomas Pynchon, Kurt Vonnegut, and others) and cinema (from Kurosawa to Buñuel and Hitchcock) were more advanced in their understanding of the centrality of self-referential creative praxis in the history and organization of human experience.

Given that these cross-disciplinary and transdisciplinary concerns overlapped and interacted, what had first appeared as a mere irritant – the *contextual* fly in the scientific ointment – ended up provoking different conceptions of inquiry, alternative ontologies and anti-ontologies and, with these new kinds of question, intellectual projects and distinctive styles of social thought.

Following the meandering course of these encounters the thematics of self-reflection and the constitutive reflexivity of everyday life began to be used strategically as a symbol of discontent – a kind of Trojan horse – embodied in the disarming and recurrent question: 'From what *grounds* are you speaking/reading/interpreting/investigating?' Or in its proto-punk version favoured by obstreperous students: 'What *right* have you to...?' ('Where *exactly* are you coming from?') and, finally, cynical reason's nihilist questions, 'So what?' and 'Why speak *at all*?' In its populist version this drift from relativism to tragic cynicism and nihilist truculence was condensed in the mantra, 'Turn on, tune in, and drop out' and elevated into a subversive principle by the many countercultural utopias of the day. Anti-establishment theory and action frequently assumed the form of 'anti-theory' movements.

2.2 Situated theoretical contexts: seven species of reflexivity or 'the revolt against positivism'

In what follows we can understand the expressions 'reflexivity' and 'self-reflexivity' not only as iconic banners for alternative interpretive frameworks but as markers for different ontological commitments responsive to the idea of thought turning back, returning and recovering its own constitutive, historical, and dialectical presuppositions, its core values and way of being-in-the-world. The ancient metaphysical idea of the 'unity' of theory and practice – of thought and being – returned in the appearance of theorizing and practical action exploring the interplay between constructed versions of reality and particular modes of thought. The result of these developments was an increasing awareness of the dialectical complexity and historical mutability of social worlds. It was this renewed awareness of complexity that prompted the many attempts to appropriate the legacy of radical reflection as one way of renewing neglected traditions of critical thought.

While philosophy had, at least as a *credo*, pursued radical reflection on its own metaphysical concepts and imagined the 'deconstruction' of the history of metaphysics, in 1970s social theory critical self-reflection on ideological and normative presuppositions became the only game in town. In this critical atmosphere the idea of *reflection* was inevitably transformed from a resource into a topic of social inquiry. This led many radicals to turn away from academic life to locate 'theory-in-practice' on the streets (finding that not just 'Beauty' but Theory 'is in the street') or even to abandon Western thought as a lost cause and embrace Eastern religious traditions and practices. To pursue theory and social research without reflection was to admit the failure of the sociological and historical imagination. Theorists who pursued their profession with little thought to their own conceptual and discursive presuppositions – their own operative 'theory of mind' and communicative aims – were in fact helping to reproduce thoughtless versions of human speech. As with the mainstream social sciences, philosophy without radical reflection had become a purely inward-looking and instrumental discipline (exemplified by the detached pursuit of 'conceptual analysis' and 'logical positivism').

Risking the dangers of a 'summarizing Proust' competition, the following *models of reflection* (and their associated *styles of thought* and associated *modes of praxis*) in the field of 1960s and 1970s academic sociology can be distinguished. When viewed as analytic versions of self and community, each of these perspectives may be located on a continuum ranging from 'weak reflection' (committed, so to speak, to revisionary metaphysics) at one extreme to 'strong self-reflection' ('radical dialogue' questioning orthodox metaphysical frameworks and their institutional armatures) at the other. I will argue that the Analytic theorizing developed by Alan Blum and Peter McHugh and their colleagues in a series of publications through the 1970s and into the 1980s intervened on the radical side of this spectrum.

1 First, the model of reflection as a *methodological technique* to *reform* positivism and behaviourism and reinstate then-influential value-free paradigms of social science and epistemology, leading to the design of more context-sensitive quantitative protocols, sophisticated mathematical modelling, and general systems models of social phenomena. This revisionary gesture remained firmly committed to the descriptive and explanatory aims of metaphysical naturalism and survives to this day in the procedural instruction provided by most departments of social science (the division of 'scientific methods' training into 'quantitative' and 'qualitative' branches is one of its lasting educational legacies). Here we might mention influential American figures such as George C. Homans, Paul Lazarsfeld, Robert K. Merton, David Riesman, and Edward Shils in the development of standard American sociology (it is now difficult to understand the popular reception that greeted Homans' polemical *ASR* essay 'Bringing Men (*sic!*) Back In' in 1964). But it was perhaps Talcott Parsons' intrepid journey as an 'inveterate theorist' that was the most sustained attempt to rescue naturalistic social science from the limited framework of empiricism and behaviourism. With Parsons, the literal understanding of the social as a stable normative order and functioning system – a thinly disguised vision of an imaginary, harmoniously stratified American society – remained unquestioned, as did the monadic ideal of the *theorist-as-hero*. Parsons was, however, a conduit to older European theorists and problematics. Parsons' analytic version of self, his way of being-in-the-world, is displayed in the image of *convergent intellectual synthesis* of European social theory that authorized and informed his work as this developed from his integrative reading of predominantly late nineteenth- and early twentieth-century theorists in *The Structure of Social Action* (1937) to his grand project of constructing a systemic conceptual

framework as a heuristic representation of society and its sub-systems in *The Social System* (1951). This culminated in Parsons' later speculations about the cybernetic principles of a general theory of action systems grounded in a structural-functional systems paradigm that might unify all the 'human sciences' under a transdisciplinary framework of scientific inquiry (for example in Parsons, 1966). Essentially the same objective was pursued in German sociology by Niklas Luhmann, but with more philosophical rigour and guided by the master themes of communicative reflexivity, societal differentiation and systems integration (Luhmann, 2013a, 2013b).

Under this heading we might also include the appearance of humanist, ethnographic, and qualitative alternatives to the dominant naturalist tradition of American social science. For example, Reflexive Anthropology's emphasis on the confessional acknowledgement of the role of researcher self-involvement and the ethnographic methodology of 'thick description' (associated with the work of the anthropologist Clifford Geertz) and the distinction that many researchers began to routinely draw between *etic* (external and taxonomic categories) and *emic* (functional and meaningful categories) methodological strategies), the revival of interest in the self-oriented theories of Symbolic Interaction associated with the humanist writings of Kenneth Burke and George Herbert Mead and the 'Chicago School' of social science (from Robert Park and Ernest Burgess to Herbert Blumer and Howard Becker), the context-defined project of 'grounded theory' formulated by Barney Glaser and Anselm Strauss (1967), a renewed interest in naturalistic pragmatism defended by Charles Sanders Peirce, William James and John Dewey, and the inspiration of the later 'pragmatic turn' and neo-pragmatism associated with Richard Rorty, the early dramaturgical sociology of Erving Goffman (*The Presentation of Self in Everyday Life*, 1959), Aaron V. Cicourel's *Method and Measurement in Sociology* (1964), Abraham Kaplan's *The Conduct of Inquiry* (1964), Max Black's *Models and Metaphors* (1962), Paul Goodman's *Growing Up Absurd* (1960), among other critical voices. In the wider American philosophical field we should also note the appearance of *revisionary naturalisms* explicitly crafted to avoid the reductionism of traditional empiricism and logical positivism (linked to the names of post-analytic philosophers like Willard van Orman Quine, Hilary Putnam, Donald Davidson, John Searle, Stanley Cavell, Paul Feyerabend, and Charles Taylor). Not surprisingly such reflections focused on the ambiguities of *method* framed in scientistic forms as restricting the pursuit of knowledge. All of these intellectual currents were concerned to expand the field of what was conceptually possible in philosophy, the social sciences and humanities (cf. Bernstein, 1983; Davidson, 1984; Dewey, 1958; Putnam, 1981; Quine, 1971, 1976; Rorty, 1979, 1991; Searle, 1969). Many refocused philosophy upon questions of meaning, interpretation and subjectivity.

2   Second, reflection understood as an *epistemic opportunity* grounded in alternative philosophical traditions of interpretation, exemplified by the

Sociology of Everyday Life, Ethnomethodology and Conversation Analysis. Here the mundane operations of language and reflexivity *in practical action* were invoked in the context of the discovery of the self-referential complexities of the micro-worlds of everyday activities and mundane social interaction. The interpretive reinvigoration of micro-sociology – the invention of the social role and ideal of ethnomethodological indifference – opened a polemical space for programmes of descriptive research associated with the early ethnomethodological movement (Garfinkel's programmatic *Studies in Ethnomethodology* (1967), Cicourel's *Cognitive Sociology* (1973), McHugh's *Defining the Situation* (1968), Sacks' early 'Sociological Description' (1963) and his then-unpublished lectures on Conversation Analysis (Sacks, 1992), and the 'Left-turn' of radical ethnomethodology (Pollner, 1991)).

Human beings were liberated from their earlier status as objects and granted properties unique to subjective agents. Rather than applying external methods (and objectifying methodologies) ethnomethodology turned to study the everyday 'methods' used by members in organizing their social worlds. With this shift toward human contexts reflexivity is transformed from a *technical* or *methodological* issue of research to a rich and complex resource used in the construction of social orders by knowledgeable agents. This resulted in accounts of the self-referential complexities of ordinary language as constitutive of the *substance* of social interaction itself, known and addressed by members in the orderly co-production of their routine social interactions (in social practices of meaningful action, accounting, labelling, excusing, glossing, justifying, pleading, reformulating, etc.). Where Garfinkel's seminal 'Studies of the Routine Grounds of Everyday Activities' (1964) sketched its paradigmatic sociological definition, Pollner's *Mundane Reasoning* (1987) was, perhaps, its most articulate philosophical formulation.

The outcome of this development – 'working out Durkheim's aphorism' to treat social facts as things (Garfinkel, 2002) – was a renewed sense of the reflexive complexities of the realm of practical activities exemplified empirically, for example, in the organizational studies of Egon Bittner, Harvey Sacks, Melvin Pollner, David Sudnow, Lindsey Churchill, Don Zimmerman, Emanuel Schegloff, and others – for samples from the late 1960s and 1970s see Turner (1974). Rather than imposing methods *upon* social phenomena the task was to investigate the methods that *produced* such phenomena. Unfortunately the complex *historical* problematics of everyday talk, embodied awareness, and organized discourses were typically confined to questions of local sense-making and organizational accounting practices. The broader structures of human historicity and the fundamental location of individuals and communities as beings-in-language were occluded. While this is not the place to review the radical implications and ramifications of this insight for the practice of social inquiry and sociological education, we can observe that the turn to the interpretive procedures of everyday language and the concrete negotiated orders of ordinary life not only founded the many programmes of descriptive ethnomethodology and, later, Conversation Analysis but indirectly led to a renewed interest in the writings of such notable non-sociologists as Ludwig Wittgenstein, John L. Austin, Gilbert Ryle, John Wisdom, Peter Winch, Paul Grice, Stephen Toulmin, Ferdinand de Saussure, Edmund Husserl, Martin Heidegger, Noam Chomsky, Jean Piaget, Kenneth Burke, Roland Barthes, Alexandre Kojève, Stanley Cavell, D.S. Schwayder, Hannah Arendt, Leo Strauss, and Stanley Rosen. We should also note that this generalized account of 'indexical expressions' in semantic theory and associated problems of the replacement of indexical by 'objective' expressions dates back to the famous paper of Yehoshua Bar-Hillel (*Mind*, 1954) with antecedents in the paradoxes generated by the formalization projects of Bertrand Russell, Gottlob Frege, Kurt Gödel, and others logical theorists in the first half of the twentieth century. We might also mention the emergence of Transformational Generative Grammar in the work of the American linguist Noam Chomsky (his breakthrough works *Syntactic Structures* and *Aspects of the Theory of Syntax* appeared in 1957 and 1965 respectively). Chomsky was one of the key sources for the idea of deep-structures operating as a generative nexus of linguistic and cognitive competences (or, in Saussure's terms, the rules of *langue* as the generative matrix of performative speech (*parole*)). The renewed interest in the complexity of natural language and everyday cognition led to a more semantically rich conception of the cognitive sciences of mind influenced by Lev Vygotsky, Jerome Bruner, George Miller, and others. This development culminated in Chomsky's reflections in *Language and Mind* (1972) on the general significance of the linguistic revolution for the social sciences and philosophy.

3   Third, the notion of self-reflection as an incentive to create a reformed 'Sociology of Knowledge' building and revising the classical work of Karl Mannheim, Robert K. Merton, and C. Wright Mills. 'Knowledge', its history, institutional mediations and situated societal contexts, was located as an important field of sociological and cultural research in its own right. The idea of recursive investigation as a 'knowledge of knowledge', would subsequently find expression in the 'Sociology of Sociological Knowledge' (Friedrichs, 1970), and, more broadly, in the 'Sociology of Scientific Knowledge' and eventually 'Science (and Technology) Studies' as these disciplines and programmes are practised today. The protracted 'debate' about the place of self-reflexivity in empirical science studies would later bifurcate the field into antagonists (Barry Barnes, David Bloor, Trevor Pinch, Michael Lynch) and protagonists (among these the most constructivist orientations of Steve Woolgar, Mike Mulkay, Malcolm Ashmore, and Bruno Latour). Unfortunately, more radical meanings of reflexivity and self-reflection were covered up in the sterile debates that polarized the field into critics of 'vicious circularity' (antagonists) and defenders of 'virtuous circularity' (protagonists). The default relativist idiom of the day became 'the social

construction of reality' (an expression borrowed from the work of Peter Berger and Thomas Luckmann, 1966), 'reconstructions of sociological knowledge' (Douglas, 1971), and 'new directions in sociological theory' (the title of the collection published by Paul Filmer *et al.* in 1972). Indirectly this celebration of sociological relativism and recursive reflection would provide an incentive for later Social Constructionist theorizing and more generic programmes of research into the sociocultural construction of orders of facticity and their sustaining social worlds (Burr, 1995; Latour and Woolgar, 1979; Lock and Strong, 2010; Potter, 1996; Potter and Wetherell, 1987). These anti-empiricist developments were also reinforced by independent developments in the history of science and research focused upon the investigative practices of particular scientific communities. Here the path-breaking text was Thomas Kuhn's historically informed analysis of 'normal science' and scientific revolutions in his seminal work *The Structure of Scientific Revolutions* (1962). After Kuhn the term 'paradigm' became as central (and over-extended) as the word 'reflexivity'. To contextualize Kuhn's work we should also cite the influential writings of Pierre Duhem, Henri Poincaré, Karl Popper, Imre Lakatos, Gerard Holton, Paul Feyerabend, and Stephen Toulmin among other thinkers involved in the historicizing of scientific knowledge. Paul Feyerabend's 1975 text *Against Method* is a crucial document of these contested versions of science and method. This development was complemented by a broader European tradition of thought focused upon the idea of a rigorous *science of sciences* (*knowledge of knowledge*) from which emerged the project of a *genealogy of knowledge formations and scientific discourses* (associated with the rationalist tradition of Gaston Bachelard, Georges Canguilhem and Michel Foucault). A powerful conception of self-reflection as meta-science (*metatheory*) continues to draw its inspiration from both Kuhn's theory of paradigm change and the broader Continental rationalist tradition (for example, Foucault, 1970, 1972, 1977; cf. Dreyfus and Rabinow, 1983).

4   Fourth, reflection as an activity of *self-reporting and autobiographical confession.* Alvin Gouldner's quest for a 'Reflexive sociology', traced in a series of texts published in the 1970s, is the most prominent example of this idea of *personal reflexivity.* Gouldner's rejection of the positivist grounds of the then-influential mode of doing sociology dominated by the 'world of Talcott Parsons' appeared in his 1970 book, *The Coming Crisis of Western Sociology*; Part IV of the *Coming Crisis* ('The Theorist Pulls Himself Together Partially'). Identifying a paradigmatic struggle between Parsonian structural-functionalism and alternative radical Marxist frameworks, Gouldner articulated a vision of reflexive sociology as a *value-laden confessional genre* (1971: 481–512) which he expanded and defended at length in his influential 1973 work, *For Sociology: Renewal and Critique in Sociology Today.* In this way Gouldner's advocacy of personal self-reflection upon theorists' values, ideological beliefs, and political commitments opened a path for a spate of attempts to return self-experience and agency to the

centre of sociological work and with this existential turn to foreground the fundamental role of story-making, metaphor, irony, doubt, contestation and, *in extremis*, radical political self-assertion in creative sociological work.

5   Fifth, reflexivity as a critical theory of *practical reasoning and creative praxis* in the context of neo-Marxist and post-Marxist theories of everyday life, discourse and communication. With the demise of the 'Old Left', the New Left took refuge in theories of everyday life, communication and discourse, and a revaluation of the 'relative autonomy' of culture and other 'superstructural' formations. We might illustrate this development with the pragmatic-communicative turn in the work of second-generation Frankfurt School theorists such as Jürgen Habermas, Karl-Otto Apel, Albrecht Wellmer, and their students, in Hannah Arendt's *Human Condition*, Agnes Heller's theory of everyday life, the heterodox work of the 'Bakhtin Circle', Niklas Luhmann's systems theorizing, and Henri Lefebvre's critique of everyday life. All of these disparate projects are implicitly unified in rejecting the reductive logic of dialectical materialism and mechanistic conceptions of self, culture, and society. All would develop alternative 'critical theories' by stressing the relative autonomy of ideology and cultural forms. Habermas continued to articulate the linkages between rational discourse and emancipative politics as a general theory of 'communicative action' and normative political judgement throughout his later work. Alvin Gouldner had already formulated its basic maxim: 'Of the many who hear the call to this new mission for sociology [that is, the creation of a radical, reflexive sociology] only those will be 'chosen' who understand that there is no way of making a new sociology without undertaking a new praxis' (1971: 512). One of the products of these debates was the reinterpretation of the central task of social theory in terms of 'solving' the difference between the dynamics of micro-interaction and the structural determinism of macro-structures or, as this was later expressed, as resolving the problem of the relationship between 'agency' and 'structure' (cf. Giddens, 1979, 1984; Dallmayr and McCarthy, 1977). Each of these perspectives helped to open dialogues around the intersubjective relationships between motivated action and understanding (*Verstehen*), knowledge, truth and values, communication, power, and politics (dialogues that would draw into their orbit the Frankfurt School of Critical Theory represented in America by Douglas Kellner, Stephen Eric Bronner, and Martin Jay and intersect productively with the Nietzschean current of post-structural explorations in the work of Michel Foucault, Gilles Deleuze, Jean-François Lyotard, Michel Serres, Pierre Bourdieu, Jean-Luc Nancy, and others).

6   Sixth, the tradition of Husserlian transcendental phenomenology radicalized around the life-world or *Lebenswelt* problematic:

6.1   as a transcendental theory of pre-predicative perception and embodiment ('lived experience') as the ontological ground of reason and rational praxis. The key figure was the French phenomenologist,

Maurice Merleau-Ponty and his argument for the centrality of perceptual life, the primacy of incarnate knowing grounded in pre-reflective ontological relations, the interfaces between language and the symbolic order, and his remarkable efforts to transcend the 'philosophy of consciousness' by radicalizing the dialectical figure of the lived body and humanly constituted space (1962, 1964a, 1964b). Many who were young academics at the time retain a vivid memory of reading Merleau-Ponty's *Phenomenology of Perception* (1962), *Signs* (1964b), and his posthumous text, *The Visible and the Invisible* (1968) in the late 1960s. Some – like John O'Neill – would undertake to translate little-known texts from Merleau-Ponty (for example *The Prose of the World*, *Humanism and Terror*) and work these ideas into their own conception of a reflexive sociology (O'Neill's *Sociology as a Skin Trade* (1972) being one of the first engagements with a critical sociology of embodiment as the dialectical interface of self and world);

6.2 the development of a sociocultural theory of the life-world construed as the intersubjective world of everyday life or what *OBSI* called (at p. 110) 'phenomenological social psychology' (Alfred Schutz, 1964, 1972), and other phenomenologically-inspired thinkers concerned with the descriptive analysis of the structures of the life-world and human agency (among the most prominent exponents being Aron Gurwitsch, Maurice Natanson, James Edie, George Psathas, Don Idhe, Calvin O. Schrag, and Fred Dallmayr); and

6.3 as a way of exploring ontic forgetfulness, the ontological difference between beings and Being, loss of 'world', and the larger project of ontological recovery in the then-current writings of Martin Heidegger (the worldly status of *Dasein*, the *Seinsfrage* or hermeneutic question of the meaning of Being, and the impact of 'fundamental ontology' in the work of what critics at the time disparagingly termed 'Heideggerian sociology' and *partially* exemplified in some of the texts in Sandywell *et al.*, *Problems of Reflexivity and Dialectics in Sociological Inquiry* (1975/2014).

7 Finally, reflexive strategies derived from a range of critical practices that might, with the risk of some distortion, be called the *hermeneutics of reading*. Most of these developments sought to revive the critical impulse of earlier accounts of reading and interpretation or what Paul Ricoeur called 'the hermeneutics of suspicion' (1970, 1974). Among the most influential of these projects were structuralist re-readings of Marx and Freud (initiated by Louis Althusser, Jacques Lacan, Paul Ricoeur, and their students), the hermeneutics of the subject and 'care of the self' in Michel Foucault's later work, reflexive reading practices as deconstructive acts (Jacques Derrida), the exploration of alternative practices of writing and narrative linked to the political, ethical and feminist turn in post-metaphysical science and philosophy, Jean Baudrillard's announcement of the 'end of the social' and the

triumph of the virtual, and, perhaps most significant of all, the exploration of more radical dialogical models of knowledge, self, and truth (associated with a diverse range of figures such as Martin Buber, Mikhail Bakhtin, Hans-Georg Gadamer, Paul Ricoeur, Walter Benjamin, Emmanuel Levinas, Julia Kristeva, and Hélène Cixous).

3 The project of Analytic sociology

Something like this climate of discontent and intellectual change was in play in the concerns of early Analysis. Understanding this profoundly polemical context is necessary if we are to reconstruct the categories and 'game rules' that Analysis both presupposed as a resource and negated as an integral part of its commitment to a radically 'other' mode of speech and relationship with language. Throughout we need to keep the core question in focus: In what sense was the project of *Analytic sociology* a game-changing text? Or more simply expressed: What is the *problem* for which Analytic theorizing is a *solution*?

I will explore these questions by means of a series of interrelated thematic constellations.

3.1 Language and speech as ontological events

What is *the reflexive imperative* and how should we practise self-reflexive speech?

Where many theoretical perspectives developed in the 1960s and 1970s had recognized the irreducible and ubiquitous operations of self-reflexivity and the mediations of signification and language in their various constructive enterprises, and had begun to imagine alternative forms of speech and writing (alternative curricula and syllabi, cross-disciplinary journal debates, alternative lecture styles, and so on), few of these 'alternatives' were discourse-centred and even fewer were discourse-decentred in actively embracing the fundamental *reflexive theorem* that *all* acts of speech could – and in an ethical sense *must* – be able to articulate and exemplify their own categories and social commitments as a *principled* concern.

While American social science produced a range of alternative 'sensitizing concepts', 'conceptual frameworks' and 'methods', it engaged in minimal reflection on the *linguistic, existential and ontological commitments* involved in these alternative conceptual schemes. The notion that such discourses were commending and promoting *particular forms of life* was literally unthinkable. As if to protect themselves from this kind of self-involving dialectic the world of theory and the world of everyday practices were understood as discrete 'spheres', operating in complete isolation from one another. Theoretical description and explanation was understood as a categorial representation of pre-existent objects and practices. Given this ancient separation of 'theory' and 'practice' the Word and the World could not be articulated as a radically dialectical process. Something called 'life' (or 'everyday reality') was opposed to something called 'thought' ('theory', 'analysis', 'knowledge', 'science', 'philosophy'). As theorizing was taken to be completely indifferent to 'life', so subjectivity, contextuality, and reflexivity could only appear as epistemic irritants, the anecdotal intrusion of 'values' from another alien 'sphere'. And that sphere was to be carefully cordoned off as a no-go zone. In place of a more thoughtful analysis of the interplay of analytic language and phenomenal contexts we find a deep-rooted rhetoric of speech as a 'view from nowhere' and of epistemology and methodology from a 'God's-eye perspective' (Nagel, 1986; cf. Haraway, 1991; Harding, 1991). Value-free social research painted itself into the aporetic corner of a context of no context.

Where conventional critical sociologies treated reflexivity as *anecdotal*, Analysis commended self-reflection upon the grounds of speech and language as a *principled* concern for *every kind of inquiry*. In other words, Analysis embraced the imperative obligation that flowed from recognizing the intrinsic self-referentiality of words and language, of thought and life. If all speech originates as a particular form of language, every responsible speaking must involve some acknowledgement of the 'grounded' legacy of language and the intrinsic violence involved in the 'separation' and 'differentiation' of acts of speaking within the wider normative contexts of linguistic and cultural engagements. The idea of nature speaking itself or a God's-eye view of the world was internally incoherent and indefensible. Expressed more politically, unreflective versions of speech and inquiry that ignore or evade this process of self-recognition and indebtedness must be radically challenged. Even the celebrated 'neutrality' of objective science was to be reframed as a topic for radical historical reflection.

In contrast to many influential forms of interpretive and critical sociology, Analysis's fundamental question – its *originary problematic* – is to remind readers that every act of speaking belongs to (and unintentionally commends) a *form of life*, or, even more existentially expressed, that speaking reflectively is not only a specialized *rhetoric* or *way of talking*, but more profoundly an *inventive communal pursuit* and principled *way of life*. The same question can be asked of every *social* and *philosophical* theory: would you want to live in 'the social' posited by the assumptions of this method or theory? To speak and write is not merely to convey a message, defend a cause, represent facts or reveal a world, but to *self*-represent, to *imagine, construct, display, defend*, and *personify* a particular *relation* to a world, tradition, and way of being-in-the-world, to implicitly *promote* a particular normative *identity* shaped in and by transactions within a specific historic legacy. In short, no speech is possible outside the relation that *OBSI* formulated with the metaphor of *grounding*. The force of this elementary insight into generative grounds moves reflection from the commonplace fact that speaking is a socially motivated and interested activity (expressed, for example, in the various language-games constructed by the human sciences and humanities) to the idea that speech tacitly *encodes* powerful ethical, ontological, and ideological commitments which, once disclosed, can disturb and transgress the existing *status quo*. This is where the questions, Whose text? and Whose context? become politically consequential (cf. Schegloff, 1997).

Analysis, in other words, asks the elemental question about the *ethicality of reflection*: *what kind of moral world and political order is implicit in your way of talking, researching, writing, educating*? Given this principled concern with the 'positive negativity' of all acts of speech, it followed that every form of social theory – indeed every act of theorizing and form of writing when viewed as a *rhetorical* and *social achievement* – is itself an instance of the kind of phenomenon it seeks to describe, analyse, and explain. This principle, of course, resonated with the 1960s *Zeitgeist* that every kind of knowledge and every knowledge claim are in some deep sense value-driven, interested, and political (the question 'Whose knowledge?' can be raised with regard to every epistemic discourse in the human and physical sciences). And asking 'Whose knowledge?' suggests alternative and conflicting forms of analysis. The implicit 'conflict' internal to speech and writing simply replicates the conflictual concerns that empirical discourses seek to address. Rather like the social anthropologist Claude Lévi-Strauss admitting that his work on South American myths is, in its own way a myth (cf. Derrida, 1972: 257–258), all speech (*qua muthos*) reveals a form of life in its desire to articulate and explain other forms of life. In this way the violent *rhetorical* projection of imagined communities in the course of social life sustains both the practices of everyday life and the specialist projects of reflection and theorizing irrespective of whether these are described as 'scientific' or 'humanistic'. Interrogating this inescapable *dialectical* relativity, reflecting on the pre-reflective *complicity* that forms the normative horizon of every move within a symbolic order, is one of the first tasks of any discourse that aspires to be reflexive.

For most scholars and researchers, however, what was understood by the term 'reflexivity' (and implicitly by *ethicality* and *sociality*) simply named a routine *problem*, *puzzle*, or *paradox* associated with the conventionality or 'arbitrariness' of language that was better kept hidden or actively excluded from 'responsible' social-scientific discourse (this standard response would be frequently invoked in construing the imperative of self-reflection as an 'irritant' or 'obstacle' in the pursuit of objective knowledge and scientific responsibility (and subsequently as something to be excised from any possible sociology of scientific knowledge (SSK) and the sociology of the sociology of scientific knowledge (SSSK)). From this position 'self-reflexivity' was something to be confessed and footnoted before returning to 'business as usual'.

The elementary metanarrative fact that we can speak about things but also speak about our own speech (its 'grounds' and categorial architecture) was taken as a fortuitous happenstance and, for all intents and purposes, ignored. Occasionally the 'problem of reflexivity' in many of these disputes was reduced to the status of a viral danger that demanded careful intellectual management with appropriate policies of screening, quarantine, and systematic immunization. At all costs the normal work of cognitive representation had to be protected from self-reflection. As *OBSI* itself pointed out, there are innumerable forms of evasion in social life as well as in theoretical work. In an era that celebrated the death of the author and the end of the social, becoming 'overly' preoccupied with self-reflection was judged to be a kind of infantile abrogation of serious objective research and narcissistic regression to self-obsessed and self-refuting habits of thought. In a further act of self-violence, the ruling norm of positivity demanded that all speech about the grounds of speech was to be ruled out of court in deference to the 'serious' speech that reflected the order of things without mediation or the 'corruption' of existential values and evaluative judgement. Social analysis would ideally like to appear as the outcome of a purely transparent conceptual language. In the light of this election editors of journals and other gatekeepers imagined their work to be one of filtering out discourse that failed to comply with an imaginary canon of representational speech.

In other words, *serious inquiry was equated with objective speech as the language of science liberated from mediation.* In interrupting the interdiction that flowed from this equation Analytic sociology was distinctive not only in being deeply concerned with the singularly reflexive character of theoretic speech, but also committed to implementing ways in which forms of speech and representation (along with their *authorial functions* and *imagined communities*) could be problematized and, by exploiting this irreducible recursivity, how more dialectical procedures might be developed to deconstruct conventional investigative practices and forms of inquiry. As we shall see later the concern with the implicit *politics of form, style,* and *media* – and indeed with the reality of *mediation* per se – as value-shaping forms of our inherited language-games would remain a central preoccupation of Analytic work.

3.2 The reflexive imperative and the ethicality of speaking

This principled concern for the covert violence and reflective singularity of speech and ways of talking, however, was merely one phase of a radical critique of the institutional logics of social research and social science as a form of life itself. Analytic sociology's fundamental insight was to understand 'the problem of reflexivity' (as this was typically phrased in the vocabulary of 1970s sociology) as a *positive incentive* to shape a version of creative theorizing oriented to the desire to speak responsibly and to pursue a life of thoughtful inquiry as a way of being-in-the-world. In this sense what initially began as an apparently straightforward task of 'speaking about speech' – for example, to uncover the negativity of positivism's putative positivity – became inseparable from the desire to expand the realms of intellectual reflection and discursive possibilities that would encompass not only the dominant course of modern thought but the historical origins of Western culture itself. In practice, of course, we can no more evade the reflexive imperative that relates grounds to forms of speech than we can transcend the horizon of language or escape from the tacit moral and social frameworks that sustain the possibility of intelligible speech. Trying to 'evade' the dialectical structure of reflexivity is like running away from one's own shadow or 'trying to walk in the snow without leaving footprints' (Baudrillard and Valiente Noailles, 2007: 125). Analysis embraces the idea that a deep logic of indebtedness – the inescapable *fact* of self-exemplification – is part of the human condition itself.

If we have unconsciously inherited an instrumental or representational conception of language the first analytic task is to examine the covert violence at
work in the tradition and history of representation itself, of how such forms of
speech have excluded all reference to grounds and thereby occluded the radical
sociality of thought and learning. The ethical imperative of contestation is
expressed in Alan Blum's thesis that theorizing 'is the speaking which understands itself as inescapably rhetorical, and which acts upon such an understanding by preparing its very speech as an argument for the rationality of that
commitment' (Blum, 1974: 169). Blum's thesis is a particular version of the
ontological claim that analytic speech is speech that is concerned with recovering its principled indebted relationship to the symbolic order of language, itself
construed as a metaphor for our inescapable orientation to the collective order of
the human condition and, ultimately, to the enigma and ambiguity of our *being-
in-the-world*. What concrete and objective speech neglects is that to exist as
human beings is to exist thoughtfully, to tacitly display the ambivalent tensions
and *aporia* that order our being alive here-and-now *in medias res*. By opposing
this forgetfulness analytic speech can be described as language that *recovers* and
relocates the grounded character of concrete speech by revealing the sources and
origins of its limited rationality as a distinctive form of life.

From this perspective the recognition that *reflexivity* and *self-reflexivity* were
not simply local 'problems' or technical 'issues' to be confessed (Gouldner),
sociologically described and glossed (Garfinkel), or reformulated in metalinguis-
tic or metalogical terms (as in the approach of logical theory from Russell and
the early Wittgenstein to contemporary set-theoretic discourse – for example, the
work of Alain Badiou today (2009, 2013)), but a clue to the dialectical movement of language itself led Analysis to engage with and appropriate earlier ways
of thinking that had struggled to articulate these kinds of problem (in this context
Hegel's life-long reflection on the dialectic of categories and forms of consciousness, Wittgenstein's concern for the conventionality and self-referentiality of
language use, and Heidegger's creative re-writing of the self-involving *logos*
that appear in the texts of Heraclitus and Parmenides became particularly
important provocations).

Heidegger's notion of *Destruktion*, his radical path of 'thinking' (*Denken*),
and his preoccupation with the ontological difference (scission) between Being
and being(s) became a consequential horizon for early Analytic sociology. But
Heidegger's work is also to be treated as an *instance* or *example* and not as the
standard of reflexive thought. Heidegger's deconstructive thinking was also to
be contested with respect to its confinement to a self-imposed ontotheological
horizon – what other critics would later call its commitment to the *metaphysics
of presence* – and as a consequence its failure to develop a radically social and
ethicopolitical problematic. As post-phenomenological thinkers like Adorno
(1973b, 2005), Arendt (1958), Derrida (1973, 1978), and Levinas (1969) had
also argued, Heidegger's 'overcoming' of European nihilism was insufficiently
self-reflexive and, as a consequence, necessarily defaulted to another, if more
subtle and dangerous, variant of nihilism. At root the Heideggerian path failed to

respond to the question of ethical indebtedness and human fragility and in that failure inevitably occluded the vital problematics of natality, community, politics, and symbolic obligation. Heidegger had failed to ask how his own thinking displayed the kind of person he wished to be (and, more consequentially, the kind of community he would wish to live in). In this respect Heidegger's critique of 'the forgetting of Being' and the subsequent course of ontotheological metaphysics fell behind the self-analytic critiques of Kant and the dialectical thought of Hegel with their concern for the existential mediations of categories, of self-recognition through the manifold forms of symbolic consciousness and the historical deformations of ethicopolitical life. What Heidegger had theorized as the polysemic history of 'Being' (*Sein*), in other words, was still locked into the European logocentric quest for a grounding event (*Ereignis*) understood as a foundation (*Grund*), and as such this kind of hermeneutics still actively concealed the more radical horizon of corporeal finitude and dialogue that makes any kind of self-reference, reflection and communality possible. Like Nietzsche before him, Heidegger misconstrued the Platonic texts as the fateful source of the metaphysical tradition, failing to understand the Socratic idea that dialogical reflexivity or the agonistic play of dialectic is an *intrinsic political horizon* of the self's being-in-the-world.

3.3 The failure of positivism

What was Analysis against? We can say immediately that the papers gathered and published as *On the Beginning of Social Inquiry* were locally concerned with addressing the limits of sociological reasoning ('the failure of positivism' and the authors' retrospective gloss that 'the paper on motives is really about sociology' (43)). The immediate adversary is the method and language-games of positivist social science, but the larger horizon is an influential version of language understood as *mimesis* (or what we might call the ethos of *representationalism*). For Analysis, positive method is merely one late-modern form of *representational thinking* that continues to misconceive the life of dialogue in creative experience (cf. Auerbach, 1953). Establishing the inherent limits of representation is itself a metaphor for thinking through the mimetic desire that inaugurated the Western tradition of dialectical thought.

'Failure' in this context might be heard as metonymic for the situation of instrumental and mimetic speech as language alienated from its grounds, speech separated from its sustaining horizon, speech that silences the question of its own ontological and ethical possibility. For Analysis, speech loses its principled reflexivity in evading reflection on the prior possibility of reference and representation. If all speech reveals its indebtedness to some principled commitment, speaking that elides such auspices reveals the process of alienation at work in language. For this attitude, speaking and the community of dialogue appear as simply items on a list of discrete things. Positivist conceptions of representation no less than deconstructive versions of anti-mimesis display this alienation in extreme forms. Indeed the pursuit of theory – whether in functionalism, critical sociology, survey research, or postmodern thought – inevitably poses the question of self-representation in revealing its own version of authoritative discourse as 'speech that corresponds with the real'.

In uncovering this deep logic of evasion and forgetfulness Analysis displays its own alternative sense of anamnetic method. Analysis' method only achieves responsibility by producing its own version of itself as a principled concern. By concealing its commitment beneath representational images of language and thought, unreflective discourse hides and devalues the very grounds that make its own project possible. Given its ubiquity this order of irony has sedimented as a routine part of the essential rationale of modern social science research, whether functional, critical, or ethnomethodological in form. Within a wider historical frame the temptations of reductive, descriptive, representational and essentializing styles of speech turn out to be real possibilities of our own modernity, seductive forms of speech and displays of a particular way of being-in-the-world. At this critical juncture the method of Analytic sociology interfaces with an even more radical critique of forgetful modernity and its generative ideologies.

More creatively, *On the Beginning of Social Inquiry* was motivated by the aim of demonstrating – concretely 'showing' – an alternative conception of rational thought grounded not in the security of method, instrumental technique, theory convergence, or unmediated facticity but in the differential process of collaborative praxis itself. As the authors emphasize, their version of inquiry makes *conversational* collaboration a *necessary* feature of analytic work: *no dialogue, no analysis.* As the authors of *OBSI* make plain, collaborators 'remind us of that which we have to forget in order to speak. Without collaborators we would either have no reason to speak … or else we would have to give up our commitment to analysis' (4).

We have suggested that as a *subversive event, OBSI* intervened in a particular historical moment of sociological discord and philosophical change. One of the startling features of the book – *startling* in the historical context of American sociology in the 1950s and 1960s or what C. Wright Mills famously described as 'dust-bowl empiricism' (1970) – is that readers are actively encouraged to disengage from *all extant versions of social inquiry* and to disavow any kind of common focus or identity that might gather the papers into an alternative 'perspective'.

OBSI goes even further: we are to leave the polyphony of perspectives and opposing worldviews to their own devices. This explicit breach of expectations still resounds as a radical gesture. Readers are instructed that the collection of topics that make up the book have nothing *substantial* in common, not to look for repair work or methodological *fixes*, and to be prepared to distinguish Analytic work from any and every kind of descriptive, interpretive or structural sociology.

The chapters are thus not intended to be read as *samples* of phenomenology, ethnographies or ethnomethodological studies. Unlike ethnomethodology, for example, Analysis does not propose to describe and reconstruct common sense knowledge or the situated rationalities of members' activities. Its interest in the work of members' reasoning and membership conventions is ironic. Unlike normative sociology, the task of speaking about the ordinary is embraced as an extraordinary possibility of language. Indeed, the received meanings of 'membership', 'description', 'reconstruction', and 'representation' are to be recovered and reformulated as indices of more fundamental analytic concerns. Here the symptomatic *silences* of mainstream social science and philosophy are where we should begin to ask critical questions. What is at issue here is the very *idea* of the everyday, common sense, and descriptive correspondence that operate as an unacknowledged epistemology and normative paradigm for all forms of conventional social science. The dominant conception of 'theory' – namely disinterested conceptual *representation* or descriptive *mimesis* (and their version of 'failure' depicted as partiality, bias, and the like) understood as methodic *imitation* – is part of the problem and not the solution. Abstract theory-building – whether in the style of a Parsons, Merton or Habermas – should certainly be questioned and subject to phenomenological and political critique. But phenomenology and ethnomethodology are also in their own way artful discourses that construct their phenomenal objects but conceal their analytic versions of self and community. From the analytic perspective the socially organized conduct of theory and research – indeed the practices of *all* versions of rationality – need to be understood as indebted formations embedded in implicit language-games, narrative strategies, and forms of life that invite more radical analytic attention. We can readily see how this general *attitude* would resonate with many radical feminist approaches to science, epistemology and the gendered organization of everyday life (for example, Henriques *et al.*, 1984; Haraway, 1991; Smith, 1987; and Pollner, 1987).

For certain purposes any and every act of description, narration and representation can be viewed as an *indebted praxis* – a praxis that projects and invokes an idealized version of self ('I' or 'ego') and other ('Thou', the collective, generalized other, community, etc.). In producing this *double* every act of speech entails a conception of grounds ('objectivity', 'value', 'significance', 'relevance', 'order', 'identity', 'self-importance', and so on) that stands in need of *dialectical* justification. Expressed more directly, no act of speech, no account (*logos*) or theoretical discourse is analytically viable without a tacit relation of radical grounding. The *lack* of interest or concern for groundedness reveals the *aporetic* character of unreflective speech, the manifest irony displayed by theoretical discourses that are committed to description and analysis of the real and the 'everyday' while exempting their own signifying practices, rhetorical stratagems and stylistic life from reflection and critique. Unreflective speech that fails to examine its own *form* of description, analysis, and explanation might be likened to a Möbius strip that implicitly denies its self-involving structure, or a social game insisting that it is not a game, or an Escher drawing that has a logical resolution.

As practices insulated from and indifferent to radical reflection, many investigative frameworks contain an *aporetic* core of silences and, as such, are destined to have a half-life in the academic marketplace as they perform their work as temporary 'fixes' of some substantive, methodological, or epistemological trouble. The 'rhetoric of science' centres around concealing or disguising such silences as products of objective procedure. By bracketing the dominant paradigm of science that justifies this kind of disembodied mimetic speech and recovering the classical idea of self-engaged *theoria*, Analysis argues that we need to develop ways of transcending these self-limiting perspectives as an ethical imperative.

In the light of this principled commitment to reflexive grounding, readers are cautioned not to expect any kind of conventional 'overview' or 'introduction' to sociological work. Analysis in principle cannot 're-present' or replicate *any* phenomenal objects. Unlike ethnomethodological studies it has no abiding interest in the surface conventions and operative rules that organize social *phenomena*. Its principal interests are not in mimetically 'mapping' such phenomena, but rather in locating the *principled grounds of phenomenality* as social achievements, and in particular as 'grammatical' and rhetorical products of representational practices that conceal their own mediating work and 'political' ramifications. Readers who are committed to mimetic and technical versions of speech will therefore look in vain for concrete instructions on how to construct a more technically precise or instrumental recovery of the real.

In general, then, speech about concrete phenomena, worldly events, or 'topics' becomes analytic in recognizing the operation of social categories and other rule-constituted formations that operate prior to explicit reflection. The fundamental point, of course, is that as speakers – as lay theorizers – we have already 'begun', we are always already 'on the way', following well-worn rhetorical tracks in an apparently stable, but in reality chaotic, ideologically fraught discursive topographies. In other words whether we recognize it or not we are parties to unacknowledged language-games, implicit rhetorical contracts, and tacit metaphors that have been variously proposed as 'reality', 'common sense', 'everyday life', 'commonality', 'shared culture', and 'the moral order', but which, under analysis, turn out to be the outcome of constructive operations that belong to the imaginary institutions of society.

Not surprisingly, the first efforts to formulate the categories and grounds (auspices or imaginary institutions) of phenomena – for example, by uncovering their conceptual architecture – remain an incomplete resolution of analytic desire, an incomplete cure of forgetfulness, silence, and alienation. We have seen, for example, that interpretive approaches that preclude self-reflection risk being ironic instances of sublimated forms of thoughtlessness. In contrast to versions of speech that understand themselves as imitation or copies of the real, the identification of generative rules and the explication of forms of life need to be understood as *occasions* to engage in *self*-reflection – to ask how analysts' authorizing versions of self, community, reality, and so on are possible. In this context the silences of unreflective speech are recovered and indexed with the thematic status as *symptomatic occasions for analytic work*. 'Topics', 'usage', 'everyday commonplaces', and so on have the status of examples that provoke reflexive investigations. What have been hitherto spoken about as 'topics' or 'phenomena' are recovered as grammatical incentives, as indices marking the sites of possible dialectical histories.

3.4 Radical self-reflection

Analysis begins with deceptively simple questions: How did you get to think like *this*? What *kind* of practice, what *form* of life, authorizes *this* kind of speech? What possible *world* licenses you to speak (and write) about phenomena in *these* ways? What hidden *ethical* practices or *normative* order ground your theorizing activities? What other forms of speech were foreclosed by this election? Or, at its most generic, what was the *problem* for which this kind of speech and writing is commended as a *solution*?

What Marxists back in the day called the *unity of theory and practice* was thus a principal concern of Analytic sociology. In keeping with its Socratic ancestry, Analysis also calls for a radical change in our conventional ways of thinking about 'theory' and 'practice' that might precipitate a wider change in social and cultural institutions. But the change envisaged by Analysis was fundamentally different from the language-games played by Marxism, Phenomenological sociology, and Ethnomethodology (cf. *OBSI:* 122).

This is best seen in the idea of theorizing as transformative *self-reflection*. Reflection becomes *self-reflection* through the work of the other, the friend or community of friends who articulate an account of the limits of our own speech. Reflection becomes *radical* self-reflection by recovering the 'wholly other' source of intelligibility. Whatever the ghostly 'I' or 'self' may be, it is no longer a secure site of instrumental, authoritative or coercive speech, but fundamentally a conditional 'selfhood' already linguistically indebted to the other and continuously sustained and transformed in dialogue with the language of the other. In this context *friendship*, *generosity*, and *reciprocity* are part of a transformed attitude toward collaborative life.

With this single move Analysis disturbs and interrupts every received model of subjectivity and language (and of the 'subject in language'). Whatever language may be, it is first encountered as the language of others, of real and imagined voices, of delayed and dispersed signification that mediate our being-in-the-world. To use 'I' – to speak of the self, to speak of things – is to participate in a form of life governed by grammatical conventions. To refer descriptions and accounts to an 'I' is to stage a discourse where selectivity, distortion, bias, and 'subjectivity' become possible. Ironically, what orthodox science is eager to diagnose and condemn as 'distortion', 'bias', 'inadequacy', or 'ambiguity' turns out to be the spirited expressions of the finitude of all discourse, icons of a *human-all-too-human* indebtedness that undermines the myth of transparent, neutral, anonymous, and perfect speech. Non-authored speaking – the anonymity of objective truths – is revealed as a particular rhetorical stratagem. Even the most routine acts of referential speech implicate mediating layers of indebtedness as their sustaining condition. Ultimately how speech 'works' is not in the governance of individual decision or personal volition understood in naively psychological or sociological terms. Speaking – like every other form of social action – is a *situated* or *conventional* freedom indebted to horizons of alterity. In reality *every* speech act, every *convention* presupposes a grammar and secretes a hidden debt to darker ethical horizons. The assemblages we call 'referents', 'social reality', 'the world', and so forth are constituted in language (or, more precisely, in certain *kinds of language*). We might then say that the very *idea* of critical reason is itself a situated historical response to the desire to recover speech's moral indebtedness as an existential imperative. Like the motivating occasion of Hegel's dialectical philosophy of Spirit, Gadamer's celebration of the historicity of tradition, or Merleau-Ponty's later philosophy of the incarnate *logos*, Analysis is a *movement* 'toward a reason which would embrace its own origins' (Merleau-Ponty, 1993: 69; cf. Hegel, 1977; Gadamer, 1991).

As a strategy of *defamiliarization* and *derealization* the very ideas of 'narrator', 'reader', 'reading', and normal 'reader expectations' are breached and 'phenomenalized' as *rule-constituted* achievements. What was previously taken for a real 'unity' turns out to be the effect of grammars and related imaginary functions. 'Readers' ('subjects', 'reader-*positions*', 'interlocutors', 'audiences') are themselves imaginary and historical achievements and *like all such signifying practices* invitations to further cycles of self-reflection and *dialectical* critique.

In sum: language is first *mediation* not *mimesis*. With this shift of perspective, every variant of academic social science – as putative descriptive 'sciences of the real' – may be 'bracketed' and approached as local 'topics' or analytic 'phenomena' with regard to their constitutive norms and historical genesis. In historical terms, forms of mimesis are particular modes of remediation. It follows that any possible social science that aspires to explain the social world necessarily forms one part or moment of the world it seeks to represent. Without self-reflection representational and impersonal discourse risks repeating and reproducing the phenomenal world it describes: *Sic transit theoria mundi*.

But this act of de-realization, this 'putting out of play' is merely the other side of a 'putting into play'. What is put 'in play' here is a distinctive version of inquiry that insists on a radical difference between *doing membership* and *doing analysis* (or between *concrete* speech and *analytic* discourse). Every 'subjectivism' – every attempt at grounding speech in some privileged *subjectivity* or *intersubjectivity* – is to be treated, just as much as every 'objectivism' in the human sciences, as a local achievement of interested sense-making practices and institutional imperatives that conceal the grounds of their partiality and indebtedness.

Understood as rhetorical formations, every species of 'subjectivism' and 'objectivism' is self-positioned as an indexical achievement of local sense-making practices and rhetorical stratagems. Unsurprisingly, each 'resolution' of sociology's primary 'objective' generates contradictions and *aporiae*. Indeed from an Analytic perspective the very intelligibility of conventional social science is now viewed as grounded in an unacknowledged commitment to particular membership conventions that implicate their own coefficient of violence.

The investigative procedures of normative sociology (Parsonian structural-functionalism, Phenomenological sociology, Goffman-style dramaturgy, Ethnomethodology, Reflexive anthropology, and so on) however artful and insightful, all presuppose mimetic notions of 'objective description', 'explanation', 'evaluation' (and 'bias'), 'meaning', 'identity', 'motivation, 'normative order' (and so on) without asking and inquiring into the rule-governed conditions of their own *re-presentational* procedures as 'interested' displays of sociality.

The genealogy of such mimetic practices – now understood as artful social achievements – is disclosed as a kind of subterranean history of elided and occluded grounds. As *OBSI* explains: 'Our procedure is never to do a description of what actually is the case but rather to generate for any potential description – motives, bias, art, snubs, evaluation – the deep grounds that make it possible' (7). Unlike descriptive and mimetic social theory, Analysis deconstructs the grounds of the possibility of mimetic gestures and representational formations. Being successful in their own terms, many such alternative visions remain blind to a deeper order of indebtedness occluded by their commitment to methodic, instrumental, epistemic, or confessional versions of reasoning. In fact all such foundational gestures already presuppose a darker horizon of articulation experienced as the interminable task of self-grounding itself. It follows that the pursuit of 'alternative histories', 'new beginnings' and 're-foundings' of the sociological enterprise *without radical self-reflection*, will be chronically prone to corrosive ironies. We are tempted to say that if it can be *represented* it is no longer a *ground* but a strategic move in an administrative order.

Little wonder that the simple gesture of problematizing this correlativity of surface performance and deep structural auspices would be viewed as subversive. By identifying and publicizing such ironies – here lies the comedic moment of analytic work and its affinity with Socratic irony – Analysis requires its practitioners to avoid deepening the debt, mortgaging speech to established formulae in order to encounter indebtedness and the freedom it discloses in its full ontological and ethical significance. The genealogy of social practices – now understood as reflexively engineered social phenomena – is disclosed as a kind of subterranean history of elided and occluded grounds. The interpretive violence *On the Beginning of Social Inquiry* enacts with regard to the whole spectrum of established 'quantitative and qualitative traditions' and the sustaining usages of everyday life they presuppose goes to the heart of reflexive sociology, its fundamental commitment to display how any kind of methodic inquiry, technical speech, or evidence-based 'science' is possible and coherent as a recognizable language-game (indeed as a recognizable *social* game in a conflicted force-field of related games).

3.5 Generativity and depth grammar

Analytic speech begins with the question of the conditions of the possibility of apparently inconsequential mundane topics (various expressed as 'usage', descriptive 'phenomena', 'normative conventions', 'ordinary speech', and the like). But from an Analytic perspective *everydayness* – the *ordinary* – is not seen as a *domain of phenomena* framed for descriptive investigation in the style of phenomenological sociology or as ethnomethodological 'reverse engineering' practices, but as an ironic occasion to inquire into the extraordinary network of discourses and historical procedures that narratively organize, articulate, and structure the flow of everyday experience. Analysis necessarily views usage, convention, everyday speech, language, traditions, and so on, as situated ways of resolving fundamental problems of ambiguity and ambivalence that pervade *every* social activity. From an analytic perspective there is already a *dialectical struggle* operating within the life of ordinary language.

A crucial formulation of this principle appears in the first pages of the 'Introduction':

> Analysis, for us, is generative. It is not finding something in the world, or making sense of some puzzling datum, or answering an interesting question, or locating a phenomenon worthy of study, or resolving a long-standing dis-agreement or any other essentially empirical procedure. To analyse is, instead, to address the possibility of *any* finding, puzzle, sense, resolution, answer, interest, location, phenomenon, etcetera, etcetera.

> (*OBSI*: 2)

We might recall an analogous formulation of the analytic attitude described in Section 90 of Wittgenstein's *Philosophical Investigations* (1968):

> our investigation, however, is directed not towards phenomena, but, as one might say, towards the '*possibilities*' of phenomena. We remind ourselves, that is to say, of the *kind of statement* that we make about phenomena.... Our investigation is therefore a grammatical one.

> (Section 90: 42e–43e)

Or even more concisely: 'Essence is expressed by grammar' (Wittgenstein, 1968: Section 371).

Like the anamnetic impulse of Wittgenstein's 'return' to the constitutive con-ventions of ordinary usage and the forms of life they presuppose, Analysis aspires to uncover the depth grammars not only of familiar social worlds but of the forms of life and principled selfhood that makes these possible. This is the source of a minor but crucial distinction between the concept of reflexivity as a pervasive infrastructure of everyday language and mundane sociality – continu-ously informing the common sense accounting practices of everyday interaction and sociality – and the *idea* of *self-reflection* as *desire, irony* and *institutional imperative* with a disparate and conflictual history that leads back to pre-Platonic Greek culture and forward to the historicizing pursuits of Vico, Herder, Hegel, Marx, Nietzsche, Simmel, Heidegger, and beyond.

The desire exemplified by dialectical speech – speaking about speech as a conversation within the soul – is not merely a *way of life* but a *way of being-in-the-world* (cf. Hadot, 1995). By making this move, we see that irony and

ambiguity are no longer minor literary tropes, but the existential levers of dialectical thought and the vital medium of every form of critical appraisal and self-
recovery.

3.6 Collaboration as dialogical self-reflection

To summarize, we have argued that Analytic speech is speech that presupposes
the other, and with the other the irreducible reality of dialogue, generosity, and
collaboration. Dialogue understood as a medium of linguistic reflection is necessary to the work of recovering and formulating the grounds or auspices of any
social practice. The fundamental impulse of self-reflection is to resist the
amnesia of concrete and unreflective speech by asking how particular conventions, evaluations, appraisals, formulations, and the community displayed in
such speech acts are themselves possible. Rather than accepting conventions or
evaluations as secured 'solutions', Analysis uncovers the *problem* – or *problem-
aticity* – for which these formulations are citable as solutions. If what are called
self, existence, desire, and *language* are dialectical correlates we must continually ask: How has language unwittingly shaped our sense of 'problems' and 'res-
olutions' and framed our discursive existence? What are the norms constitutive
of any kind of problematic thought and inquiry? How do such forms of life function as the 'conditions of possibility' of their varied manifestations and operations? How can reflection explicate itself without destroying the very tension and
movement of thought? How can we speak responsibly about what makes speech
and conversation possible?

An awareness of the inability of speech (and writing) to formulate its own
auspices is what separates analytic speech from both common sense discourse
and conventional sociological reasoning. The task is no longer one of faithfully
describing 'reality' or reverse engineering the ordered character of ordinary
usage and conventionality. Rather, the analytic moment begins by ironically
'alienating' the self from its mundane engagements and turning the soul toward
the horizon of alterity. The act of speaking/writing is then seen to implicate the
other in the sense that all acts of speech and writing 'face away from one's own
fundamental grounds through which those formulations come about' (3). The 'I'
posited by ordinary self-consciousness that enacts the rules of conventional
speech actively masks the conversational grounds of selfhood and identity. Anal-
ogously, without depth-analysis the investigative 'I' also displays the unreflective status of another 'I' (the 'I' as resource disclosing the 'I' as topic). Yet it is
only the operation of alterity in the dialectic of *inter*locution that offers an escape
from this circle. The very limitations and inadequacy of ego's efforts to speak
intelligibly become the occasion that invite the reformulation work of alter. In
this sense a *collaborative* other – and a *rhetoric of collaboration* – is a vital
occasion for re-collecting and recovering grounds in ways that disrupt and
deconstruct the dominant representational conception of grounding that has
shaped the course of Western science and metaphysical discourse. Whoever
speaks from within the metaphysical framework with its roots in Graeco-Latin

grammar and its network of philosophical metaphors turns out to be a lay theorist operating within the normative framework of a particularly resilient conception of self, knowledge and truth. Ultimately it is this 'grammatical' tradition that Analysis seeks to disrupt. In inquiring into the grounds of phenomena Analysis is in the same position as Wittgenstein's philosophical architect: 'I am not interested in constructing a building, so much as in having a perspicuous view of the foundations of possible buildings' (1980: 7).

The studies in *On the Beginning of Social Inquiry* necessarily locate the reader as a compassionate interlocutor who is integral to the project of dialectical work and co-responsible inquiry. As 'papers which seek a conversation' each chapter is an act of *interlocution*, a dialectical invitation: 'We hope, by providing our auspices to enable you, the reader, to see snubs and bias dialectically: by taking on the collaborative role of alter, you can formulate the auspices that lead you to see how it is *possible* that they come to look like whatever they look like' (9).

'Auspices' function like the foundations of possible (conceptual, social, discursive, interactional) buildings.

3.7 The grounds of conventionality

By exploiting this distinction the imperative of self-reflection shifts from an unreflective acceptance of normative conventionality ('ordinary self-consciousness') with regard to descriptive and explanatory 'adequacy', to first-order reflection upon the operation of such conventions, and on to radical questions about the *need* and *limits* of conventionality itself (this 'shift' from ordinary language (everyday speech) to reflective language (e.g. the discourses of science) to self-reflexive discourse (prefigured in irony, dialectic, philosophic discourse, poetry, compassion, etc.).

This movement of radicalization might be seen as a strategic way of shaming the other into self-reflection. Practically enacted as a concrete process of thoughtful reformulation it also has the effect of generating more disturbing conceptions of language, identity, community, and truth. For example, in provoking the other into self-reflection an *ethical* ideal of reflection is revealed as the subversive desire to question the various historical shapes of rationality, including what now passes for common sense (objective reality) and reason (logic, argument, evidence, judgement, accountability, and so forth) in our own neck of the wood:

> Analysis is the concern not with anything said or written but with the grounds of whatever is said – the foundations that make what is said possible, sensible, conceivable. For any speech, including, of course, speech about speech, our interest is reflexive.... Our interest in what we call the grounds or auspices of phenomena rather than in the phenomena themselves is exemplified in every chapter in this volume.
>
> (*OBSI*: 2–3)

Analysis' first task is to remind readers that all speech – including theoretical discourse as a particular mode of social life – is a *socially constituted* and *rhetorically crafted practice*. And there are, moreover, endlessly different forms of social practice. The traditional puzzles of philosophical and ethical discourse begin to look as though they had origins in literal understandings of grammar and usage (and their consequent translation into one-sided versions of literary practice and writing). The founding questions that animated metaphysics and theology, for example, might even be viewed as 'problems' or sociopathologies internal to the operations of ordinary language where, for example, everyday idioms have illegitimately extrapolated figures of speech to create the prose of abstract thought.

A similar theme is a recurrent concern of Wittgenstein: 'In philosophizing we may not *terminate* a disease of thought. It must run its natural course, and *slow* cure is all important. (That is why mathematicians are such bad philosophers)' (1967, Section 382). The analytic attitude is to *endure* and *follow* the course of a deep-rooted linguistic problem, to understand its seductive hold on ordinary consciousness and to re-locate its genesis in another way of speaking and being-in-the-world. Above all we must avoid being one more instance of the unexamined life.

From an analytic perspective the phrase 'social practice' is a pleonasm. Practices always already display their indebtedness to publicly identifiable ways of speaking and forms of life. Speech and communities of discourse are to be approached as historically situated ways of being human, as parts of the unending conversation that constitutes traditions and forms of life. As imaginary collective formations we find implicit versions of 'ethics' and 'politics' – imagined communities – already embedded in the many different versions of reason and the values and judgements these versions license. For example, the imaginary communities of representational discourse always and everywhere desire the solace of the real (when all conversation falls silent there is always the real – what neo-Marxism designated as the referent 'in the last analysis'). Yet even this zero-degree of dialogue ('consensus', 'established truth', 'absolute evidence', 'facticity', etc.) with its violent stratification of insiders and outsiders still remains a form of dialogue, a particular language-game.

3.8 Historicity

We might formulate these observations in the idiom of *historicity*: where unreflective investigations conceal or cover-up their dialogical grounds and history, Analytic discourse has a deep and principled concern for dialogue and temporality; for example, where 'motive talk' or 'bias talk' conceals the hidden categorical work embodied in rule-governed 'procedures' (the implicit grammars governing the language-games of 'identity', 'person' ('personal identity'), 'biography', 'guilt', 'responsibility', 'subjective bias', 'representation', 'misrepresentation', and so on), Analysis identifies such categories and the 'phenomena' they index as icons of possible historical practices, dialectical institutions and symbolic worlds. In general: the genesis of speech within language has its communal origins in forgotten relations of temporal indebtedness and co-responsibility.

Members' competent use of motive talk (operative 'theories of mind', lay-conceptions of identity, attribution, reason-giving, etc.) or bias talk (distortion, error, partiality, opinion) can then be recovered as a surface clue to deeper structural competences (for example, the intersubjective narrative competences required to operate in everyday possible worlds – in the social domains of science, legal practices, education, and so on – where ascriptive rules are routinely invoked as collectively available rhetorics and, indeed, commonplace reading 'procedures'). Such procedures – whether as autobiographical, legal, political, or cultural idioms – turn out to be grammatical achievements sustained by the tacit world-work of local communities. In a slogan: *behind every fact a convention; behind every convention a grammar; behind every grammar an imaginary history; behind every history some form of implicit or explicit dialogue.* As the paper on 'Motives' concludes, from an analytic perspective motives: 'are a procedure for organising an historic and regular interactional future' (42).

Similarly, the empirical recognition and intelligibility of the phenomenon of 'bias' (and 'bias repair work') secures its local coherence and 'currency' from within the sustaining language-game of empiricism, the form of life of positivism (55ff.) that subjects inquiry to the judgement of 'facts', 'empirical evidence', and the authority of scientific expertise. And, of course, all of these objects are already internally differentiated and articulated as historically situated 'imaginary formations' that help to reproduce a mimetic conception of reality. When instituted as a collectively accessible grammar 'positivism' can operate as a shared universe of objects, representations and operative procedures. At root the failure of positivism is the failure of a dominant conception of causality (more precisely, of a limited and literal *view* of *causal necessity*) that occludes the pre-reflective causal configurations of temporality and existential embodiment. In this manner, positivism may fail as an epistemology but end up successfully embodied as a powerful ideology and way of life.

Expressed more generically, Analytic sociology treats the 'world of everyday life' not as *phenomena* but as an occasion or 'impetus' for theorizing (11): 'Our analysis then seeks to dissolve what is in hand by treating the security of the example as covering over and concealing its history' (11). Here 'phenomena', 'topics', 'problems', etc. are indices of the generative work of silent grounds.

3.9 Misunderstanding analysis

I speak from personal memory here. Undoubtedly the first students of Alan Blum and Peter McHugh in the 1970s resisted their work as disorienting and, given the tenacity of theoretical positions already painfully 'mastered', invariably tried to 'translate' and 'locate' the pedagogic and literary activities of Analytic sociology in the terms of already-established versions of inquiry and reflection (and the associated conceptions of self, learning, teaching and community implicit in those versions). Their invitation to travel along another path was resisted by already-established commitments embedded in other conceptual frameworks. The unfamiliar was veiled by the familiar.

It was (and perhaps still is) rare for doctoral students to be asked to provide grounds for their 'interests' or to formulate the possible world that such investigative interests exemplify. It was even more unusual to read texts where their authors admitted that their own accounts were provisional and revisable (Wittgenstein's *Philosophical Investigations* and Heidegger's post-*Sein und Zeit* work being notable exceptions).

In this context it is important to note that the collective 'authors' of *OBSI* formulated their own auto-critique of the 'Motive' paper (originally published in 1971) in the 1974 Addendum (43–46). The 'breakthrough' paper on motives is glossed as a *work-in-progress* whose concern for sociological treatments of motive actively covered up the 'deeper' topic of self-collection or *collectability* that was now (i.e. in 1973/1974) rephrased in terms of the immanent 'belonging' of speech with the horizon of language (the other, the *Logos* or the ambivalent relationality of alterity itself).

Here the theme of *indebtedness* as both an ethical and ontological horizon returns. The very *topicality* and *readability* of members' rules, conventions, interpretive procedures, etc. – reflecting some of the preoccupations of 1970s sociological work – both revealed and occluded these 'objects' as modes of 'indebtedness' to a wider tradition and a structure of ambivalence intrinsic to the relationship between speech and language, reason, and its 'origin'.

For students of later Analytic work, it became clear that the *ego-alter paradigm* of interaction formulated in the early 1970s was itself no more (but no less) than a temporary resting place of thought and an iconic incentive to recover a deeper (and older) dialectical paradigm of Self and Other and the ethicality of 'reciprocal recognition' and, therewith, more consequential notions of language, dialogue, friendship, temporality and history, justice, and moral life.

With this move the fundamental concept of *ground* shifted decisively from referencing the local *conditions-of-production* of mundane topics and phenomena to articulating the anonymous horizonal 'giving', the tense unity of *Dasein* and Being, that both grants and withdraws all ontic experiential possibilities (the *es gibt*, or 'Language speaks', to formulate this in the idiom of the later Heidegger). Heidegger implicitly asks how our fundamental orientations to self and world would change if we think of speech constitutively, viewing language in non-mimetic and non-instrumental terms as 'the house of Being':

> Language, by naming beings for the first time, first brings beings to word and to appearance. Only this naming nominates beings *to* their being *from out of* their being. Such saying is a projecting of the clearing, in which announcement is made of what it is that beings come into the Open *as*.... Projective saying is poetry: the saying of world and earth, the saying of the arena of their conflict and thus of the place of all nearness and remoteness of the gods. Poetry is the saying of the unconcealedness of what is.
>
> (Heidegger, 'The Origin of the Work of Art', 1971b: 71)

By participating in the drama of self-understanding, by struggling to say, the self is eternally beholden to the other (as the absent ontological horizon of all possible articulation, what *has* to remain absent in all presence). Correspondingly, we displace the meaning of 'conditions of possibility' from the local grammars of everyday experience/ordinary language to the unrepresentable horizon of Being, of the 'relation' of beings (the Many) to the One. This was also the path that would lead the semiotic tradition from the structural nexus of *signifier* and *signified* to the thought of *différance* and *intertextuality*. Heidegger had already spoken of the *ontological difference* as a kind of non-reflective, pre-predicative relationship between speech and language, sense and silence, multiplicity and unity:

> The peal of stillness is not anything human. But on the contrary, the human is indeed in its nature given to speech – it is linguistic. The word 'linguistic', as it is here used means: having taken place out of the speaking of language. What has thus taken place, human being, has been brought into its own by language, so that it remains giver over or appropriated to the nature of language, the peal of stillness. Such an appropriating takes place in that the very *nature*, the *presencing*, of language *needs and uses* the speaking of mortals in order to sound as the peal of stillness for the hearing of mortals. Only as men belong within the peal of stillness are mortals able to speak in *their own* way in sounds.
>
> (Heidegger, 'Language', 1971b: 205)

In effect, the limits revealed by the actual practice of Analytic work in formulating the auspices of 'motive', 'travel' or 'art' provoked and invited other ways of thinking about self, friendship, communality, justice, finitude and world. We then see that the initial motivation of Analytic work to formulate 'beginnings' and 'grounds' should itself be recovered as a first experiment in reflexive speech confronted with the ultimate ambiguities of living and being-in-the-world. In subsequent writings this would be rephrased as the irresolvable question of 'fundamental ambiguity' and the 'grey zone' shadowing personal and collective existence.

3.10 Between logos *and dialogue*

The questions *Why speak?* and *Who speaks?* are fundamental issues for Analytic sociology as they are for the dialectical tradition of philosophy and critical theory more generally. Where concrete responses to this question typically nominate the 'speaker' or 'I' of enunciation as a conventional anchorage of speech, Analytic sociology thematizes the *concept* (and *conception*) of the speaker as an idealized version of reasonable speech. It follows that the question *Who speaks?* must be answered in *principled* rather than in *concrete* and *contingent* ways. The '*Who?*' in question here turns out to be an icon and display of a certain kind of 'speaking-life', an indebtedness to language or logos rather than to a concrete set of linguistic rules or games. Recovering this difference is also the vital motivation behind both Hegel's and Heidegger's concern with language as the indebted eventfulness of speaking formulated in the thesis '*Language speaks*':

> Language speaks. Its speaking bids the difference to come which expropriates world and things into the simple onefold of their intimacy. Language speaks. Man speaks in that he responds to language.... It is not a matter here of stating a new view of language. What is important is learning to live in the speaking of language. To do so, we need to examine constantly whether and to what extent we are capable of what genuinely belongs to responding: anticipation in reserve.
>
> (Heidegger, 'Language', 1971b: 207)

Somewhat paradoxically, the 'flow' that makes discourse possible cannot be controlled or directed by speech. Human arrangements are already indebted to the event of Being and what Heidegger symbolized as 'the Open', the articulation of World and Earth that grounds social activities. The idea was already present in Heraclitus: 'It is wise, listening not to me but to the logos, to agree that all things are one' (Fragment 50, Sandywell, 1996 vol. 3: 245). For Heraclitus, as for Heidegger, speaking is already an oriented relationship and an existential response to the gathering of language:

> For, strictly, it is language that speaks. Man first speaks when, and only when, he responds to language by listening to its appeal. Among all the appeals that we human beings, on our part, may help to be voiced, language is the highest and everywhere the first. Language beckons us, at first and then again at the end, toward a thing's nature.
>
> (Heidegger, '...Poetically Man Dwells', 1971b: 214)

Similar considerations might be formulated with respect to the basic idea of conversational *work* and dialogical *writing* that flows throughout *OBSI*. 'Dialogue' is itself polysemic and ambiguous (at once interlocution, desire, travel and art). Wherever the word is invoked as a term of art we need to locate particular *conceptions* of dialogue (or in the language of *OBSI*, particular *elections*). The innovative idea of radically collaborative writing exemplified in *OBSI* entered a relatively established 'field' of dialogical theorizing within the social sciences and philosophy from the late 1960s through the 1970s. The many misconceptions of Analysis' radical version of dialogue were perhaps inevitable given the proliferation and variability of ideas concerning *self-reflection, language, critique, semiosis, dialectic, deconstruction*, and so on circulating during this period of ideological contestation.

We can inventory some of the variant conceptions of dialogue and dialogical work that may have both facilitated and reinforced such misinterpretations. Indeed 'dialogue' had already been understood and represented in a number of mimetic forms:

1   as 'merely' another topic for sociological analysis (understood as cultural simulacra of dialogue exemplified by Socratic/Platonic dialectic: the tradition of 'spiritual exercises', Stoic moral 'reform', casuistry in Christian ethics, Calvinist self-inspection, and so on);

2   as the 'dialectic' of master and servant in the Hegelian odyssey of consciousness and self-consciousness (popularized by the humanist reconstruction of Hegel in the work of Alexandre Kojève (1969) for example);

3   as an idealist irrelevance disabling 'real' social analysis (the 'descent of consciousness' toward the absolute materiality of the signified in Marxism and Critical Theory);

4   as the dialogical medium of the 'talking cure' in psychotherapeutic contexts;

5   as the communicative medium of symbolic interaction and semiotic exchange in structuralist epistemologies;

6   as a version of the hermeneutic circle (dialogical understanding as a 'fusion' of disparate horizons in the transmission of tradition as formulated by the hermeneutic philosopher Hans-Georg Gadamer);

7   as Rorty-like pragmatic conversation (the appeal to the 'conversation' of Western liberalism, the faith in the progressive value of disparate dialogues within and between communities);

8   as a concrete image of the life of interminable dialogue (Buber, Marcel, Bakhtin);

9   as the societal equivalent of *intertextuality*;

10   as the site of 'negative dialectics' (Adorno, 1973a; Jameson, 1971; Jay, 1984).

3.11 Dialogical existence (the 'tu quoque' principle)

In relation to these different concepts and contexts it comes as no surprise that Analytic sociology should display its commitment to the idea of co-responsible dialogical speech/writing in a number of different ways in a related (and evolving) series of contexts:

> our conception of sociology is different from conventional ones which consider collaboration unnecessary or even unnatural.
>
> (*OBSI*: 2)

Dialectical speech is speech that suspends conventional usage and everyday consciousness to assume the obligation of theoretic speech, a 'collaboration' animated by the Good that shines through speech.

To continue in this Platonic idiom: analytic speech is speech that respects the difference between the quest for essence or idea (*eidos*) and the image of ground as the Good that lies beyond Being and Non-Being. Speech that reminds a community of this difference is speech that is on-the-way to becoming self-reflexive. Here lies the *jouissance* and creativity of analytic discourse:

The creative character of analysis is its re-creation of the difference.... The re-creation which is analysis is a way of making reference to the original creation as the possibility of any creation.

(19)

What we have called 'radical dialogue' creates a distinction between thoughtless speech (Heideggerian *rede* or 'chatter') and reflective philosophical discourse:

Thoughtful speaking is essentially historical and the history it shows is the tension of a contest – a contest between origin and achievement – rather than the linearity of method.

(15)

The desire to speak reflexively is the desire to enter an agonistic space of creative tensions and ambivalence, to be open to the ambiguity and irresolution of all discourse, to enter the play of language itself.

Readers of the original book would also have heard this claim as an echo of a view of radical dialogue formulated in different ways by theorists such as Martin Buber, Gabriel Marcel, Mikhail Bakhtin, Jacques Lacan and Hans-Georg Gadamer:

True dialectic is not a monologue of the solitary thinker with himself, it is a dialogue between *I* and *Thou*.

(Ludwig Feuerbach (1843), cited in Buber (1961: 46))

To enter the reflexive attitude requires 'an ego who speaks and thereby denies his auspices and an alter who formulates the auspices ego forgets by speaking.... Any actual formulation of ego by alter can raise the same problem which it solves, namely how *it* is possible.... We have collaborated in ego-alter fashion, and now we ask that the reader collaborate in the same way.... Readers are asked to treat our papers reflexively. They are asked to become our collaborators. This is our version of how to read' (7–8).

But there is also an even more radical conception of dialogue (and with this, of dialectical writing) that leads reflection on grounds back into the 'conversation' that precedes and pervades the movement of language itself:

our primordial notion of collaboration makes reference to the conversation within language and in this sense the 'relation' between ego and alter can be re-presented as the dialectical engagement between the speaker and his tradition which is exemplified in his course of thought.

(14)

The 'difference' and 'tension' between self and other operate as an icon or metaphor for the ontological difference that opens a site for any kind of relation and relationship. Yet this 'difference' is never tangible or concretely given (the ontological difference is not another topic among an inventory of topics: 'Being' that appears in 'beings' is not itself a being). The 'work' of difference is always-already operative and can only be recollected and displayed by acts of thinking that explicitly attend to this 'granting' or 'gifting' that makes any kind of collection or unity possible. In this sense analytic writing is a writing that attempts to re-create the *arche-écriture* of *différance* (to borrow the idiom of Derrida). This is the pervasive tension that animates the writing practices assembled in *OBSI*. This is also the point where the original Socratic *elenchos* (and the work of *ironic* dialectic) is re-appraised as a play space of difference.

What Alan Blum would develop in two remarkable books (*Theorizing* (1974) and *Socrates* (1978)) is already prefigured in *OBSI*: 'The Socratic dialogue is then preserved in speech as a movement which evokes the tension and irregularity of the contest within the soul idealised as true thinking' (19).

3.12 The status of analytic speech

We have seen that one of the lessons of *OBSI* concerns the ethical question '*Why speak?*' (and with it the more existential question *Who speaks?*): What are your grounds for speaking and what is revealed about the psyche and self-identity in the performances sustained by such grounds? The question is not merely, What are your (contingent) *interests in* or *reasons for* speaking?, but What are the principled *grounds* that warrant just *this* (and *this type of*) speaking? How is your sense of self '*oriented*' and what frames your desire to talk *in this way*?

The force of these questions was initially aimed at the representational canons of sociological speech ('the failure of positivism'), asking these discourses to recognize their own interested status, compelling a member of such communities to formulate their own grounds, and provide for their 'authority' to inquire and research in *these* particular ways and through particular metaphoric strategies. Here the particular irritant of the question '*Who are you (in speaking thus)?*' discloses the unavoidable (and to this extent universal) question '*How do I/We always-already belong to a community in and of language?*'

The 'failure of positivism' turned out to be one element of a deeper societal – and indeed civilization-wide – crisis that had already been diagnosed by Nietzsche in the late nineteenth century under the rubric of *nihilism* and in the twentieth century by Heidegger as the *age of the world-view* and the *technological era of enframing*. Analogous demands for a radical *Destruktion* of the course of Western thought had already been advanced by phenomenological, hermeneutic, and interpretive criticisms of the canon. Of course, Analytic sociology was not initially (and is not today) locatable wholly in terms of a competition with Phenomenology, Hermeneutics, or any other variant of philosophic speech. Indeed Analysis might reasonably claim that a truly radical phenomenology of alterity would be literally self-defeating in eliding and effacing the radical ethical grounds of experience.

Unlike conventional 'interpretive sociology' *OBSI* begins with an acute awareness of the analytic status of its *own* rhetoric and the need (and desire) to 'ground' its own modes of speaking in ways that had evaded both mainstream social science and their philosophical critics (other than in established autobiographical, methodological or narrowly-conceived epistemological terms).

Take for example the self-description of Ethnomethodology as a quasi-naturalistic science or 'reverse-engineering' ethnography of everyday practical reasoning. Unlike Ethnomethodology's professed research rhetoric – which, of course, displays its tacit answer to '*Why speak?*' – Analytic sociology approaches 'the everyday world as a proximate occasion for initiating inquiry and not as a "fact" to be reproduced'. The *agôn* in question here is not one of competitor 'perspectives' in the academic market place of social science, but the struggle to recover the other, the violence required to loosen and explicate the grounds of speaking. Ethnomethodology – like other brands of micro-sociology – is essentially committed to mimetic or descriptive reason, while Analytic sociology locates its grounds in the *logos* that makes any kind of rationality possible: 'In our respective attitudes toward ordinary language and the everyday world, we have about as much in common with ethnomethodology as Heidegger shares with Austin' ('Motive': 22–23).

While at a superficial level both Ethnomethodology and Analysis begin with quotidian 'phenomena' or instances of usage, the former pursues a descriptive micro-sociology of the everyday, while the latter problematizes the very idea of 'phenomena' and 'everydayness'. Ethnomethodology criticizes sociology's image of the actor as a 'judgmental dope' and grants everyday agents with intricate reflexive-cultural competences to 'pull off' sensible environments through practical reasoning procedures. But ethnomethodological protocols fail to see members as genuine – that is, radical – theorizers. In limiting theorizing to 'practical concerns' and 'impression management' (let us say at best the kind of activities Aristotle signalled with his notion of *phronesis* or practical reasoning), they overlook the kind of transformative reason that Aristotle and Plato called *theoria*. Ethnomethodology thus speaks-*for* the everyday and the *present* (and thereby exemplifies another cycle of mundane membership and the repetitive reification of object-facticity) while Analysis suspends mundane rationalities in order to address the dialectic of reason that makes *theoria*, imagination, and principled transformation and possible *futures* possible.

For Analysis the task is not to mimetically *describe* but to *transgress* and *transform* the ordinary, to restore a richer *theoreticity* to agents, and to change everyday life. We could re-write the famous Thesis XI in Analytic terms: 'Philosophers have hitherto only described … the ordinary … the task is to formulate and change it'.

OBSI claims that speech's authority is not controlled by speech, but lies elsewhere, and that this 'elsewhere' is of supreme analytic interest to the theorist; this is the 'elsewhere' or 'Other' of 'unspeakable auspices' (134), of an unrepresentable relation that is always-already 'other-than-being'; it is the 'unspeakable Other' signalled by the metaphoric images of 'grounds' and 'auspices' throughout the papers in *OBSI*. Here again we hear the echoes of the 'groundless ground' that preoccupied Heidegger after the so-called *Kehre* (or 'turn'). In Heidegger's formulation: 'Everything spoken stems in a variety of ways from the unspoken, whether this be something not yet spoken, or whether it be what must remain unspoken in the sense that it is beyond the reach of speaking. Thus, that which is spoken in various ways begins to appear as if it were cut off from speaking and the speakers, and did not belong to them, while in fact it alone offers to speaking and to the speakers whatever it is they attend to, no matter in what way they stay within what is spoken of the unspoken' (Heidegger, 1971b: 120).

This insistence upon the transcendence of the other also recovers the Socratic insight into speech's irreparable 'inadequacy' that necessitates a re-writing 'other' (or moment of alterity as *internal* to and *constitutive* of the analytic commitment). All of these observations can be folded into the emerging language of community or communality ('*Who speaks?*' being a symptomatic correlate of '*Which community?*').

Indirectly, then, the immanent critique of Ethnomethodology (and by implication *all* descriptive positivisms and philosophical empiricisms) produces the idea of *constitutive rhetoric* as a sphere of analytic interest: *why-speak-like-this* (*rhetoric*) is a surface clue to *why-be-like this*? (*ethics*). While positivism and empiricism are superficially epistemic frameworks, on a deeper level their lack of reflexivity helps reproduce a particular model of speech and community. In this way the positivist solution to the question '*Why speak?*' already implicates a communicative politics or ethicopolitical utopia. The positivist idea of a rhetoric-free form of representation – speech untouched by the artifice of figuration and metaphor, objective speech as the speech of nature – ironically displays its own rhetoricity as a commitment to un-mediated discourse. This imaginary dissociation of speech from language operates as a kind of involuntary alienation from the principled ideal of responsible selfhood. The same conclusion appears in the Sandywell collection (1975) influenced by the early work of Analytic sociology: 'Ethnomethodology is a prime example of the practical rhetorical accomplishment of a research discipline which refuses to think through its rhetoric; refuses to move from its research object, which it locates as everyday members' practical, indexical accomplishments of sensible environments to the grounds of its rhetoric' (1975: 14). With this insight into the reified movement of unreflective speech it is also possible to imagine other investigations where the implicit 'history' (say in the genealogy of the leading imagery and metaphors at work in positivism and empiricism) can be subject to genealogical critique – where we might map out reflexive studies of the cultural history of 'self-reflection' and the many attempts to construe truth as 'objective discourse'. This opens up a domain of reflexive self-inquiries not directed primarily to the question of the 'phenomenality of phenomena' but to the question of the 'rhetoricity of rhetorics', the conditions of the possibility of discursive sites, narrative desire, and techniques of description, representation, and self-reflection. In this way the history (or histories) of the origins, development and dominance of re-presentational language, and the hegemony of visual models of experience – of language-games that ground themselves in a reductive *structure of mimesis* – becomes a history of the pursuit of objective science, philosophical certainty, and perfect self-identity (Sandywell, 2011).

4 The genealogy of grounds and auspices

This awareness of active *amnesia*, the unwillingness or inability of speech (and writing) to formulate its own auspices is what separates analytic speech from both common sense discourse and conventional sociological reasoning.

The Heideggerian parallel here is the idea of a fundamental distinction between the life of concrete reflection (for example, the representational speech of science) and the project of ontological reflexivity (the self-grounding speech of *Denken* or 'thought'):

> ...science is not an original happening of truth, but always the cultivation of a domain of truth already opened, specifically by apprehending and confirming that which shows itself to be possibly and necessarily correct within that field. When and insofar as a science passes beyond correctness and goes on to a truth, which means that it arrives at the essential disclosure of what is as such, it is philosophy.
>
> (Heidegger, 'The Origin of the Work of Art', in 1971b: 60)

The act of speaking/writing implicates the other in the sense that all acts of speech and writing 'face away from one's own fundamental grounds through which those formulations come about' (3). Analytic work distinguishes between rhetoric as a concrete 'medium' or 'happenstance' of inquiry and analytic speech as a desire to formulate the primordial grounds of acts of speaking (and all possible styles of speech). Given the sociality of truth, a fundamental motive of Analysis is the cooperative pursuit of grounded speech, its *telos* governed by an insistent 'engagement with grounds' (*OBSI*: 48).

This in turn poses the question of whether the preoccupation with 'grounds' (let alone 'fundamental grounds': 3–4) risks replicating traditional images of the quest for demonstrable 'grounded speech' that has characterized large stretches of the Western tradition of philosophy from Aristotle to contemporary Critical Theory. Is philosophy's traditional desire for 'original beginnings', 'ultimate causes', 'security', and 'universality' a rhetoric of foundational grounding, indeed a theocentric rhetoric of First Principles, First Cause, Divine Being, and their equivalent metaphorical images in more recent forms of European thought? Does changing the question to the disclosure of 'forms of life' or the *logos* as the sustaining horizon of unreflective practices transform this traditional approach? The question of indebtedness and ambivalence becomes unavoidable where the language of 'groundedness' seems to divide into the idea of *contingent* grounds (assumptions and terms of reference required to occasion and motivate any mind of productive work) and *transcendental* grounds (as the 'hidden' matrix of speech, the unavailable auspices of speaking, or quasi-transcendental *desire*)?

The ghost of the 'transcendental' or 'quasi-transcendental' lingers in formulations like the following:

> Analysis is the concern not with anything said or written but with the grounds of whatever is said – the foundations that make what is said possible, sensible, conceivable. For any speech, including, of course, speech about speech, our interest is reflexive.... Our interest in what we call the grounds or auspices of phenomena rather than in the phenomena themselves is exemplified in every chapter in this volume.
>
> (2–3)

Perhaps, like other radical frameworks, *OBSI* interweaves insight and blindness. One of the risks of commending radical alternatives to conventional sociological speech, for example, is the danger of being confined by the language of the adversary. Would it be unjust to say, with hindsight, that the papers assembled in *OBSI* are constrained by the triangulation of '*rule, grammar and form of life*'?

The outlines of this kind of auto-critique appear in the response at the end of the 'Art' paper to the criticism that Analytic sociology is solipsistic and only concerned to see 'rule, grammar and form' in every topic it treats (180–182). In rejecting the charge of deprecating the other, the text articulates the beginnings of a stronger version of alterity – that despite the threat of foundationalism only a 'discourse of grounds' is in a position to conceive of and address the dialectic of Self and Other. How this notion of radical alterity should be developed remains an outstanding question.

OBSI argues that 'grounds' (and 'grounding') cannot be essentialist or transcendental in the traditional sense of establishing universal and necessary 'conditions of the possibility' of phenomena (for example, in the sense that Kantian criticism aimed to establish the *a priori* forms of intuition (space and time) and formal categories of judgement as the necessary framework of all phenomenal experience or in the manner in which phenomenology traces the pure eidetic structures of phenomena to intentional correlates and life-world formations (Husserl, 1970b)).

However, in strategic terms the concern with the archaeology of 'auspices' is *quasi*-transcendental in striving (1) to uncover the generative grounds of everyday practices and phenomena ('bias', 'motives', 'snubs', 'travel', 'art', etc.), (2) in providing a motivated version of self and community that makes such phenomena conceivable, visible, describable and intelligible in the first place, and (3) in articulating the need for more radical self-reflection capable of deconstructing the claims of both foundationalism and anti-foundationalism.

5 Multiple voices in *On the Beginning of Social Inquiry*

The theme of creative ambivalence or fundamental ambiguity has appeared throughout this chapter. It goes without saying that in this context 'ambivalence' – the interplay of two or more undecidable 'moments' in a given structure – should not be read as 'finding fault', indexing 'repair work', or even marked as one phase of a dialectical movement that terminates in a unifying synthesis. Rather, ambivalence appears as an irreducible structure of paradoxicality across all acts of speech and throughout forms of life. This irreducible dialecticity cannot be stabilized by any kind of 'absolute' or unmediated ground. Where deconstruction speaks of the generic *indetermination* and *seminal* adventure of the trace (Derrida, 1972: 264), in the Analytic context *ambivalence* marks the tension inherent in the movement of conversation, the *agôn*, as a site of responsible speech (the ontological ambivalence marked by the '/' in *speech/language*) or in the play of forms (*eide*) that conjoin human speech to Being itself.

Given this generic exigency it would certainly be surprising if the texts composing *OBSI* did not display such tensions as a vital part of their orchestrated achievement. One concrete example is the use of collegiate pronouns throughout the text ('we', 'us', 'our', etc.) that binds the voice of authorship to a common *telos* while tracing the polyphony of speech and difference to the occasions of their manifold appearances. Another instance is the *interplay* of different *idioms* set in play in describing the task of recovering 'grounds', 'auspices', 'generative rules', 'deep structures', 'auspices', 'forms', and so on.

Without engaging in a full deconstruction of the text we may consider the differential voices at play in the textual fabric of *OBSI* as one of its lasting provocations and innovations. Here *voice* should be understood in its concrete and grammatical senses. Compare, for example, the differences that can be traced between the Garfinkel/Chomsky/Saussure imagery of grounds as unavailable 'depth' structures that organize the everydayness of everyday life and the Platonic/Heideggerian/Lacanian image of ontological sites of manifestation sustaining ontic formations (*idea* and *exemplars*, *Being* and *beings*, *speech* and *Language*, *thatness* and *whatness*, etc.). Even the distribution of the 'collective voice' of the 'Introduction' symptomatically divides along the lines of these different voicings: pages 1 to 14 exemplifying the conventional idiom of interactional recovery of auspices through ego/alter dialogue (what the text later identifies as an 'introductory' ploy responsive to 'the terminological constraints that attend conventional speech in social science' (14)) and the release from these conventions (from page 14 onward) with a voice invoking the 'unconstrained' language of Socratic theorizing, Platonic *erôs*, the *logos* as re-collecting the idea, *aporia*, Socratic *elenchos*, ironic speech, ontological difference, and so on.

If we can borrow Bakhtin's term *heteroglossia* (or the *polyphonic* interplay of different voices) we might also note the resonances of voices that have 'played' into the composition of the 1974 text: the voices of British ordinary language philosophy (usage), Wittgenstein (*Sprachspiele*, forms of life, grammar), Chomsky (surface and deep structure, the Ideal Speaker, generative competences, etc.), Heidegger (the ontological difference between Being (*Sein*) and beings (*seiende*), language as *logos*, *No-thing* and *nothing*, *Dasein*, and so on), Parsons and Schutz and their preoccupation with accounting for the normative grounds of social order, Hans-Georg Gadamer (the dialogical principle), among such traces:

We make reference to our grounds by showing that any concrete activity can be conceived of as a move in a game.

(178)

Analysis, as we practice it, is concerned with constructing for any behaviour its rationality, but not with producing rational behaviour.... Our position is closer to Chomsky's.

(7; also cf. 29, 30, 32)

...our principle of analysis which requires seeking the form of life of a phenomenon ... our method was always to seek the intelligibility of surface instances through the deep ground which generated them.

(176)

motive acquires its analytic status by virtue of the fact that it requires for its use certain deep structures for conceiving of 'person', 'member', 'responsibility', 'biography', and the like.... It is through these deep conditions that an analytic conception of the ordinary sociological use of motive is provided.

(30)

True speech recognises the difference between time and eternity.

(15)

Examples are then the same (displays of the original difference between Being and being) and different (intelligibly distinct displays).

(18)

6 Reflexive sociology as collaborative dialectics

The shifts and resonances – what Alan Blum would call the necessary *tensions* – marked by the polyphonic play of these voices – are rhetorically designed to move the reader from the idiom of *social interaction* and concrete *intersubjectivity* to the Socratic idea of *inter*-action as an *anamnesis* of the grounds of speech, a re-collection of the desire animating the theoretic life. The dialectical image of 'interplay' also functions to problematize received conceptions of *dialectic* and to radicalize the meaning of dialogical existence exemplified by these studies. We might say that the topics, usages and local descriptive problems of 'everyday life sociology' are sublated into the *erôs* of philosophical speech as the desire to speak the truth about responsive and unresponsive modes of human existence.

In this transposition, what is called 'Analysis' itself becomes an exemplary metaphor for a life of radical dialectic displayed in the art of philosophical conversation. The 'principled agency' of theorizing as a formulation of the *idea* or *logos* within quotidian examples and metaphors is a heuristic device that turns the ordinariness of mundane thought to the great problem of the One and the

Many. Here the dialectical figures of 'dialectic' and 'dialogue' themselves – once recognized as self-limiting notions – are reunited with the Platonic 'inner conversation of the soul' as the pursuit of analytic speech reorients a prospective audience to the profound textual achievements (and invitations) of the Platonic *Dialogues*.

We have called this anti-metaphysical strategy the quest for 'radical dialogue', the interminable desire to find a perfect dialogical partner, to renew the life of theorizing through spirited friendship, to de-reify the Present and the Real in the name of (im)possible futures.

This strategy ensures that the reflexive imperative of radical dialogue is no longer tied to concrete interaction or the topicality of current issues and themes. What contingently *occasions* analysis is ultimately never the final or authentic issue. Thus in beginning with and attending to particular topics ('bias', 'motive', 'friendship', 'travel', 'snubs', 'art', and so on) the analytic interest lies in how such intelligible 'unities' (*qua* common sense 'topics') achieve their collective topicality. The analytic issue at play here lies in replicating the very movement from concrete accounts to their sustaining horizon (by revealing their debt to an inheritance, to language, the manifestation of Being, the Good, and so on). The ideal analytic conversation would be something like the dramaturgy of the soul displayed in the polyphonic texts of Platonic writing in its revelation of the forms (of existence, being, unity, goodness, and the like) and of the interrelationships between these forms, and ultimately of the 'form of the Forms' that Plato names 'the Good'. The voice that articulates this Socratic-Platonic turn warns of the danger that 'it is easy to imagine that such a situation [of concrete conversation between persons] would draw us away from language in the interests of our own speech' (15). Expressed in a Platonic idiom, 'concrete speech (at its best) formulates its grounds as ideas, forgetting that the ground of speech is that which surpasses idea' (15). Concrete speech convinces its audience (and itself) that topics are simply *there* for the taking. For Analysis, however, topics are constituted in and by their methodic treatment. In sum: while beginning with concrete commonalities of everyday usage, Analysis discloses the ground of all possible communality and a radically different conception of the communality of reflexive inquiry.

7 Concrete and analytic community

The work of Analytic reflection should ideally not only 'produce' analytic *accounts* but also produce 'others' – real and virtual collaborators – who are invited to assume dialogical positions with regard to these analytic formulations. The 'products' of Analytic work are thus necessarily open-ended, social and promissory; their 'point' is to occasion other and alternate acts of interpretation and communities of theorizing and, in a projective tense, future traditions of analytic responsibility.

In this context the act of reading or 'reception' cannot be one of 'confirming' or 'rejecting' the results of analysis, but rather of entering into the play and *jouissance* of dialogue, of participating in the unending reflexive processes of ego and alter formulation and re-formulation, of responding existentially to aporetic situations and problematics.

If we can gloss the term 'community' as shorthand for 'moral community', then analysis has an explicit and principled 'moral' conception of open communality, occasioning 'ways of seeing', topics, and concrete phenomena 'such that you could see those affairs in some grounded way, not necessarily in just the way we do' (8–9). This celebratory and, perhaps Nietzschean, version of moral communality is explicitly codified in the principle 'that behind every practice lies a concealed morality that animates the practice...' (95). How to orient toward that which 'animates' speech, the spirit (*anima*) of language's openness and heteroglossia, then become the central impetus and initiative of theorizing.

This notion of principled ethical commitment also accounts for the lack of totalization, closure and finality in the texts of reflexive sociology. As 'open texts' (and fallible analyses), incompletion is a necessary structure rather than an epistemic failure of dialogical reflexivity. Other interlocutors are not to be 'faulted' or 'downgraded' for being partial or for 'deforming' data in their struggle to articulate a distinctive voice. Analysis has no need for the notion of faltering 'attempts' as 'stages' along the way of perfect description and theory. In fact, 'partiality' – existential finitude – is a shared condition of both speaker and auditor, of writer and reader. Analysis strives to exemplify this non-evaluative stance in the very *form* of its writing practices. This concern with the give and take of reason is, so to speak, the categorical imperative of reflexive work. It is, therefore, not a damaging accusation to say that such texts are *essentially* incomplete (10) or *descriptively* limited; recognizing the 'limits' of all possible acts of speech is precisely the starting-point of theorizing; hence every analysis, every formulation and textual response, is necessarily an open *work-in-permanent-progress*. As speaking can never be representationally closed, each topical essay is indexed with an invitation to creative re-formulation: each formulation is itself a display of the process of communal 'ordering'. Analyses are provocations and invitations to speech and thought rather than final words or finished products.

This may give the indolent reader the impression that these texts are insubstantial or, ultimately, about nothing in particular, or even 'unintelligible' ('Evaluation B': 99–100). In one sense this could not be further from the truth. In another sense, however, this kind of 'criticism' contains a more subtle insight: 'for while it is true that the so-called object of analysis is no-thing in the sense that it is not a thing, it is not true that this object is nothing' (16). Heidegger – and we might even say, the radical spirit of phenomenology – is re-visited and recollected at this point: 'Being does not show itself in itself but announces itself through phenomena which show themselves. The analyst is one who is committed to this re-cognition and who seeks to speak under its auspices' (*OBSI*: 6).

7.1 Who or what is 'the other'?

In its most immediate sense the community implicit in analytic collaboration is 'consummated' in the constitution of real and virtual communities of analytic readers and co-responsible workers: 'These are papers which seek a conversation, as it were' (9). In the terminology of Mikhail Bakhtin, analytic investigations are dialectical, heteroglossial, and polyphonic, the products of multiple voices that open up possible futures for 'other voices'. Once again the accent is upon *futurity*. This version of theoretic speech is premised upon the impossibility of both a 'first word' and a 'last word'.

But why '*as it were*'? Well, the tension of ambivalence in this '*as it were*' holds open the idea of 'conversation' in its threefold sense as *method* or *medium*, as the *topic*, and as the primordial *resource* of theoretic work. Once more the partial 'appearances' and situated displays of dialogue must be taken seriously, but not as an aid or heuristic to descriptive inquiry; rather dialogical 'appearances' makes reference to their own hidden methodic 'history' and 'conditions of possibility'. In principle, no 'dialogue' enjoys a determinable 'origin' or 'terminus'. Dialogue is more like the mobile affective media of desire circumstantially shaped into recognizable practices and forms of life for *these particular interests and ends*. Dialogue – and hence dialectic – never sheds this moment of *haecceity* or contingency.

Analytic sociology consequently posits ego and alter – whether actual and virtual – as *conversational* partners in an interminable dialogue:

> Ego, for us, is the speaker who, by speaking, necessarily forgets his reason for speech. Alter reminds ego why he speaks by formulating ego's auspices.... Conceiving of both ego and alter together, which is to say conceiving of collaboration, is our method for being able to produce an analysis which is reflexive, which addresses its own possibilities, and yet is at the same time speakable, do-able, distinct from chatter, a denial of nihilism. Alter and ego collaborate to generate analysis.
>
> (4)

What are the unexplicated philosophical (ontological, ethical, political?) assumptions embedded in the choice of terms like 'ego' and 'alter' for dramatizing dialogical self-reflection? Such an 'option' is not a neutral action. Far from it. The decision to prioritize 'ego' (even in the decentred pairing of *ego/alter*) is already overdetermined by the normative interactional contexts of Analysis's own history and, as such, unwittingly suggests an ego-centric image of the world. Could, for example, the terminology of 'Self' and 'Other' be substituted for 'ego' and 'alter' or would this simply be a notational variation of Analytic sociology's preferred idiom? 'Ego' (*Ich*), we might recall, already imports psychoanalytical motifs and theorizations of psychic life as well as more distracting connotations of 'egoism/egotism'. Incidentally, the Freudian language of ego and alter was also the terminology that Parsons favoured in working out some of the basic concepts of normative social interaction, socialization, social order, and systemic structure (the 'Snubs' paper cites the Parsonian precedent at 124–126).

Perhaps 'Self', with its much older Indo-European roots (*s(w)e – swami*) would have opened up other metaphorical paths (for example, in its translation into Latinate culture as *sui* (as in suicide) or *sui generis* (Durkheim's representation of social facts as realities *sui generis*)). Analogous possibilities arise with respect to the etymological resonances of 'other' (*Hetero-*, alter, alterity, difference, differentiation, and so on). Like one moment in a process of dialectical recognition, the paper on 'Snubs' commends something like this terminological change, where the idiom of *ego/alter* is displaced by 'the dialectic between Self and Other and the complex of problems connected with togetherness and separateness, unity and difference' (109–110).

This possibility of this 'shift' returns us to the more general issue of technical terminology or 'terms of art' and the privileging of certain recurrent metaphors in analytic work ('work' being one of these metaphors). How might analytic work have been constructed if the authors of *OBSI* had experimented with 'desiring subject', 'speaking subject', 'writing subject', 'divided self', and so on rather than the figures of 'ego' and 'alter'? Are there also not other models of 'mutuality' and 'friendship' that would lead beyond the European frame of reference and to non-European conceptions of thought and inquiry?

7.2 The structure of alterity

'A philosophical problem has the form: *I don't know my way about.*'
(Wittgenstein, 1968 sec. 123: 49e)

Framing conversation in this interactional style automatically produces the questions: Do 'ego' and 'alter' designate separate selves (*inter*personality) or are they terms for 'conversations' within the self (*intra*personality)? What are the 'limits' and 'borders' between 'ego' and 'alter'? Are the notions of separation and division here only heuristics to begin the 'real work' of analysis or more consequential traces of the 'cuts' and 'separations' that are inseparable from the inherited language and methodological stipulations of academic philosophy and social science?

Clearly, complex ontological and ethical questions of conceptual identity, unity, and difference are implicated in this way of understanding conversation and responsive friendship as principled notions. For example, can the dialogical roles of ego and alter be performed by an individual 'empirical self' (Plato's voiceless conversation of the soul)? Plato's inner division of the speaking soul is affirmed in the following terms: 'Others' [other initial or original formulations] formulate themselves to some extent, which is to say they do the work of both ego and alter' (6). Here there are no literal delimitations, but only an anecdotal 'division' and 'interplay' *within* the talk of the 'inner self' (once again we are both liberated and constrained by the problematic spatial metaphors of 'inner' and 'outer', 'inside' and 'outside', 'we' and 'others', 'friends' and 'enemies', 'familiarity' and 'strangeness', etc.).

On the side of alterity. A strong conception of non-substantial selfhood entails an equally principled conception of the other (and alterity). How is alter and the formulation work of alter projected as a responsive interlocutor and co-writer? Is 'alter' to be construed as autonomous or a dependent *persona* of ego, ego's avatar interlocutor (the other with a small case 'o' or the Other with a capital case)? This raises further questions: Are there authentic and inauthentic 'Thou's' (interlocutors)?, ephemeral and loyal 'Thou's' (contingent acquaintances or life-long friends), enemy 'Thou's'?, indifferent 'Thou's'? What is the role of friend-ship and enmity and the process of amicable struggle that orders adversarial dialogue? ('we have the *Thou* in opposition because we truly have the other who thinks other things in another way' (Buber, 1961: 46)). Where does 'otherness' in dialogue become total incomprehension? In what ways can we preserve the radical 'difference' of the other in such dialogical practices? How might we return to other attempts to theorize dialogically and emancipate their frozen interlocutors? We return to Plato's and Aristotle's conceptions of the 'genuine' friend as 'another self', but now with the courage to criticize and judge the limits of Platonic/Aristotelian versions of the other-*qua*-interlocutor. How should we re-listen to a Protagoras and Gorgias?

Even more concretely, what version of response, responsibility, and friend-ship is presupposed by the actual *physical* processes and *material* circumstances involved in doing Analytic sociology? How do these pre-reflective conditions shape the normative life of responsible speech? In what ways is Analysis itself a form of moral conduct? By what criteria are we to separate (evaluate?, grade?, criticize?) responsible from irresponsible analytic responses (and, thereby, dia-logical collaborators)? In sum: is there a favoured dialogical method appropriate to the ethical demands of analytic work and communality? Would the project of Analytic speech be modified by embracing the multiplicity of voices (Bakhtin's heteroglossia) or celebrating the polyphony of fractured, untotalizable and, perhaps, undecidable character of adversarial dialogue? Are their limits that no act of speech can cross?

7.3 Dialogical method

Did Analytic sociology (as it was exemplified *c.*1974) have a principled account of dialogical existence (the principle that all analysis, even the most concrete and empiricist, is essentially indebted to the ethical moment of dialogue)?

Something like this conversational deep structure is coded in the notion of exemplariness where topics or formulations of phenomena are approached as contingent exemplifications of the method that made them possible. Expressed inversely, topics (as formulated texts) are occasions to 'reverse engineer' their auspices (where 'auspices' is to be read as a metaphor for way of being or 'form of life' (107)). Thus a 'topic' such as the intelligibility, ordinariness and conven-tionality of everyday life experiences or the unnoticed normative background of scientific practices has the status of an iconic example hiding a founding problem or ambiguity, which, once recognized, creates a constructive occasion that *initiates* reflexive work as a genealogy of concealed grounds. What kind of *labour* is involved here? The orientation toward auspices is analogous to phenomenological *epoché* that transforms the natural attitude into a phenomenological problem or, more textually, to the attitude of deconstruction that 'brackets' the logocentrism of language to explicate the conditions of its (im)possibility. Is this still not to be fascinated by *theoretical* work?

While not invoking terms like 'intentional sedimentation', 'genealogy', or 'deconstruction' in the 1970s, Analytic sociology certainly formulated this kind of reverse engineering as a genetic inquiry into the problematics and problem-resolving texture of 'history': 'Everyday life is then not a phenomenon but an impetus; it provides the practical and concrete incentive for reflexive inquiry' (11). For example, the 'surface' interaction of collaborative teaching, writing, administration, and so on becomes an occasion for examining the idea of 'true collaboration' and the value of a 'true friend'. What, in this context, is the concrete machinery of writing – *inscriptive work* – involved in producing a collective 'analysis'? How are the everyday attributes of friendship co-opted and 'merged' in the co-production of analytic texts? What kind of in-mixing of labour is involved in such work? In the *Introduction* to *OBSI* we learn that the 'method' involves a number of phases; first the stage of concrete discussion and conversational voices, then a heuristic draft of a possible paper, followed by re-drafting by other collaborators, finally a 'finished' version?

This prompts the question as to the nature and function of disagreement, interruption, and non-congruent versions of a given topic. How is the voice – and person – of the interlocutor to be respected in this process? In keeping with the ethical spirit of reflexive transparency should these dissonant voices and 'non-congruent' formulations have been published together as dialectical 'variants' of a given topic? Without these acts of friendly reformulation we are left with a product without its process. We also note that the published texts chose not to experiment with alternative styles of dialogical production and presentation. There is no attempt to replicate the Platonic dialogue or other dialogical texts in the tradition. How did the authors of *OBSI* move from working drafts to publishable papers? What are the working assumptions concerning the procedural interplay of multiple voices in the crystallization of an analytic text? How is disagreement and the interplay of dissonant voices 'merged' to produce an apparently univocal paper? More politically, how were the manifest conflicts and interruptions that accompany such distributed acts of composition laundered from the finished article?

In establishing the 'deep auspices' of a phenomenon – for example, in claiming that the form of life of positivism is the ground for the recognizable phenomenal status of *bias*, *distortion*, and 'reason-giving' *evaluations* – who has the casting vote that decides whether the 'final text' or 'last word' on grounds has been secured ('Then someone edits the full collection of material into a "finished" paper': 4)? How is the terminal and compelling character of a finished paper negotiated and recognized?

Clearly these questions raise both practical and analytic issues that are not the unique preserve of Analysis. It is the virtue of Analysis to have fore-grounded these problems as universal issues that are typically ignored or actively repressed from the conduct of theoretical work.

7.4 The community of analytical work as a promissory life of dialogue

If collaborative writing (re-writing) only occurs 'between' ego and alter, what is the 'lesson' taught by *OBSI* about the difference between ontic and ontological dialogue, speech, intertextuality, writing? Given Analysis's focal concern with problematic auspices and ambiguity we might suspect a range of tensions between the experimental exercises of 'speech' and the unexplicated emergence of a series of 'written' versions prior to the 'finished' text. Like ripples in a stream, embodied voices seem to disappear into the materiality of the text.

In *OBSI* 'speech' frequently (necessarily?) appears as a synonym for 'writing': 'Second papers formulate for the originals the auspices under which the latter were produced' (5).

But is this picture of the 'community of analysis' still presented abstractly as a collectivity of *intellectual* co-writing (located in self-critiques of and interventions in the programmatics of post-ethnomethodological sociology)? Or is the projected community of analytic work more like the temporary ensemble of ethically oriented selves (selves intervening in the practices of everyday life, what passes for 'academic politics' and perhaps wider horizons of political involvement – the radical reflexivity or 'left-turn' of post-Garfinkel ethnomethodology in Melvin Pollner's well-known paper (1991)). Or are none of these mundane and academic models of collective speaking/reading/writing fully consonant with the aspirations, concrete pleasures and pain of analytic work as a distinctive human activity?

Analysis, in its silence about these processes and dynamics, has brought to our attention a whole complex of problematics that apply to *all* forms of socially organized research and writing – opening a wide range of transdisciplinary questions that can be asked of the dramaturgy of speaking and writing in the history of thought.

Consider another instance. At numerous points in *OBSI* the relationship between provisional formulations (or preliminary *phases* of writing) is presented in the 'holistic' language of 'deepening': in the writing process 'second papers should always be deeper than first. But not because the response writers are cleverer or even because science marches on. Second papers are deeper than first by their very nature. The fact of a first paper makes possible a second which formulates the auspices of the first' (5).

Here the terms inviting deconstruction are 'depth' and 'deepening'. How are formulations 'graded' in terms of being 'more useful' or 'deep' than others (6)? What are the criteria of evaluation here? Or, perhaps more consequentially, is there something like an implicit measure of 'completion' (and 'truth') in operation? Is it satisfactory that the analytic process of 'deepening' should be simply grouped under the catchall notion of being 'ad hoc' solutions to collaborative problems? If first versions are somehow identified as 'inadequate' what would *adequacy* look like? Is there a distinction between 'repairable inadequacy' and 'absolute inadequacy'? Is not all speech, in some fundamental sense, *inadequate*?

Is there something like an analytic equivalent of the 'hermeneutical circle' at work in the concrete procedures of analytic collaboration and writing? Clearly notions like 'deepening', 'adequacy', and 'useful' understood as implicit evaluation criteria require further in-depth consideration and clarification.

7.5 *Dialogical transformation and the question of criteria*

We have argued that one of the fundamental aims of Analytic speech – comparable to psychoanalytic dialogue – is the transformation of self through the collaborative process that formulates the problematic occasion of mundane experiences and interactions. The 'Snubs' formulation is that the provision of grounds 'transforms us all from mutual substitutable two's or ego's into a differentiated collection of ego and alter' (134). The transformative vicissitudes of collaborative writing form a process that gathers the other into a promissory community of recollective dialogue. Dialogue is the process that reconfigures strangers into possible friends.

Can we map this transformation in terms of the relation between first and subsequent formulations? That is, in what ways is the 'self' displayed in formulation one 'deepened' through the second (or subsequent) formulation(s)? Again this suggests an unexplicated version of 'ground' as a projected ethical community or 'moral order' (or, more cautiously, a promise of ethical communality oriented to shared problems, ambiguities, and concerns).

What are the operative criteria for this 'deepening' in self-descriptions of the type: 'All papers include ideas which are, in the course of the papers themselves, deepened' (5)?

If such criteria cannot be depicted as 'better descriptions', more 'acute analyses', 'getting closer to the truth', etc. how is the dynamic or *deepening* process to be judged (whether by ego or alter) – the implicit reference to the demand that the editorial 'final' draft should recover 'the dynamics of the relationship between the original and the response' (6). Working criteria that are mentioned include (i) originals that cannot be responded to; (ii) responses that 'seem irrelevant to the original'; (iii) unusable 'material' ('Often we give up on some material in midstream') (6).

This leads to further questions concerning the ethical matrix of dialogical transcendence and self-transformation. How are we to understand 'self' as both an analytic *topic* and the *telos* of analytic speech/writing? In what way does the activity of 'doing' analytic writing make participants ('members'?) different, more self-reflective selves? In what ways is the promise of Analytic speech some version of reflexive selfhood or a future image of non-centred self and communality? Is 'the other' (*alter*) assumed to remain identical through this process? What are the assumed criteria for the 'otherness of the other'? What responsibilities (and responses) are involved in addressing shared problems, traditions and existential concerns? What responsibility does Analytic work owe to its possible audiences?

7.6 The difference between dialectic and dialogue

Thinking in common might be the motto of the dialectic. Rhetoric is a dialogue of love.

(Roland Barthes, 'The Old Rhetoric: an aide-mémoire', 1988: 19)

Clearly any critical genealogy of different conceptions of speech and community, insofar as these have informed philosophical traditions and the human sciences, raises the question of the ethicality of analytic conversation. In what ways is the disclosure of the auspices of powerful modes of speaking and writing (for example the analysis of the prescriptive form of life of positivism) already a display of other ways of speaking an ethical process? If positivism (as both epistemology and form of life) is a variant of philosophical empiricism how should we deconstruct this form of life? Or, otherwise expressed, what 'other site' are we invoking in commending a more responsible way of life?

These questions echo and run parallel to the ethical dialogism of a Buber (1961) and Levinas (1969) who were both concerned to critique and deconstruct the objectivist traditions of Western thought as inimical to genuine ethical communality: Buber thematizing the prevalence of the attitude of 'I–It' over the 'I–Thou' relation, Levinas rejecting the idea of logocentric totality (and totalization) grounded within the tradition of ontotheology from Aristotle to Hegel and Heidegger and prioritizing the themes of self-transcendence and ethical responsibility against the claims of totality and absolute truth.

Like these earlier dialogical traditions, Analytic work rejects the framework of fundamental ontology and projects an image of collaborative speech and community as an alternative ethic of responsible discourse. Consider, for example, the last sentences of the 'Bias' paper which conclude by saying, 'we have asked whether such a life [positivism/objectivism] is worth living, whether such a world is worth our commitment, and we have brought an alternative world to view' (75). If we accept that human life is in some sense radically dialogical this needs to be demonstrated in the very conduct of social inquiry. And, as we have repeatedly underlined, engaging in science, philosophy, or theorizing more generally is not merely *theoretical practice* but a paradigmatic instance of dialectical rationality. The reconciliatory impulse of dialectic needs to be reconfigured in the context of the radical 'loving-friendship' of dialogue. As Buber asks: 'When will the dialectic of thought become dialogic? (Buber, 1961: 47).

This movement from disinterested dialectic to the differential *ethos* of dialogue is, perhaps, displayed in the auto-critique of the 'Motive' paper, which depicts itself as a stage along the path toward a more responsible version of analytic speech, representing 'the inarticulate and underdeveloped conception of analysis of earlier works in order to make available a clearer sense of our own analytic commitment now' (46). But this 'movement' also prompts a broader question: Is there an analytic-sociological-philosophic equivalent of *erôs* and *philia* that might reactivate the great problematics of desire and friendship, perhaps 'the *erôs* of dialogue' as a paradigm for the *jouissance* of Analytic speech and writing (cf. Buber, 1961: 48–50)?

How in a post-foundational, post-metaphysical, and anti-formalist culture are we to recover 'the ethical' not primarily in the epistemological question of what it means to speak and write, but in the concern for what it means to be alive, to live together, to transform what passes for everyday life? Can the ironic strategies of Analytic theorizing foster a new form of ethics and politics? In other words, what kind of positivity is immanent in Analysis' engagement with the negativity of secure topics and conceptual frameworks?

8 The politics of Analysis

No doubt something like an analytic politics is necessarily at work in the idea that grammars code ontologies that are lived as forms of life shaping the contingent appearances of experience and everyday life. In effect, from an analytic perspective everydayness is congealed ontology. What passes for 'the ordinary' (what has been called 'the myth of the everyday' (Sandywell, 2004)) now becomes an occasion for radically rethinking the complex and interweaving symbolic forms of power, life, and experience. The everyday as background context and the everydayness of research are no longer secure base-camps for social inquiry. To treat the world as such a resource is to deepen the generic forgetfulness of unreflective language and the forms of life that are sheltered by language. Here the possible future of a different kind of politics beyond every form of representationalism returns. This shift toward a more radical understanding of 'life with the other' (alterity) and the possibilities of other conceptions of power ('the political') generate a range of unfinished problems.

How should Analysis formulate the grounds of different forms and understandings of power? How should we distinguish 'the political' in both concrete from analytic terms? What are the implicit power asymmetries contained in the formulation of grounds and grounding? In a profoundly nihilistic, monological, and phallogocentric culture is collaborative praxis and radical dialogue still possible as viable forms of life? What would be the preferred language-game for rethinking the idea of *history* and recovering more radical senses of *temporality* and *historicity*? Does Analytic sociology adequately formulate the dimensions of the present crisis? We might ask why there was no paper on 'Alterity' or 'Power' in *OBSI* and no formulation of the history of self–other problematics in the rich tradition of reflexive and dialectical discourse about the grounds and ethics of 'open dialogue'.

In the work carried out from the late 1960s to the end of the 1970s we can note the absence of an explicitly reflexive account of the *horizon of metaphysics* – the *metaphysics of presence* – that 'grounded' much of what passed for social theory and sociological analysis during that period. We might also note the lack of a theory of speech's concrete *embodiments* and *inscriptions* (in work, writing practices, social relations, technologies and material culture, urban life, the apparatuses of the state, political organizations, cyberculture, and so on). And, finally, the question of the institutional constraints on dialogue and the broader ethico-political horizon of theorizing are absent from the 1974 work. It should be said, however, that many of these enduring issues would be addressed in later writings; notably with the publication of the papers in *Friends, Enemies, and Strangers* (Blum and McHugh, 1979), *Self-reflection in the Arts and Sciences* (Blum and McHugh, 1984), and most explicitly in Alan Blum's remarkable text on the modern city (*The Imaginative Structure of the City*, 2003), and more recently his investigations of the ambivalent zones of embodiment, health, and illness (*The Grey Zone of Health and Illness* (2011)).

9 Conclusions

> *animum debes mutare, non caelum* ('you must alter your mind, not the sky above you')
>
> (Seneca, *Letters*, Letter 28)

Over the course of this brief history I have shifted from a relatively well-defined essentialist and ahistorical question '*What* is analytic speech and writing?' to the more existential questions '*When* does speech become reflexive?' and '*What* are the forms of desire that motivate reflexive speech?'. The chapter has traced the movement from a more-or-less traditional ontological *paradigm of reflection* where thought is construed as a mimetic 'mirroring' of its objects and its presupposed version of the monological self to a *radical dialogical or relational paradigm*, where thought is understood as an active social *engagement* and *praxis* provoked by the reflexive imperative itself. In this movement it is the unending dialogue between thought and language itself that comes to the fore. We have shifted from an *ocularcentric* vocabulary of reflection as a cognitivist term for questioning, thematizing, or, generically, *problematizing* experience to a sociolinguistic conception of reflective acts articulated in convention-constituted language-games, to sociopolitical conceptions of individual and collective *styles* of reflection institutionalized as organized patterns of reflexivity, and finally to radical dialogical images of reflection understood as modalities of *desire* and *phronesis* (dialectically occasioned practices of experience, judgement, imaging, inscribing, speaking, describing, documenting, archiving, writing, recording, photographing, symbolizing, etc.) as distinctively human activities oriented to the endlessly variable problem-solving contexts of human living.

By working through this itinerary we come to the conclusion that Analytic rationality is grounded on an imaginative conception of reasoning that responds to this process of radicalization as a distinctive way of formulating existential and ethically immanent phenomena without resorting to any type of concrete authority or transcendent guarantees. Perhaps the most resonant question of Analytic investigations today is how new styles of qualitative and critical inquiry can be imagined and invented without resorting to any of the established ontological commitments and traditional theoretic perspectives. In other words, how, in Kieran Bonner's resonant terms, can transdisciplinary inquiry institutionalize the life of 'good troublesome company' and restore the ethical integrity and diversity of radical inquiry as a way of practically implementing a fully reflexive programme of critical research.

As an agenda for the future we can briefly summarize some of the more general implications of this style of analytic-reflexive work.

1   First, I have suggested that the *project* of Analytic sociology initially began as a critique of objectivism and as a radical intervention in American social theory by returning practitioners to questions concerning the grounds of practices and social interaction. But, in contrast to all other variants of interpretive, qualitative, and critical sociologies, Analysis embraces a principle of *radical reflexivity* that requires that any analytic formulation must be able to recover its own principled orientation and creative grounds through a process of collaborative dialogue. The force of this ethical imperative led the analytic project to a more radical reflection on the ontological significance of language and community as the horizon of all theoretical speech. This unavoidable engagement with older reflections on language and existence, if you like, is a *version of desire, memory*, and *historicity* reformulated, and displayed in Analytic work.

2   Second, before it is an *epistemological principle* this commitment to collaboration needs to be understood as an *existential demand*: speech becomes reflexive when it recognizes its own limits, and in that recognition its indebted status as a partial and ambiguous achievement sustained by an ongoing community, legacy, or tradition. In this way human speech – whether as qualitative phenomenological inquiry or as quantitative mathematical model building – reveals its fragility and its unfulfilled promise to speak the truth.

3   Third, as a *project of anamnesis* we need to think of Analytic desire itself in *temporal* terms as an unfinished and perhaps interminable process of dialectical thought rather than as an application of some secure method to pregiven problems in the style of orthodox philosophy and social science. Here the difference between concepts and language as *existentially constitutive* rather than *epistemologically reflective, instrumental, or representational* comes into play. If in general it is more useful to think of discourse *conceptually constructing* its problematics and interlocutors this also applies to the language-games of analytic inquiries. From this perspective there are no self-sufficient problems (as it were, 'problems-in-themselves'), subject matters, or phenomena independent of the questions and constitutive practices shaping their discursive articulation. This conception of discursive *composition* also underlines the importance of imagining questions and researchable spaces unthinkable – indeed unrecognizable and untheorizable – within established discursive topographies: questions and problems, like

concepts and works of art, have to be first imagined, invented, and stylized (analytically speaking, you *are* the questions you ask), and inventive practices are vital clues to the symptomatic silences and glosses that routinely organize social worlds and forms of life.

4 Fourth, the studies assembled in *On the Beginning of Social Inquiry* are in important ways 'before their time', in the same way that the thought of Nietzsche, Heidegger or Wittgenstein was *untimely*, involving (1) a *making strange* or *defamiliarization* of what passed for common sense, objective reality, and everyday usage, (2) a *principled suspension* of frameworks organized around the subject/object opposition of traditional social theory, philosophy, and liberal ideology, and (3) a *theoretical experimentalism* in search of alternative ways of thinking about the dialectical processes of word- and world-making. Not surprisingly, the task of imagining other analytical pathways, formulating the silences of traditions, and determining the precise meaning of *transcendence* and *critique* as a revelation of speech's ethical indebtedness remain very much in play today as open questions.

5 Fifth, it is, perhaps, only in retrospect that this interpretive 'openness' and 'experimentalism' can be recovered as one of the most responsible voices of a transformative approach to the programmes of modern philosophy and the human sciences; here *untimeliness* is perhaps another version of the principle that difficult texts should be allowed time to breathe and live (this will also reveal the limits of particular analyses, operating as a reminder that the dialectic that creates ambivalent zones fosters both unity and difference, insight and blindness, illumination and misunderstanding).

6 Finally, the *jouissance* of dialectical collaboration open to the celebration of difference and radical responsibility promises nothing less than a transvaluation of what passes for self and social reality. Extrinsic criteria of knowledge and truth are no longer able to sustain the grounds of rational inquiry. No supra-temporal Regulative Ideal, Nature, History, Independent World, Spirit, God, Transcendental Ego, Perfect Communication, or whatever, can be treated as a secure 'signifier' and founding principle of reasoned discourse. In rejecting these metaphysical versions of transcendence, Analytic inquiries reveal their own indebtedness to an older dialectical politics of thought committed to the critique of dogmatisms while resisting the temptations of cultural relativism (anything goes), cynical reason (nothing matters), and nihilism (nothing goes).

In this respect the idea of returning and recovering the spirit of these texts not only provides an opportunity to engage in the collective work of recuperation and re-interpretation but, looking to the future, to reaffirm and recreate the idea of an international community of reflexive inquiry as an ongoing project of transdisciplinary research.

Bibliography

Adorno, T.W. (1973a) *Negative Dialectics*. London: Routledge and Kegan Paul.

Adorno, T.W. (1973b) *The Jargon of Authenticity*. London: Routledge and Kegan Paul.

Adorno, T.W. (2005) *Minima Moralia: Reflections on a Damaged Life*. London and New York: Verso.

Arendt, H. (1958) *The Human Condition*. Chicago: University of Chicago Press.

Arendt, H. (1977) *The Life of the Mind*, vol. 1, *Thinking*. New York: Harcourt Brace Jovanovich.

Auerbach, E. (1953) *Mimesis: The Representation of Reality in Western Literature*. Princeton, NJ: Princeton University Press.

Bakhtin, M. (1981) *Rabelais and His World*. trans. C. Emerson and M. Holquist, Austin, TX: University of Texas Press.

Badiou, A. (2009) *Logics of Worlds. Being and Event. 2*, trans. A. Toscano, London: Continuum.

Badiou, A. (2013) *Being and Event*. trans. O. Feltham, London: Bloomsbury Academic.

Bar-Hillel, Y. (1954) 'Indexical Expressions', *Mind* 63 (251) pp. 359–379.

Barthes, R. (1988) 'The Old Rhetoric: An Aide-Mémoire' (1970), in *The Semiotic Challenge*. Oxford: Basil Blackwell, pp. 11–94.

Baudrillard, J. and Valiente Noailles, E. (2007) *Exiles from Dialogue*. trans. Chris Turner, Cambridge: Polity.

Beckett, S. (1984) *Collected Shorter Plays*. New York: Grove.

Berger, P. and Luckmann, T. (1966) *The Social Construction of Reality*. New York: Doubleday.

Bernstein, R. (1983) *Beyond Objectivism and Relativism: Science, Hermeneutics and Praxis*. Philadelphia: University of Pennsylvania Press.

Black, M. (1962) *Models and Metaphors*. Ithaca, NY: Cornell University Press.

Blum, A.F. (1971) 'Theorizing', in J. Douglas, ed., *Understanding Everyday Life*. London: Routledge and Kegan Paul, pp. 301–319.

Blum, A.F. (1974) *Theorizing*. London: Heinemann.

Blum, A.F. (1978) *Socrates. The Original and Its Images*. London: Routledge.

Blum, A.F. (2003) *The Imaginative Structure of the City*. Montreal, Kingston, London, Ithaca: McGill-Queen's University Press.

Blum, A.F. (2011) *The Grey Zone of Health and Illness*. Chicago: Intellect Press.

Blum, A.F. and McHugh, P. (1971) 'The Social Ascription of Motives', in *American Sociological Review*, no. 36, February, pp. 98–109.

Blum, A.F. and McHugh, P. eds. (1979) *Friends, Enemies and Strangers: Theorizing in Art, Science, and Everyday Life*. Norwood, NJ: Ablex Publishing Company.

Blum, A.F. and McHugh, P. (1980) 'Irony, the Absolute and the Notion', in *Maieutics: Centre for the Study of Social Theory and Moral Education*, vol. 1, no. 1, Spring, pp. 136–144.

Blum, A.F. and McHugh, P. (1984) *Self-Reflection in the Arts and Sciences*. Atlantic-Highlands: Humanities Press.

Bourdieu, P. (1993) *Outline of a Theory of Practice*. Cambridge: Cambridge University Press.

Buber, M. (1961) *Between Man and Man*. trans. R.G. Smith, London: Collins/The Fontana Library.

Burr, V. (1995) *An Introduction to Social Constructionism*. London: Routledge.

Carlisle, C. and Ganeri, J. (2010) *Philosophy as Therapeia. Royal Institute of Philosophy Supplement, 66,* Cambridge: Cambridge University Press.

Castoriadis, C. (1987) *L'Institution Imaginaire de la société* (Paris: Seuil, 1975), *The Imaginary Institution of Society,* trans. K. Blamey, Cambridge: Polity Press.

Castoriadis, C. (1991) *Philosophy, Politics, Autonomy: Essays in Political Philosophy,* ed. D.A. Curtis, New York and Oxford: Oxford University Press.

Castoriadis, C. (1997a) *The Castoriadis Reader,* ed. D.A. Curtis, Oxford: Blackwell.

Castoriadis, C. (1997b) *World in Fragments: Writings on Politics, Society, Psychoanalysis, and the Imagination.* Stanford: Stanford University Press.

Chomsky, N. (1957) *Syntactic Structures.* The Hague: Mouton.

Chomsky, N. (1965) *Aspects of the Theory of Syntax.* Cambridge, MA: MIT Press.

Chomsky, N. (1972) *Language and Mind.* San Diego: Harcourt Brace Jovanovich.

Cicourel, A.V. (1964) *Method and Measurement in Sociology.* New York: The Free Press.

Cicourel, A.V. (1973) *Cognitive Sociology.* Harmondsworth: Penguin.

Dallmayr, F. and McCarthy, T. eds. (1977) *Understanding and Social Inquiry.* Notre Dame, IN: University of Notre Dame Press.

Davidson, D. (1984) *Inquiries into Truth and Interpretation.* Oxford: Clarendon Press.

Derrida, J. (1972) 'Structure, Sign, and Play in the Discourse of the Human Sciences', in R. Macksey and E. Donato, eds. (1972) *The Structuralist Controversy: The Languages of Criticism and the Sciences of Man.* Baltimore and London: The Johns Hopkins Press, pp. 247–272.

Derrida, J. (1973) *Speech and Phenomena and Other Essays on Husserl's Theory of Signs.* trans. D. Allison, Evanston, IL: Northwestern University Press.

Derrida, J. (1976) *Of Grammatology.* Baltimore: Johns Hopkins University Press.

Derrida, J. (1978) *Writing and Difference.* trans. A. Bass, Chicago: University of Chicago Press.

Derrida, J. (2005) *The Politics of Friendship.* London: Verso.

Dewey, J. (1958) *Experience and Nature.* New York: Dover.

Diels, H. and Kranz, W. (1951–1952) *Die Fragmente der Vorsokratiker,* 3 vols, 6th edn Berlin: Weidmann.

Douglas, J.D. ed. (1970) *Understanding Everyday Life: Towards the Reconstruction of Sociological Knowledge.* Chicago: Aldine; London: Routledge and Kegan Paul.

Dreyfus, H. and Rabinow, P. (1983) *Michel Foucault: Beyond Structuralism and Hermeneutics,* 2nd edn 1982; reprinted 1983, Chicago: University of Chicago Press.

Feyerabend, P.K. (2010) *Against Method,* 4th edn. London: Verso.

Filmer, P., Walsh, D., Phillipson, M., and Silverman, D. (1972) *New Directions in Sociological Theory.* London: Collier-Macmillan.

Foucault, M. (1970) *The Order of Things,* trans. A. Sheridan, New York: Random House.

Foucault, M. (1972) *The Archaeology of Knowledge.* New York: Pantheon Books.

Foucault, M. (1977) *Discipline and Punish: The Birth of the Prison.* trans. A. Sheridan, New York: Random House.

Friedrichs, R.W. (1970) *A Sociology of Sociology.* New York: Free Press.

Gadamer, H.-G. (1976) *Hegel's Dialectic: Five Hermeneutical Studies.* New Haven: Yale University Press.

Gadamer, H.-G. (1985) *Philosophical Apprenticeships.* Cambridge, MA: MIT Press.

Gadamer, H.-G. (1991) *Truth and Method,* 2nd revised edn, trans. J. Weinsheimer and D.G. Marshall, New York: Continuum.

Garfinkel, H. (1964) 'Studies of the Routine Grounds of Everyday Activities', *Social Problems,* vol. 11, no. 3, Winter, pp. 225–250.

Garfinkel, H. (1967) *Studies in Ethnomethodology.* Englewood Cliffs, NJ: Prentice-Hall.

Garfinkel, H. (2002) *Ethnomethodology's Program: Working Out Durkheim's Aphorism,* ed. A. Warfield Rawls Lanham, BO: Rowman & Littlefield Publishers.

Garfinkel, H. and Sacks, H. (1970) 'On Formal Structures of Practical Action', in J.C. McKinney and E.A. Tyriakian, eds., *Theoretical Sociology: Perspectives and Developments.* New York: Appleton-Century-Crofts, pp. 338–366.

Giddens, A. (1979) *Central Problems in Social Theory: Action, Structure and Contradiction in Social Analysis* Berkeley, CA: University of California Press.

Giddens, A. (1984) *The Constitution of Society: Outline of the Theory of Structuration.* Berkeley, CA: University of California Press.

Glaser, B. and Strauss, A. (1967) *The Discovery of Grounded Theory: Strategies for Qualitative Research.* New York: John Wiley.

Goffman, E. (1959) *The Presentation of Self in Everyday Life.* New York: Doubleday.

Goodman, P. (1960) *Growing Up Absurd: Problems of Youth in the Organized Society.* New York: Random House.

Gouldner, A.W. (1970) *The Coming Crisis of Western Sociology.* London: Heinemann.

Gouldner, A.W. (1973) *For Sociology: Renewal and Critique in Sociology Today.* London: Allen Lane.

Hadot, P. (1995) *Philosophy as a Way of Life: Spiritual Exercises from Socrates to Foucault,* trans. M. Chase, Oxford: Basil Blackwell.

Haraway, D. (1991) *Simians, Cyborgs, and Women: The Reinvention of Nature.* London: Free Association Press.

Harding, S. (1991) *Whose Science? Whose Knowledge? Thinking from Women's Lives.* Buckingham: Open University Press.

Harvey, D. (1973) *Social Justice and the City.* London: Arnold.

Hegel, G.W.F. (1977) *The Phenomenology of Spirit,* trans. A.V. Miller, Oxford: Oxford University Press.

Heidegger, M. (1967) *Being and Time,* trans. J. Macquarrie and E. Robinson, Oxford: Basil Blackwell.

Heidegger, M. (1968) *What is Called Thinking?* trans. J.G. Gray and F.D. Wieck, New York: Harper and Row.

Heidegger, M. (1971a) *On the Way to Language* trans. P.D. Hertz, New York: Harper and Row.

Heidegger, M. (1971b) *Poetry, Language, Thought.* New York: Harper and Row.

Heidegger, M. (1993) *Basic Writings,* ed. D.F. Krell, London: Routledge.

Henriques, J., Hollway, W., Urwin, C., Venn, C. and Walkerdine, V. (1984) *Changing the Subject: Psychology, Social Regulation and Subjectivity.* London: Methuen.

Husserl, E. (1970a) *Logical Investigations,* 2 volumes, trans. J.N. Findlay, London: Routledge and Kegan Paul.

Husserl, E. (1970b) *The Crisis of European Sciences and Transcendental Phenomenology,* trans. D. Carr, Evanston, IL: Northwestern University Press.

Jameson, F. (1971) *Marxism and Form: Twentieth-century Dialectical Theories of Literature.* Princeton, NJ: Princeton University Press.

Jay, M. (1984) *Marxism and Totality: The Adventures of a Concept form Lukács to Habermas.* Cambridge: Polity Press.

Kaplan, A. (1964) *The Conduct of Inquiry: Methodology for Behavioural Science.* San Francisco, CA : Chandler Publishing Company.

Kojève, A. (1969) *Introduction to the Reading of Hegel.* New York: Basic Books.

Kuhn, T. (1962) *The Structure of Scientific Revolutions*. Chicago: University of Chicago Press.

Lacan, J. (1977) *Écrits: A Selection*. London: Routledge.

Lacan, J. (1978) *The Four Fundamental Concepts of Psycho-Analysis*. New York: Norton.

Latour, B. and Woolgar, S. (1979) *Laboratory Life: The Social Construction of Scientific Facts*. Princeton, NJ: Princeton University Press.

Levinas, E. (1969) *Totality and Infinity*, trans. A. Lingis, Pittsburgh, PA: Duquesne University Press.

Lock, A. and Strong, T. (2010) *Social Constructionism: Sources and Stirrings in Theory and Practice*. Cambridge: Cambridge University Press.

Lodge, D. (2014) *Lives in Writing: Essays*. London: Harvill Secker.

Luhmann, N. (2013a) *Introduction to Systems Theory*, trans. P. Gilgen, Cambridge: Polity Press.

Luhmann, N. (2013b) *Theory of Society, Volume 2*, trans. R. Barrett, Stanford, CA: Stanford University Press.

Macksey, R. and Donato, E. eds. (1972) *The Structuralist Controversy: The Languages of Criticism and the Sciences of Man*. Baltimore and London: The Johns Hopkins Press.

McHugh, P. (1968) *Defining the Situation: On the Organization of Meaning in Social Interaction*. New York and Indianapolis: Bobbs-Merrill.

McHugh, P. (1970) 'On the Failure of Positivism', in J.D. Douglas, ed., *Understanding Everyday Life: Towards the Reconstruction of Sociological Knowledge*. Chicago: Aldine; London: Routledge and Kegan Paul, pp. 320–335.

McHugh, P., Raffel, S., Foss, D.C., and Blum, A.F. (1974) *On the Beginning of Social Inquiry*. London: Routledge and Kegan Paul.

Merleau-Ponty, M. (1962) *The Phenomenology of Perception*. trans. C. Smith, New York: Humanities Press.

Merleau-Ponty, M. (1964a) *The Primacy of Perception*, ed. J.M. Edie, Evanston, IL: Northwestern University Press.

Merleau-Ponty, M. (1964b) *Signs*, trans. R.M. McCleary, Evanston, IL: Northwestern University Press.

Merleau-Ponty, M. (1968) *The Visible and the Invisible*, trans. A. Lingis, Evanston, IL: Northwestern University Press.

Merleau-Ponty, M (1993) 'Cézanne's Doubt', in G.A. Johnson and M.B. Smith, eds., *The Merleau-Ponty Aesthetics Reader: Philosophy and Painting*. Evanston, IL: Northwestern University Press.

Nagel, T. (1986) *The View from Nowhere*. Oxford: Oxford University Press.

O'Neill, J. (1972) *Sociology as a Skin Trade: Essays Towards a Reflexive Sociology*. London: Heinemann.

Parsons, T. (1937) *The Structure of Social Action*. New York: Free Press.

Parsons, T. (1951) *The Social System*. London: Routledge and Kegan Paul.

Parsons, T. (1966) *Societies: Evolutionary and Comparative Perspectives*. Englewood Cliffs, NJ: Prentice-Hall.

Pollner, M. (1987) *Mundane Reasoning: Reality in Everyday Life and Sociological Discourse*. Cambridge: Cambridge University Press.

Pollner, M. (1991) 'Left of Ethnomethodology: The Rise and Decline of Radical Reflexivity', in *American Sociological Review*, vol. 56, no. 3, June, pp. 370–380.

Potter, J. (1996) *Representing Reality: Discourse, Rhetoric and Social Construction*. London: Sage.

Potter, J. and Wetherell, M. (1987) *Discourse and Social Psychology: Beyond Attitudes and Behaviour*. London: Sage.

Putnam, H. (1981) *Reason, Truth, and History*. Cambridge: Cambridge University Press.

Quine, W. van Orman (1971) *From a Logical Point of View*. New York: Harper and Row.

Quine, W. van Orman (1976) *The Ways of Paradox and Other Essays*. Revised and enlarged edition. Cambridge, MA: Harvard University Press.

Ricoeur, P. (1970) *Freud and Philosophy: An Essay on Interpretation*, trans. D. Savage, New Haven: Yale University Press.

Ricoeur, P. (1974) *Conflict of Interpretations*. Chicago: University of Chicago Press.

Rorty, R. (1979) *Philosophy and the Mirror of Nature*. Princeton, NJ: Princeton University Press.

Rorty, R. (1991) *Objectivity, Relativism, and Truth: Philosophical Papers Volume 1*. Cambridge: Cambridge University Press.

Sacks, H. (1963) 'Sociological Description', *Berkeley Journal of Sociology*, vol. VIII, pp. 1–16.

Sacks, H. (1992) *Lectures in Conversation*, ed. G. Jefferson, 2 vols, Oxford: Blackwell.

Said, E. (1978) *Orientalism*. New York: Vintage.

Sandywell, B. (1996) *Logological Investigations*, 3 volumes London: Routledge: *Reflexivity and the Crisis of Western Reason* (volume 1), *The Beginnings of European Theorizing: Reflexivity in the Archaic Age* (volume 2), and *Presocratic Reflexivity: The Construction of Philosophical Discourse* (volume 3).

Sandywell, B. (1998) 'The Shock of the Old: Mikhail Bakhtin's Contributions to the Theory of Time and Alterity', in M. Bell and M. Gardiner, eds., *Mikhail Bakhtin: Alternative Dialogics*. London: Sage, pp. 196–213.

Sandywell, B. (1999) 'Specular Grammar: The Visual Rhetoric of Modernity', in B. Sandywell and I. Heywood, eds., *Interpreting Visual Culture: Studies in the Hermeneutics of Vision*. London: Routledge, pp. 30–56.

Sandywell, B. (2000) 'Memories of Nature in Bakhtin and Benjamin', in C. Brandist and G. Tihanov, eds., *Materializing Bakhtin: The Bakhtin Circle and Social Theory*. London and New York: Macmillan and St. Martin's Press, pp. 94–118.

Sandywell, B. (2000) 'The Agonistic Ethic and the Spirit of Inquiry: On the Greek Origins of Theorizing', in M. Kusch, ed., *The Sociology of Philosophical Knowledge*. Dordrecht: Kluwer, pp. 93–123.

Sandywell, B. (2004) 'The Myth of Everyday Life: Toward a Heterology of the Ordinary', in M.E. Gardiner and G.J. Seigworth, eds., *Rethinking Everyday Life: And Then Nothing Turns Itself Inside Out, Cultural Studies*, London: Routledge, 18 (2/3), pp. 160–180.

Sandywell, B. (2011) *Dictionary of Visual Discourse: A Dialectical Lexicon of Terms*. Farnham, Surrey: Ashgate.

Sandywell, B., Silverman, D., Roche, M., Filmer, P., and Phillipson, M. (1975) *Problems of Reflexivity and Dialectics in Sociological Inquiry: Language Theorizing Difference*. London: Routledge and Kegan Paul, reissued in 2014.

Schutz, A. (1964) *Collected Papers: Studies in Social Theory*. volume 2, The Hague: Martinus Nijhoff.

Schutz, A. (1972) *The Phenomenology of the Social World*. London: Heinemann.

Schwayder, D.S. (1965) *The Stratification of Behaviour: A System of Definitions Propounded and Defended*. London: Routledge and Kegan Paul.

Searle, J. (1969) *Speech Acts*. Cambridge: Cambridge University Press.

Seneca (1969) *Letters from a Stoic*, trans. R. Campbell, Harmondsworth: Penguin.

Schegloff, E.A. (1997) 'Whose text? Whose context?, *Discourse and Society*, 8 (2): 165–188.

Sica, A. and S. Turner, eds. (2005) *The Disobedient Generation: Social Theorists in the Sixities*. Chicago and London: University of Chicago Press.

Smith, D. (1987) *The Everyday World as Problematic*. Boston: Northeastern University Press.

Touraine, A. (1981) *The Voice and the Eye: An Analysis of Social Movements*, trans. A. Duff, Cambridge: Cambridge University Press.

Turner, R., ed. (1974) *Ethnomethodology*. Harmondsworth: Penguin.

Wittgenstein, L. (1967) *Zettel*, ed. G.E.M. Anscombe and G.H. von Wright, trans. G.E.M. Anscombe, Oxford: Basil Blackwell.

Wittgenstein, L. (1968) *Philosophical Investigations*. Oxford: Basil Blackwell.

Wittgenstein, L. (1980) *Culture and Value*, ed. G.H. von Wright and H. Nyman, trans. P. Winch, Oxford: Basic Blackwell.

Wright Mills, C. (1970) *The Sociological Imagination*. Harmondsworth: Penguin.

Part III
Topics in analysis

3 Analysis and sincerity

Warding off relativism

Gregor Schnuer

Introduction

The following contribution will explore some of the implications of the explicit and persistent critique of positivism in *On the Beginning of Social Inquiry*, also with reference to Habermas' charge of relativism brought against Blum and McHugh's work in the 1980s. It will suggest that the collapse of truth, and the related loss of a particular version of honesty, does not necessarily result in a nihilistic moral relativism. In order to pursue these implications the chapter will look at honesty as a topic. At first this might appear to be a peculiar choice, especially given that honesty is theoretically or philosophically an almost antiquated concept, closely associated with virtue ethics, and also deontology. Nonetheless, honesty will be regarded as relevant in this case as it bridges a concern for factual truths and the moral desirability, or even the necessity, of adhering to such truths. Put differently, honesty is founded, on the one hand, on the understanding that truth is speakable and communicable – that is, that a speaker can be truthful about some *things* – and, on the other hand, on the claim that doing so is somehow morally relevant and preferable to not being truthful. Consequently, I will draw on *OBSI* to speak of honesty as a topic of analysis, but furthermore, this chapter will also outline how McHugh *et al.* not only critique a particular form of deceptiveness relating to positivist social inquiry, but also relativize universalist moral claims about honesty, and propose, or even recommend, a particular version of honesty. This combination of both formulating and relativizing honesty will be shown to be commensurable, rather than self-destructive.

This engagement with honesty will begin by looking at intuitive usage of this concept, drawing particularly on two sources: the fable of the shepherd boy who cries wolf (Croxall, 1792: 263) and the deontological example of the honest shopkeeper (Kant, 2003: 11). These are used both to draw out facets of honesty's intelligibility, and to set up two cases that can be returned to on occasion to collect the argument. The second part of the chapter will take Kant's shopkeeper example as a universalist moral premise from which to draw a connection to McHugh *et al.*'s exploration of bias and positivist social inquiry. The applicability of their critique of positivism to Kant's enlightenment formulation of rationality and autonomy, and with that, deontological ethics, makes the third part of the chapter a short exposé of the charge of relativism leveled at Blum and McHugh by Jürgen Habermas in 1981. The fourth part outlines McHugh *et al.*'s explicit claim that their formulation of analytic speech is necessarily truthful, juxtaposing this with their critique of positivism for formulating a claim that, superficially at least, appears similar, namely that the application of scientific methods necessarily produces truths. The final part will then differentiate these two claims, arguing that McHugh *et al.* not only allow us to treat honesty as a topic of analysis, exploring its intelligibility as a convention, but that they also formulate a particular version of honesty that will be referred to as *sincerity*, which describes the way in which analysis makes reference to its own grounded-ness. The paper concludes that *On the Beginning of Social Inquiry*, by making a claim to truthfulness that orients to and lays bare the nature of speech, formu-lates the grounds of a way of acting that is *sincere*, and that has an explicit moral dimension.

A short glance at honesty

'To be honest is to be truthful'. This intuitive definition, in its simplicity, is helpful, since it does not require honesty to involve exclamations of truths, but it also accommodates the avoidance of deception or lies. The negative definition, where honesty is not lying, not being deceptive, and not being fraudulent, points us to one key aspect of truthfulness, namely that it is more about the intention and desire to speak the truth, than actually being correct, that is, in speaking the truth is some objectifiable sense.

I want to recount two well-known stories that deal with *honesty* explicitly and highlight how fine the line is, between honesty as stating a factual truth and honesty as being truthful, that is, not deceiving someone. The first example is from Aesop's fable 'The Shepherd's Boy' (otherwise known as 'The Boy who cried Wolf'):

> A certain shepherd's boy kept his sheep upon a common, and, in sport and wantonness, would often cry out, The Wolf! The Wolf! By this means he several times drew the husbandmen in an adjoining field from their work; who, finding themselves deluded, resolved for the future to take no notice of his alarm. Soon after, the wolf came indeed. The boy cried out in earnest. But no heed being given to his cries, the sheep are devoured by the wolf.
>
> (Croxall, 1792: 263)

This young shepherd is quite clearly dishonest, since he tells a blatant untruth, that is, that there is a wolf, when in fact there is not. An honest shepherd's boy would instead sit alone, albeit bored, watching the sheep as the day goes by. It is worthwhile noting that the boy deluded the other shepherds several times before they decided to no longer trust him. In Croxall's commentary, or 'Application', of this particular fable he states that 'though mankind are generally stupid enough to be often-imposed upon, yet few are so senseless as to believe a no-torious liar, or to trust a cheat upon record' (1792: 264). Interestingly, this almost implies that, in spite of people's supposed stupidity, the shepherd boy poses no real risk, except unto himself. Indeed, the most common 'moral of the story' tends to focus on the boy and the detriment to himself that is brought on by his lies. Croxall, however, adds another aspect, pointing out that the repeated lies might also adversely affect others by prohibiting the shepherd's boy from warning them about the wolf, disrupting social relations more broadly.

The second story is that of Immanuel Kant's shopkeeper, which he uses not just as an example of dishonesty, but also to make a case for being honest for the right reason:

> for example, it certainly conforms with duty that a shopkeeper not over-charge an inexperienced customer, and where there is a good deal of trade a prudent merchant does not overcharge but keeps a fixed general price for everyone, so that a child can buy from him as well as everyone else. People are thus served *honestly*; but this is not nearly enough for us to believe that the merchant acted in this way from duty and basic principles of honesty; his advantage required it; it cannot be assumed here that he had, besides, an immediate inclination toward his customers, so as from love, as it were, to give no one preference over another in the matter of price. Thus the action was done neither from duty nor from immediate inclination but merely for purposes of self-interest.
>
> (Kant, 2003: 11)

The first example would certainly be a poor fable in the eyes of Kant, since lying is discouraged because it is counter to self-interest, rather than lying failing to conform to duty and the categorical imperative. The shopkeeper's tale, to return to the above intuitive definition of honesty, shows how it is not necessary to speak an untruth to be deceptive. Charging inexperienced customers more does not require a shopkeeper to lie about this practice, he can simply avoid mention-ing it. The self-interest, much like the shepherd's boy, revolves around a reputa-tion, since a shopkeeper who acts like a crook and might be overcharging his customers slyly risks the trustworthiness of his business.

Both of these stories share three facets that relate to honesty. First, there is a factual reality, namely the presence or absence of a wolf and the money taken from various customers for a product. Second, there is a convention, namely that shepherds call for help when dealing with wolves and that shopkeepers charge set prices to all customers. Third, the stories make a moral claim. In the first example, the moral of the story is that repeated lying is not desirable for either the liar or those that are lied to since it undermines the trust necessary to effect-ively deal with wolves. In the second example, the moral claim is more compli-cated, since Kant does not only argue that lying is morally wrong, but he claims that being honest is also problematic when it is motivated by self-interest and not motivated by a duty to honesty: that is, a disinterested pursuit of truth for its own sake, rather than the actor's sake. For Kant, the example is not about being an honest shopkeeper, but it is about being an honest person per se.

We might also differentiate these two examples, formulating two versions of honesty: in the first example, honesty is part of the adherence to the particular duty of a shepherd, and it can thus be related to other virtues, particularly *honour*, since the boy has a duty to fulfil, but also arguably patience (although the latter is more particular to this example, whereas the former can be linked to virtuous honesty more generally); the second example is honesty in a much more contemporary (read: modern) form, where it refers to a much simpler dictum 'Do not lie!' that holds some universal moral relevance, and also rests more heavily on a universalist version of duty.

Honesty, positivism, and bias

Kant's example and his concern with a dispassionate adherence to generalizable and independently true moral imperatives (2003) shows a striking similarity with positivism as a form of inquiry. Even though Kant is mostly concerned with *a priori* analytic truths rather than *a posteriori* truths arrived at through empirical study and observation, both Kant and positivist social inquiry share the assumption that certain fundamental truths are knowable, and that coming to know them is a process of applying certain logically sound methods to uncover independently existing truths.

In *On the Beginning of Social Inquiry* McHugh *et al.* (1974) apply their version of theorizing to positivist science as a social practice and topic, critiquing its objectivism by looking specifically at bias as a trouble or problem that positivist social inquiry faces, since its influence on the application of scientific method might lead to a false account or description of the independent factual reality. Bias is not considered as an 'object', but the chapter of the same name explores, rather, 'how this troublesome character of bias is intelligible by asking what idea generates the possibility of such a view of bias in the first place' (1974: 49).

The idea that generates this possibility includes some of the key tenets of positivism: there is an independent factual reality that can be discovered through dispassionate inquiry and observation using appropriate scientific methods in order to produce valid, reliable, and repeatable results and answers. Given that the researcher cannot be eliminated and is a subject, bias is the difference between the influence of the researcher that is problematic on the one hand and the influence that can be overlooked on the other. It is, however, difficult to argue that the process by which bias is recognized and identified is itself not also subject to the same potential influence of interests, that is, it is hard to recognize an objective or natural criterion for recognizing bias. In other words, positivist inquiry presumes both its own methods and the methods used to identify bias to be objective and beyond personal influence. It is supposedly merely the application of these methods that can be fraught with the dangers of personal interests.

McHugh *et al.* not only charge positivism and its integral practice of bias, which it itself makes possible and necessary, with hiding or covering-up its own commitment to non-commitment (or its own interest in disinterestedness) in order to 'protect this very question (the question of commitment) from being explored', (1974: 75) but they also explore bias as a practice that relates to a community of actors, and that also implies a particular formulation of what a social actor is at his or her best. It is this version of an actor that reveals a particular indebtedness of positivism to Kant's conception of the rational and autonomous actor, the same actor who, as shopkeeper, chooses to charge the same price for all products for honesty's sake.

McHugh *et al.* summarize this 'every man' as follows:

> To say that 'every man is the measure' is therefore to open yourself to the question of what kind of measure a man is: if the every man is the measure, this means that any single, particular man, in order to be seen as an adequate measure, has to be the measure of all men or of any man.... This is nice, because the best man is the man who typifies the community: the collective.
>
> (1974: 68)

In the case of the positivist charge of bias we are seeing something resembling a Kantian charge of being irrational, that is, the speech or action does not adhere to a categorical rule (nature or reason) accessible to all. Just as it is insufficient to apply scientific methods passionately (for personal reasons, rather than disinterest) in the pursuit of scientific inquiry, it is also not enough to apply the maxims of honesty passionately in the pursuit of universalist morality.

There is, nonetheless, a distinction to be made here between nature and rationality as two distinct universal premises, given that the former is a premise for empirical truth and the latter is a premise for autonomous action entire. Science, even though implying a definition of the 'every man' does not explicitly make the adherence to scientific methods in life a condition of personhood. This cannot be said for Kant, who defines a *person* as 'a subject whose actions can be *imputed* to him' (Kant, 1996: 16) and must therefore be autonomously exercised.

> *Moral* personality is therefore nothing other than the freedom of a rational being under moral laws (whereas psychological personality is merely the ability to be conscious of one's identity in different conditions of one's existence). From this it follows that a person is subject to no other laws than those he gives himself...
>
> (1996: 16)

It should, however, be mentioned that Kant does not state that all action *must* adhere to a categorical imperative, since there are *permitted* actions that are simply not 'contrary to obligation', but since these are only cases where there is *no* obligation to adhere to, the shopkeeper's lesser version of honesty is arguably not permissible, since there is a categorical imperative applicable. Kant's universalist concept of *reason* and *autonomy*, therefore, presents us with a far stricter version of *membership*, or, put more accurately, Kant's *membership* is more encompassing, since it does not only concern the 'scientific' community (that the 'every man' in the above quote refers to), but membership of *persons* per se.

Truth and relativism

In spite of this critique of the scientific premises for telling the truth, McHugh *et al.* nonetheless draw on an implied formulation of honesty in their work, both in their treatment of bias (47–75), but also when speaking of snubs (109–136). The honesty that is being considered is quite evidently different from Kant's version, meaning the dispassionate adherence of truthfulness in a way that is universal. The treatment of positivist scientific inquiry as a social practice that follows certain conventions also turns positivist notions of truth into conventional, rather than objective, knowledge. Bias is one of the positivist conventions, rather than a break from them, yet the argument that positivist truths are conventional, that is, do not come from something objective and external, also begins to expose analysis to the charge of relativism. Similar to various other critiques of positivism, particularly in the postmodern and poststructuralist tradition, McHugh *et al.* (1974) and later Blum and McHugh (1984) deny the researcher a privileged access to 'reality' through the use of methods that render the researcher a mere messenger, unlike, so they claim, positivism (McHugh *et al.*, 1974: 70). Instead, the positivist method, including its charge of bias, are considered as a conventional social practice that permits the discovery of positivist truths, yet these truths are not objective in the manner that positivism claims. This claim itself is also already part of the positivist convention and internal to its very intelligibility.

This denial of positivist truths, which even leads McHugh *et al.* to suggest that the positivist way of life is either ignorant or deceptive (75), has led to their claim of the unprivileged theorist being described as 'self-destructive relativism' (Habermas, 2004: 127). Habermas repeats this charge of relativism in reference to McHugh's claim that:

> We must accept that there are no adequate grounds for establishing criteria of truth except the grounds that are employed to grant and concede it – truth is conceivable only as a socially organized upshot of contingent courses of linguistic, conceptual, and social behaviour. The truth of a statement is not independent of the conditions of its utterance, and so to study truth is to study the ways truth can be methodically conferred. It is an ascription.... Actually, this principle applies to any phenomenon of social order.
>
> (McHugh, in Habermas, 2004: 126)

This is not the objection of a positivist social scientist, but arguably of a neo-Kantian (or quasi-Kantian), at least in reference to the *Theory of Communicative Action*, where he formulates his concern with Blum and McHugh's relativism.

This relativism, that is, the claim that the scientist's application of rational and/or systematic methods of inquiry does not attain a privileged position, is, of course, not only a concern for knowledge claims, but also for moral claims in the deontological tradition. The formulation of moral duties in this approach to morality requires a version of reason and autonomy exterior to and independent of the derived moral duties, which in turn maintain an exteriority to the actual context of their respective application. Habermas also makes this connection between rationality important to knowledge construction through communicative action on the one hand (2004), and the moral importance of this communicative action (1992). It, therefore, is irrelevant in Kant's example that the person described is a shopkeeper, since the practice of running a business and having a shop has no bearing on the outcome of the moral imperative. The claim that the deontological shopkeeper has no privileged access to moral conduct, but merely access to a different set of practices and conventions is, therefore, a threat to universal moral claims.

It is, however, misleading to turn this into a false dichotomy. The reduction of objectivist and subjectivist claims into the only two options, one delivering universal laws, the other nihilistic relativism, too quickly results in the claim that the critique of positivism and an external rationality is 'self-destructive', as Habermas calls it. This critique, or conflation, appears as a consequence of the presumed requirement of an independent point of reference in order to assess the validity of a moral claim, or scientific truths. We require, in other words, some measure, to decide on what is correct or false. To the positivist and neo-Kantian, McHugh's claim cited above sounds self-destructive, since the claim declares itself to be no more or less right than any other, and it suggest that 'interpretive sciences must give up the claim to produce objective knowledge at all', and furthermore (this point being particularly relevant to the idea of bias), that making 'an explicit theme of the interpretive processes on which the researcher draws does not dissolve its situational ties' (Habermas, 2004: 126).

McHugh *et al.*, even though they clearly critique positivist approaches in social research, do not appear to be nihilists, nor do they avoid explicit moral claims. The avoidance of nihilism is not, however, based on an understanding of speech's self-sufficiency, that is, access to something external and independent. In spite of these claims lacking a universalist basis, they differentiate speech, in general, from nihilism. 'In speaking we are denying that we are doing an inadequate activity. Otherwise our speech would be no different than chatter, than silence, than … nihilism' (McHugh *et al.*, 1974: 3). In other words, by necessity, speaking already covers up the auspices that make that particular speech possible and intelligible, but it is not rendered meaningless as a consequence of this inadequacy. They differentiate their own approach by reference to this aspect of speech, which is not covered over, but is referred to, realized and even utilized. The focus of their work shifts from factual descriptions of 'objects'– e.g. what is bias – towards the grounds of practices and speech, e.g. what is it that makes bias possible as a conventional/intelligible practice.

Returning to honesty

The presented reading of the bias chapter in *On the Beginning of Social Inquiry* and the outline of the charge of relativism directed at Blum and McHugh invite the reader to consider honesty in two particular ways.

First, McHugh *et al.* repeatedly refer to truthfulness as important and desirable to analysis. This moral dimension of their work is evident in the introduction, where they write, for example, that

> Speech is analytic when it is consistent with itself. For us this means: since the very accomplishment of speech makes reference to its achieved character, speech which is true to itself makes reference to the fact (and mystery) of its grounds. Speech that is *truthful* to itself is not self-centred because it is faithful to the analytic conception of speech as grounded speech and this very idea points beyond speech to that which causes all things to endure, to persist, and to be. Speech which is true to itself is speech which re-cognises that it is not self-sufficient…
>
> (McHugh *et al.*, 1974: 15)

They follow this passage with a juxtaposition of analytic speech (speech that is true to itself) with concrete speech (speech that is self-contradictory). The latter, rather than making reference to itself being grounded, is speech that 'ignores its achieved character' through the 'delusion' that it is self-organizing (1974: 15). Through reference to this distinction between 'truthfulness' and 'delusion' in relation to the nature of speech, McHugh *et al.* already anticipate Habermas' subsequent critique, when saying that 'When concrete speech does not see analytic speech as narcissistic or capricious it will often see it as nihilistic, because the unformulability of grounds *seems* to mean that the object of analysis is nothing (is silent)' (McHugh *et al.*, 1974: 16).

Second, beyond thinking of analysis as principally truthful about the groundedness of speech, the method proposed by McHugh *et al.* also permits us to consider honesty not as an object of research, but as a social practice that is itself grounded and a possible topic for analysis. Honesty, in this case, is conventional, and as such, it can also be engaged with in the *truthful* manner pursued by McHugh *et al.*

We have already touched on the conventionality of honesty in reference to the two above examples, outlining three facets: factual reality; social reality or convention; and moral claim. Whereas universalist approaches to ethics might disregard the second facet as the mere setting within which the other two take place, the realization that honesty is itself conventional, and that the claim of being honest is *made* intelligible, that is, its intelligibility is an achievement, shifts the focus towards its grounds.

In addition to the two examples above, McHugh *et al.* permit us to look at two further instances of dishonesty, in this case, two instances that they charge with dishonesty: bias and snubs. The former is a more tenuous charge of dishonesty, and also more complicated, since the charge of bias itself alludes to the scientist being either ignorant or deceptive. McHugh *et al.* charge positivist social science with being dishonest, or at least ignorant. 'We have sought to show how the requirements which we have located through their talk (and for their talk) are out of tune with whatever their talk recommends' (1974: 75). The charge of bias is deceiving in so far as it recommends a particular form of speech; one which the charge of bias itself is unable to produce itself. As we have already seen, analysis juxtaposes its own approach by insisting that it is 'in tune' or 'true to itself'. The second example, snubs, according to McHugh *et al.*, 'appears as a pure case of the diabolical' that 'denies "what is"' (1974: 130). However, despite appearances, snubs are not as clear a case of dishonesty as it might appear at first, since, unlike positivist social science and its charge of bias, it is not at odds with itself in the same way. In order for a snub to be a snub it must be recognized as such, and in this requirement of recognition, it is necessarily a failed non-recognition, or, it is a bad lie. Instead of the denial of recognition, that is, the snub, being the cause of injury and upset, McHugh *et al.* suggest that it is the deliberate recognition of difference in a segregating manner that is at the heart of a snub. It 'is a deliberate, calculated sort of impropriety ... a decision to segregate, rather than collect' (1974: 134). Yet the hurt of the snub and the snub itself become intelligible through the same grounds, namely the same understanding of alter and ego, or greeter and snubber, as concrete objects that can be differentiated or compared. In much the same way as was the case with positivism and bias, McHugh *et al.* exclude their proposed analytic way of life from this morally problematic practice of hurtful snubbing, since their interest is not in concrete speech that segregates, but in collecting the grounds of speech. To put this differently, both bias and snubs are similarly intelligible: the actions disguise and cover over their grounds in a manner that disguises their conventionality and also disguises the particularities of the convention that is covered over.

The question that this permits us to ask is whether the differentiation that McHugh *et al.* formulate between their work and positivism, as well as concrete speech, is one that can itself be collected in a way that shows shared grounds concerning the intelligibility of honesty, or whether their proposed analytic way of life also suggests a different understanding of honesty altogether? The final part of this paper will explore this question, trying to show that they formulate a distinct version of truthfulness or honesty. McHugh *et al.* encourage us then to regard two versions of honesty: one is the social practice advocated in various guises as 'truth telling', and the other, which I will refer to as *sincerity*, is a way of speaking or acting conventionally recommended by the 'way of life' called Analysis.

Honesty and sincerity

So far, this chapter has introduced two examples of honesty and dishonesty, to then show that one of these examples, the shopkeeper, at first glance appears to be concerned with an external and objective understanding, similar to positivism.

Both, so the chapter argued, are concerned with independent rules in order to produce particular versions of the truth that are not subject to any-*one*. Much the way that positivist approaches regard it as mere coincidence, when a passionate and personally engaged scientist produces valid, reproducible and reliable results, so the shopkeeper who is charging everyone the same out of a personal passion for the well-being of his clientele and business is only coincidentally honest.

McHugh *et al.* can thus be drawn on to critique Kant's universalist ethics in much the same way that they explicitly critique positivist social inquiry: both the deontologist and positivist are covering up their commitment to non-commitment, or, put differently, they are covering up the grounds of their own conventionality. We might even be in a position to argue that both positivism and deontological ethics cover up the grounds of membership in their respective communities, as briefly discussed above. In Kant, this community is universal, in positivism the community is scientists, both shifting *where* objectivism and universalism are located in a manner that formulates these particulars as entire-ties, phrasing the edges of these communities as limits.

The chapter, however, continues by pointing towards the charge of relativism and the self-destructive appearance of their argument, particular in relation to the chosen aspect of 'truth', namely honesty. McHugh *et al.* formulate clear moral claims, particularly relating to truthfulness, yet nonetheless appear to also reduce any grounds such a claim might have to be little more than convention.

In one sense, then, McHugh *et al.* permit us to formulate honesty as a concern with following conventions competently, whereas dishonesty is a particular form of failing to follow conventions. The shepherd's boy is not competently follow-ing the established expectations of a shepherd, that is, guarding the sheep and intervening, or calling for help, when they are in danger. Similarly, the shop-keeper who is honest out of a concern for his business is honest through the adherence to certain practices associated with being a shopkeeper. If he were to charge different prices to unknowing customers, he would not be a shopkeeper, since that is not what shopkeepers ordinarily do. This also aids us, to some extent, in understanding how honesty is intelligibly relevant to some dishonest actors: a spy who is honest and truthful about his or her mission to the 'enemy' and chooses to be a double-agent, would nonetheless be considered dishonest by those to whom he or she only appeared a conventional spy.

Honesty, as adherence to expected and shared conventions, is no longer a cat-egorically morally desirable virtue, but it is possibly a relevant facet of social order, an aspect hinted at by Croxall's fear that repeated disruption of conven-tions causes a destructive ambiguity. Kant's deontological formulation of an honest shopkeeper can now also be formulated as the adherence to a particular convention, namely the categorical imperative. Kant's shopkeeper is first and foremost an honest deontologist. He might even be a poorer shopkeeper, since it is hard to explain why a deontologist would encourage his customers to spend money in his shop. If our shepherd, on the other hand, were a deontologist first and foremost, it is clear that he would not call 'wolf' in the absence of the animal, since that action cannot be motivated by a universal maxim, but it is equally difficult (or unusual) to formulate a maxim to call 'wolf' when there is in fact a wolf. Can we formulate a 'perfect duty' for calling upon others to help defend our property, when universalizing this duty would also compromise our own ability to defend our property when called by others?

McHugh *et al.* do not critique this form of conventionality. It is, in many ways, a premise for their formulation of analysis. To some extent, the boy who cries wolf and is dishonest is also part of this premise, rather than being antithetical to it. There is little to indicate that McHugh *et al.* object to *or* condone this version of dishonesty, even if the boy's deviation from convention might in some way even be understood as his realization that shepherding is a convention. It is not a limit, but a boundary: that is, something that can be transgressed and that can be done otherwise.

If McHugh *et al.* are only tangentially speaking about honesty as adherence to convention and meeting conventional expectations, then it is not this form of dishonesty, that is, acting differently than is socially or contextually expected or implied, that they associate with positivist social inquiry. As has been shown above, the positivist social inquiry's dishonesty is more particular: positivism does not merely abandon one convention for another without being forthright about it, but instead it claims that its own conventionality is not conventional at all, but is objective. To phrase this differently, McHugh *et al.* charge positivist social science not with lying about its conventionality, but with covering over positivism's capacity to lie in the first place, furthermore projecting its own standards of truthfulness onto other ways of life. It is perhaps in this projection that we can also make a connection to snubbing as the deliberate recognition of difference in a way that renders that difference incommensurable. Universalism, be it in relation to rationality or scientific method, has little conceptual room for accommodating difference. Difference becomes a problem, much in the way that the snubbed is a problem: the snub is not only the recognition of difference, but it is *only* the recognition of difference that refuses to even recognize that recognition. This segregating force renders difference inert, where the other is separated through an absolute limit, affirming the universalist's incapacity to do anything differently.

Understanding McHugh *et al.*'s objection to positivism and concrete speech as an objection to covering up the possibility of being wrong, permits us to juxtapose this to their formulation of analysis as 'true to itself'. It is important to note that positivism has a clear understanding of 'false', however, this, in its entirety, denotes 'other than positivism'. Positivist social inquiry posits that the correct application of the methods delivers, or more aptly, uncovers, 'truths'. This also explains how McHugh *et al.* do not charge positivist social inquiry with being wrong in spite of their charge of it being deceptive, since positivism is deceptive about the very possibility of being wrong in the first place.

We can return to their claim that analysis is 'truthful to itself'. We have established that this truthfulness cannot be to an external veridic measure, such as nature, since the externality of such a measure is precisely the deceptiveness mentioned above. The claim that analysis is truthful to itself might at first, however, return us to the above argument by Habermas, that analysis is self-destructively relativist, that is, radically subjectivist. This concern is, however, grounded in the assumption that the lack of a privileged position disassembles speakers into solitary atoms, overlooking the implications of the claim that speech that is truthful to itself in this manner is *not* self-centred, because it 'points beyond speech to that which causes all things to endure, to persist, and to be'. Analytic speech, or so McHugh *et al.* argue, points towards that which makes it possible, rather than that which makes it true, and this possibility always already makes reference to others. This version of truthfulness, which is distinct from honesty as conventionality, might be described as *sincerity*, especially since it tries to make reference to, and lay bare, its own character. Unlike *honesty*, which refers to truthfulness about that which the speech is about, *sincerity* more concretely refers to truthfulness about what is said. To be sincere, more so than honesty, can be described as the speech being 'meant' or 'meaningful'. In contrast, positivists, in the way they were described above, are insincere, since they speak 'truth' in a manner that glosses over the conditions under which this truth is spoken or formulated. Snubbers are insincere, since the snub glosses over the requirement of the recognition that it proceeds to deny.

Conventional honesty, commitment, and conclusions

Sincerity, here understood as the attempt to speak in a way that makes reference to the character of speech as shared, as not self-sufficient, and as grounded, might at first appear as tangential to the topic of this chapter, which aimed to explore *honesty* as conventional, drawing on *On the Beginning of Social Inquiry* to engage with the quandary of whether a critique of positivism and universalism also leads to moral relativism. Honesty was chosen because its intuitive use and examples such as the shepherd's boy and the shopkeeper combine claims about a factual reality and about moral desirability or even necessity.

This has allowed us, so far, to claim that honesty is best understood as the adherence of members to shared conventions. In many ways it is even a commitment to these conventions, since, other than ignorance, dishonesty requires a wilful choice where, for example, the shopkeeper knows that shopkeepers conventionally have fixed prices. It is easy to imagine a community where an honest shopkeeper conventionally charges different prices, or conventionally barters with customers. Commitment can here be understood as sticking to one convention rather than another, especially when the other can be understood as tempting. The committed shepherd boy endures the boring hours as expected and the committed shopkeeper does not overcharge the inexperienced customer – doing differently, as mentioned above, would not be an unconventional action, but it would be the adherence to some other convention for action, such as a conventional crook or a conventional bored or lonely boy. Understanding the shepherd boy in this manner also helps us explain why his poor shepherding no longer resulted in a response when the wolf did eventually show up, since by then, the shepherd boy was quite consistently behaving like a bored child. Unless the shepherd boy expressed some malicious intent the previous times, it is more plausible to imagine the other shepherds as saying 'Don't worry, he is just bored again', rather than exclaiming 'He's a liar, not to be trusted'.

If McHugh *et al.* have been drawn on in this chapter to explain honesty as an adherence to particular conventions, rules and expectations, then they have also made it harder to recommend honesty as morally desirable per se. It is this move away from clear moral prescriptions and their own insistence on being truthful that has brought sincerity into the discussion of honesty in a manner that is anything but tangential. Their work encourages a critique of universalistic ethics, without, however, reverting to either nihilist, or even particularist ethics. Instead, they allow us to avert our gaze from the question 'Is this morally good? (universally or particularly)', turning instead to the question of the nature of speech and action in a way that reflects on its own possibility. This move removes McHugh *et al.* from the dichotomous juxtaposition of true and false, and universal moral rules and nihilism, by exposing the rather murky and ambiguous grounds of these positions. But they do so, without turning this exposition of the grounds into a privileged claim, since they explicate the lacking self-sufficiency of their own speech. *Sincerity* is the open reference to the ambiguity of one's own speech, pointing out that it is also grounded in something that is rather murky and inaccessible to the speaker.

McHugh *et al.*'s claim that analysis is truthful about its own groundedness, pointing to an externality of which speech is nonetheless necessarily part, not only shifts universalist morals into the realm of convention, socially grounding them, but also implies a necessary relatedness to others through speech that sincerity makes an explicit reference to, outlining very different grounds for moral desirability. This relatedness to others that is intertwined with the conventionality of speech is developed much further in Blum and McHugh's later work, especially in *Self-Reflection in the Arts and Sciences* (1984), which begins with outlining consciousness as a social achievement. In this later text we also see a formulation for social action that is *sincere* in this manner, that is, action that references and reflects on its own conventionality, or its own possibility. This 'principled action' (Blum and McHugh, 1984: 135) goes beyond formulating the moral desirability of sincere, read analytic, *speech* by opening up the implications of this theoreticity to conventional *actions* more generally. It is, however, beyond the scope of this chapter to explore whether the sincerity formulated here can be found in the latter book in such a way that it permits us to formulate not only an honest shopkeeper, but a principled shopkeeper who is concerned with more than competent membership of a community, or who is concerned with the possibility of being a shopkeeper through the membership of a community. Instead, this chapter will conclude with the claim that *On the Beginning of Social Inquiry* is not only an engagement with the groundedness of speech, but is also a move away from moral universalism, instead recommending (or formulating the grounds to be able to recommend) an ethics of commitment and membership.

Bibliography

Blum, A. and McHugh, P., 1984, *Self-Reflection in the Arts and Sciences*, Atlantic Highlands: Humanities Press.

Croxall, S., 1792, *Fables of Æsop and Others*, London: Printed for A. Millar, W. Law, and R. Cater; and for Wilson, Spence, and Mawman, York.

Habermas, J., 1992, *Moral Consciousness and Communicative Action*, Cambridge: Polity Press.

Habermas, J., 2004 [1986], *The Theory of Communicative Action – Vol. 1 Reason and the Rationalization of Society*, Cambridge: Polity Press.

Kant, I., 1996, *Metaphysics of Morals*, Cambridge: Cambridge University Press.

Kant, I., 2003 [1997], *Groundwork of the Metaphysics of Morals*, Cambridge: Cambridge University Press.

McHugh, P., Raffel, S., Foss, D., and Blum, A., 1974, *On the Beginning of Social Inquiry*, Boston: Routledge & Kegan Paul.

4   Reunions

Standing and turning relationships

Eric Laurier

This chapter supplements the 'Snubs' chapter in *On the Beginning of Social Inquiry* (*OBSI*) by pursuing a similar episode, documented by LeBaron and Jones (2002), where a snub does not happen and, instead, a chance encounter leads to a reunion between former acquaintances. Unsurprisingly, the question of each party's standing toward the other does not have a simple answer in the reunion. How they stand in relation toward one another brings with it the remembering and reconsideration of their former relationship and their former characters. The reunion, at a hairdressers' salon, with third parties witnessing it, calls upon each party's senses of discretion over what of their or the other's intimate details they will reveal. Finally, the chapter underlines the ambiguity of the reunion as an event where each party is caught between proximity and distance, between acknowledging or avoiding the other.

> failure to have singled you out appropriately in passionate utterance characteristically puts the future of our relationship, as part of my sense of my identity, or of my existence, more radically at stake. One can say: The 'you' singled out comes into play in relation to the declaration of the 'I' who thereby takes upon itself a definition of itself, in, as it may prove, a casual or a fateful form. A performative utterance is an offer of participation in the order of law. And perhaps we can say: A passionate utterance is an invitation to improvisation in the disorders of desire.
>
> (Cavell, 2005: 194)

Reunions and re-visitings

You bump into someone you once knew, after many years apart. A chance encounter has brought together two people that once had a relationship. It may be that each is delighted to see the other, or that there is a certain dread from one, or from both, or that there are only polite and perfunctory inquiries. It may be that one finds the other to be just the same, or to have changed dramatically in appearance or manner. It may be that one has a debt toward the other, or carries an injury inflicted by the other. What happens during such encounters raises the shared problem of the reunion. A shared problem that proliferates in contemporary lives, where relationships are begun, interrupted, pursued, avoided, or ended but then returned to us by mobility, migration, and social media. Reunions are occasions that open up the possibility of the rekindling, maintenance, transformation, beginnings, and extinguishing of relationships. Their very basis and their central trouble is that whatever the relationship with the other person might become, they begin from an encounter where their relationship is a former relationship. The reunion provides them with a more or less substantial history but, as yet, no future relationship. Each person's standing toward the other is a former standing where to either rekindle or extinguish the relationship requires, first, a returning toward them.

My chapter in this collection takes the form of three re-visitings. First, it is a re-visiting of *OBSI's* chapter 'Snubs' which is itself a response to an earlier work by Roy Turner (1970). The 'Snubs' chapter is one of the texts where Self-Reflection makes clear not only the warrants for its departure from ethnomethodology but also how it analyses everyday encounters, through its engagement with Turner's description of the same type of encounter. Second, my chapter revisits the description of a reunion in a conversation analysis study by LeBaron and Jones (2002) which I first read with an interest in the endings of encounters, though not, as I will touch upon later, the endings of relationships. In responding to LeBaron and Jones' idea of the reunion my chapter tries to emulate the move made in the 'Snubs' chapter, which was to supplement the first description of an action made by Turner, by looking into the conditions of possibility for that sort of action.

Finally, this chapter was occasioned by the reunion of the community behind *OBSI* on the 40th anniversary of its publication. Members of the community were, during that event, themselves revisiting the book. To revisit a book or a person, while it might be related to the idea of a reunion, is quite a different matter. The reunion acquires its ambivalence and its sense of vulnerability from its parties reflecting upon their former standing with one another. It may be that they find themselves drawn to the enjoyment of the reunion that works out what the other person has become and what they might be for themselves. As it was, the community of authors and readers at the *OBSI* reunion found themselves comfortable with the development and working out of themselves found at the reunion (Blum and McHugh, 1984: 148). It led to future plans for future meetings and future conversations, this edited collection being one of them.

Snubs

To snub someone is one solution, then, to the problem of the reunion – rather than allow a reunion to take place, one denies any standing with the other on encountering them. In his original work 'Words, Utterance and Activities', Turner examined the complaint made, during a self-help meeting of former mental hospital patients, by one member of the group (Bert) of being snubbed by another former mental patient. In Bert's story of the encounter, he characterized the other patient as someone he had 'always buddied around with' (1970: 176).

But when he met this old acquaintance some time later in a city street, Bert was snubbed by him. The old acquaintance was walking with another person unknown to Bert. In explaining why one former mental patient would snub the other, Turner reminded us of the expectation that persons on being reunited should 'bring one another up to date' and/or 'talk over old times' (1970: 183). In Bert's case he would reveal that they were once both patients in a mental facility to the third party or, if he did not, it would be something that his former acquaintance would be obliged to reveal later. Turner argues that, for those with a former identity that they are trying to hide from their new acquaintances, they have reasons for both trying to avoid other former mental patients and snubbing them if they do bump into them.

In 'Snubs', McHugh *et al.* summarized Turner's version of the snub as a refusal of recognition accomplished through a set of conversational conditions. When one acquaintance greets another and the other does not return the greeting, the rule violation that obliges a greeting to be returned with a greeting is broken. McHugh *et al.* (1974: 114) provide Turner's components for carrying out a snub:

(a) a greeting to an acquaintance
(b) which is not returned
(c) when the absence of such a return shows itself as a denial of recognition, and
(d) where the denial of recognition can be seen as a snub.

McHugh *et al.* point toward the limitations of Turner's analysis of a snub: 'Turner's analysis is just a description of some features of a particular snub rather than an analysis of how a snub is possible' (1974: 113). McHugh *et al.* then pursue the further conditions that make each of these four parts possible. For the first component, they remind us that it turns upon the knowledge that the other is a person whom we have rights to greet (see also Sacks, 1992). Not only does it rely upon rights to greet the other but also that we know that a greeting should be produced to make it a recognizable greeting. For the second component – absence of a return greeting – the person making the greeting is required to assume that the other has mutual knowledge of the obligation to produce a greeting when greeted. The complexities of the snub deepen when McHugh *et al.* go on to add that it is not simply that the greeting is absent but, to satisfy the third requirement of a 'denial of recognition', the other party has to have intended such an absent response, rather than merely failed to notice the greeting. Finally, for the fourth feature, to see the denial of recognition as a snub, the person snubbed has to know more about the situation than merely that each of the previous three conditions was broken, to be confident that the other is snubbing them. Moreover, as they continue, refusal to recognise an acquaintance does not go far enough; a snub 'must in some sense be seen as insulting' (1974: 117).

McHugh *et al.*'s (1974) analysis deepens our understanding of snubbing by reminding us that it is not that the snubber denies that they recognize the other, it is that they do recognize the other. A snub assumes that the snubber shares the mutual recognition of the other and then, by their refusal, formulates the snubbed as someone they do not care for. In Turner's description of the self-help session, for the former mental patients listening to Bert's story of the snub there is a yet more complex judgement of the earlier event. The absence of a greeting and the denial of recognition suffered by the storyteller, began a reflection by other groups members of the difficulties of dealing with their shared identity as former mental patients. In other words, the problem of chance encounters and whether snubs were insults or not was the very inquiry that the self-help group in Turner's study were pursuing. While they show sympathy toward Bert's suffering they also consider the fact that the other former mental patient might have been avoiding remembering or admitting that he had once been a mental patient. Either of these interpretations would lessen the likelihood that the absence of response was done with the desire to insult Bert.

Turner only mentions in passing that the snub was a way of avoiding a reunion, and consequently there is little material on reunions in his writings. However, thirty years later, Curtis LeBaron and Stanley Jones provided a detailed description of the features of a reunion and how those features are put to use by its participants. Paralleling the role of the snub in Turner's work, LeBaron and Jones' primary focus is not on how a reunion is possible, nor is it focused primarily on reunions. It is, instead, on how encounters are closed, and, relatedly, how they are concluded in relation to: (a) the third parties to that encounter; (b) 'the social and material surrounds as a resource' (2002: 560) and (c) how the encounter was begun.

While it might seem that the precise nature of a reunion will disappear entirely into a more general concern with closings as part of an underlying interaction order, LeBaron and Jones do hold on to the reunion as a 'programmatic whole' which closings are required to relate to. In other words, it is a member's resource for organizing the initiation, progress and ending of the encounter. Consequently they do not grapple further with the problem of the reunion itself, they collect it as one of the many forms of ritual in everyday life. What they risk in treating reunions as 'ritualistic' is, by following Erving Goffman, taking an 'ironic cast' (Watson, 1992) on reunions as ritualistic in the sense that they follow known-in-common and well-established patterns. Equally, by staying with Goffman, they place the parties to the reunion in a distant, if awed, relationship to one another which then seems to rule out pursuing and accomplishing intimacy with one another (Raffel, 2002, 2013a).

While LeBaron and Jones' concern with the participants' perspectives and care around the event largely reprieves them from Goffman's ironising of the reunion as an insincere performance (Raffel, 2013a), a trace of irony nevertheless remains in LeBaron and Jones' concern with revealing 'potential resources for interaction' (560) where the reunion becomes just another resource to get the work of ending encounters in general done. The reunion is left interchangeable with closing a business meeting, ending a phone call or getting off the bus. However this is not at odds with LeBaron and Jones' desire to 'augment research on departure behaviour' (559) though it is in tension with their claim that 'gener-alisability is not their goal'. How we depart from a reunion is not how we depart from just any encounter, not even ritualistic encounters, and quite how it is closed can help reveal the auspices of reunions. We can analyse a reunion as an event for inquiring into 'the grounds or auspices of phenomena' (McHugh *et al.* 1974: 1–2) where those phenomena here are, as they were with snubs, remem-bering what each party's former relationship was to the other and from that returning to that previous standing, what our standing to one another might be and might become. To begin to understand the reunion is to begin to understand events where relationships are remembered rediscovered, reinitiated, destroyed, or in other ways transformed, even if only minimally.

Discretion

One of the surprising qualities of snubs that is disclosed by *OBSI* is that snubs have a protective quality. While we might see the snubbed as damaged by the snubber's action, they note that the snubbed is also protected by the snub. The snubbed is left unrelated. They are left on their own island rather than having to establish their shared place – their common ground. The temptation to snub rather than reunite is something that we can begin to understand through the hes-itancy we feel on recognizing certain old acquaintances. A hesitancy around 'offering oneself up to the other' (McHugh *et al.*, 1974: 131) which leaves oneself vulnerable to being snubbed, mistaken for someone else, barely remem-bered, remembered all too well, tolerated, subsequently pursued, exposed, and so on. In the face of the hazardous landscape of the encounter with past friends and acquaintances, the idea of the snub and the reunion 'resonates with ideas of restraint, discretion and limit' (1974: 136).

In his essay on secrecy and social relationships Simmel picks out acquaint-anceship as the form of relationship 'which is the peculiar seat of "discretion"' (1906: 452). Acquaintances lack the insights of intimates into one another's personality, and the rights to have those insights, even as they come to know facts about the other person which they 'did not positively reveal' (ibid.). Restraint is required by acquaintances not to come too near to the other. For an acquaintance to intrude further into what the other has not revealed (e.g. their fears, their loves, their mistakes, etc.) is to risk violating the personality of the other. Simmel notes that what is private to the person is not defined by its topic (e.g. fear of spiders, their first love, shooting their neighbour's donkey by mistake) but that knowledge of those matters has been restricted to, for instance, friends rather than acquaintances. Former inmates of mental institutions and pupils and teachers both find themselves with forms of friendship, but more par-ticularly acquaintanceship, where the facts they know about one another can be substantially more than were positively revealed.

OBSI develops the idea that to snub the other was to deny their freedom by denying them a relationship that is formed with the self and with the other. An obscure point, the authors add, but one that begins to take shape here when we consider discretion. Turner, in seeking to find the reason for the snub, points out that it is a feature of reunions that the shared history is revealed. Yet the snubbed's freedom would have been to exercise discretion (or not) about the secret that he knew about his acquaintance. As Simmel puts it 'discretion is nothing other than the sense of justice with respect to the sphere of the intimate contents of life' (Simmel, 1906: 454). Judging the boundaries of what the other person regards as a violation of their privacy, as Simmel then goes on to warn, 'leads … into the finest mesh of social forms' (454). To snub the other was also to not trust the other to exercise their discretion in front of a third party.

Let us begin to consider the 'finest mesh' that is discretion in LeBaron and Jones' (2002) analysis of the unfolding of a reunion between two persons acquainted many years previously. In this reunion (as it was with Turner's snub) there are third parties present and there is a former institutional relationship. In LeBaron and Jones's article, it is a school teacher (Wilcox) and her former pupil (Katie) who have a chance meeting in a hairdressers' salon, many years after their time together at school. Katie is sitting having her haircut when an older woman (Wilcox) approaches her. Initially they struggle to remember one another's names. As their encounter continues, Katie tells her former teacher about events that took her away from their town and of the death of her brother that brought her back again. In the excerpts provided in the article, Wilcox reveals little about herself by comparison. As LeBaron and Jones show, this is in part because Wilcox, the former teacher, continually asks Katie questions while also engaging with the other customers and staff. It is Katie's public character that thereby remains the object of attention for Wilcox and for the others.

Wilcox indicates that Katie had a reputation at school that others in the hairdressers' might like to learn about. And Katie, in turn, orients to the jointly remembered reputation as requiring further qualification by her.

```
 96   WILCOX:  Katie was something else
 97            ((group laughter))
      (lines omitted around hairdressing)
102   KATIE:   Okay, but it wasn't like see…
```

As the reunion continues, LeBaron and Jones provide an excerpt of the comments that are made by the other hairdressers and customers about the former pupil:

```
115   DINA:    She looks like she's in
116            elementary school again doesn't she
               …
122   MS Y:    …hh she sounds like a five year old…
```

Even with only the minor revelation that Katie is Wilcox's former pupil, this knowledge reshapes how the hairdressers see and hear Katie. They say that Katie both 'looks like' and 'sounds like' a young child. It is not just that by the very mention of her once having been someone's pupil that they find these similarities, it is in the details of how Wilcox and Katie are addressing one another (as we shall see later). They find comparisons with a five year old through metaphors (Raffel, 2013b) that in illuminating Katie's conduct also reveal aspects of her character that she had not imparted.

The accidental reunion has brought with it, then, a change in how Kate appears at the hairdressers; she is seen in terms of similarities to a small child in, and as part of, how she relates to her former teacher. Until this reunion Katie was known through the personal history that she volunteered during her small talk with her hairdresser, through the hairdressing-relevant aspects of her external appearance: her style of dress, her shoes, her age and her ambitions for her hair (Laurier, 2012; McCarthy, 2000; Toerien and Kitzinger, 2007). With this in mind it becomes clearer why the presence of other acquaintances, that do not share the history that is the basis for that reunion, touch upon discretion and indiscretion, upon the senses of privacy, and upon the public character each has established. It seems, from the material presented by LeBaron and Jones, that in remembering their relationship, Wilcox does not enter into a one-to-one conversation with Katie. By the use of 'Discreet Indiscretions' Wilcox thereby aligns herself more closely with the hairdressers than with Katie (Bergmann, 1993) providing an early hint of Wilcox's balance between acknowledgement and avoidance of intimacy with Katie.

Between knowing and acknowledging former acquaintances

Drawing on earlier work by Troll (1988) and Seltzer (1988), Jones and LeBaron (2002) describe a formal reunion as an event of collective remembering that brings together individual histories, events and groups. LeBaron and Jones argue that the chance encounter takes on 'ritualistic' qualities of a formal reunion because, even when unplanned, it follows the same prescribed order. What then produces the chance encounter as a reunion (rather than a snub) is a collection of prescribed elements which LeBaron and Jones list from the earlier studies of formal reunions:

1   Greeting and acknowledging the past relationship
2   Returning to the history of the relationship
3   Ending the reunion through turning to the present and planning for the relationship's future

In identifying the features of the reunion that its participants need to achieve to constitute their encounter as a reunion, they then miss much of the delight, anxiety, dread, and ambivalence that prefigures planned reunions and accompanies accidental ones. Reunions sit in a realm of encounters beset by perlocutionary concerns: lived through as events where we are embarrassing and embarrassed, boring and bored, charming and charmed, inspiring and inspired, confusing and confused. The trouble and delight of reunions is that, as Cavell

(2005) argues for the passionate encounter, while, for instance, one former friend might be trying to embarrass the other, the other is instead bored, or perhaps charmed. Following Cavell further, reunions are encounters where one and the other show (and perhaps hide) their standing toward the other and tries to single just this other out (e.g. as Katie) or place them in a collection (e.g. another former pupil). In the accidental reunion the other in public is not anyone, they are just this one and this one has a greater claim to find a relationship with the other.

Katie and Wilcox's reunion is not driven by deep desires, as Cavell's passionate encounters are, though, by its end, desire is at work. If we return to Wilcox and Katie's first noticing of one another, it is marked by uncertainty over who the other is ahead of any more sustained interest in the other. Katie has pointed toward Wilcox on the other side of the hairdressers and Wilcox has then walked toward Katie's chair in response. They begin without being able to put a name to one another's face which then begins to produce a context of their limited recollection of one another:

28	KATIE:	Your name Ms [Bridges?
29	WILCOX:	[No no Wilcox
30		(0.3)
31	KATIE:	Wilcox?
32	WILCOX:	Um hm
40	WILCOX:	What's your name?
41		(0.2)
42	KATIE:	It used to be Katie Crumby
43		(0.4)
44	WILCOX:	Katie?
45	KATIE:	Yes ma'am

At line 28 Katie offers a tentative remembering of the name of the other woman: 'Ms Bridges?' one which, in fact, fails to correctly recall the other's name. Rather than the details rushing back to Katie (e.g. expressed in 'Ms Wilcox, right?') she is only feeling her way back toward who this other person was. In selecting a surname rather than a first name, Katie marks a past relationship which was not on first name terms, for Katie at least. Calling someone only by their surname indexes a likely institutional and/or hierarchical relationship.

Where the formality of surnames is a marker of distance, it becomes more clearly a marker of something else when Katie offers her name as 'Katie Crumby', thereby providing both first name and surname for Wilcox, whereupon Wilcox selects 'Katie'. Not only does their dialogue re-instate their former relational pairing of teacher–pupil through surname for one and first name for the other, Katie's further affirms this through a respectful 'yes ma'am'. While it is tempting to see this as the only the re-instatement of Wilcox's authority and seniority, the surname+first-name is bound up with their joint task here of collective remembering. If we move back to line 42, Katie says 'it used to be'. The name she is offering is not one that should be taken to be her present name and that question of why it is no longer Katie Crumby is left hanging for later. It is the extended form of name that she had when she was a pupil which then offers her former teacher the best resource for recalling the former pupil now in front of her at the hairdressers.

The unexpected reunion is a Proustian moment where eating a madeleine has been replaced by talking to Madeleine. An unbidden remembering, this time with one of the parties to that past and from that past, with each party seeking to recall that past to the present. Yet it is not at all Proustian, because neither person has the liberty of several weeks spent at their writing desk reconstructing and inscribing their memories. With an audience and a hairdresser waiting to continue cutting Katie's hair, the re-united parties have to move quickly toward remembering the period of their lives where they once knew one another and remembering the person in that period. Moreover, their current possibilities for a relationship turn less upon knowing with certainty what that past relationship was, and more upon acknowledging that there was a past relationship. There is a clear difference here between the snub and the reunion. The person that snubs the other, knows them but refuses to acknowledge them, the person that returns the greeting, knows the other and acknowledges them. Reunions turn not upon questions of claiming to know one another (where the snub was a claim not to know the other), but as Cavell (1976) argued, a question of what one does or reveals on the basis of that knowledge.

For a reunion to be possible there has to be a separation, an apartness and a passing of time, that breaks the continuity that characterizes any ongoing relationship. The break changes what the relationship is, what it was and reopens questions of acknowledgement. Terminations of ongoing relationships are at their most apparent in divorces, dissolutions, splits, and annulments, yet they happen also through shifting circumstances. For Kate and Wilcox, part of being a former teacher and former pupil is that the question over what ended their relationship need not be raised. Part of how acquaintances inside and outside institutions relate to another is that they can depart with or without account nor special ceremony. Pupils naturally exit the institution of the school each year and commonly change their teachers year by year. They need not examine why their relationship ended and the fact that it did, does not mark them as having special concern for one another. However, the very fact of the chance reunion means that the relationship with the other can mean more in the present than its ending did in the past.[1]

While the school allows for the annual beginning and ending of pupil–teacher relationships, it also creates a problem of the few and the many. Each teacher has many more former students than she could name or remember. The former student has only a few former teachers though they will, of course, also recall only the memorable ones. Recalling the other is not only asymmetrical because of the few and the many, it is also that there is an asymmetry of recognizability. The former teacher remains recognizable to the former pupil but, in growing from a child to a woman, the former pupil may not be immediately recognizable from her appearance (those very changes becoming a topic later in their encounter). The problem of the many and their changing appearances for Wilcox may also be one that leads to her routinely avoiding new relationships with her former pupils. An asymmetry that leaves her in a lifeworld of avoidance that we find in its extreme in the paradigmatic case of stars that 'just want to be alone'. If we detect a certain avoidance of relationships with former pupils in the teacher it grows out of that institutional life.

Standing and trying to turn the former relationship

As we saw earlier, across the hairdressers' floor, Katie had successfully remembered her former teacher by her appearance, if not by her name. Once they are up close, holding one another's arms in an expression of the reunion's intensity, their appearances are re-examined. Each face is itself a resource in remembering. The re-examination takes in a face to compare the face that is seen now to the face from the past that it helps in recalling. An extended taking-in of the other's appearances as indexing their age now, their age then, and those appearances in a course of mutual ageing. There is more than the face of the other to take in. As Katie and Wilcox step back from their hug, they continue to look at one another, seeing the face in a wider context of shoulders, arms, clothing and, of course, hair. Having regarded each other, they are then in a position to say, with the authority of that intense mutual regard:

57   KATIE: You look good
58   WILCOX: You look good too
59   ((Group laughter (1.2)))

LeBaron and Jones point out that 'Katie's assessment "You look good" (Line 57) is more than a compliment, it acknowledges a prior relationship to the extent that it relies upon a recollection of how Wilcox looked before' (2002: 548). While it relies upon that recollection it also marks that, at least in terms of appearance, neither bears the marks of misfortune through illness or poverty, neither has to immediately account for the loss of an eye nor for sleeping on the street. Yet in each person saying that the other 'looks' good, looking good rather saying they 'are good', leaves open that they might be suffering now or have done so in the intervening years. LeBaron and Jones begin to explore these mutual assessments: 'the women sound like social equals', though we should note the caution of 'sound like', because they more clearly reveal later that they have not escaped the force of their previous relationship. Katie, as LeBaron and Jones argue, re-enacts their former institutional relationship by regularly addressing Wilcox as 'ma'am' as she does above at line 45 above and at line 83 here:

82   WILCOX: You been doing all right
83   KATIE: Yes ma'am, I been doin pretty good, pretty good

In these lines we also witness the shift from how each appears to the other (i.e. looking good), to how their lives are (i.e. doing all right). Reporting on their lives is initiated through an inquiry from Wilcox that attends to and allows Katie to begin bringing her story up to date and to prefigure the quality of that updating. It would also appear that the teacher–pupil relationship is further sustained over the longer course of their reunion by Wilcox continuing to pursue Katie 'as the topic of conversation, as the subject of inquiry, the interviewee' (2002: 551). What has been accomplished is that by the end of their reunion it is only Katie that sketches out her history in the period since they were pupil and teacher.

While there is no snub here, there does seem to be the avoidance of establishing a new relationship. Wilcox has not revealed anything about her history in the years since they were teacher and pupil. The absence of personal history may not be driven by Wilcox, given that, in the material presented by LeBaron and Jones, Katie did not seek updates from her former teacher nor make assessments of her beyond their first mutual assessment. As Svennig (1999) reminds us, Katie by her extended self-presentation, could have been taken to lack interest in Wilcox, were it not for the fact that Wilcox played such an active part in keeping Katie and her story as the topic of conversation.

In building a brief narrative of the accountable events of her life between school and re-encountering her school teacher, Katie singles out Wilcox for the influence she has had on her life. She can pay tribute to the influence of her former school teacher.

88	KATIE:	I- I'm hanging, I remember a lot of things
89		[y'all told me when i was growing up
90	WILCOX:	[Yeah yeah yeah

Wilcox is the kind of teacher that has passed on lessons for life that Katie has reflected upon as an adult. It was not that the arithmetic helped her with her job or that she never forgot how to use semi-colons. The former teacher cannot offer a similar compliment back, though there might be ways in which she claims Katie as a memorable student. Though when she does this – which we saw at the outset of the extract – it is designed for entertainment of the onlookers as a discreet indiscretion (Bergmann, 1993).

If we consider what is done by Wilcox not becoming the topic during the reunion, it has allowed them to return to their former identities as teacher and pupil and prevented them turning the former relationship into a new one. In fact their reunion resembles the pre-break-up of a dating couple studied by Hopper and Drummond (1990). In their analysis of a conversation preceding a break-up, one party is making 'small gambits toward possible intimacy' (1990: 52) where 'each gambit gets an un-promising uptake' (1990: 52). What was only an emerging, and as yet fragile, relationship as a couple turns toward a break-up through minimal responses. For Katie and Wilcox's reunion, Katie is trying to turn the former relationship into a new if as yet unfounded and unfound relationship. What they might become for one another between acquaintances and friends remains to be discovered. Wilcox, meantime, in keeping Katie as the object of attention and in artfully keeping the encounter itself one in which the hairdressers and other customers are involved, makes no move to change her standing toward Katie. The reunion is an occasion for one party to leave the relationships as a former relationship by neither updating their history nor revealing their current status, for the other they show their desire to find a new standing toward the other.

To open the possibility for approaching a new form of acquaintanceship, the parties need to track and make available the kinds of shared enjoyments they might have, and what kind of value each might have for the other or what they might do for one another. Going to the hairdresser might be the beginnings of shared enjoyment, though only in a limited sense. The encounter is not in the realm of shared pursuits that bumping into another at a reading group or running club are. It is closer to simply passing one another in the street. Katie has found the value that Wilcox had for her as a teacher, yet that cannot be a value that she has for her now in a new relationship because there is no new relationship. The relationship has yet to be and the encounter is happening in an inclement place for its cultivation. It is an unplanned reunion in a place with onlookers, over-hearers and the limits that they incur. As LeBaron and Jones (2002) bring to the fore, it is also a place with other business to do. Jane the hairdresser interrupts their talk, turning Katie's chair away from Wilcox, spraying Katie in the face and 'when Katie begins to stand so as to hug Wilcox, Jane continues to operate her comb and scissors' (LeBaron and Jones, 2002: 556). To find a better place for beginning a relationship requires agreeing to and planning a future encounter and the accidental reunion would then become a preliminary to that event.

Endings and beginnings

In their careful account of the reunion LeBaron and Jones always also have their eye on the closing moves being made through the structurings of talk, gestures with objects and movements through the environment of the hairdressers. Wilcox turns and looks into her handbag which 'projects her departure' (LeBaron and Jones, 2002: 552) and Katie returns to sitting in her hairdresser's chair. When Katie finishes telling the story of the intervening years it 'presages the reunion's end' (LeBaron and Jones, 2002: 552). It need not presage the end, though. Wilcox is at a point where she could respond, if only briefly, with her own story of her intervening years. Given that Katie has disclosed her personal troubles, Wilcox is in a position where she could take that as an invitation to intimacy. It is not that Wilcox has not offered sympathy and that is what a former teacher ought to do. Yet as the ending ends, Katie is likely left with no strong sense that her former teacher has changed from being her former teacher. Wilcox though is equally likely to have a sense that her former pupil is looking to continue their relationship. A sense that would be confirmed when Katie asks for contact details for Wilcox:

180	KATIE:	I te- I would like to get your telephone number
181	WILCOX:	Okay
182	KATIE:	And you address when you have the time
183		Cause I gotta get over here with Jane
184	WILCOX:	Okay

The request for a telephone number and address is a more obvious, if still oblique, request for permission to continue pursuing a relationship with the other party. Katie requests Wilcox's contact details in the indirect request format 'I would like to' and 'when you have the time' rather than the direct 'can I have your address' which shows a limited sense of entitlement (Curl and Drew, 2008; Ervin-Tripp, 1976). Her request acknowledging the time it will take to do this task does not fit with her hairdresser's desire to hurry her back to her haircut. Yet, as researchers in conversation analysis have documented, requests of this form are based also on the speaker's entitlement to make them. In this case of requesting the continuance of a social relationship, a former pupil's entitlement to ask this of a former teacher is minimal. It is of quite a different order to Katie asking of Jane 'I would like to get a haircut and a blow dry when you have the time'. It is a request to turn this former relationship into a new relationship though built in such a way that not giving the telephone number need not be treated as refusing a relationship with Katie. If we compare this indirect request for indirect information with either 'I would like you to be my friend' or 'can we become friends' it also then shows Wilcox that Katie is avoiding pressurizing her and indeed recognizes Wilcox's entitlement to decline her request.

In thinking about this request as more tightly tied to relationships, it might better be considered as an 'advance' even though that term is more often used in reference to the pursuit of a romantic and/or sexual relationship. Katie has disclosed her recent biography which marks her development, through a number of tough experiences and expanded commitments to family members, to have become a fellow adult. She has given Wilcox a sense of her changed status that would then allow Wilcox to judge whether she would accept an advance in the light of a disclosure which was already a way of advancing toward Wilcox. Katie was not so much pursuing intimacy with Wilcox as she was sharing stories of her difficulties, to offer an intimacy to Wilcox.

Wilcox's response to Katie's advance – 'okay' and 'okay' – is not a refusal, though it is not all that enthusiastic either. Wilcox does not ask for Katie's number in return, nor for a pen and paper. The coolness is something for Katie to assess around pursuing a further meeting with her former teacher. As I have noted earlier, LeBaron and Jones treat the reunion as a resource for closing this encounter as if it were any other encounter. In other words, the participants can analyse the completion of a reunion's recognizable features and then use them as a resource to finish this particular encounter without orienting toward its particularity as a reunion. Because it is a reunion and not a daily meeting, closing the encounter that is a reunion could either hold the beginning of a series of encounters which could begin to cement a new friendship or be avoiding a new relationship.

Having been separate and then meeting one another again, the ending of a reunion raises the question over whether we will, or desire to, meet again. For formal reunions, by their very formality, the reunion happens with only a minimal concern for its desirability. In LeBaron and Jones' description of the chance encounter, the question of whether one or the other will pursue a new relationship with just this other arises, it is part of what Cavell refers to as the 'disorders of desire'. In closing a reunion, the question is raised, then, of whether we would, or should, want to meet again. Each party makes its analysis across remembered, former, and current commonalities, concerns for one another, virtues of the other (e.g. 'I remember a lot of things y'all told me'), shared interests and affections, disorderly desires, to find their desire to pursue or retreat.

Conclusion

Just as a reunion offers each person the chance to recover, renew, or transform a former relationship with the other person, it offers also to each the occasion to avoid recovering, renewing, or transforming it. Because of the break in our relationship we no longer know how we feel about this particular person nor they about us, and in the light of change or the absence of change, we may no longer know them nor they us in the sense both of one another's inner lives and of what they are for us. These then are the further problem of the reunion that the pairing of our social categories will need re-examine, because we are no longer teacher–pupil or acquaintance–acquaintance. In that indeterminate state and reflexively tied to it we disclose or hide the constituent events and experiences that could transform those former tied categories. A former teacher might become a mentor or a friend or an acquaintance or just remain a former teacher. Consequently, how the reunion is begun, acted through and ended carries more significance than the routine encounters that constitute the continuance of each and any ongoing relationship. Each party to a reunion more or less carefully monitors the other, as they begin to greet, fill in gaps, and then make their partings, for their desire for another meeting and may then also come upon their own desire, or its absence, for another meeting.

As I remarked upon earlier, LeBaron and Jones (2002) suggest that reunions have a ritualistic character and that does begin to move toward how they are differentiated from the repetitious character of the other encounters that maintain relationships of acquaintance, friend, and intimate. In understanding what a reunion means we need to go farther than 'ritual' and place the reunion in the family of events which transform relationships (e.g. introductions, break-ups, dates, births, graduations, marriages, divorces, and re-marriages in Cavell, 1981). From within those rituals, we need to locate the reunion within those events where it is ambiguous whether it will lead to the beginnings (or ending) of a relationship. The unplanned reunion is all the more ambiguous while touched by the music of chance because neither party has sought the other out, nor accepted an invitation to a formal event.

Unlike the routine encounter, the reunion carries a weight that might be a burden because it has returned what was once a relationship to us after we had been freed from it either by transformation or circumstance. In returning this relationship to us, it poses a fateful significance through the reappearance of each party in the other's life. In the face of this feeling of significance, the reunion takes its participants from a consideration of their former relationships, their histories, and their appearances to the desire to single out this other party as someone who one wishes to find a standing with and toward or to merge them back into the crowd of former acquaintances and friends (Cavell, 2005). To echo the closing of *OBSI* on snubs, the reunion, in its potential for making and extinguishing new relationships, requires discernment and imagination to recover what was shared and to renew or avoid the relationship.

Note

1 From comments by Stanley Raffel on an earlier draft of this chapter.

Bibliography

Bergmann, J.R. (1993). *Discreet indiscretions*. New York: Walter de Gruyter.

Blum, A. (2015). 'The border between intimacy and anonymity in innocuous action: The greeting as a social form', in *Journal of Classical Sociology*, Online first. http://doi. org/10.1177/1468795X15574410.

Blum, A. and McHugh, P. (1984). *Self-reflection in the arts and sciences*. Atlantic Highlands NJ: Humanities Press.

Cavell, S. (1976). *Must we mean what we say?* Cambridge: Cambridge University Press.

Cavell, S. (1981). *Pursuits of happiness: The Hollywood comedy of remarriage*. London: Harvard University Press.

Cavell, S. (2005). 'Passionate and performative utterance: Morals of encounter', in R.B. Goodman, *Contending with Stanley Cavell* (pp. 177–199). Oxford: Oxford University Press.

Curl, T. and Drew, P. (2008). 'Contingency and action: A comparison of two forms of requesting', in *Research on Language and Social Interaction*, 41(2), 129–153.

Ervin-Tripp, S. (1976). 'Is Sybil there? The structure of some American English directives', *Language in Society*, 5(1), 25–66.

Hopper, R. and Drummond, K. (1990). 'Emergent goals at a relational turning point: The case of Gordon and Denise', *Journal of Language and Social Psychology*, 9(1–2), 39–65.

Laurier, E. (2012). 'Encounters at the counter: The relationship between regulars and staff', in P. Tolmie and M. Rouncefield, *Ethnomethodology at play* (pp. 287–308). Farnham: Ashgate.

LeBaron, C.D. and Jones, S.E. (2002). 'Closing up closings: Showing the relevance of the social and material surround to the completion of interaction', *Journal of Communication*, 52(3), 542–565.

McCarthy, M. (2000). 'Mutually captive audiences: Small talk and the genre of close-contact service encounters', in J. Coupland, *Small talk* (pp. 84–109). Harlow: Pearson Education.

McHugh, P., Raffel, S., Foss, D.C., and Blum, A. (1974). *On the beginning of social inquiry*. London: Routledge & Kegan Paul.

Raffel, S. (2002). 'If Goffman had read Levinas', *Journal of Classical Sociology*, 2(2), 179–202.

Raffel, S. (2013a). 'The everyday life of the self: Reworking early Goffman', *Journal of Classical Sociology*, 13(1), 163–178. doi:10.1177/1468795X12474055.

Raffel, S. (2013b). *The method of metaphor*. Bristol: Intellect.

Sacks, H. (1992). *Lectures on conversation*. Oxford: Blackwell.

Seltzer, M.M. (1988). 'Reunions: Windows to the past and future', *American Behavioral Scientist*. 31 (5) 644–654.

Simmel, G. (1906) 'The sociology of secrecy and of secret societies', *American Journal of Sociology* 11(4), 441–498.

Svennevig, J. (1999). *Getting acquainted in conversation: A study of initial interactions*. Amsterdam, PA: John Benjamins Publishing Company.

Toerien, M. and Kitzinger, C. (2007). 'Emotional labour in action: Navigating multiple involvements in the beauty salon', *Sociology*, 41(4), 645–662.

Troll, L.E. (1988). 'Rituals and reunions introduction', *American Behavioral Scientist*, 31 (6) 621–632.

Turner, R. (1970). 'Words, utterance, and activities', in *Understanding everyday life: Toward the reconstruction of sociological knowledge* (pp. 169–187). Chicago: Aldine Publishing Company.

Watson, R. (1992). 'The Understanding of language use in everyday life. Is there a common ground?', in G. Watson and R.M. Seiler, *Text in context* (pp. 1–19). London: Sage Publications, Inc.

5 Rethinking art

A borderline case

Stanley Raffel

For E.S.

This chapter revisits the terrain of the 'Art' paper in *On the Beginning of Social Inquiry*. It explores a case where a critic argues that the noted novelist, Philip Roth, produced a work that, according to her, was not worthy of him. I suggest that her argument revolves around whether and how it is appropriate to mine real-life material for art. I argue that, with an alternative understanding to this critic as to the possible role of such material in the creation of art, Roth's novel can be seen as not, in the end, a failure. Some general observations are derived from this specific case to the effect that one of the powers of art is to enable what I call its ability to help us visualize events.

The paper 'Art' in *On the Beginning of Social Inquiry* (McHugh *et al.*, 1974) depicted art's distinctiveness by comparing it to other phenomena also discussed in the book, e.g. common sense, science, and the authors' own activity, Analysis. None of these activities aspire to be art. Here I adopt an alternative strategy, seeking to depict art by analysing a case of what at least one critic argues is something other than art because it is a failed attempt at art. The case to be discussed is a novel by Philip Roth, *I Married a Communist*. However, before we can directly address the novel's claim, whether failed or not, to be art, it will be necessary to describe, in detail, the circumstances of its creation.

Interpreting Bloom

In 1996, the actress Claire Bloom published what she described as 'a memoir' (Bloom, 1996). While its nominal subject was her life as a whole, its real focus and major selling point was her description of her relationship with the novelist, Philip Roth. Her account caused severe damage to his reputation. According to one critic, she 'outed the author as a verbally abusive neurotic, a womanizer, a venal nutcase' (Sara Nelson, cited in Roth, 1999: 1). In strikingly similar terms, renowned fellow novelist John Updike writes that Bloom's book shows him 'to have been neurasthenic to the point of hospitalization, adulterous, callously selfish, and financially vindictive' (Roth, 1999: 1 citing Updike, 1999).

In a letter to the *New York Review of Books* published three years after Bloom's book, Roth explains that while he has 'become accustomed to finding Miss Bloom's characterization of me taken at face value' (Roth, 1999: 1) the fact that someone of Updike's repute has written in such terms does require a response. He suggests what he calls a 'slight revision' to Updike's version. He asks it to read: 'Claire Bloom, presenting herself as the wronged ex-wife of Philip Roth, *alleges* him to have been neurasthenic to the point of hospitalization, adulterous, callously selfish and financially vindictive' (my emphasis added) (Roth, 1999: 1).

In his letter that is all Roth says. Therefore, while he is clearly implying that it is actually a mistake to accept Bloom's book at face value, he offers no guidance as to how we can do otherwise. As both Updike and the other less well-known figure arrived at their conclusions thanks to Bloom's book, it could seem that we will not be able to reach different conclusions in the absence of additional material.

However, the nature of Bloom's book is such that it is possible to separate when she is reporting facts from when she is offering (as facts) what can be more accurately defined as her interpretations of those facts. Updike and the other writer tend to treat not just the reported facts but also her interpretations of them at face value. By reflecting on and not merely accepting these interpretations, it begins to be possible, even while working only with Bloom's text, to see that, at the very least, it really is a mistake to accept her conclusions at face value. Or, to put it another way, fully appreciating the possible, indeed credible, meaning of her text requires doing what the deconstructionists call a close reading. This is what Updike and others have failed to do.

In her review of Bloom's book, Zoe Heller makes a good start on doing exactly this. For example, she remarks on the 'princessy tone' of the book. (Heller, 1997: 2). She notes the 'contrast between Bloom's wounded, more in sorrow than in anger postures with the hawkishness of some of her marital revelations' (Heller, 1997: 2–3). She is dubious concerning the 'plaintive aside' (Heller, 1997: 2) with which Bloom accompanies her description of their divorce settlement. Referring to the long section in which Bloom depicts Roth's stay in a mental hospital, she says: 'It is one thing to take revenge on your husband by telling the world what a shit he is – quite another to offer painful snapshots of his mental collapse'. (Heller, 1997: 3). And finally, quoting Bloom explaining at one point that 'I felt unfairly misunderstood and started screaming' (Heller, 1997: 3 citing Bloom, 1996: 196). Heller guesses that, in their marriage as a whole 'the pain may have been more evenly spread than Bloom would have us believe' (Heller, 1997: 3).

What is very stimulating about Heller's observations is that they do begin to show that there are aspects of Bloom's text that it is very unwise to take at face value. Much more can be done in the same vein. Bloom says they fell in love during a trip Bloom, then living in London, made to New York. She says her 'first glimpse' (Bloom, 1996: 160) of Roth's character was when he refused to cancel a pre-arranged trip to the Caribbean so that he could spend more time with her during her visit. She wants us to conclude that the 'fact' she was glimpsing was his 'rigidity: he had arranged to go and he was going' (Bloom, 1996: 160). But it can certainly remain true that he stuck to a plan without this (as she thinks) letting her glimpse rigidity, particularly if we note the additional fact, mentioned by Bloom but without attaching any significance to it, that the trip that she expected him to cancel was not one he was making on his own. He was going with, as she tells us in passing 'a close male friend' (Bloom, 1996: 159). Even people who are not at all rigid can be determined to go through with what they have arranged in advance, particularly when changing those prior plans would be likely to inconvenience significant others.

Bloom tells us that the living arrangements they settled on were to live six months a year in Roth's house in Connecticut and six months of the year in Bloom's house in London. The main point of the latter arrangement was so Bloom could spend half the year in the company of her daughter by a previous marriage. Updike's idea that Bloom shows Roth to be 'callously selfish' makes most sense as derived from the fact that, according to Bloom, Roth told her that he was unwilling to keep to the London phase of their relationship so long as the daughter stayed in the house. The passage in Bloom's book where she depicts the events concerned is worth quoting in full:

> It was a choice between the security of a companion and the welfare of a daughter. Anna was asked to move out. She was eighteen. The circumstances were terrible: Anna witnessed someone she viewed as an outsider calling the shots in her own home, and her mother unable to set any boundaries – understandably she felt angry and betrayed. In addition, Henry Wood House, the student hostel, was located across the Thames in one of the least salubrious neighbourhoods of London.
>
> (Bloom, 1996: 172)

If we do take this passage at face value, certainly we can see why Updike concludes that Bloom has shown Roth to be callously selfish. That is, there is no doubt that the 'facts' that someone forced a mother to choose between them and her child's welfare and/or created the circumstances in which a mother was visibly unable to set limits that would have safeguarded the child stand as near textbook cases of callous selfishness. However, what is a good deal less clear is if this is the most credible or even (as Bloom implies) the only way to interpret what, on reflection, are the actual facts, namely that the proposed solution arrived at was for an eighteen year old to live, across the river from her Chelsea home, in a dorm room at her university.

Whatever impression of Philip Roth and his likely excesses that we could have gathered from his novels, that he would be revealed to be a materialistic money-grubber would not feature. Therefore, Updike's conclusion that Bloom shows him to be 'financially vindictive' is particularly damaging to his reputation. In this case, the facts refer to an incident that occurred after they separated. Bloom reports that:

On my lawyer's advice, I wrote out a list of furniture, china, and linens from my former home, items I considered to be my personal property. I was scrupulously careful not to include anything I hadn't paid for myself.

(Bloom, 1996: 250)

Some weeks later, because Roth said he had not been told of the list by his lawyer: 'I offered to fax it over to him right away' (251). In reply Bloom says she received 'a fistful of faxes' (252). She reports that: 'In rapid, staccato succession, Philip demanded the return of everything he had provided for me during our years together' (252). The list she details for us starts with things that perhaps sound reasonable such as '$100,000 of his money used to buy bonds in my name' (252) but then becomes more and more absurd, for example 'half of the costs incurred on our holiday to Marrakech in 1978' (252) finally culminating in the total absurdity that 'for refusing my prenuptial agreement, he levied a fine of sixty-two billion dollars, one billion for every year of my life' (252).

In this case, the reminder not to take things at face value is not going to save Roth from being shown to have misbehaved but is it credibly seen to be the form of misbehaviour Updike assumes? His interpretation of these facts begins to make less and less sense as Roth's so-called 'demands' become more and more absurd. Unlike a true money-grubber, he is not really requiring Bloom to return what he paid for. What he probably had in mind was an (admittedly not very nice) parody of her fax. If she is going to be so 'scrupulous' as to list everything she paid for, he decides to be so 'scrupulous' as to list everything she hasn't paid for.

Heller is much closer to the mark in her interpretation of this event. She says it 'evokes the scary wrath of Roth' (Heller, 1997: 2), not at all nice to witness but, it has to said, not much of a surprise to those familiar with his novels and so not nearly so sure to ruin his reputation as what Updike claims Bloom's story reveals.

It is fair to conclude that Roth's 'slight revision' has been a helpful stimulus. Not taking Bloom's conclusions at face value, even when having to work only with her own versions of the facts, does make her interpretations seem more doubtful. But why does Roth not give us his side of the story? It must be that whatever he says would just be what he alleges and so just another presentation that we would be foolish to take at face value. However, while everything discussed so far (including Roth's letter to the *New York Review of Books*) leaves the impression that, quite unlike Bloom, Roth never put forward his version of their marriage, that impression is wildly at variance with the reality. Whatever else it may be, his novel *I Married a Communist*, published in 1998, most certainly draws on events, including events we are familiar with from Bloom, from their marriage.

Assessing Grant's critique

What to make of what he did do, including the important and difficult question of whether what he did amounts to a serious mistake that damages his standing as an artist, is now our problem. Is Roth merely doing his own version of alleg-ing? If not, what differentiates a novel or, better, this particular novel, from the act of merely alleging things as Bloom does in her book? At least one critic thinks 'not very much' and therefore concludes that Roth's big mistake was not to remain silent.

According to Linda Grant, Roth should have 'taken what was coming to him on the chin. Kept his mouth shut. Pleaded the Fifth. Bloom's book didn't diminish him; he's done it himself' (Grant, 1998: 2). Grant is not referring to his few words of self-defence in the *New York Review of Books*. She is referring to *I Married a Communist*. Her review of it begins:

> It is hard for an admirer of Roth's novels not to see *I Married a Communist* as a howl of rage about fact, which has bullyingly usurped the self-appointed task of fiction to tell the truth.
>
> (Grant, 1998: 10)

We will need eventually to consider the rather large claims Grant is making about rage, fact, the relation of both to fiction and, especially fiction's relation to truth. For example, cannot rage be a valid motivational tool for at least some forms of fiction? Can fiction not draw on facts? Is it really the job of fiction to tell the truth and, if so, in what sense? But what can be clarified straight away is that Grant is pointing to something that it is impossible to deny. *I Married a Communist* is, as we said, a novel that draws on the very material that Bloom has drawn on for her 'memoir'. So, even if it remains true that we never learn what Roth alleges went on between him and Bloom, Grant is right that he did not exactly merely 'take it on the chin and keep his mouth shut'.

Grant's view that Roth did not really remain silent arises because she has noticed various parallels between facts she has gathered from Bloom's book and features of Roth's book. For example, the main female character in *I Married a Communist*

> Eve Frame is a Jewish actress, so is Bloom. Frame's second husband is a financier, so was Bloom's. Eve Frame has a daughter who is a harpist; Bloom's girl is an opera singer. Ira (Frame's husband) tells the daughter to move out. Roth did the same. Ira has an affair with the daughter's best friend. Roth, Bloom alleged, came on to her own daughter's best friend. Frame comes to see her husband in the hospital where he has had a nervous breakdown and gets so upset she has to be sedated – so did Bloom.
>
> (Grant, 1998: 2)

It would be foolish in the extreme to treat all this as mere coincidence but the ques-tion is what to make of it. Grant's conclusion is that what Roth has produced 'is an angry, bitter, resentful mess' (Grant, 1998: 2). Whatever a mess is, especially an unintentional mess, unlike, say, Tracey Emin's bed, it is surely not art. Judging from the fact that what immediately follows her observation of all the parallels is her statement that 'the taste in one's mouth gets worse and worse' (Grant, 1998: 2), we gather that, according to Grant, the failure of an artist who Grant admires to (this time) produce art arises from how Roth is utilizing real-life material.

To be more specific, while Grant is aware that Roth has, in a sense, changed the material, e.g. characters' names, opera singer to harpist, changing what was an actual affair into a near one, and so has not done the precise sort of 'alleging' that Bloom did, we get the sense that she thinks this is little more than a device to avoid a libel suit. Therefore, her underlying point is that certain sorts of relation to real-life material, in this case Roth's use of his failed marriage, are inconsistent with and even ruinous to art. While he was wise, unlike Bloom, not to even attempt to provide his side of the facts, he was very unwise to think he could make a decent form of art out of (his version of) the facts.

But the important and difficult question that can now be raised is exactly this one, the relation of artistic products to the material out of which they are composed. The 'Art' paper did insist that 'art is certainly never the things it recapitulates' (McHugh *et al.*, 1974: 156) but that should not be taken to mean that art cannot be based on material that is external to the artistic product. Hannah Arendt's analysis of art becomes relevant at this point, as she has managed to produce what is still one of the best discussions of this issue. First, she distinguishes the activity she calls 'work' from the activity she calls 'labour' on the basis that work potentially results in lasting products. Art is a subcategory of work. All work produces products using 'material worked upon' (Arendt, 1958: 139). For example, a table is a product whose material could be wood. In order to work to produce a product, the 'material is not simply given and there like the fruit of field and trees' (139). Instead the material must, as we said, be worked on, in some sense developed. She remarks on the 'element of violation and violence' (139) of this process. In the case of a wooden table, this violence would include killing the tree to produce the wood and then the furniture maker further violating the wood to produce the finished product.

So all work products both require source material and violate it in the sense of transform it. A wooden table is, indeed, a transformation of wood. Art, too, both has its raw material and transforms it to produce products, in most cases ideally lasting products but in its case there is 'more than mere transformation' (Arendt, 1958: 168). Citing the romantic poet, Rilke, Arendt suggests that what happens to the raw material in art is 'transfiguration, a veritable metamorphosis in which it is as though the course of nature which wills that all fire burns to ashes is reverted and even dust can burst into flames' (168).

The notion that art's material could be dust captures very well the sense that sometimes the artist can transform even the most mundane raw material into a great work. It also captures the fact that, as with a table, there is no art that merely leaves the material out of which it is composed intact.

Now, applying Arendt's conception of art to where we are in our consideration of Grant's critique of *I Married a Communist*, a first point is that we should now see that Grant must do much more than just point to material that Roth is clearly using to construct his book in order to demonstrate it is not art because all art uses material to produce its product. His life with Bloom, even if or perhaps especially if it leaves a bad taste in the mouth, could, in this case, be his particular dust.

However, Grant could legitimately object that the problem, certainly with regard to the source material referred to so far, is that Roth has barely trans-formed it, much less transfigured it, not to mention make it burst into flames. In other words, her valid objection could be not (as it first seems) just that he is using the material of his marriage but that his way of using it is not consistent with art. The points to be developed now are that this potential objection will seem much less cogent once we have both further refined our sense of what some art's relation to its material can be and further elaborated what, contrary to the impression created so far by the limited examples chosen by Grant, Roth's full relation to his material actually is in *I Married a Communist*.

In order to develop these issues, we will need to entertain a view of what art can be that is not available in Arendt. Possibly because it is so influenced by Romanticism, one problem with Arendt's conception is that it tends to imply that by the time art has done its work, all the material out of which it has been pro-duced will be so transfigured as to be virtually unrecognizable. Certainly this is true of some art but there are also forms of art in which not only does it remain easy still to see some of its raw material but where the aesthetic experience actu-ally partly depends on a continuing relation to some of what it has been pro-duced out of. Arguably the 'Art' paper, by formulating art's rule as 'see it' (McHugh *et al.*, 1974: 156) did not have this type of art as its primary focus.

To take a well-known example, Arendt's conception of art does not manage to capture the kind of art that Picasso's *Guernica* displays. While not in any way being 'realistic' and so therefore certainly involving a transformation of the material out of which it has been produced, i.e. the bombing of a town, yet the aesthetic experience surely depends on us experiencing a continuing relation to the material the painting refers to, i.e. civil war.

Georges Didi-Huberman's view of art, largely developed by contemplating how certain paintings work, can help us here. Without in any way committing himself to a view of art as mere copy – indeed by denying the effectiveness of so-called realism – he has suggested that the artfulness of some paintings con-sists in the fact that they enable us to visualize some event (Didi-Huberman, 2005: 17). We can think of whatever the event is as some of the material out of which the painting is composed and the power and art of the painting as that which enables us to visualize the originating event. Picasso's *Guernica* would be an instance, in this case enabling us to visualize, by its transforming techniques and certainly not by just copying, civil war.

Roth's visualizing work

Philip Roth is no painter but might his work in *I Married a Communist* consist in enabling us to visualize some things? If so, this would be significant because it would mean that Grant's observation that he is clearly drawing on real-life

events, even events that he is 'angry, bitter, and resentful' about, does not necessarily militate against the product amounting to art. But of course this defence of
the work will only be viable if the book can be seen as helping us to visualize
the events it draws on.

The book contains many scenes which, as is clear from both Bloom's book
and Grant's critique, draw on the material of their marriage. Because it probably
represents the most damning charge against him, I will focus on how the novel
treats the event concerning the daughter that according to Bloom and Updike
made Roth seems 'callously selfish'. In the novel, before the event, 'Ira' (the
Roth character) was becoming more and more isolated in the house' (Roth,
1998: 172). Eve would be 'up in Sylphid's (the daughter character's) room …
listening to the record player. The two of them in bed, under the covers, listening
to *Così Fan Tutte*. When he'd go up to the top floor and hear the Mozart blaring
and see them together, Ira felt as though he were the child' (172–173).

Already we can begin to visualize why Roth might have thought the daughter's moving out might be quite a good idea. But when he proposes it, 'all Eve
does is cry. This is unfair. This is horrible. He is trying to drive her daughter out
of her life.… No, around the corner, he says … she is twenty-four years old, and
it's time she stopped going to bed with mommy' (173). Apart from the fact that
Roth changes the daughter's age, it could have happened like this and if so we
are still further along toward visualizing what even Bloom herself admitted was
an over-dependent relationship.

The Roth character tries to tell Eve that the daughter moving out could be
healthy for all concerned. He argues that 'there is going to be a considerable
improvement in Sylphid's outlook on life' (173). But the Bloom character won't
listen and replies in language that is quite close to what, as we saw, Bloom, in
her book, tried to portray as the objective reality. According to Bloom 'It was
the choice between the security of a companion and the welfare of a daughter'
(Bloom, 1996: 172). Roth has Eve say:

> Why are you doing this to me? To make me choose between my daughter
> and you, to make a mother choose – it's inhuman.
>
> (Roth: 173)

As Bloom presumably did, eventually Eve 'gathered her courage' (174) and told
Sylphid she must move. Ira hears screams and goes

> racing up the stairs to Sylphid's room. He found them in bed together. But
> no Mozart this time. Bedlam this time. What he saw was Eve on her back
> screaming and crying, and Sylphid in her pyjamas sitting astride her, also
> screaming, also crying, her strong harpist's hands pinning Eve's shoulders
> to the bed.… There, on top of his wife, sat Sylphid screaming: 'Can't you
> stand up to anyone? Won't you once stand up for your own daughter against
> him? Won't you be a mother, ever. Ever?'
>
> (174–175)

We are now being enabled to visualize a daughter with such a knack for manipulating/intimidating her mother that what at face value did seem inhuman (and so, on reflection, actually hard to picture unless we do assume inhumanity on Roth's part) now seems, however unpleasant, quite possibly the only way forward.

But we do notice that, assuming Bloom's version of the facts is accurate, Roth made the events occur six years later than they really did. Of course, this change makes it much easier for us to visualize him acting in this way rather than treating his deed as the sort of thing we cannot picture anyone short of a monster doing. Also, of course we have no way of knowing how many other facts Roth changed to help us visualize the event.

On the one hand, given that, as Arendt argued, art must change its material and, as Didi-Huberman argued, some of art's function is to enable us to visualize things, it is tempting to say that it does not matter how much Roth changed reality. On the other hand, it does seem important that the factual changes do serve (as we suspect) more to help us visualize how the event could have happened rather than just to offer a one-sided defence of Roth against Bloom.

As some evidence that what Roth changes could primarily be serving the former – what we can now call the artistic – purpose, it is worth noting that whatever liberties he is taking with reality, the book as a whole does not make the Roth character seem all that much more admirable than the Bloom character. There is in the book no male equivalent of the wronged ex-wife. For example, if the Bloom character is portrayed as having 'no idea how to conduct herself in a dispute or disagreement ... every conflict is perceived as an assault, a siren is sounded, an air raid siren, and reason never enters the picture...' (Roth, 1998: 161) about the Roth character it is said 'no one in the world had less talent for frustration ... or was worse at controlling his moods' (286). Given the balanced judgements, we can begin to believe the facts are not changed merely to portray Roth in a better light.

The overall sense the novel conveys of the marriage can be summarized by one character's verdict that it 'was a mismatch from the start' (54). The scenes of the novel, as written by Roth, tend to confirm this impression. What makes it unlikely that whatever changes to the reality he has made are devoid of artistic merit is how distinct and more easy to picture this verdict of mismatch is from the impression Bloom tried to create. As we have noted, she presents herself as the wronged ex-wife. Both because Bloom's idea of herself is just the sort of thing individuals, in the aftermath of a divorce, typically allege and because our own scrutiny of what even Bloom herself reports casts doubt on it, only the novel's version (mismatch) seems to manage to produce what we said art can do, the work of enabling us to visualize-picture-something rather than merely announce what someone happens to say-think-allege about the thing in question.

What Roth does here, unlike Bloom (and what we argue constitutes his art) is surpass a merely adversarial exchange. To visualize is to eschew sheer advocacy in favour of imagining a plausible scene for their intimacy. By so doing he achieves a degree of impersonality and separation from the conditions they both faced.[1] As an alternative to Bloom's one-sided advocacy, we are offered the chance of seeing their relationship, such as it was, as a beginning for reflection. We see that reflective option in for example the analysis of both of them as flawed and of the relationship as a mismatch.

Roth's metaphor

What is perhaps most compelling about the visualizing work of the novel is that it has a way to challenge the validity of Bloom's book even without resorting to factual counter claims. There is at least one point in the novel where it is undeniable that Roth departs from – indeed even violates – the facts but without his revisions' efficaciousness depending on their factual plausibility. As we have seen, Bloom wrote what she describes as a memoir. In the novel, what the Bloom character does is described by Grant as writing 'a book during the McCarthy years which exposed her ex-husband as a Red' (Grant, 1998: 1).

As Grant sees it, the difference here is just another case of Roth slightly changing the facts so that his book will appear to be a novel rather than merely his version of the events. That is, she thinks it is of a piece with renaming Claire 'Eve' or making the daughter a harpist rather than an opera singer.

Before we accept Grant's view, it is worth noting the nature of the typical books published by acquaintances of communists and alleged communists during the McCarthy era. Even when they contained aspects of the truth, they were inevitably sensationalized accounts, designed to put their subjects or, better, victims in the worst possible light. Hence their authors, even if not outright falsifiers, tended to be disparaged as 'informers'. And the books, in line with their purpose of discrediting someone, tended to have attention-grabbing titles, *I Married a Communist* being a perfect example.

There is a passage in the novel where Roth offers an apt description of the nature of these books. Even when they did portray facts, they were grossly inadequate because they

> Empty life of its incongruities, of its meaningless, messy contingencies, and to impose on it instead the simplification that coheres – and misapprehends everything.

(305)

Can we not say that, whereas Bloom certainly prefers us to see her book as a memoir, it is better described as suffering from exactly this problem? It is much more trying to be an exposé (of Roth) than a memoir. As such it is fair to say that this factual change by Roth is both legitimate and much more significant than Grant realizes. It enables us to better visualize what Bloom, in publishing her book, has done.

And note that this critique of Bloom is credible irrespective of whose facts about the details of the marriage are more accurate because the critique is grounded in the point that the very genre in which she has chosen to write makes it impossible that what she is presenting could capture much in the way of the reality.

The specific artistic technique that Roth has used here to help us visualize a reality is to invent a metaphor. We better see the nature of what Bloom has done by understanding that, in terms of Roth's metaphor, it is like what informers did to communists or supposed communists in the heyday of McCarthyism. It is in her treatment of this point that we perhaps see how much Grant is misunderstanding Roth's achievement. Her reaction to this aspect of the book is to complain that 'the whole enterprise of examining the McCarthy period collapses under the weight of Roth's vengeful agenda' (Grant, 1998: 2). While I would dispute her specific judgement that the book does not offer a useful exploration of the period, the far more basic objection to Grant's point is that a metaphor's main function is to help us see something else, not itself. If we say my love is like a rose, it would normally mistake our enterprise to object that we are failing to explore roses.

Unlike Grant, we are managing to see this novel as other than a mess because we have identified certain changes, one of them taking the form of the invention of a metaphor, that do seem to be the work of an artist, precisely because they do enable us better to visualize both the marriage and Bloom's book about it.

However, even as he achieves what we argue is artistic distance, this is not to deny that affect has animated his book. The 'Art' paper suggested the part of the power of art was its freedom 'from any dependency on externals'. (McHugh *et al.*, 1974: 175). In this case, the freedom resides in not merely acting out the obvious frustration, anger, and resentment, all the residues of their failed relationship. Angry Roth no doubt is but the anger seems not to have militated against (and may even have inspired) his art.

But, even if the novel has been shown not to lack art, nothing said so far can serve to challenge another of Grant's critical points, one just mentioned but with which we have not yet engaged, that what Roth has written is 'a novel of revenge' (Grant, 1998: 1). While I am sure she is right about this, certainly – whatever else it is – his novel being payback for Bloom's exposé, do we need to go along with her corollary, that so doing 'diminishes him?' (Grant, 1998: 2). The question here is not whether he has produced art but whether revenge, even revenge that qualifies as art, could ever be worthwhile.

Along with all its other visualizing work, arguably the novel even offers some help toward enabling us to visualize the nature of at least this specific act of revenge. I refer to the scene in which the Roth character is talked out of doing what he really wanted to do in response to Eve's exposé of him. It is reported that

> He was going to garrotte her. And the daughter. He was going to garrotte the two of them with the strings off the harp. He had the wire cutter. He meant it. He was going to cut the strings and tie them around their necks and strangle the two of them to death.
>
> (Roth, 1998: 303)

A revenge novel may not be great, perhaps because it would typically contain too much resentment and not enough of the ability to visualize we have identified with art, but if, as here, we are encouraged to visualize it as a substitute for a particularly grisly act of double murder, it certainly does not seem as bad as it otherwise would. And note that it is by another case of Roth's art, in this case the invention of the passage just quoted, based, we can surmise, on the 'material' of his first impulse when he read or heard about Bloom's book, that this further visualization has become possible.

Conclusion

It was indicated at the outset that the method of reflecting on art adopted here is different from the one utilized in *On the Beginning of Social Inquiry*. There, the work of formulating art took the form of considering what differentiated the form of life of art from other activities, namely science and common sense. Here I asked instead what differentiates art from what a critic saw as a failed attempt at art. It is worth asking what the benefits might be of the differing approach taken here.

> The earlier paper begins as follows: Art is art in so far as we can recognise that artistic activity shows some rule which is required for it to be called art in the first place. Even to be rejected, the artist's work must be seen to be an attempt at art, whether it turns out to be good art, poor art, successful art, innocuous art, or whatever.
>
> (McHugh *et al.*, 1974: 154)

In that, as it is rightly said here, even poor art is an attempt at art, there is the danger that an exclusive focus on what is art in the first place might make the question of what does make for poor art seem not to be a proper focus for Analysis. Certainly, it is true that the original paper never explicitly addresses this question.

I would argue that there is no reason why Analysis needs to avoid evaluating an art work and that it can do so by addressing what I have called a borderline case, i.e. an example where the claim is made, that someone, unlike a scientist or common sense person, is indeed attempting art but is also said, wrongly in my view, to be failing in that attempt.

Note

1 This point was suggested by Alan Blum.

Bibliography

Arendt, Hannah (1958) *The Human Condition*, Chicago: University of Chicago Press.
Bloom, Claire (1996) *Leaving A Doll's House*, London: Virago Press.
Didi-Huberman, Georges (2005) *Confronting Images*, University Park: Penn State Press.
Grant, Linda (1998) 'The Wrath of Roth' from *The Guardian*, 3 October, 1998, sourced on the internet, www.theguardian.com.

Heller, Zoe (1997) 'An Emerald Ring, a Portable Heater and $150 an Hour' from the *London Review of Books*, 20 February, 1997, sourced on the internet, www.lrb.co.uk.

McHugh, Peter, Raffel, Stanley, Foss, Dan, and Blum, Alan (1974) 'Art' in *On the Beginning of Social Inquiry*, London: Routledge and Kegan Paul, pp. 154–182.

Roth, Philip (1998) *I Married a Communist*, London: Jonathan Cape.

Roth, Philip (1999) 'Slight Revision' from the *New York Review of Books*, March 4, 1999, sourced on the internet, www.nybooks.com/articles/archives.

Updike, John (1999) 'One Cheer for Literary Biography' from the *New York Review of Books* February 4, 1999 sourced on the internet, www.nybooks.com/articles/archives.

6   Expats

Richard Feesey

Expats are a bold bunch to turn their back on so much – kith and kin, the whole country – even if 'did they ever really leave?' seems always to follow them as well. Who wouldn't change a cold and rainy, over-taxed, immigrant-swamped going-to-the-dogs motherland for a place in the sun? Or who would, with all the visiting if grandchildren are not to miss out on grandparents? No matter, there they are – younger ones working online, female timeshare touts, male plumbers, and barmen servicing other expats – but for the greater part a scatter of greying couples with enough life to follow a trail around the wider Mediterranean, Croatia, southern Ireland (not so sunny), or Bulgaria. These are not just any émigrés. Excluded will be migrant contractors in Qatar or Dubai and drug money fugitives stuck in Marbella for their sins, while the genteel who go somewhat native in their adopted Dordogne, Tuscany, or Provence will be classed as exceptions proving the rule. 'Expat', more broadly than when it meant chiefly old colonial-looking types, means the rest. This is Cataluña or Corfu but by a whisker was Mallorca or Malta not called home, if indeed 'home' is how the new site of domicile is actually reported back. Not only Brits, Germans, and Dutch – it can be Finns, Japanese, or Russians. Ireland is not so bothered by its 'blow-ins' but unsureness is also abroad. Doesn't the accepting country see, in essence, tourists who stayed on, even if the latter might claim other identity? We cringe that it should be ambassadors of ourselves living the holiday but leave it unexamined that cringing is not quite saying good riddance. We smugly enjoy accounts of the dream turning sour and then admire the lack of homesickness when it doesn't. We settle for an unsettled sobriquet, half endearing, half censorious. We call them expats.

So what might collect all the dispersion and firmly place this exit from patria, this challenge to the idea that roots, belonging, or loyalty to history any longer make the slightest claim? Re-domiciling, skyping home, and a five year postal vote strike patriots, nationalists, and the civic-minded variously as desertion, insolence, or ingratitude, of which any strange expatriate flag-flying seems to them a confirmation. Deprive a home country of you and your pension money, abandon what nurtured you when the deterioration isn't that bad or even reflects you rationalizing the exit? Never! Then again, why not if the possibility of dwelling in global place is ever more asserted, if not itself dwelled on as a possible impossibility?

In Spain there is an official category of Residential Tourist. It is also a sort of sigh. Beyond garbage collection, road upkeep, and healthcare, what greater stake or interest in the affairs of the place have these particular anonymous faces than the visitors they usually were earlier? Doesn't expats' *there-ness* in the locale, their intense non-involvement and non-contribution, particularly suggest tourists frozen by a large pause button, strangely arrested mid-trip? All this expats must live down. But how? What quality of *plaza, piazza* or *place* – what character of collective self-reflection – will have started to resound if only one dwelled on what it all might represent?

I come to the topic via two stimuli at once.[1] The immediate occasion is Karen O'Reilly's (2000) ethnographic study of certain British on the Costa del Sol, a cluster marginal to the larger diaspora taken in here. But my debt is to a tradition of inquiry that always made a difference to the idea of being investigatively limited in any such way;[2] questioning for example whether modestly bearing witness to the nature of the events shows one to be enough of an inquirer. Data one needs for sure, and side by side with sun-belt hedonism and unsustainable boredom O'Reilly identifies community and social structure making for new identity which exerts its hold. In this she retrieves some data in creditable form in a way in which those upholding this other tradition (McHugh *et al.* (1974) writing on a similar defiance of roots and belonging – travel), do not. The latter only manage to sound snooty. Propelling them on the other hand is no prospect of final speechlessness in modest fascination for what the world is like, fascinations discrete like any blow-ins that settle. It was never as if such-and-such research findings on tourism and travel's figures *or* vivid ethnographic pictures of mass-touristic or individualistic travel culture would be what the world thereabouts was finally like with purely such findings left to speak for what brought them to the topic. Indeed they collected a form of life – holidaying from commitment and conceiving somewhere as anywhere – as the topic's reflexive self-applicability and, paradoxical as it sounds, the commitment a theorist reflects in accomplishing the feat of passivity by which, inter alia, cautious field trippers manage to observe and record and so show their non-obtrusive selves.

Just like O'Reilly we *provide* a theme of special problematic identity and belonging. How to be and belong in liminal space, as she calls it? (Liminal: standing on or on both sides of a boundary or threshold.) Like her we would add there is no straddling an important defining boundary. Unlike her, however, we immodestly presume to *provide for*, in one commensurate form (economy of discourse/formulation/theory) the solutions expats regularly come up with, solutions grouped together here either as their affirmation of what for us would be the *place* of the place in the sun, allowing them decisively to stay and not for example repatriate personal ashes, or alternatively to identify their foreign spots' failure to foster a habitable concept of place when the zone of personal relocations is rather the dislocation or homeless ozone of anonymous demographics where 'strong expat community' reflects mere head count or survey, supporting the opposite outcome of going home ex-expats, ultimately to die ex-ex-expats embosomed perhaps in the same underfunded immigrant-dependent NHS which in the Brits' case at least once drove them away.

'Our place suits us, it's good enough for us, we've never looked back'. Such talk is common in sun-belt coupledom, and the last phrase notably contradicts itself by its utterance, perhaps seeking to forestall the kind of interrogation not very welcome in a life of ease. But what of larger common place now? Common place would seem a substitutable convenience, an outer environment amenable in sheer toleration terms to plural sovereign places/places for sovereign I's or twinned I's. Time was when 'my place' meant my abode ironically and humor-ously, but not now and certainly not here. And this Me suited by its nice spot, reflecting like any me an indefinite anterior Us impersonally providing my or anyone's sense of it might just worry 'Is the region maybe harmed as much as benefited if this kind of presence rather consigns it to being a service economy?' Natives never used to look forward to being maids, waiters, or geriatric nurses. Us-and-our-place talk quietly unsettles us now. Me and my life on a journey or not in a good place until moving on etc. is talk similarly seeming to put my thoughtful dwelling quite elsewhere. And more concretely, where would be the wisdom in letting a dotage of me and the missus join a pathetic twilight of quiet pining for ordinary human society, the *bon viveur* delights becoming empty of delight if one is honest; the vitamin D in the skin only that? Then again, it was the right move. It all depends.

So it is a divided experience. Roughly by halves expats stay or drift home again. Which way the one who 'didn't need Britain in his life just then' goes may come as a surprise. And restocked all the while is the undecided middle, the dilemma the idea here is to appropriate and relish.

I

Push and pull factors of seasonal or permanent economic migration do not begin to apply, the few working expats cause little fear of a brain drain, there is nothing of colonial diaspora about it and it could not be less like urgent exodus. Standing in relation to other migration types as a war of choice stands to other war the expat drift is entirely and exhaustively elective, a sum of personal movements some temporary and some permanent. Couples of maturing years are saying they are better suited by environment bubbles to relocate to when features 'tick their boxes', as worked out in loosening certain affective ties and defying certain claims of belonging. We tend to know the boxes: temperatures good for arthritis, soothing views, golf, pension-stretching prices with alcohol duty agreeably low, not too many other expats around, not too few for moral support either, and authentic country folk good at leaving retirees like these in peace to keep them-selves to themselves and to be no more adoptively something, not foreigner-local for example, than they the expats need or expect *los del lugar* to be more than shadow neighbours. Discreteness is the physicality of it and discreet 'live and let live' is the social tone, a tone neither cold nor warm but as we shall hear, tepid. And low guilt levels about leaving are matched by how little dread catches up with this zero expectation of naturalizing in the new place when distinctive identity does turn abstract aggregations of lifestyle émigrés into transmitters of normative order.

The forwardness in backing off from thoughts of new roots is that of sidling in *qua* cunning squatter. Expats are there provisionally, perched for now, and the nice spot's substitutability in principle applies as much to a squat decades long with boats truly burned as to waverers slinking home to a *pied-a-terre* for the contingency. In either camp the experience is lived by quasi-squatters. It is a rigorous individualism of couples missing a couple as little as locals notice one's arrival sometimes. It is fine for the stunning Shangri La of a Dunroamin to resemble that curious chained-down Winnebago not unknown in the USA, dominated by motility and resale value in all the stasis of the pitch. The given vehicle of view must only not be too soulless, the fabric also not too kitsch or inept. Does X property enjoy the better view, is Y the prettier identical vantage point? Ask an expert in perspective contingent on position with an eye for what others have got. Ask one whose point of view *is* that all points of view are equal in the contingent aspect of the ground stood on for the duration.

Looming large is the accidental aspect of what we stand on in taking a position on a matter and the revocability of the position-for-now or tendency becomes important. It is reminiscent of the erudition game in pedagogy. One is alert to other authorial ways of seeing still out there for the sampling and collecting, other whole corpuses, always a diversion from the inherent offer of perspective and purview potentially immanent *here*, here where we are, restless that the next viewpoint occupant might have a better view of X, relieved they have an untempting angle on Y but finally comfortable to shrink from ever really appropriating the matter we have perspective on since of course it could show one as too incomplete. Circumspect squatting, rather than taking up residence with a splash, is diffident about owning except as co-occupancy forward with its reserve of judgement as to what finally belongs with what, how a thing stands, what it *is*. Good viewing positions could have been better, we have the castle but those aerials are regrettable and it's all rather committal to expect much actual change of perch. (This does not complete a form of life for expatriate living however. Expats do vacate often enough, sitting less well with the exegete who has no position to abandon.)

Rural expats in particular can be discerning to a fault. Here, if natives find blow-in privacy and its non-interference almost stand-offish and the lack of need of the local tongue almost shrill (capable types like these would learn it in other situations) an appreciation of environs deserted by the place's youngsters these days may redeem the unnerving inscrutability, the confinement of things to a *Buen día* returned from the terrace.

Locals more generally, with little to go on, unmoved even if their own intensity of life is envied given how parochial they themselves might deem it, can see these ciphers setting themselves up to be caricatures of Brits in Cyprus, Krauts in Mallorca, etc. as never before. To be stuck with being 'nationals' was not in the plan, anything but, but the would-be egregious Brit or Kraut does well to particularly confound the stereotype (reserved/excessive with drink; humour-less/ditto) in the gregarious soiree of the tribe spied, with relief, in the gravitation of Cockneys to the Pheasant Plucker, Glaswegians to the See You Jimmy, or others to the local bar on expat night.

Expat recognition on discovering common travail with the same dodgy agent or poor builder may or may not lead to much but it is very hard to signal that you wouldn't have gone near half those appalling people with a barge pole back home, it's excruciating, what commonality does a replica passport signify? Then it is belied by the whole triumphant succession of centre-stage interaction enfolding even the non-communicators the scene throws up – the compatriot near-neighbours in the middle of nowhere saying it would take an earthquake to bring them together and there they are where it matters, comporting themselves and their non-communication *echandose una mirada sesgadamente* at Saturday morning market, neither party backing down from attending. Next to the gruff native way of doing things the delicate avoidance management is a small diversion in the heaving scene. They are Britons then; but will they be adequate expats, Britons with a difference?

In relations locally, expats could not be less like Georg Simmel's Stranger (Wolff, 1950: 402).[3] This stranger, usually a visiting trader, arrives to find his unfamiliar origins and impersonality putting him at a special premium. A stranger like him, still of the same language community, will best take the role of non-partisan listener the whole parochial place wants to engage by turns, speaking freely, almost confessional, all ears as well, in a trusting subjection to impartial balancing of different cross-cutting interests their speech inevitably presents. *This* he will do for nothing, the reward is doing it, and before gaining much reputation to be vain about he's off again. Neutral as to side-taking, Simmel's stranger is not conceded neutrality as to the potentially good repute of a place that arises with the need of a figure like him: someone abstract because representing a possibility of self-scrutiny for the collective, but corporeal for the time that the figure is embodied in conduct or, in other words, the aspiration re-embodied, if it is. Simmel's slightly bemused merchant from 'away', wise and balanced when to him it's trite sometimes, is the dignified anyman they make themselves known to while inhibiting from being a known person in kind, which would detract from what is hopefully reflected in the confidence invested. A known person not yet elevated as biographical (not yet conveying sublime possibility in any of the mundane you-or-I doings, which is how biographical authorship inscribes itself) is only banal, only a diaspora of fascinations collecting no dwelt-on behaviours as a figure's ambiguous presence would. A place's Strangers, like the Unknown Warrior a plain flagstone can evoke, are only a way for it to see how a collective aspiration could be said to be held for itself.

New expat arrivals, exited apparently from the whole idea of possibly dying for a patria (or dying for much else beyond certain consumer products 'to die for'?) can, however, display a form of this Stranger status within an *expat* community when that, properly speaking, comes about, as we see shortly. And, very separately, 'foreigner-turned-adoptive-local'[4] can also parallel Simmel here in a re-presentation of the same evergreen question of the soul of community and its humane modes of compelling recognition in boundary-flexing forms of sociation.

If the inscrutability of expats understandably leaves natives detained in national typing at times then our would-be trans- or supra-national dwellers were sometimes already returning the compliment. Only the Portuguese could manufacture a water heater so useless, etc. etc. It is no way for a guest to talk but these are no guests and to hell with what's notionally demeaning, it's only a bit of fun or cathartic. (Hence, something still *could* demean: the potential call of a public sphere, however distorted, is still present.) But the devil makes work for idle hands and other-nationality expats become grist as well. Back home it was well known what a category mistake it is to speak of what's in or not in a 'national character', and too much racism at home was even why you got out, but now look at those well-heeled Dutch, how they are tragically missing out on really delicious village fare because Lidl is ever so slightly cheaper. They would have their separate Spanish bank accounts to monitor if the charges weren't so extortionate. Just so Dutch...

The whole relocation was to have left inauthenticity, and all else bad for the individual, behind in bad Britain (or wherever) so as to be yourself and live the authentic life like the free and ultimately conventional and circumspect actor who would be the realizer of Rawlsian life-plans,[5] fostering the dwelling of possibly fair-minded individuals across citizenship divides and, in the European instance, valuing porous borders for upping comfortable consumers' numbers (rather than testing the nature of the collective) and yet here you are, reviving something medieval. Expats both as rusticators needing to get out more and the ghettoized who could use more space to reflect, in these moments are finding it hard not to laugh (is it the lack of children?) at the old chestnut about hell. Hell is where the cooks are English, the comedians are German, the lovers are Swiss, etc., and it's all organized by the Italians. Facetious humour takes a corny facet and tugs at our weakness for envisaging full face, seeing ourselves in the facet's image, multi-faceted and deep as it would alternatively be if a decent character impression and not a self-caricature or identity impression taken in by its own actor. Facetiousness's development towards a wit we would call our own is an arrested development, its Jeremy Clarkson-type reflex of systematic self-disavowal ever averting it from the mirror reflecting the mix of humours in the *piazza* or *agora* where its very own 'nothing is serious' opinion would risk exposure if only it showed its face there. As it is, facetious dwelling presents neither interested mind nor open soul. It sits at the parked table of simplistic nationalism and its gaunt unironic face (its own obverse), not at expats' diffidently shunted-together tables in the *plaza* they pussy foot around in, their face at least appearing wholesomely torn.

Needless to say, no embrace of deracination is going to manage the action or capacity of 'human beings' identity-wise, any more than the next maverick did. Even absurd allusions to a 'national culture' or occupationally convenient invocation of home-land security for the-people-as-one (keeping the world safe for democracy) privately know it well. A collective identity like any other is not conferred without drawing boundaries and making exclusions, as true in hybrid or trans-national identities (if such there be)[6] as in any other. Human beings' presence is just too little heard of outside of barbaric treatment or disaster areas and expat zones are very secure. Souls, human beings, people, species members, global citizens, any would-be candidate for non-exclusive identity – forget it, there is no relocating to *that* as material for re-working one's sense of identity as one action of an I who is an I to itself and so at once a Me reflecting an Us that can only be it-self in a particular nurturant place in common.

As for what defines and distinguishes expats in their own view, they are more vocal on what they are not. They are not old colonials, not foreign plants thriving unchanged in local gardens or importers of culture totally intact. Thus the resolute stayer-in-the-making takes exception to the jibe that we see essentially tourists who stayed on or, again, Spain's official Residential Tourist category. Call us mindless-eyeball travellers arrested mid-trip or comical-turned-reprehensible with our phrase-book level language, but only look and you will see identity, social distinctiveness with themes all its own. Hence the deeper-than-tourist skin-tan employing sunlamps on top of the ample natural sun to that end. Skin is not that of the nice old man on the donkey. Style of dress is semi-local. Car scratches are left unpainted. Cheeks are always continental-kissed, never singly. Backs are slapped after a fashion. It signifies being not indigenous and not visitor (and quite likely only 'expat' in jest) but us here, sort of local, us to take as you find us. But what does *that* mean or what greater social specificity is indicated? That at least was O'Reilly's question and her stress on some nicely unpredicted slices of life, albeit at the border of the phenomenon proper, we are glad to recycle shortly.

II

Fascinating data having the last word speak to an author shying away, second-thoughts expat fashion, from authorizing why they fascinated. As to the authority to have selected *those* data the drawn ethnographer is as modest as expat contribution to place is, in the common prejudice, modest to downright non-existent, a problem in turn being how virtuous modesty ever was.

This is not to knock ethnographic visits to sociocultural curiosities with care and awe for what the world is like, special-interest tourist fashion. There is no knocking how what happened had to happen as it did for members' procedures and accounts to take the documented form they did. There is even a dearth of good documentations. We only insist in addition on deriving perspective in the not unprepared visit; on venturing to formulate the *place* of the place in the sun, ipso facto the habitable concept of place, as the centrally stimulating area of a topic's reflexive self-applicability, the activated resource-area of the topic. Back comes a wry remark now: what 'in addition' is there when a purely allusive interest in 'grounds' of members' accounts to imaginatively hold them to suggests, if anything, the no-lose strategy of those who will never know a disappointed study, probably never fail to find what they are looking for, never know what it is to have been essentially wasting time as it might turn out? We would say, if no-lose means risk-free and infallible, unable to be wrong, then alertness to how an activity finds it essential to itself as human activity that it *could* be wrong bodes well for analysing it; bodes well for that loosening of an assemblage to re-view how it coheres (called analysation in a former time and here termed Analysis for short) naturally prone to misreading along 'breaking up into simple elements' lines which however is others' problem not ours.

Or again, a 'hall of mirrors' image flashes our way. In this image the analytic inquirer leaves his armchair only to fall victim in the same room, in something akin to perceptual or neural mishap, to misapprehending as substantive or warrantable life-world reference what is so much multiplying cross-reflecting artifice of the apprehender's own eccentric apparatus. Pity rather than blame this private derangement, unshared in detail although looking modestly contagious when the cute or not so cute jargon, a shared idiomatic distinctiveness going nowhere except back to its own hallmark lexicalities, is a declared symptom. Not *too* nasty, the hall of mirrors syndrome is a health warning to the few at risk; humane advice to take the air of a pedagogic equivalent of the healthy hallucination-free olive terrace work benefiting certain mental health émigrés on the Mediterranean.

Back on topic, so far we have what resembles a squat in a site of domicile more than a home, occupying a location instead of being part of a place, contingently ticking preference boxes rather than stealing hearts utterly, against regional backdrops characterized by passive acceptance or bemused tolerance as against hosting in any sense, all as a normative order's so far tepid endorsement, a situation asking for resolution in either cold rejection or warm embrace.

The same ostensibly bad Britain O'Reilly's first-few-years residents regularly run down they keep tuning into. Sound-wallpaper backdrops of rolling Sky news and even weather of the mother country are sometimes dipped in and out of in turn with the pool. Things that mattered before belonging somewhere was headed for being a memory were never really going to stop mattering the moment the removals van left. And so neither smug wallowing in the wise move nor exactly a pained nostalgia captures very well how varieties of scandal, outrage, and the rousing 'things we do well' can be as acutely meaningful and significant, if not more so, than when one's actual address or TV set was back there. Here is something to get worked up about and if home is where the heart is then affairs in political, civic, and public life generally, hallucinated as in some small measure potentially influenceable in turn, will never be fully banished from what one is belonged with, e.g. home and particular sense of place. It would be intolerable for a pleasure like civic pride, however vicariously experienced in mass-mediated daily living it always was and still is now, to be suddenly never on offer again; a dreadful mistake of self-banishment. The thematic dilemma takes a new form: would it be a sadist who snuck round and snipped that life-saver of a Sky cable, or someone cruel to be kind, i.e. the kind clarifier of a very important practical decision?

Is that five-year postal vote enough, in other words, or given the betwixt and between space is it indeed more a sort of civic insolence?

III

Absurd and yet helpful I feel is to impute to the hard-core isolates among expats, those discrete and discreet, circumspect and innocuous, aesthetic materialists to a man and woman in choosy control over everything from climatic environment to minute interior and garden design to precisely who one's social set will comprise, an extravagant demonstrative exercise in irony. Where does affluent liberal democracy in modern/postmodern culture with civic conduct ever side-lined send the very idea of place-habitation and belonging, so, they considered, pre-expat, if not on this trajectory now: neither to old loci of collective identity in public minded acts, patriotic moments, election campaigns, or traditional memberships, nor any promise of international or transnational status never culturally accredited in all honesty, but towards stabilizing the shifting sands of subscription and identification through that inhabiting of common place which conceives and maintains it as though eternally hierarchical with me and my place at the top. The sunlit uplands offered therein are where we contented bronzed *individuals*, more than anyone, can say we now are; we out of anyone live the prescribed life, we *are* the I's basking atop the common place, serene even in dipping down into the anterior Us enabling the self- and other-concepts and interpretations etc. of one and all, with the Us in like manner mastering and managing all it surveys in outer politico-economic contexts and natural environments. Places in the sun are so many culminations of personal journeys and with 'journey' being anything but geographical movement these days we light-treading squatters are also the splendid exception by no means at odds with rampant self-help however much some like to sneer about Nero fiddling while Rome burns.

Like all serene hierarchy it is Apollonian. Apollo needed neither skin-fed vitamin D nor Factor 30 but beamed the changeless and entirely formalistic ratio of how things are – which was also the joke about the Dutch in their Lidl branch on the Med tragically exchanging immanent principle for external standard (euros and cents) as the criterion of good. Conversely the Dionysian tendency, usual part of recognizing the Apollonian, helps us supply the particular expat version of moderation here in the phenomenon of tepid convention-fearing British tut-tutting about compatriot visitor lager lout-ism or drunken sex in public (very Dionysian) where indigenous locals only shrug, even Catholic conservatives more flexible than this other conservatism adjacent and so distant. The question is of course are we yet the reality, is any kind of life together in a social, habitable environment actually to be *lived* in the image of this prescription?

The overarching contemporary imperative to pursue and have *fun*, unashamedly frivolous fun so often, as per the whole New Left/Baudrillard axis of critique of our western consumer culture, can be seen to culminate in one form topically germane, and that epitome is expat golf. This actor it is who takes a tepid and tame ultimate pursuit, with the logic par excellence of a sovereign ego or *égoïsme-a-deux* made flesh, to of all places, places of perennial water shortage. Desertification threatens already and still they putter their days in spacious, speechless mid-spectrum green when, as that Apollonian-of-sorts Kant would point out, if the generality of water users in the vicinity insisted on a Third Age pastime in like manner with irrigated tracts of theirs then all quite literally starts to evaporate and scorch in frivolity unbounded, placeless dust replacing placeless grass blades, one uninhabitable silence for another. It would seem to be the parting note, the suicide note, of the ironic expat self-inquisitor.

We still suggest more rationale for getting out than abiding there, but bear with me.

Expat spots being rather pleasant on the whole does not preclude some ghastliness in the pageant, and the greater ultimate repellence resides in what had every environmental accoutrement of potentially convivial community but supports social desert instead. One passionate commentator in reacting to a sample of Europe's most physically blighted and ecologically raped stretch of coast (not yet the worst thing about it) glimpses in the jumble of architectural kitsch and excess, so often twinned with nouveau riche deficiency, what Peter McHugh affirms as the pretence or impossibility of creating a real place in the image of the ontologically prior individual (2005: 144–147). Giles Tremlett sees there

> ...the outer suburbs of a coastal city in Florida, Australia or any of the white-dominated suburbs of South Africa's Indian Ocean coast. It was, essentially, a new place. It had been invented out of nothing and answered to nothing more than its residents' desire to live a life of leisure.
>
> (2012: 120)

What else would you expect, chirps the zeitgeist dialectician entertained above. The rhetorical question on real lips is more likely to be 'why not if no one is getting hurt?', returning us again to the centrality of the tepid and what to do about it. Real expats are by common consent, we recall, a variant of society's marginals; national deserters, total civic life absconders and shirkers, shameless familial unfaithfuls, AWAL. But McHugh suggests that, among other ways, it is in how the given model of society guides actual public engagement with marginals' challenge to the community and the kind of place the society is aiming to be that the persuasiveness of the model is tested. What then is the response of our prevalent individualist model to deviant politics, personal habits, sexual preference, or indeed generic disreputability if not precisely, as he says, 'of the tepid "Live and let live" variety that shunts them into anonymous privacy, the community attic, where the issue can be hidden rather than publicly engaged'. It is par excellence our innocuous actor circumspect in his and her foreign neighbourhood and for whom the principle of personal autonomy means 'refusal of entanglement in divisive argument of the kind that includes sociocultural risk ... (which is) not moderate as it first may seem, but rather careful, vaguely impartial, and prudently remote, however significant the issue' (McHugh: 145).

An activity is not illegal, no one's getting hurt and the choice-rich life is lived. Is that to endorse the activity? Implicitly it is when further principle like the intrinsic justice or virtue of a matter sounds too antiquarian amidst freedoms and entitlements exercised by autonomous I's, all such rights and privileges being in principle equal contenders for value and the means to find balances as need arises neutral as to ends. US procedural justice is quite explicit there, as McHugh's succinct look at his country's historical performance on justice emphasises. John Rawls among others was not intellectually confrontational here, avoiding the issue as he was at liberty to do. But Rawls' paradigmatic human actor, a distribution- and competition-minded possessor of personal spending priorities – a variant on 'the consumer' in all frankness – is only nominally interested in the justice of a matter, equating both justice and fairness with formal equivalence of opportunity to realize this Rawlsian actor's *life-plans*. Diasporic expats are life-plan realizers par excellence and Rawls would approve of them (naturally a sub-continent of a country like his doesn't feature them). Neither would Ronald Dworkin manage any hint of censoriousness, nor any who devote the sum of their considerable intellectual endeavour to something as definitively *devolved already* (devolved: rolled down, departed from centre or sense of immanent means of deriving principle) as 'rights'. It is tepid endorsement, and Rawls would presumably search our expats' intellectual passion for any sign of his Aristotelian Principle. The latter affirms for Rawls the formalizing hierarchy whereby the justice/fairness-minded agent realizes and expresses herself/himself quintessentially through nothing like the drink-induced agreeableness of everything nor terribly well through healthy vitamin D in the skin, nor yet golf but, at the azimuth, chess. But we won't go there.

IV

The point is the place concept. Expats are not the point but a way of making it, and it is worth reviewing the development of the concept of place in the tradition commended here.

Place in McHugh *et al.*'s 'Travel' piece was usage and not concept at all. Site was mostly as good a word in that analysis. Their one figurative play with place following a famous predecessor's attempt failed and they let it go. They would not be like Alice strutting about in Wonderland – 'From now on words may only mean what *I* want them to mean,' – which sent the later Wittgenstein so beside himself. 'Travel' noted the underlying equivalence of places in travel and how the typical example of travel's sense of place boils down to place without context (McHugh *et al.*, 1974: 138) Those equating change of place with necessarily educative change are very severely questioned. The question of why then browbeat an interlocutor so weak and untempting as their traveller was not addressed, and one answer is that technical Anglo-American empiricism's tepid holiday or self-absenting from questions of value and commitment invites a heated up companion. 'Travel', like the other papers in the collection except for the last, reads as furious.

Blum and McHugh calm down by the time of their nationalism article (1978) in a progressive move, a move back etymologically, to an explicit interest in the habitable concept of place; a notion of place ceasing to be particularly accessible to anywhere and everywhere like the pure geographics of any and the next region or universalistic nation-state features. Canadians in a Canada decent and enlivening would be in a place, a conversational site at last, strong precisely for how its defining features stood as expressive reminders of Canadians in their own nature, exerting its hold in that way. Yanks locally flooding in would seem unthreatening in such a Canada just like Ireland's blow-ins. Ironically, the worried nationalists the paper addressed struggled to locate what actually made them particularly and importantly Canadian at all. They were not American but what were they? But if huge influxes should happen and Canadians feel turfed out it would still be their own strong *place* that drew them decisively to any new place of cultural asylum. In general terms it becomes perfectly imaginable that

> ...some would have to go into exile in their own (strong) place, and others would drift into immigration in their own (weak) place.
>
> (Blum and McHugh, 1979: 332)

Place completely ceases to be subject in turn to context in the way travel's touristic site after site and place-name after place-name made it call out for context. Immigrant drift within one's weak place here actually refers to expat Americans in Canadian academic posts for the money and job security rather than the pedagogy, though other examples suggest themselves, not least a chunk of the European drift alluded to. Drifting homewards *only* because boredom with shallow secluded expat comforts has set in keeps the terms weak, as does the onset of decrepitude in rural isolation. Much more auspicious is that pining for normal involvement in ordinary human society with one's former deserted roots now forgiven for whatever was too limiting. It is the decisive expat stayers we still have to hear about, breaking the mould of non-interference and non-involvement, who would express the strong version of place, suggested now as the good although rare nationalist sense of nation evoked with enough playfulness and humour for key proud traditions bearing the sense of it (when there *is* lively pride rather than modestly going through the conventional motions) to be serially figurative of transcendent Tradition itself. For that read: soul of community non-negotiably subscribed to when, as in this example, motherland respect or lack of it is what is made to make the difference absolutely. Or again read: fertile place. Or: the transcendent *logos*; language itself; the indivisible common ground of which we cannot speak and yet go right ahead and refer to as what probe-ably (or probably) confines a terrain of speakers producing no complete speech yet still vociferous and potentially influencing affairs of the place for the better. So what might the expat stayer, our non-homesick blow-in totally at home with dying so far from cosy roots and just as far from any foreign country's cold indifference have to say, generatively and habilitatingly?

Subsequent work of McHugh and Raffel revisits the human person as 'I' and 'Us' and 'Common place' all at once. The porous boundaries between these and the elastic limit to the collective signified are only that within, among and between all of which the acting individual or human agent exists and moves. From a stay with soul of community always suggestive of the immanence of standard, which is to say the inescapable anthropocentricity of value, place's emphasis moves on and back an era or two to being, well, place: a focal public space in our age apt to be cast as an institution or organization or more amorphously a polity so long as members thereof are locatable through its version of what it aims to be, not as their selfless identification with something otherwise impersonal but as a need with which they arise if they are adequately recognized and described. Common place infuses the same us it shelters; the us always anterior to I's interpreting it for themselves for good or ill, trying to idealize themselves as I's alone for good or ill, and so on. Is the place on whatever salient definition still being helped to be what it is supposed to be?

V

And so to those decisive stayers, confounding the idea of being non-involvement and non-contribution personified. They always ran the gauntlet of censoriousness which says it is wrong and they abscond indecently, and allegiance and loyalty whether to mother, or personal history, or wider place of nurturance are not nothing but, rather, are positive virtues. More than lost Sky reception or collapsing sun loungers *isn't* there trouble in realizing that civil involvement is now not on offer ever again; that if they pine for reunification with all that created them pre-expat, dumb coercive conditions very much included after so much freely elective ticking of boxes exercised only by couples' compromises, didn't they have it coming, is not an institution of expatriate support pockets abroad a sort of garage chain servicing the needs of a throughput in decline mechanical and otherwise, staffed by more old crocks alive and well purely in the sense that throughput numbers happen to increase like the whole demographic?

These are the musings O'Reilly's field trip interrupts (2000: chapters 6 and 7). Her Fuengirola-Mijas bunch sees far too few slinking home to validate any myth of return, though in the zone proper the numbers will be up. For the few it was all clearly a mistake, hard to admit. But for the mainstay it is the right move, marriage-saving often enough. The mainstay social ambit and community patters out no demoralized twilight of nostalgia for when gratitude for one's history included influencing one's local world in turn because just that is being done. These greying jolly are pleased to be there for one another, they monitor who's around and network and share. They lend, cadge trustingly, barge in, freely break former norms of punctuality. It is how one behaves in 'Spain', their Spain. New arrivals almost can't not have a special talent to contribute, on top of a set of wheels for the carless whose knowledge of where's a good dentist or dog groomer is payment enough. Everything is first-name terms, surnames unremembered even when there was a brief need to know them. Tracey and Tony – Bob and Barbara: Bob and Barbara – Tracey and Tony. Take them as you find them because little baggage of biography came in the removal van. A former Chief Inspector finds he was once investigating his now favourite barman. Former illustrious careers are suddenly not worth the effort trying to impress with. Kudos would need earning again from scratch now. The past counts for little in a fresh start with a veil of ignorance over it all, each couple or individual a Simmel-type stranger to the rest so there can be almost an excess of the candid and confessional. The natural troubles of newcomers attendant on recent losing of affective ties and the way that affects the sense of self find real mitigation in this community-building, this new levelling possibility of what people might yet be, personally and together, all so much more than discoveries of common travail with the same town hall bureaucracy or dubious builder, etc. although even that easily leads to another soiree.

Almost hard to remember is that the one absence is of course youth – literally speaking let alone an actual baby; that this is Amish community only without the solemnity, its reproduction a similar matter of attracting new staff.

The Full Resident and Returning Resident categories, top of O'Reilly's four-fold division of British migrant identity, as presented to ethnographic study around Fuengirola at least (scientists are cautious to imply generalizability but the stray implication of it escapes out of O'Reilly) find additional social reward in the way voluntarism and being there for one another leads to some formaliza-tion. Clubs, societies, charities, hospices, Ecumenical Church coffee mornings spring up. Ballroom dancing groups of less than a hundred members have twenty five on the committee. Certain familiar old imperatives of organizational life re-appear benignly. With novel social structure and a seeming anthropological uni-versal of hierarchy itching to be thought about (but it would say more than field notes can) the use of surnames in formal deference to status, related to length of time 'served' in whichever Fuengirola institution, makes its distinctive and fas-cinating entry.

Thus the place of the place in the sun, the forum of collective discussion now starting to be inherited, is helped in the furtherance of the same principles by which it nurtures: principles like others' interests coming first, and this convinc-ingly what I can hold dearest as a 'me' in a situated and historicized community; the networking and informal support evolving as traditions brought forward for the sake of it and outside of coercion, guilt-tripping, or threats of the cold shoul-der (although it is no utopia either and, in a little replay of tradition's big trans-ition to modernity, possible discontents of anomie and rationalization may seem to loom on the horizon). Blaming 'bad Britain' for the time being at least gives way to 'how can we help in Fuengirola-Mijas?'

All seems like a happy success story of functionalist sociology. But still there's a but; concurrent all the while is possible disillusion and bathos. Take that updated Contacts list on the phone, the people around. Natives are not 'around', they are décor setting off the cohort, those with handy tool to borrow, gold dust knowledge of the lingo you exploit for translation services as need arises so you keep especially them sweet. What is it suddenly but people using people? Expat community is one spectre more of the prison ship, that floating curio of systematic and exhaustive instrumentalism where being, specifically, objects of one another's designs *is* the moral order.[7] Pleasing the prison guard = obsequiousness towards the bureaucrat selling building permission = cultivating the expat-friendly mayor who helps restrict further structural development detrimental to amenities enjoyed by those whose presence brought it to that level and are now allied in the cause for the time it is expedient. Good will is after all the impression of it, another delivered persona among the managed impressions the stage exhaustively is.[8]

Tremlett adds passion to one O'Reilly datum regarding the effect of a habit popular and prevalent among both the foreign full-time resident and returning owner-resident categories. It is the habit of declining to register in the local town as resident. Failing to register is not illegal but scarcely welcome when nearly everyone has to know that regional financial support from central government is awarded by registry numbers, with obvious detriment to public services they enjoy like the rest. A certain wider opportunistic avoidance of an officialdom less competent than in cool-temperate Europe explains the seeming shot in the foot. These tax and other charge avoiders feel they are individually better off compromising the general good in this way, and aren't the locals at it as well with the whole economy half a black economy, no one holier than thou, which is why objections are sullen rather than loud on the few occasions you hear them. Don't we only mirror in our polite self-containment the so-called exploited indigenous; and since they know the net economic benefit of our presence why not leave it at a happy pact of forgetting? Tremlett by contrast, a principled man awed and lovestruck by lively endogenous Spanish struggle to both recover, evoke, and live principle as the life-enhancing work of a nurturant common place, the Spain still uncompleted he sees it selectively bringing itself towards, is going to pander to no one and nothing holding the process back (of which there is plenty). Where an O'Reilly will keep quiet (stay modest, stay scientific) and let the reader judge the facts for themselves as to moral value (her own inclination or bias is for that minimal inferred insinuation that might escape sequestration) Tremlett's reward is to dwell where he lives; to put his dialectical money where his mouth is as a critical commentator on the country he loves, whether welcomed in open arms or threatened with being concretely sequestered ('disappeared') from the place.

So it remains unsettled. *Is* a place, concretely now this region of a province tied to this form of economy, pursuing the betterment of all in it; being helped to be what it is supposed to be?

Notes

1 Or three – a third would be living in Welsh-speaking Wales as an English person, whom language sticklers would like to call Immigrant but have to settle for In-migrant.
2 Stanley Raffel put me on to the nascent tradition in 1973 and Alan Blum, Peter McHugh and students furthered the involvement in Canada. Raffel's help in keeping the interest cemented for me subsequently has been such as to make acknowledgement of instances of it seem to me too arbitrary.

3 Barry Sandywell helpfully pointed out Simmel's relevant insight here, among further themes.
4 Journalist and historian Giles Tremlett is awed and humbled in a parallel way by his adoptive Candelada home. See his *Ghosts of Spain* (2012: 451).
5 I allude to John Rawls' paradigmatic human actor as US middle class consumer.
6 Although O'Reilly supposes the usage or validity of 'transnational identity' without her field notes supplying it literally (ethnography not yet being neopraxiology/ethnomethodology) it doesn't drop her into those who for Garfinkel (1966) 'imagine behaviour in any damn way they like *as* a perfectly normal and expected procedure'.
7 This heuristic metaphor from a McHugh undergraduate lecture helped students grasp what drier Weberian social-historical description might have left divested of animating dynamism.
8 Interpreting C. Wright Mills as much as Erving Goffman here, McHugh was asking whether a Salesroom model of society is what the formers' materials are very instructively seen as pursuing; or in later language, how particularly well would a limitation to authenticity vs. sincerity concerns reflect potential improvers of a common place?

Bibliography

Blum, A. and McHugh, P. 1978. 'The risk of theorizing and the problem of the good of place: a reformulation of Canadian nationalism', *Canadian Journal of Sociology* 3 (3), 321–347.

Garfinkel, H. and Sacks, O. 1966. Purdue Symposium on Ethnomethodology (Unpublished Proceedings).

McHugh, P. 2005. 'Shared being, old promises and the just necessity of affirmative action', *Human Studies* 28 (2), 129–156.

McHugh, P., Raffel, S., Foss, D., and Blum, A. 1974. *On the Beginning of Social Inquiry*. London: Routledge and Kegan Paul.

O'Reilly, K. 2000. *The British on the Costa del Sol*. Oxford: Routledge.

Tremlett, G. 2012. *Ghosts of Spain*. London: Faber and Faber.

Wolff, K. 1950. *The Sociology of Georg Simmel*. Toronto: Collier-Macmillan.

7 The complaint

An analysis

Saeed Hydaralli

The complaint, upon a little reflection, proves to be an irresistible topic for analysis. This has everything to do with the feeling of dividedness that it tends to engender in any thoughtful interlocutor. More specifically, the complaint is arguably a meaningful component of any social member's repertoire. At the same time, it has long faced much resistance, articulated as moaning and whining. Yet, despite this tension that pervades the very being of the complaint, it has little been theorized, whether by sociology, or the human sciences in general. It is precisely that absence that this paper aims to satisfy.

> Wonder is the foundation of all philosophy, inquiry its progress, ignorance its end. […] an ignorance that requires no less knowledge to conceive it than does knowledge itself.
>
> (Montaigne, 1970: 314)

Introduction

It is hardly uncommon these days to hear, both inside and outside the university, a significant amount of complaining about the failings of the current generation of students in the human sciences, and beyond. It is said of those students, especially in the human sciences, that they for instance: cannot write, are distracted and dominated by social media and hand-held technology, are overly coddled, have a sense of entitlement, and more (cf. Starnes, 2009: 770–771). After having listened to these complaints for some time, I began to find them annoying, even though some of those complaints are arguably legitimate. However, this annoyance seemed to be informed by more than my sense that these complaints might just be another instance of that seemingly timeless ritual where an older generation expresses its disappointment about the decline of civilization represented by one or more of the inadequacies of a younger generation.

So I started to ask myself, an asking which takes shape in this paper, from whence does my annoyance originate about these complaints – despite the fact that they might have some truth to them, and apart from my feeling that they reflect a kind of generational rite of passage on the part of an older generation – especially in view of the fact that I am hardly immune from complaining about a variety of things in everyday life, both great and small. For instance, I complain about people who choose to stand on the left-hand side when going down escalators as if they have not only developed temporary paralysis, but also temporary cognitive impairment in relation to the social obligation of consideration for others – because they make it impossible for others to go past – only to be revived, at least from their temporary paralysis, when the escalator has run its course. It is as if the escalator is a transitory reprieve from both the seemingly onerous character of walking and the need to be aware of the responsibility to the other (that s/he might in fact need or desire to keep moving at a pace that exceeds that offered by the escalator).

That division in me that the complaint animates was the provocation for the inquiry that is this paper. Indeed, in the *Republic*, Plato's Socrates tells us the following:

> ...reflection is provoked when perception yields a contradictory impression, presenting two opposite qualities with equal clearness, no matter whether the object be distant or close at hand. When there is no such contradiction, we are not encouraged to reflect.

> (Plato, 1945: 239)

The devaluation of the complaint

The complaint as an ordinary and everyday practice[1] seems to enjoy little affection and tolerance, if we were to look at popular references to this phenomenon.[2] Hence, the exhortation to 'stop complaining' or 'this is a no complaining zone', widely found on bumper stickers and frequently uttered in workplaces and living rooms, especially in the USA and Canada (Ehrenreich, 2009). Indeed, a 2007 bestselling book (over two million copies sold to date) is called *A Complaint Free World: How to Stop Complaining and Enjoy the Life You Always Wanted*. What is more, the author of that book, Bill Bowen, has also sold over ten million purple 'Complaint Free' bracelets primarily through his three *Complaint Free World* websites. Complaining, in this view, as a form of life, is seen as an inability to recognize and appreciate all that is good about one's current situation. Hence the popular, and widely circulated, online image that shows two service windows in an office building, one of which says 'complaints' and the other which says 'gratitude'. There is an interminable line-up for the window that says 'complaints', while the 'gratitude' window is devoid of anyone. The complaint is seen as a preoccupation that blinds us from recognizing and seizing the opportunities for a rewarding life that the everyday makes available. Thus, the complaint is understood as an impediment to experiencing the world as pleasurable.

Similarly, there is the widespread demand, relentlessly uttered in various media, that we 'stop complaining and do something', where the complaint is seen as not making, or having the potential to make, a difference in relation to the call for change that might be said to be implicit in its utterance. Further, we are told that, rather than complain, we must 'leave the situation, change the situation, or accept it'.[3] Here, the complaint is seen as a form of inaction, a refusal to developing a strong relationship to the situation, which might include accepting that the best course of action is to live with the situation, that it is impossible or too onerous to escape or change. Such a demand understands the challenges of social life as always and entirely in need of, and amenable to, resolution. That injunction also proposes that the time to act is now as there is no time to be wasted.

What is more, such an exhortation seems to suggest that complaining fails to recognize the power and freedom we each possess to take the kinds of actions or to make the kinds of changes that are necessary for a satisfying life, a life that is free of the need for complaining. A world in which we have the power and freedom to influence our fates is a world where one has absolutely no reason to complain, and to do so fails to accept the responsibility of one's freedom.

Yet, Simmel (1950) reminds us that a world in which freedom is available to all of us such that we would have no reason to complain is a world where inequality would be rampant since freedom means precisely the freedom of the strong to exploit the weak, the clever to exploit the stupid, the grasping to exploit the timid. He goes on to say:

> …since in all power relations an advantage once gained facilitates the gaining of additional advantages (the 'accumulation of capital' is merely one specific instance of this general proposition), power inequality is bound to expand in quick succession, and the freedom of the privileged always and necessarily develops at the expense of the freedom of the oppressed.
>
> (Simmel, 1950: 66)

Simmel thus reminds us that in a world such as ours, where the freedom of the individual is sacrosanct, inequality naturally follows, which then, ironically, means that the complaint is inevitable and inescapable.

Nonetheless, the prevailing sentiment essentially tells us that the complaint does not have any perceived benefit or value. Rather, the complaint amounts to a burden to all concerned. Let's listen to one who identifies as a social psychologist and who corroborates this view:

> Instead of bringing relief, complaining may actually lead to the deterioration of affective states in both the complainer and the listener.
>
> (Wojciszke, 2005: 51)

He goes on to say,

> Productivity loss may be yet another component of the negativity trap resulting from or maintained by the culture of complaining. There are several reasons to expect such a productivity loss in chronic complainers. First, preoccupation with negative emotions and recurring negative thoughts

(rumination) consumes mental resources and hinders their use for task solving and instrumental functioning.

(Ibid.: 55–56)

This is perhaps why the one who is seen to have license to complain (say, someone with a debilitating chronic condition) but does not do so is celebrated with sentiments that might take the following form: 'despite the hardships and injustices to which s/he was subjected, s/he never complained'.

It is such an understanding of the complaint that might account for why many preface their impending complaint with the following disavowal, 'I'm not complaining, but....' This conventional resistance to the complaint has come to be seen as a component of the larger criticism that ours is a culture of complaint (Hughes, 1993), or a 'grievance culture' (Baggini, 2008: 3), where many are said to believe that they are entitled to privileged access to collective resources. They are said to not have the appetite for doing the necessary work in order to secure whatever it is that is eluding them. In other words, complainers are said to blame other people for their situation, or any challenges they encounter, rather than facing up to the ways in which they might be responsible for their predicament, or the ways in which they ought to be responsible for their choices and how life has unfolded for them (cf. Baggini, 2008: 104).

In a grievance culture, one's own deficiencies are always someone else's fault. If you do badly at school, it is because the system failed to cater to your special educational needs.

(Ibid.: 114)

What is more, the complainant is seen as self-absorbed, focused on privatized concerns, without any interest in the good of the collective. According to this view, the complaint is typically 'associated with self-serving pleading, not a cry for an end to general injustice' (ibid.: 109).

Let us listen to some instances of the complaint being treated as exemplary of the so-called grievance culture. These examples are from readers' comments in relation to a social justice issue reported by a local Toronto newspaper, *The Toronto Star*. The sub-heading for this particular news story is, 'Protection against discrimination on the basis of family status includes child care and other family obligations, Federal Court of Appeal says' (Monsebraaten, 7 May 2014).

Having children is a lifestyle choice. Please don't ask for my tax dollars to support that choice. Childcare is not an entitlement.

(Muffin – Monsebraaten, 7 May 2014)

Instead of child care in college, maybe you could have taken basket weaving. It might have a higher value in the job market. If you want a decent wage, don't take mickey mouse courses.

(Muffin – ibid., 2014)

Oh yes, let's keep asking the government for more free stuff! Full Day Kindergarten, Green Energy, and a new pension! And then get surprised that taxes went up, electricity rates went up, and withholding taxes go up. What an entitled class we are!

(Socialism is Evil – ibid.: 2014)

If you are envious of Quebec's Child Care Program, then move to Quebec.

(Ronly 2 – ibid.: 2014)

In each instance, the readers' comments tell us that the complainer (the protagonist in the original newspaper article) needs to be put in her place, otherwise she will continue to claim more and more concessions for herself. In this view, the complaint is directed to demanding special status and preferential treatment for an exemption from what others must endure, a situation that is common to all, yet only protested by a few. The complaint is seen as the speech of the special interest group. The upshot it that members ought to 'grumble less and work more'.

Further, the very changes in the political dynamic that made it possible for more generally marginalized groups to raise the alarm about the ways in which they have been and/or continue to be oppressed and excluded is treated as a function of a culture of complaint. What is especially fascinating about such a view is the way in which a 'culture of complaint' is used as a means of dismissing the concerns of the variety of so-called complainers. Not to be missed is that in this view, thinking, reflection and analysis are also consistent with complaining, and therefore to be avoided, as given in a very popular self-help book. Here is a brief description of the thrust of that book:

Two little maze-dwelling, cheese-eating people named Hem and Haw – for the human tendency to think and reflect – arrive at their 'Cheese Station' one day to find that the cheese is gone. The 'Littlepeople' waste time ranting and raving 'at the injustice of it all,…' But there are also two mice in the maze, who scurry off without hesitation to locate an alternative cheese source, because, being rodents, they 'kept life simple. They didn't overanalyze or overcomplicate things'.

(Johnson in Ehrenreich, 2009: 117)

The message here is that one should not 'waste time' examining and understanding the challenges with which we must contend, asking the difficult questions; nor should we have the temerity to inquire as to their ethical implications. Rather, we must conceive the prevailing conditions as always ripe with opportunity.

Consequently, it has been noted that such widespread distaste for what is received as complaining tends to shut down dissent and debate, leaving the status quo untouched. Thus,

Interest rates get more play than social justice these days. In fact, instead of outraged idealism, I hear more outrage at idealism.

(Wexelblatt, 1986: 84)

So rather than complaining about gross and increasing inequality, we are invited to aspire to join the ranks of those who make that inequality palpable. This is exemplified in the following instruction contained in a best-selling book about achieving financial independence:[4]

Place your hand on your heart and say ...

'I admire rich people!'
'I bless rich people!'
'I love rich people!'
'And I'm going to be one of those rich people too!'

(Eker quoted in Ehrenreich, 2009: 93)

We are reminded that the only complaints that are sanctioned are ones that are only ostensibly so, meant to show the subject in a positive light via her connection with something that the culture affirms. For example, one is permitted to complain about being busy and exhausted:

While earlier elites flaunted their leisure, the comfortable classes of our own time are eager to display evidence of their exhaustion – always 'in the loop,' always available for a conference call, always ready to 'go the extra mile.'

(Ehrenreich, 2009: 76)

Similarly, one is permitted to 'complain' about the precociousness of one's children, or an over-active social life, and so on.

Yet, the force of a good complaint might be irresistible, as exemplified here by a resident of a nursing home:

The diminutives! The endearments! The *idiotic we's*. Hello, dear, how are we doing today? What's your name, dear? Eve? Shall we go into the dining room, Eve? Hi hon, sorry to take so long. Don't we look nice today?

(Corbet in Ehrenreich, 2009: 48)

Here, the complainant is able to artfully provide a glimpse of the infantilization to which residents of old age homes are subjected, and thus secure our engagement with the problem.

The complaint according to psychology

Psychology says that the conventional condemnation of the complaint and the complainer misses the important fact, in its view, that the complaint, rather than being a function of a culture of grievance, is simply a very effective means of venting, a strategy for catharsis, for the release of the frustration that is inextricable with everyday life (cf. Kowalski, 1996, 2002; Alicke *et al.*, 1992).

> 'Complaining allows people to vent, to get their frustrations off their chests,' something psychology calls an intrapsychic function.
>
> (Kowalski, 1996: 185)

Psychology's view is seemingly confirmed by this excerpt where someone wrote in to an advice column (The Urban Diplomat) in *Toronto Life* magazine:

> Two of my coworkers live near me in the suburbs, so we drive to work together. Our boss just moved into the neighbourhood and is poking around for a carpool. He hasn't straight-up asked us yet, but it's only a matter of time. The problem is the commute is the only chance we get to *vent* about him. We can't swap that *cathartic bliss* for two hours of awkward silence. What should I say if he asks?
>
> (*Toronto Life*, April 2014: 34; my emphasis)

What is more, psychology tells us that to not complain is to risk self- and self-other harm.

> Type C personality refers to the cancer prone personality. The inhibition of emotional expression is what distinguishes Type C individuals from other people. [...] people with a Type D personality are at increased risk for coronary artery disease because of the stress associated with the inhibition of emotional expression.
>
> (Kowalski, 2002: 1029)

Similarly, here is a prison inmate speaking to the supposed risk of self-other harm from not being able to complain due to the general intolerance of complaining in a prison setting:

> I've always noticed that complaining in a prison setting caused big problems. If the guys kept in their complaints, they tended to end up in mental health wards. If they were too vocal in complaining, they ended up on lock up. [...] If you complain to fellow prisoners, they brand you as a weakling or a sissy. [...] So,... I can see why the return rate to prison is so high. Instead of voicing any complaints, they would tend to 'act out' this suppressed rage when released.
>
> (Ibid.: 1029)

Despite psychology's tolerance for, and general affirmation of, the complaint, it seems to understand the complaint as simply a coping mechanism for dealing with life's frustrations, and nothing else. In this way, the complaint is conceived as a weak form of social interaction where the speaker needs to vocalize without any interest in meaning making or problem solving. It is monological, rather than dialogical or conversational. It cannot adequately imagine social life. So the complaint, in this view, is entirely about affect. It does not wish to register or demand any meaningful change in one's situation or in collective life. Thus, the psychologist would point to the common sentiment of 'stop complaining' as misrecognizing the function of the complaint. Here s/he would say that the complaint is not entitlement and grievance speech, but rather affective speech. The complaint in this view has only the responsibility of making a difference in one's well-being by making available opportunities for the release of frustration.

Similarly, a certain strand of sociology also affirms the function of the complaint, but in this case emphasizing its social qualities of providing for group cohesion, fragmentation, and the socialization of members (Hanna, 1981: 298–311).

The analysis has so far provided a glimpse of four different relationships to, and understandings of, the complaint, and each of those views have been unequivocal in their stance, either as advocates or detractors. This means that the paper has yet to adequately come to terms with the division that the complaint inspires, a division that sees one practice complaining, and yet often experience the complaints of others as misguided. It is to that necessary work that we now turn.

Making sense of the division

Conversational analysis, usefully, tells us the following:

> [C]omplaints are the result of a collaborative and progressive move and complainants do quite elaborate work to prepare the ground for a potential complaint in order to secure the recipient's affiliation. As a consequence, the recipient often ends up being the one who in fact explicates the complaint proper.
>
> (Heinemann, 2009: 2383)

This suggests that the complaint that is represented in ways that invite conversation and dialogue is able to escape censure and resistance. What is more, this imagines the complaint as a form of life that is organized around being-with, and as therefore fundamentally social (cf. Nancy, 2000). This contrasts with the psychological view, which sees the complaint as cathartic and therefore reflective of being-in-the-world as being-for-oneself. So perhaps it is the form the complaint is given that is the crucial dimension in terms of how we respond to it, whether we are engaged by it or whether we find it irritating (reflective of whining, grumbling, moaning and the like). In our desire to persuade and convince the other of the legitimacy (truth) of our complaint, we often resort to the rhetoric of polemics; such polemics risk alienating the listener, especially one who is not necessarily sensitive to nuance. Could it be that the resistance to the complaint has something to do with how the complaint is typically registered, as if there is little need to represent it in ways that reflect the complexity and ambiguity of the problem it references, and to do so with some artfulness? Here, we might do well to listen to Benjamin (1968) when he tells us art and artfulness, unlike what he calls information (which would include the typical complaint), preserves and concentrates its strength and is capable of releasing it even after a long time. The story (which exemplifies artfulness), he goes on to say, invites an investment from its audience in ways that makes of its audience an interlocutor. The story, through its artifice, seduces us into reflection. The complaint, in the form of a well-told narrative, is likely to get past the resistance to engaging that which is taken for granted and secure.

This is what, I think, Calvino wants/means to say in his essay, 'Lightness' (1986: 3–30). Even the weightiest of tasks, Calvino tells us, must be handled with a light touch, what he calls the 'secret of lightness' (Calvino, 1986: 12).

> To cut off Medusa's head without being turned into stone, Perseus supports himself on the very lightest of things, the winds and the clouds, and fixes his gaze on what can be revealed only by indirect vision, an image in a mirror.
>
> (Ibid.: 4)

Is this not a recommendation for how we ought to approach what is in need of being problematized? Calvino further wants us to remember the ways in which such lightness not only makes it possible to slay the Gorgon (that is, invite reflection), but also produces new life, which in its turn, is also generative.

> Medusa's blood gives birth to a winged horse, Pegasus – the heaviness of stone is transformed into its opposite. With one blow of his hoof on Mount Helicon, Pegasus makes a spring gush forth, where the Muses Drink.
>
> (Ibid.: 5)

So perhaps what the 'grievance culture' narrative represents as ingratitude might be reformulated as the debt we owe to each other, and to pleasure, (cf. Lanchester, 1996); to problematize social life in ways that stimulate reflection, and that invites the other into becoming a potential collaborator in a project of collective self-reflection oriented to the question of the ethical. In this way, the foregoing analysis reminds us of the crucial role of the complaint as a vehicle for reflection, for asking difficult questions, directed to a concern with the ethical. Second, it invites us to think about the variety of forms the complaint might take, and whether certain forms might be more effective in permitting for dialogue, that is, for sustaining a conversation in relation to a problem. And third, it raises the question of whether the kind of complaint we find most engaging, and therefore most likely to provoke questioning and reflection, takes the form of sublimation into art and artfulness.

Notes

1 Complaining has mostly been studied in relation to consumer psychology and behaviour. Here the complaint is typically understood as instrumental, as directed to seeking redress or accountability (cf. Alicke *et al.*, 1992).
2 It is perhaps because the Bible teaches us not to complain, to trust in god, regardless of the atrocities visited upon us, as in the example of Job (see Girard, 2011), or of social injustice, that Nietzsche understands Judaism and Christianity as exemplary of slave morality (Nietzsche, 1989), a form of moral resignation and compliance that brooks no complaining. Similarly, we are reminded that, St. Paul even encourages slaves to know their place and keep in it: 'Exhort servants to be obedient unto their own masters, and to please them well in all things; not answering them' (Baggini, 2008, 9). So some might be inclined to argue that it should not be entirely surprising that we have little tolerance for the complaint.
3 This sentiment is widely attributed to Eckhart Tolle, a best-selling self-help author.
4 The book is called *Secrets of the Millionaire Mind*. It has sold over one million copies and has been a #1 New York Times bestseller.

Bibliography

Alicke, Mark D., Braun, James C., Glor, Jeffrey E., Klotz, Mary L., Magee, Jon, Sederhoim, Heather and Siegel, Robin. 1992. 'Complaining Behavior in Social Interaction'. *Personality and Social Psychology Bulletin*, 18 (3), pp. 286–295.

Baggini, Julian. 2008. *Complaint: From Minor Moans to Principled Protests*. London: Profile Books.

Benjamin, Walter. 1968. 'The Storyteller: Reflections on the Works of Nikolai Leskov'. *Illuminations*. pp. 83–110. Translated by Harry Zohn. New York: Schocken Books.

Boxer, Diana. 1993. 'Complaining and Commiserating: Exploring Gender Issues'. *Text* 13 (3), pp. 371–395.

Calvino, Italo. 1995. 'Lightness'. *Six Memos for the Next Millennium*. pp. 3–29. Toronto: Vintage Canada.

Drew, Paul and Holt, Elizabeth. 1988. 'Complainable Matters: The Use of Idiomatic Expressions in Making Complaints'. *Social Problems*, 35 (4), Special Issue: *Language, Interaction, and Social Problems*, pp. 398–417.

Edwards, Derek. 2005. 'Moaning, Whinging and Laughing: The Subjective Side of Complaints'. *Discourse Studies*, 7 (1), pp. 5–29.

Ehrenreich, Barbara. 2009. *Bright-Sided: How the Relentless Promotion of Positive Thinking Has Undermined America*. New York: Metropolitan Books.

Gilmore, J.R. and Trow, J.F. (Publishers). 1863. 'The Complaining Bore'. *The Continental Monthly; Devoted to Literature and National Policy*, 3 (4), pp. 496–499.

Girard, René. 2011. *Sacrifice*. Translated by Matthew Pattillo and David Dawson. East Lansing: Michigan University Press.

Hanna, Charles F. 1981. 'Complaint As a Form of Association'. *Qualitative Sociology*, 4 (4), pp. 298–311.

Heinemann, Trine. 2009. 'Complaining in Interaction'. *Journal of Pragmatics* 41 (12), pp. 2381–2384.

Hughes, Robert. 1993. *Culture of Complaint: The Fraying of America*. Oxford: Oxford University Press.

Kaiser, Cheryl, R. and Miller, Carol T. 2001. 'Stop Complaining! The Social Costs of Making Attributions to Discrimination'. *Personality and Social Psychology Bulletin*, 27 (2), pp. 254–263.

Kowalski, Robin M. 1996. Complaints and Complaining: Functions, Antecedents, and Consequences'. *Psychological Bulletin*, 119 (2), pp. 179–196.

Kowalski, Robin M. 2002. 'Whining, Griping, and Complaining: Positivity in the Negativity'. *Journal of Clinical Psychology* 58 (9), pp. 1023–1035.

Kowalski, Robin M. 2003. *Complaining, Teasing, and Other Annoying Behaviors.* New Haven: Yale University Press.

Lanchester, John. 1996. *The Debt to Pleasure: A Novel.* Toronto: McClelland & Stewart.

Monsebraaten, Laurie. (2014) 'Federal Appeal Court Upholds Landmark Child Care Ruling'. *The Toronto Star.* May 7, 2014, p. A7.

Montaigne, Michel de. 1970. 'On Cripples'. *The Essential Montaigne.* pp. 309–319. Translated by Serge Hughes. New York: Mentor Books.

Nancy, Jean-Luc. 2000. *Being Singular Plural.* Translated by Robert D. Richardson and Anne E. O'Byrne. Stanford: Stanford University Press.

Nietzsche, Friedrich. 1989. *On the Genealogy of Morals.* Translated by Walter Kaufmann. Toronto: Vintage Books.

Plato. 1945. *The Republic of Plato.* Translated by F.M. Cornford. London: Oxford University Press.

Schegloff, Emanuel A. 2005. 'On Complainability'. *Social Problems*, 52 (4), pp. 449–476.

Simmel, Georg. 1950. *The Sociology of Georg Simmel.* Translated by H. Kurt Wolff. Glencoe, Illinois: The Free Press.

Starnes, Bobby A. 2009. 'These Kids Today'. *The Phi Delta Kappan*, 90 (10), pp. 770–771.

Wexelblatt, Robert. 1986. 'Complaining Before and After 1984'. *The Iowa Review*, 16 (2) (Spring – Summer), pp. 68–87.

Wojciszke, Bogdan. 2005. 'The Negative Social World: The Polish Culture of Complaining'. *International Journal of Sociology*, 34 (4), pp. 38–59.

Part IV

Dialogical and dialectical engagements

8　Dasein/Analysis

Blum and McHugh between ethnomethodological heresy and the continental tradition

Steve Bailey

Introduction – between two disappearances

The school of 'Analysis' (henceforth capitalized so as to be distinct from social analysis as such) associated with Alan Blum, Peter McHugh, and a number of likeminded colleagues and students, most particularly Stanley Raffel and Kieran Bonner, emerged in a period, the 1970s and 1980s, of great theoretical ferment within the academy. The ascendance of high theory was evident in a wide array of culturally-inclined academic fields, most notably literary studies, anthropology, and cinema and media studies, in addition to the disciplinary context of sociology in which Analysis emerges. While Analytic work, including of course *On the Beginning of Social Inquiry*, attracted significant comment within sociology, its relationship and indeed contribution to a wider range of research fields and interpretive practices has not been properly recognized. I would argue that this is due largely to the limitations associated with viewing Analysis as a sort of wayward child of the ethnomethodological tradition or, more theologically, as a heretical deviation from ethnomethodological dogma. By reframing the work, to use Goffmanian terminology, as kindred spirit to a wide range of concurrent and indeed earlier thinking from what could broadly be called the continental tradition, the line running from Nietzsche, Hegel, and Kierkegaard (and fueled by the distinct philosophical positions amongst them) to Derrida, Deleuze, and Baudrillard, a clearer picture of both the influences and possibilities of the analytical school emerges. While some of the key Continental figures important for Analysis, most notably Heidegger, are directly addressed in Analytic work, there is relatively little treatment of this larger set of thinkers, perhaps explained by the authors' interest in intervening in the North American sociological scene and in their roots in the ethnomethodological revolution.

Indeed, I would characterize the relationship with ethnomethodology as a dual movement of containment and, simultaneously, a ripping at the seams around more orthodox variations of the ethnomethodological school. Containment in the sense that Analysis can draw upon the value and technical acumen of the ethnomethodological tradition – and its prudence regarding certain interpretive tendencies in classical sociological theory – without accepting the metaphysical extension of this prudence; ripping in the sense that, in a fashion not so far removed from the Derridean enterprise, there is a refusal to let close off the work of interpretation, to let things stand or to be merely operational-ized. Perhaps as is often the case with heretics, there is a purifying impulse at work within the heresy itself, in this case related to a refusal to move with the major currents in ethnomethodology, particularly in reference to the importance of reflexivity for sociological theory and practice. As Paul Attewell (1974) points out in an article published the same year as *On the Beginning of Social Inquiry*, 'What seems clear is that each ethnomethodologist (with the exception of Blum and McHugh who nowadays decline that identification) has reduced the level of analysis, hoping to gain a scientific analysis untroubled, or less troubled by the flaws involved in standard sociology' (208). Refusing this 'reduction', though, was both a dissent from larger trends, as signaled in the protestant shedding of the name, and the maintenance of key earlier commit-ments, most particularly to a reflexivity in theory and research practices. Indeed, the question of reflexivity has dominated many treatments of the shifts in eth-nomethodological orientation as the school of thought gained traction in the 1970s and 1980s.

As an example, in 'Left of Ethnomethodology: The Rise and Decline of Radical Reflexivity', a 1991 reflection on the titular phenomenon, Melvin Pollner argues that while never completely 'extinguished' (his term), the reflex-ive impulse is muted in later ethnomethodological work. Pollner writes, 'as eth-nomethodology is codified into an empirical program concerned with interactional, conversational, or scientific practices per se, radical referential reflexivity is muted, discounted, or disowned. In short, radical reflexivity is left out' (374). In a later review of ethnomethodology's trajectory, published posthu-mously in 2012 and written a few years earlier, Pollner provides a nearly apoca-lyptic take on these tendencies:

> The discomfort of EM 2.0 [Pollner's shorthand for a more recent, non-reflexive strain in ethnomethodology] is born from its across-the-board rejection of representation and formal analysis and from its haecceity – the immediate here and now of the practitioner. Conventional modes of reflec-tion and representation – formal analysis – are either distractions from or distortions of lived presence.... If EM 1.0 risks disappearance through a reflexive dispersion, EM 2.0 – fueled by its disdain for formal analysis – risks, no strives for, disappearance through immersion into the phenom-enon.... Relinquishing or divesting itself of any and every endogenous perspective or analytic concern, EM 2.0 (if all routines are utilized) plum-mets toward and eventually *implodes* in the host world, domain or discip-line. In this respect it articulated a black hole which consumes the social and the sociologist/ethnomethodologist.
>
> (19)

Consider Pollner's vertiginous rhetoric against Jean Baudrillard's reflections on the destiny of certain Continental thinkers from 1987 (translated 1990):

And yet what are the writings of Barthes, Lacan, Foucault (and even Althusser) but a philosophy of disappearance? The obliteration of the human, of ideology. The absent structure, the death of the subject, lack, aphanisis.... They bear the mark of a Great Withdrawal, of a defection, of a calculated failure of will, of a calculated weakening of desire.... A whole generation, by contrast [with the humanist tradition] have disappeared in a manner wholly coherent with what it described, what it sensed, of the inhuman. It is ironic signs that they have left behind, and the whole labour that is left for those whom they have sumptuously disappointed will be to make positive monuments out of those signs, monuments worthy of memory, of a juicy intellectual memory, with no regard for the elegance and style of their disappearance.

(Baudrillard, 1990: 160–161)

While there is a seeming resemblance in the respective characterization of EM 2.0 and the French thinkers by Pollner and Baudrillard, attention to the ways that endogenous empiricism and 'philosoph(ies) of disappearance' enact a kind of withdrawal is important and germane. The real strength of the 'ironic signs' of the latter, despite the best efforts of some of their followers to make 'positive monuments' of them, is in their negativity, their refusal to be absorbed; wilful disappearance, in contrast to the plummet of 'EM 2.0' would be closer to the 'disappearance through reflexive dispersion' of the earlier strain in ethnomethodological thought, one that Pollner connects directly to *On the Beginning of Social Inquiry* through a brief discussion of the 'analytic nerve' required for reflexive analysis (2012: 18–19). The question of intention is most important here, as the willingness to push against the current and dictate the terms of one's own disappearance is to recognize the irony of creating a theoretical position that questions the very grounds of one's own position; this is a characteristic of Analysis and also defines a certain style of European thought, as Baudrillard so keenly elucidates.

Indeed, a type of 'analytic nerve' is at the centre of the relationship between Blum and McHugh's position and both the ethnomethodological tradition from which they emerged and the Continental thinking – and its elegance and style, to use Baudrillard's terms – to which it bears significant resemblances. One might consider this as a form of commitment to acknowledging a certain remainder in the interpretive process, the necessarily incomplete character of any interpretation, and indeed the nerve required to pursue it in the face of the inevitably (partial) failure. Such a remainder is central to the theoretical work developed within both deconstruction and psychoanalytic theory, as well as to Walter Benjamin's earlier work (see Zima, 2002: 75–76), but also to the very practice of reflexive sociological work, a remainder sacrificed in the shift from 'centrifugal' to 'centripedal' directions in ethnomethodological analysis (see Pollner, 2012: 18). Interestingly, Zima describes Derrida's and Benjamin's orientation to a remainder as linked to the 'strong theological tendencies that the latter (Derrida and Benjamin) display when they turn the "magical enchantment of language" into a quasi-religious enchantment...' (75). Just as a perfect translation of any language is impossible (as a vast body of work in the burgeoning field of translation studies demonstrates), so is a perfect or even non-representational analysis of a social practice. Sociological work, and indeed the 'documentary method' itself, is inevitably an act of translation and unable to escape the limits associated with any translation.

Irony as contact point

The religious tone that Zima references is germane to a consideration of the question of ethnomethodology and theoretical commitment, as the former is marked by its own dance around the question of theoretical agnosticism. While Garfinkel somewhat huffily remarks 'we're not agnostic' in a footnote within his 1996 restatement of ethnomethodological principles and explicitly refuses the notion that ethnomethodology is categorically different from 'FA' (formal analysis) as regards theoretical commitments, the centrality of an indifference or agnosticism is certainly a perennial question within the ethnomethodological tradition. Near the end of a chapter of *Self-Reflection in the Arts and Sciences* titled 'Irony: The Way of Life of the Principled Actor', Blum and McHugh (1984) offer the following rumination on the titular question:

> Irony revolves into enjoyment as it grasps the need to resist dualism: on the one hand, awe for the ultimate truth and its contemptuous adaptation to discourse, or on the other hand, enchantment by the notion through the inaccessibility of the ultimate truth. Irony transforms itself into enjoyment insofar as discourse reflects into its necessary togetherness with the ultimate truth as one of its many shapes and looks.... Thus, irony develops at the moment when it has the power to laugh at the notion of the enigmatic character of the whole. It is not that irony denies the enigma, but, rather that it laughs at the notion that the enigmatic character of the whole is a continuously problematic limit for man.... Irony, then, enjoys itself when it achieves the confidence needed to free itself from the guilt resulting from man's thinking of himself as being inadequate vis-à-vis the ultimate truth. The crime irony is often charged with, then, is that it enjoys itself because it does not find the enigmatic character of the whole a *problem* (i.e., it is not a topic for positive inquiry or theology), since it needs to begin with strength rather than inadequacy.
>
> (150)

In this passage and in the larger section from which it is drawn, Blum and McHugh make clear – and I do not intend irony in describing the above passage as clear, though it is certainly dense – their distance from any mode of theoretical agnosticism (even as they express an indifference to theological concerns). Through a Kierkegaardian sense of the ironic as a moral stance, one that Kierkegaard launched explicitly against a technical dogmatism, and also as capable of both recognizing limitations while acting or speaking or writing as if they did not exist, a kind of dualism that can never disconnect but also refuses unification emerges as central to the Analytic position.

The work on irony provides a strong point of contact with the work of Paul de Man, writing in very much the same era, linked to its literary theoretical vanguard, and certainly working in a context many times removed from the ethnomethodological enterprise, albeit engaged in similar dialogue with a very different sort of 'formal analysis', the legacy of 'new criticism' in post-war literary studies. In a lecture given in 1977, and later edited and published in 1996 as 'The Concept of Irony', de Man, working from the nineteenth-century philosopher Friedrich Schlegel, describes irony as the 'permanent parabasis of an allegory', identifying the possibility of an ironic doubleness at any point in discourse, an unsettling but also exhilarating prospect. De Man then focuses on the contribution of the work of Walter Benjamin to the issue, writing (and quoting from Benjamin's doctoral dissertation, *The Concept of Criticism in German Romanticism*):

> He [Benjamin] says, and he uses this Hegelian language here (it's very clear, very moving, very effective): 'the ironization of form is like a storm which lifts up the curtain of the transcendental order of art and reveals it for what it is, in this order as well as in the umediated existence of the work. Formal irony ... represents the paradoxical attempt still to construct the edifice by de-constructing it, and so to demonstrate the relationship of the work to the idea within the work itself.' The idea of the infinite project (as we had in Fichte), the infinite absolute toward which the work is under way. The irony is the radical negation, which, however, reveals as such, by the undoing of the work, the absolute toward which the work is under way. (parenthesis in original).

> (De Man, 1996: 183)

Here, the distinction between what might be considered Benjaminian (and I would argue both de Manian and Analytic) neo-Gnosticism and any ethnomethodological agnosticism seems quite stark. One could read the passage from *Self-Reflection in the Arts and Sciences* quoted above as a working through of the problem of Formal Analysis (in the Garfinkelian sense) vs. ethnomethodology through an ironic relationship to it as a kind of dualism. De Man, though, adds a rhetorical specificity to this orientation, pointing to the movement of infinite and particular, incomplete and transcendent, that Benjamin so poetically identified.

Benjamin's messianic kabbalism or, for that matter, Kierkegaard's Christianity do not seem incidental here, as the movement between the situational and the infinite, even as the latter is always out of reach, defines the ironic encounter as much as it defines a certain spiritual stance. Garfinkel (1996), of course, denounced interpretation, writing that 'enacted local practices are not texts which symbolize meanings and representative of something else. They are in detail identical with themselves and not representative of something else' (8).

Note that this position forecloses the possibility for the parabasis so central to Schlegel and de Man (and evident, aesthetically, in Aristophanes), one that depends upon the ability for the enacted practice to not be identical with itself, to open itself up to the metaphoric and the metaphysical without staking a claim to have possession of that ultimate except as – to use Blum and McHugh's language – a shape or a look. A bit later, I'll consider the poetic dimension of this style of thought, but here I want to think of it in more practical terms, as a way of both refusing an anti-interpretive orthodoxy but also of recognizing the value, to again use their preferred term, of the 'contemptuous adaptation', the very terrain of the conventional ethnomethodological investigation, an investigation that must then be wilfully blind to this very contemptuousness. By recognizing that irony is neither nihilism nor noise (in the sense of Norbert Weiner's cybernetic model, one with its own curious relation to ethnomethodology), Blum and McHugh display their shared ground with a range of thinkers and indeed of schools of thought that extend well beyond Heidegger and into a variety of late Modern European developments in philosophy and critical theory.

Blum and McHugh, though, find pleasure or at least enjoyment in the ironic, and this too provides an intriguing link with de Man's rhetorically-inclined analysis of irony. While they value that irony 'laughs at the notion that the enigmatic character of the whole is a continuously problematic limit for man', de Man provides a wonderfully mundane example of how this very dynamic operates within popular culture in his 1979 book *Allegories of Reading* (again, roughly contemporary with some of the most important early work within the Analytic tradition):

> I take the first example from the sub-literature of the mass media: asked by his wife whether he wants to have his bowling shoes laced over or laced under, Archie Bunker answers with a question: 'What's the difference?' Being a reader of sublime simplicity, his wife replies by patiently explaining the difference between lacing over and lacing under, whatever this may be, but provokes only ire.... As long as we are talking about bowling shoes, the consequences are relatively trivial.... But suppose that is a *de*-bunker of the arche (or origin), an archie De-bunker such as Nietzsche or Jacques Derrida for instance, who asks the question 'What is the Difference' – and we cannot even tell from his grammar whether he 'really' wants to know 'what' difference is or is just telling us that we shouldn't even try to find out. Confronted with the question of the difference between grammar and rhetoric allows us to ask the question, but the question by means of which we may ask it may deny the very possibility of asking.
>
> (De Man, 1979: 9–10)

Thus, the 'sub-literature' of the television sitcom offers a means for demonstrating the comic potential of irony as it provides the irreconcilable contrast between Edith Bunker's inability to recognize the figure of speech and Archie's frustration as one who 'muddles along in a world where literal and figurative meanings get in each other's way (9). De Man's reflections on grammar and rhetoric are pertinent here as well in that they identify the tension that makes things indeed representative of something else, to play with Garfinkel's polemic. Irony does not allow for containment nor for reconciliation, but it does articulate, whether comically or tragically, the tension between the specific practice and the horizons of meaning and meaninglessness linked to an absolute.

Ancestor to analysis: Ludwig Binswanger and Daseinanalysis

If the work on irony illustrates the links to Continental philosophy with a degree of specificity, there is a broader parallel that can be drawn with an earlier school of thought that also tried to work through tensions between an empirical and/or technical mode of explanation and one that attempts to grasp or at least strive for the more elusive horizons of being. In the 1930s and 1940s, Ludwig Binswanger, a psychiatrist and close colleague of Freud, developed an approach called *Dasein analysis* as a kind of existential strain of classical psychoanalysis (indeed it was sometimes referred to, tellingly, as both *existential psychology* and *phenomenological psychology* in subsequent years). Binswanger's interest was in breaking from the biologism and meta-psychology associated with Freudianism – particularly in the era – and mobilizing the thinking of both Husserl and Heidegger in conjunction with Freudian theory to provide a more complete picture of the existential condition of the individual.[1] Here the parallel between the more empirical and scientifically oriented variations of psychoanalysis and the ethnomethodological tradition is worth pursuing, while of course, acknowledging some major differences in orientation. The emphasis on the case study (and indeed the case histories are arguably Freud's greatest philosophical and literary accomplishment) within the psychoanalytic tradition bears a resemblance both to the workplace (the object of obsessive interest in the ethnomethodological tradition) and also, not coincidentally, to the case study-organization of two major works within the Analytical tradition, *On the Beginning of Social Inquiry* and the edited collection from a few years later, *Friends, Enemies, and Strangers: Theorizing in Art, Science, and Everyday Life*. More narrowly, one finds a loose parallel between forms of clinical psychoanalysis in the emphasis on working on internal dynamics (whether of the conversation or the dream, for instance) as the foundation for making interpretive claims when such claims are permitted.

Binswanger's frustration with the limits of the medical-empirical dogmatism that was a part of Freud's work (particularly in the latter's lifetime) anticipates – though certainly not through direct influence – the same drive to both open up – through classical and contemporary philosophical influences and through writerly prose – the interpretive cloister of ethnomethodology; this drive is evident in *On the Beginning of Social Inquiry, Self-Reflection in the Arts and Sciences, Friends, Enemies, and Strangers*, as well as Blum's somewhat more eccentric *Theorizing*. Indeed, in his recent address to the ethnomethodological community, entitled 'The Jouissance of Ethnomethodology', Blum offers some explanation for the heresy associated with the work of Analysis that might illustrate my positing of Binswanger as ancestral to this school of thought:

> Yet, two issues would come to haunt the inspirational impact of Garfinkel: first, there was the problem of distinguishing the practice of theorizing from other practices (playing jazz, playing basketball) as something more than a recitation of the 'tendentious detail' of each practice. Garfinkel might lead us to believe that our interest in *theorizing*, in a way analogous to any practice, would be exhausted in a concern for its detail as a local accomplishment, but this did not begin to tap the richness of the practice as we engage it even as practitioners, what Stanley Rosen calls intuition, or the surfeit of energy registered in the notion of desire. Membership has powers in excess of the practitioner's *techne*, that is, it shows in its heterogeneous appearances a grasp more profound, complex, and ironic. To appreciate that this is not just my stipulation, think of the possibility of ethnomethodology itself – of Garfinkel as a speaker – as irremediably grounded in an imaginative structure (a *writing* Derrida would say) upon which its very local production with its 'tendentious detail' depends. And isn't this what we find most compelling in Garfinkel and Sacks, what makes their writings so special and particular? So, there is something missing, something we might call the 'ghost of desire' or a trace of what Simmel calls the Ought.
>
> (Blum, 2013: 11)

Here, one sees precisely the seam-ripping drive referred to above, the drive to explode the limits of a more contained technical system one finds in Binswanger's interest in supplementing the Freudian system with the more metaphysically inclined work of existential and phenomenological philosophy. What is particularly intriguing about the Analytic deviation from orthodox ethnomethodology as characterized by Blum in the above address is that the attempt at a boundary-crossing heresy relies upon a partial reversal, in intellectual terms, of Binswanger's enterprise.

Blum's reference to the 'ghost of desire' as the missing element in classical ethnomethodological work, work that was, as Blum and many others have discussed, deeply influenced by the phenomenological tradition, suggests that in this case psychoanalytic thought might provide a wedge to pry open the ethnomethodological enclosure. Of course, in the forty or so years between Binswanger's initial forays into a Daseinanalysis and early Analytic masterworks, psychoanalysis had shed much of its scientism and, certainly, Lacanian thinking reflected a strong move away from biologism, thus making it more amenable to a dialogic and even liberating use. As Blum remarks later in his talk,

> I have been discussing the mind as if equipment in the primordial sense of imagination as a tool, relating this notion to Burke's conception of strategy and so, to Lacan's imaginary, showing how mind always implies the desire towards idealization that must ground all speech and action and the necessary

investment in the value of one's own practice that must animate the practical actor, revealing the causal force Simmel identified with value and
called the Ought. Ethnomethodology of course could have none of this talk
because the great expectations for himself as the founder of a movement led
Garfinkel to invest in the dream of being a groundbreaking scientist, tying
together his conception of self and the destiny of his research as a pattern of
symptom formation that could only foreclose other openings, rendering him
deaf to his very creativity.

(Blum, 2013: 13)

Here, Lacanian desire disrupts ethnomethodological 'foreclosure' much as
Heideggerean, Husserlian, and Buberian phenomenology and existentialism disrupt
the clinical foreclosure of the early Freudian enterprise in Binswanger's work. In
both cases, the work of opening up a closed system while continuing to draw upon
the strengths, value, and even 'poetry' of the same systems can be demanding and
can also inhibit the uptake of such work within wider academic circles. While Binswanger was a major figure in developing existential/psychology as a part of psychological thought and therapeutic practice, his influence in social and cultural
analysis – areas in which the major components of his thinking, psychoanalysis,
and Continental philosophy, have held a profound influence – has been notably
slight despite the initial prominence suggested by Foucault's translation. While the
work associated with the Analysis school attracted some very significant attention
in sociological theory circles, particularly in the 1970s and 1980s, it has attracted
relatively little attention in wider studies of cultural meaning-making, an area in
which it held and continues to hold significant promise.

Poet/teacher/theorist

Blum makes reference to Garfinkel's and Sack's 'efforts to solve the problem of
fundamental ambiguity through an impossible dream of purging the surfeit of
poetry from the ethnomethodological sensorium' and I think the poetic dimension
of theoretical work, so important to Heidegger, is worth briefly exploring as a final
connection between Analysis and the Continental tradition. Let me begin on a
perhaps somewhat whimsical note and mention that the title *On the Beginning of
Social Inquiry* triggers a curious phrase-association in my mind with 'Before the
World was Made' by W.B. Yeats, a poem famous enough to be turned into song
by both Van Morrison and, more recently, Carla Bruni. In the poem, a part of his
larger work *A Woman Young and Old*, Yeats provides another variation on the
Romantic poetic fantasy of a pure experience of the world (something central to
Wordsworth and many, many other canonical poets):

If I make the lashes dark
And the eyes more bright
And the lips more scarlet,
Or ask if all be right

From mirror after mirror,
No vanity's displayed:
I'm looking for the face I had
Before the world was made.

In the poem, Yeats' description of 'looking for the face I had before the world was made' could be read, albeit ironically, as a poetic perversion of an ethnomethodological reverse engineering of the social world. But one should not forget that poetry thwarts indifference, thwarts a more tepid agnosticism that might spring from an orthodox ethnomethodology. Heidegger's sense of the unconcealing power of the poetic resonates nicely here with Yeats' postromantic fantasy of an unmade world, but it also identifies a power in the poetic discourse that takes it beyond the confines of traditional aesthetics and makes it a vehicle for truth. Recognizing the poetry in this truth-making enterprise, whether explicitly, as in the Romantic and post-Romantic poets, or in a later process of identification, as in Blum's identification of the incipient poetry – a poetry linked to the titular jouissance of his talk – in the ethnomethodological world, however repressed, is crucial for Analysis as it reflects an uncontainable excess in any social situation.

Here the work of another Continental literary scholar, Julia Kristeva, is useful in its recognition of just how disruptive the poetic can be in relation to a presumed stable and accountable social order. In her masterful *Revolution in Poetic Language* (1974/1985) (some forty years later, still unsurpassed in its theorization of the psychodynamics of the poetic), Kristeva analyses the tensions in poetic language between the semiotic (associated with the discharge of drives) and the symbolic (the representational, meaning-making aspects of language use). As Prud'homme and Légaré (2006) point out in a recent reflection on Kristeva's early work,

> Why take poetic language as a starting point? Because it is a dynamic practice that 'breaks the inertia of language-habits and offers the linguist a unique opportunity to study the becoming of the signification of signs.' As a practice of exploration of the possibilities of language, poetic language is the only complementary system that manifests the infiniteness of the entire code (ordinary language) in its totality, or nearly so.
>
> (n.p.)

In light of the notion that, for Kristeva, poetry offers access to a kind of totality of the symbolic order through a particular literary gesture, consider the description of the teacher and her role in conversation in Blum and McHugh's introduction to *Friends, Enemies, Strangers*:

> To say that the teacher is the custodian of conversation is to say that he seeks to keep safe the recognition that it is only through conversation, as part of the One, that concealment of the One can be disclosed. This is the

strongest sense for the idea that conversation is both topic and resource. The conversation must turn towards itself – it must heed and gather itself in maintaining its place as part of the One. The revolutionary turn of heeding and gathering is the strongest sense for the idea that conversation is reflective.

(Blum and McHugh, 1979: 5)

While the language of the above is certainly distinct from Kristeva's neo-Lacanian, French feminist vocabulary, one finds here the notion that the conversation is a kind of interactional poetry that, in its 'heeding and gathering' can offer a privileged access to Being. Interestingly, in *Theorizing* (published the same year as both *On the Beginning of Social Inquiry* and *Revolution in Poetic Language*), Blum writes, 'to be a theorist is to be able to treat the partiality of speech as if it could be completed...' (116), and builds a larger case for theorizing as a kind of conversation, indeed for reversing 'the silencing of rhetoric' that has characterized the attempt to theorize (172–175). That conversation, at least in its ideal form, resembles Kristevan poetic language, thus places theorizing itself close to the poetic enterprise.

Of course, the choice of conversation as both poetic and as a foundation for theorizing in Blum and McHugh's work is surely not a neutral choice, as 'conversation analysis' was arguably the most influential subset of ethnomethodology and key, as Pollner notes, in the transformation from 'EM 1.0 to EM 2.0' (2012: 17). Paul Atkinson (1988) adds that 'it (the intellectual character of much conversation analysis) is the extreme outcome of what Mehan and Wood (1975) identify as the *logico-empirical* (as opposed to the *hermeneutic-dialectic*) tendency in the ethnomethodological project' (Atkinson, 1988: 454). Thus, in transforming conversation from the object of logico-empirical orientation into the reflexive foundation for the dialectical process of theorizing and education, Blum and McHugh quite cleverly reverse the tendency that, for Pollner and Atkinson as well as their own Analytic school, so diminished the radical spirit of ethnomethodology.

To return to the connection with Kristeva's theoretical work, this transformation might be understood as recognizing a certain negativity in the conversation, not as an unintended consequence nor as failure, but as central to its ability to generate forms of sociological knowledge. As Sina Kramer (2013), explains 'the two most important characteristics of negativity that Kristeva takes from Hegel are the emphasis on movement or process and the relationality or mediation of dialectics. Kristeva consistently describes negativity as a kind of rhythm' (469). The rhythmic quality of social life was important in an earlier age to Georg Simmel, a key figure – although not often cited directly – for the Analytic perspective, and the sense of motion that challenged any stasis in the established order was a part of social interaction and particularly social interaction within the de-naturalized rhythms of modern urban life was an important aspect of Simmel's contribution (Spykman, 1925/1984: 244–245). The nature of these rhythms and their negativity – for both Simmel and Kristeva, at least partly linked to their physically embodied character – is crucial to preserving an openness in dialogue. Interestingly, Kristeva draws upon Plato in her juxtaposition of the symbolic and semiotic that grounds her conception of the animating tension in poetic language, borrowing the term 'chora' from *Timaeus*; Blum dedicates a significant portion of *Theorizing* to an exploration of Plato's importance for social theory and particularly for his insight into the relationship of Being to non-Being (see especially 69–73), and while the two thinkers derive rather different lessons from Plato, they are united in their keen interest in the ambiguities sometimes obscured in a conventional understanding of the Platonic tradition.

Conclusion: anti-dogmatism and analytic style

My intention in exploring the poetic in the preceding section is to demonstrate that there is an orientation evident in a wide range of work from the Analysis school tradition that place it in real intellectual kinship with a range of thinkers distant from the sociological and more specifically ethnomethodological traditions – though Heidegger, certainly, is not without significant influence in some quarters – but that are affiliated with work within literary analysis and critical theory that is not only radically anti-positivistic but that recognizes the unstable charge of language and especially poetic language. Second, much of this work – and Kristeva, who has more recently turned to fiction writing, is a particularly keen example – attempts to mobilize this recognition in forms of academic prose that respect and play with the same instabilities. Of course, this is an endeavour with significant risks, as evident in a brief discussion of reflexive sociology by John Law (1975) (later a major figure in the ethnomethodologically-influenced Actor-Network Theory movement), who refers rather caustically to the 'carpet-pulling school of Blum and McHugh'. Law continues, 'reflexive sociology produces more than its fair share of obscure writing. Hitherto it has been unclear whether this is because there is something difficult about its subject matter or because its practitioners just could not write' (448). Stewart Clegg, likewise writing near the time of *On the Beginning of Social Inquiry*'s publication, 1976, expands the attack on Analysis into a moral critique of a perceived narcissism in Analysis, writing that he hopes will 'display how (Blum's) "theorizing" leads to a narcissistic indulgence with one's self, which is essentially "nihilistic"' (65). Clegg goes on to specify what he perceives to be the root cause of this narcissism,

> 'Theorizing' theorizing is doing a display of self, whereby one engages tradition (language) in dialogue – one engages oneself in one's seeing in a form of intellectual onanism, becuase (*sic*) one's self is only a moment in the history of language.... Theorizing, like fucking, ought to involve an other. And this other is not simply the analytic other that McHugh *et al.* allude to, because essentially in their terms this other is just another 'theorizing ego'.

(84)

It is worth noting that the same work won praise from others for its density and sophistication; Albert Robillard (1976), in still another contemporary review, specifically praises the treatment of otherness in *On the Beginning of Social Inquiry* (293–295), but, perhaps perversely, I think the negative reviews might say a bit more about the place of the work in a particular intellectual moment, the moment in which ethnomethodology was moving toward the its '2.0' incarnation while a wide range of European thought including Derrida, De Man, Kristeva, and Baudrillard was emerging as an alternative version of 'theorizing'.

Here, the condemnations of opacity and narcissism are telling in that they connect the work to a modernist tradition awash in numerous charges of opacity and narcissism, and one with an equal drive to inspire commitment in the reader (and the producer as well, whether it is Harold Bloom's strong poet overcoming aesthetic ancestors or the willingness to take interpretive risks in social research). Indeed, I would argue that at its best, Analytic work demands – and potentially achieves – an intimacy that exceeds the 'fucking' requested by Clegg and an intimacy produced by the shared ground created by an attention to style. Here the words of Theodor Adorno (1990), no stranger to critiques on the grounds of his 'opaque' prose and arguably the strongest critic of positivist social sciences in the 20th century, are insightful,[2]

> The indifference to linguistic expression shown in the mechanical delegation of intention to a typographic cliché arouses the suspicion that the very dialectic that constitutes the theory's content has been brought to a standstill and the object assimilated to it from above, without negotiation. Where there is something which needs to be said, indifference to literary form almost always indicates dogmatization of the content.
>
> (Adorno, 1990: 303)

The anti-dogmatic spirit of Analysis is closely linked, I think, to the pleasure and pain (or perhaps the jouissance) of encountering and working through such opacity to get to the intimacy-beyond-fucking (exemplified perhaps in Yeats' altogether erotic 'original face') that might constitute the spirit of education and theorizing as developed in the key texts of early Analysis, of which *On the Beginning of Social Inquiry* is clearly a touchstone. Understanding this work as claiming its own space between the Continental theoretical tradition and much of the ethos and spirit of the initial ethnomethodological school that it would eventually and necessarily blaspheme helps understand its contribution but also and more importantly its vitality for contemporary critical theory.[3]

Notes

1 And, just as a mild measure of Binswanger's initial influence, I would note that one of Michel Foucault's first published works was a translation of Binswanger's *Dream and Existence* with a translator's introduction. I would also note that as Ruggerone has recently argued, Husserl and Garfinkel share many commonalities in their development of a perspective on the lifeworld.

2 I realize that I may be flirting with cliché myself in the turning to Adorno, as he is frequently marshalled to defend difficult writing, most notably by Judith Butler in
response to receiving a 'Bad Writing Award' from the journal *Philosophy and
Literature*.

3 Part of this early spirit was a radical anti-positivism keenly identified by Zygmunt
Bauman, in an essay titled 'On the Philosophical Status of Ethnomethodology'. In the
essay, Bauman specifically includes Blum and McHugh in his discussion of ethnomethodology and includes both strong praise and some pointed criticism of Blum's work,
connecting it to existentialism.

Bibliography

Adorno, T.W. and Nicholsen, S.W. (1990). 'Punctuation marks'. *The Antioch Review*,
300–305.

Atkinson, P. (1988). 'Ethnomethodology: A critical review'. *Annual review of sociology*,
441–465.

Attewell, P. (1974). 'Ethnomethodology since Garfinkel'. *Theory and Society*, 1,
179–210.

Baudrillard, J. (1990). *Cool Memories*. (C. Turner, Trans.). New York, NY: Verso. (Original work published 1987).

Bauman, Z. (1973). 'On the philosophical status of ethnomethodology'. *The Sociological
Review*, 21(1), 5–23.

Bloom, H. (1973). *The Anxiety of Influence: A Theory of Poetry*. Oxford: Oxford University Press.

Blum, A. (1974). *Theorizing*. London: Heinemann.

Blum, A. (2013, August). 'The jouissance of ethnomethodology'. Keynote address at the
IIEMCA Bi-Annual Conference, Waterloo, ON, Canada.

Blum, A. 'The Jouissance of Ethnomethodology'. Unpublished talk given at the *IIEMCA
Conference: the International Institute for Ethnomethodology and Conversation Analysis*,
August 6, 2013.

Blum A. and McHugh, P. (1979). *Friends, Enemies, and Strangers: Theorizing in Art,
Science, and Everyday Life*. Norwood, NJ: Ablex.

Blum, A. and McHugh, P. (1984). *Self-Reflection in the Arts and Sciences*. Atlantic Highlands, NJ: Humanities Press.

Clegg, S. (1976). 'Power, theorizing, and nihilism'. *Theory and Society* 3, 65–87.

De Man, P. (1979). *Allegories of Reading: Figural Language in Rousseau, Nietzsche,
Rilke, and Proust*. New Haven, CT: Yale University Press.

De Man, P. (1996). 'The concept of irony'. In A. Warminski (Ed.), *Aesthetic Ideology*
(163–184). Minneapolis: University of Minnesota Press.

Garfinkel, H. (1996). 'Ethnomethodology's program'. *Social Psychology Quarterly* 59 (1)
(March 1996), 5–21.

Kramer, S. (2013). 'On negativity in Kristeva's *Revolution in Poetic Language*'. *Continental Philosophy Review*, 49 (3) (Summer 2013), 465–479.

Kristeva, J. (1974/1985). *Revolution in Poetic Language*. (M. Waller, Trans.). New York:
Columbia University Press.

Law, J. (1975). 'Extended review'. *The Sociological Review*. 23 (2) (May 1975),
448–454.

McHugh, P., Raffel, S., Foss, D., and Blum, A. (1974). *On the Beginning of Social
Inquiry*. London: Routledge and Kegan Paul.

Pollner M. (1991). 'Left of ethnomethodology: The rise and decline of radical reflexivity'. *American Sociological Review*, 56 (3) (June, 1991), 370–380.

Pollner, M. (2012). 'The end(s) of ethnomethodology'. *The American Sociologist*, 7–20.

Prud'homme, J., and Légaré, L. (2006). 'The subject in process'. *Université du Québec à Trois-Rivières, 29*.

Robillard, A.B. (1976). Review of *On the Beginning of Social Inquiry* by Peter McHugh, Stanley Raffel, Daniel C. Foss, and Alan F. Blum. *Theory and Society*, 3, 292–295.

Spykman, N.J. (1984). *The Social Theory of Georg Simmel*. New Brunswick, NJ: Transaction Publishers. (Original work published 1925).

Yeats, W.B. (1994). 'Before the world was made' in *The Work of W.B. Yeats*. Ware, Hertforshire: Wordsworth Editions, pp. 230–231.

Zima, P.V. (2002). *Deconstruction and Critical Theory*. London: Continuum.

9 The Analysis school and feminism

Intersection, explanation, and a challenge

Stephen Kemp

Introduction

In this chapter I will compare the views of reflexivity and the situated character of knowledge in *On the Beginning of Social Inquiry* and in some feminist perspectives. One of my aims is to draw out what I see as similarities between the two, which both offer insightful views about reflexivity and its role in social scientific inquiry. These similarities are intriguing insofar as they arose despite the apparent absence of an interchange of ideas between feminist thinkers and the authors of *On the Beginning of Social Inquiry*. A second aim of the piece is to analyse how these similarities might have come about. The third task of the piece is to critically probe the presuppositions of both approaches, particularly in relation to how successfully they break from the assumptions of approaches that they are rejecting. And the final concern will be to consider whether each approach has ideas that can help take the other's project forward.

Given the accounts in previous chapters an extensive introduction to *On the Beginning of Social Inquiry* (*OBSI*) is unnecessary. However, let me note here that it is an early collaborative work by writers who sometimes refer to themselves as proponents of 'Analysis'. The writers involved have gone on to build up an impressive body of work addressing questions of reflexivity, value and interpretation in the social sciences (see for example Blum and McHugh, 1984; Raffel, 2013). More relevant to this volume, however, is an introduction to feminist approaches to reflexivity. The first point that I want to make is that the writers of *OBSI* shared theoretical premises to a large extent, whereas this is less true of feminist defenders of reflexivity. For this reason, it would be quite questionable to give an outline of feminist approaches to reflexivity as if all shared a single presupposition. One, admittedly crude, way to distinguish feminist approaches is to separate those who are more sympathetic to 'realism' and those who are more sympathetic to 'constructionist' approaches to social inquiry. Of course the usage of each of these terms is complex and contested in itself. But, roughly speaking, those feminists who have realist commitments are inclined to see society as a hierarchically structured entity, the characteristics of which can be more or less successfully grasped. For such thinkers, being reflexive involves understanding one's position within this hierarchy and its bearing on the knowledge that one generates. One early contribution to feminist debates about reflexivity with somewhat realist commitments comes from Sandra Harding. Harding is best known for her espousal of feminist standpoint theory and for producing a classic typology to situate it in relation to other approaches, but her 1983 article 'Common Causes: Toward a Reflexive Feminist Theory' addressed the reflexive location of knowledge. In this article, Harding states:

> ...we must be able to explain, understand and criticize our own inquiry practices in terms of the very same kinds of causes of practices and beliefs which our theories claim structure the social order.
>
> (1983: 31)

Harding's use of the terms 'structure' and 'social order' is not misleading here, and she uses them elsewhere in the article along with the claim that the 'sex/gender system' is the key discovery of feminist research (Harding, 1983: 33). For Harding, social structures shape what can be known and reflexivity involves thinking about what these structures permit different groups to 'know' at different junctures (Harding, 1983: 38).

By way of contrast to realist-oriented approaches, feminist approaches to reflexivity which are more strongly indebted to constructionist thought are less keen to talk of structure, cause and system, and more inclined to argue for the importance of language and difference in understanding society. In particular, in constructionist forms of feminism there is a tendency to see language as a crucially constitutive part of social relations rather than as a medium which allows a better or worse representation of reality (see e.g. Miller, 2000). Arguments for this position are often linked to post-structuralist writers such as Foucault (1972) and Derrida (1976) who have, in different ways, rejected representational accounts of language in favour of arguing for its constitutive force. An acceptance of the argument that language has a constitutive role in society is closely linked to feminist enthusiasm for reflexivity because the inquirer's language-use then becomes a crucial topic to explore, and inquirers are encouraged to engage in self-examination in order to understand their contribution to the account of the world that they offer (e.g. Mauthner and Doucet, 2003). In doing so, inquirers explore the ways in which their own social positioning and background has shaped the knowledge-claims that they produce. Here I want to explore the links between feminist constructionism and the Analysis approach, because of the intriguing similarities and overlaps, although I will also be noting relevant differences.[1]

Exploring the similarities between *On the Beginning of Social Inquiry* and feminist constructionism

I want to begin my comparison between the early Analysis work and feminist constructionism by considering the status of language and linguistic utterances in each approach. Crucial to the approach taken in *On the Beginning of Social*

Inquiry, is the idea that any act of writing or speech is not independent or self-subsistent. Rather, speech is dependent on something else:

> Since we treat every finding, every speech, every chapter in this book as a mere surface reflection of what makes them possible, since no speech is in this sense perfect or self-sufficient, speaking and writing is always from the perspective of analysis an inadequate activity.
>
> (McHugh *et al.*, 1974: 3)

What is it that speech, then, is dependent on? For the Analysis school, it is dependent on its auspices, its grounds. It is these that 'make what is said possible, sensible, conceivable' (McHugh *et al.*, 1974: 2). But how are these auspices and grounds to be conceived? I would suggest that the Wittgensteinian conception of 'language-games' is somewhat helpful in explicating this. In the first place, *language* is crucial here. Speech is embedded in language that makes it possible and intelligible, rather than such speech being free-standing. Using another term that the Analysis school favour, speech is grounded in 'convention'. However, language itself is not free-standing but is grounded in interactions with others, and here we can see the relevance of the idea of *language-games*, activities that are conducted with others. These others are, for McHugh *et al.*, a community of language users. It is in understanding the way in which community is conceived of by the Analysis school that the connotative limitations of the term 'games' may become apparent. This is because McHugh *et al.* argue that communities are characterised by deeply held moral commitments, which are expressed in their speech (see for example McHugh *et al.*, 1974: 79).

This focus on the grounding of speech in community reflects what might be called the 'ontological' orientation of Analysis, which is consonant with the authors' interest in Heidegger's work. Although language-usage is crucial to their approach, proponents of Analysis fundamentally connect it to a concern with the deep character of community and relationality. As well as focusing on moral commitments, *OBSI* explores the dialectic of identity and questions of self and other, as apparent in the chapters dealing with *Snubs* and *Travel*. In their analysis of *Snubs*, McHugh *et al.* explore the deep assumptions that are revealed by reflecting on interactions where one participant fails to accept the greeting of the other. These assumptions are revealed to relate to the way in which an actor giving a greeting attempts to collect together self and other in a mutual recognition of their sameness whereas the proponent of a snub withholds such recognition. Likewise, in their considerations on *Travel*, the exponents of Analysis are concerned with the relation of the traveller both to the community s/he leaves and to the community s/he visits, exploring the superficial and uncommitted character of sociality embodied in travelling. From these examples, we can see that the Analysis approach is fundamentally interested in considering the grounds in community and relationality out of which speech and activity emerge. And it is because they argue that any speech act reflects these grounds but cannot ultimately capture them that McHugh *et al.* argue for the situated and always limited character of such speech.

In the first significant overlap that we are noting, feminist constructionists also wish to avoid the idea that speech and writing is self-subsistent. One way in which this concern has had a specific significance for feminists is that in promoting an understanding of the social, cultural and political character of gender relations, they have been concerned to challenge speech about sex and gender that presented itself as 'natural' or as simple 'common sense' (for one example see Davies, 2003: 1–2). The 'obvious facts' of sex and gender were being disrupted by feminists and this encouraged a concern to understand the non-surface, non-obvious roots of the naturalization of gender in speech and writing. In order to theorize the challenge to common utterance, feminist constructionists often drew on structuralist and especially post-structuralist writers.

Probably the most common reference point within feminist constructionism is the Foucault-inspired notion of discourse. The term 'discourse' has a wide range of meanings, of course, and some of this plurality comes through in variations within feminist approaches. Nevertheless, one common usage involves feminists referring to a discourse as a relatively structured and organized set of ideas and practices that shapes possible forms of subjectivity (see for example, Weedon, 1997). Although this is not always fully explicit, discourse in these usages seems to be seen as something underlying what is said, and thus the ground of utterances and their meaning. To use an example discussed in Cameron (1998), when analysing why the word 'Ladies' is used on a toilet door, feminist poststructuralists would not treat the meaning of the word as self-subsistent, or as reflecting nature/biology, but would look at the linguistic and practical discursive grounds which make sense of the use of the term 'Ladies' rather than, e.g. 'Women', and indeed make sense of the practice of separating toilet facilities by sex/gender.

Another line of feminist constructionism takes its inspiration from Derrida. In her work on 'Rhizovocality', Alecia Youngblood Jackson explores the non-innocent character of the voices of participants within research and states that on a poststructuralist view

> ...voice is not transparent; it can no longer express an absolute, ideal, essential meaning that is present/conscious to itself.

> (2003: 702)

Here Jackson is drawing on Derrida's idea that speech cannot be solidly grounded, but relies for its meaning on elusive traces back through previous usages (see Derrida, 1976). And this kind of argument takes the feminist challenge to 'natural' speech a step further insofar as it questions not just the authenticity of utterances that naturalize gender but also the speech of those suffering from gendering processes in society, which is not seen as grounded in the unquestionable realities of their lives.

When discussing Analysis, I referred to its ontological concern with questions of community and relationality. Although a concern with these elements is undoubtedly present in some feminist analysis, it is tempting to suggest that discourse, language, and indeed power, are the fundamental ontological entities for feminist constructionism. That is to say, for the latter approach it is the combined operation of discourse, language, and power that works to create differentiated and unequal forms of identity that are considered the key features of society. I will return to questions of inequality and community in the Concluding section of the chapter.

So far, we have considered an initial similarity between Analysis and feminist constructionism in their accounts of the non-presence of speech and writing. But in each case, this analysis of language is then developed further in order to generate a critical account of certain forms of speech and writing. In essence, what is criticised is those forms of utterance which fail to recognize their dependence on a background that is not full present within them.

For McHugh *et al.*, the form of speech that involves a misrecognition of the character of language is 'concrete' speech. They state:

> Concrete speech ignores its achieved character, violates itself and conceives of itself as first. When concrete speech attempts to locate its grounds it points to 'external' nature, to 'internal' mind(s), to the self-organizing activity of speech itself, or to past events under the delusion that such 'sources' are external to speech.
>
> (1974: 15)

In this quote, the proponents of Analysis outline two ways that those who see speech as concrete can be mistaken about their speech. One is to believe that speech is 'first', which involves failing to see that for speech to occur there need to be auspices and grounds which are the basis of its production. The other mistake occurs when proponents of concrete speech do admit that their utterances have grounds, but wrongly identify the character of these.

Let's explore one example of misidentified grounds. According to the Analysis school, proponents of concrete speech may believe that their descriptions are grounded in nature itself. We can take this to mean that concrete speakers believe that representations of natural objects are underwritten by the state of those objects in themselves. It's worth pointing out here that even concrete speakers are unlikely to hold that *all* uses of language give an accurate representation of their subject matter. If they did, the common aim of distinguishing between true and false representations would be pointless – all representations would be true. What is more typical is the idea that true belief is grounded in nature itself. Who is it that accepts this kind of position? One such theoretical grouping was only beginning to emerge when *OBSI* was published, and can be called realist, relevant sub-categories being critical realism (e.g. Bhaskar, 1975; Archer, 1995) and scientific realism (e.g. Psillos, 1999). Although realists, at times, recognize aspects of the mediating character of representation, they also have a strong commitment to the existence of real objects and processes, and see theories and beliefs as oriented to representing these.

In *OBSI* positivism is a key approach that is identified as having a concrete conception of speech. This might seem puzzling as if we look at, for example, the logical positivists, who often harbour doubts about grounding science in reality, in things-themselves, seeing these as problematic metaphysical concepts. The concern to avoid a metaphysical attempt to use reality as a ground motivates logical positivists to instead treat 'sense experience' as the basic element of analysis. And indeed, many logical positivists might be characterized as conventionalist in character, although there were disputes within the school (see Hanfling, 1981 for discussion). I think this puzzle about the accusation that positivists have a concrete conception of speech can be resolved by noting the sheer variety of uses of 'positivism' as a term, both by those who were happy to classify themselves as such, and by critics (see Bryant, 1985). Thus the term positivism can be used to refer not just to logical positivists but also to those practitioners who adopt a scientistic orientation and have an unproblematic confidence that their claims are grounded in the characteristics of reality (see McHugh *et al.* (1974: 75) for how they characterize the 'positivist' programme).

For the proponents of Analysis, the alternative to a misguidedly concrete conception of speech is speech that acknowledges its grounds. This is easier said than done. As McHugh *et al.* state:

> ...to be caught up in the activity of formulation is to face away from one's own fundamental grounds through which those formulations come about.
>
> (1974: 3)

Thus, in *OBSI* it is argued that speaking turns one away from one's grounds, making their recuperation very difficult. For McHugh *et al.* there is no way to completely resolve this difficulty. However, that does not mean that there is no way at all to avoid the perils of concrete speech. What McHugh *et al.* recommend is the value of collaboration. Collaborators who listen to ones utterances or read ones words can help to identify the grounds of that speech (McHugh *et al.*, 1974: 3–4). Of course, the response of a collaborator does not bring the analysis to a conclusion, as this response also needs to be situated in its own grounds, as part of an ongoing process. Nevertheless, this ongoing situating process is seen by McHugh *et al.* as a way to deepen one's understanding of what is spoken or written.

As with the Analysis school, feminist constructionists have been very critical of utterances, particularly knowledge claims, that do not acknowledge their situated character. One key feminist work which discusses these issues is by Donna Haraway. Haraway has written a range of insightful and provocative discussions which make connections between sex/gender, knowledge, science, technology, and animals (1990, 2003). Here I want to discuss a quote from her well-regarded piece 'Situated Knowledges: The Science Question in Feminism and the Privilege of Partial Perspective' (1988). Even the title of this article, with its reference to 'situated knowledge' cues us in to her feminist concern that knowledge claims should be located. Haraway states:

I would like to insist on the embodied nature of all vision and so reclaim the sensory system that has been used to signify a leap out of the marked body and into a conquering gaze from nowhere. This is the gaze that mythically inscribes all marked bodies, that makes the unmarked category claim the power to see and not be seen, to represent while escaping representation.

(1988: 581)

Haraway is here critiquing forms of knowledge that she presents as oriented to seeing but not being seen, forms of knowledge that do not admit to their own bases, presenting themselves as from nowhere. In this category Haraway places techno-scientific forms of knowledge including those drawn on for military purposes. But it is also worth mentioning that from feminist perspectives the limitations of existing positions are often connected with the influence of a masculine orientation to the social world. So, for at least some feminists, it is an abstract masculine mode of thought and action which tries to conceal its basis by obscuring its roots (Haraway, 1988: 577–578).

In terms of a positive response to these issues, many feminist constructionists have argued that a commitment to reflexivity is an important way to deal with the problems of the 'gaze from nowhere'. On this view, it is crucial that those making knowledge-claims situate themselves, acknowledge that they are coming from a particular position, social background and perspective. One of the questions that has arisen from this feminist emphasis on situatedness is how those in differently situated perspectives can have meaningful interactions with one another, and I want to return to this issue in the final section of the chapter.

I will return to this issue in the final section of the chapter, but now want to consider one more overlap between the Analysis school and feminist constructionism. This is that both approaches criticize the idea that moral and political commitments are 'private' matters to be excluded from research. This argument is made in quite a subtle way in *On the Beginning of Social Inquiry* and it will be interesting to explore the way it comes up in McHugh *et al*'s critique of the positivist notion of 'bias'. For positivists, bias is a problematic feature of research that features it. One important way it is seen to operate is as a form of favouritism towards a particular answer to a research question (McHugh *et al.*, 1974: 49). Where does this favouritism come from? On the Analysis account, positivists see favouritism as an intrusion of the private interests of the inquirer into public, communal, discourse:

When we fail to see community in an inquiry we are expected, according to the rules of the scientific language game, to look for his [*sic*] private interests as the means for understanding his inquiry. When we find such interests, we are charging bias.

(McHugh *et al.*, 1974: 63)

A further intriguing point that McHugh *et al.* make is that many positivist treatments argue that bias cannot be completely removed from scientific inquiry (McHugh *et al.*, 1974: 51). What this means is that positivists both deplore the influence of private self-interest on public inquiry but also admit that it cannot be removed.

The treatment of bias in *OBSI* is complex and I cannot cover all aspects of it here. For our purposes, a key move that McHugh *et al.* make is the argument that what positivists see as favouritism is, in fact, commitment (1974: 51–52). When taken this way, what positivists are recognizing in their remarks about the ineradicable character of bias is, implicitly, the ineradicable character of the commitment of researchers. And for members of the Analysis school commitment is not something that should not be disavowed or proclaimed to be problematic. Rather, it is part of the grounds of an activity which can be (at least partially) recollected through the collaborative work recommended in *OBSI*. Furthermore, these grounds are not to be understood to be private features of an individual inquirer but as shared between members of a community of language use who share forms of life.

Turning to feminism, we can see that a key tenet of feminist methodology has been a rejection of the idea that moral and political commitments are private, and best kept outside of the research process. This rejection has been made on the basis of at least two arguments. Firstly, feminists have been very critical of the public/private distinction and the idea that there is a principled division to be made between the two (for a discussion by a key feminist thinker see Pateman, 1983). This critique has been made on various grounds, but one important aspect, of course, identifies problems with the socio-cultural association of men with the public realm and women with the private realm, an association which connects men with paid work and political activity, and women with the home, domesticity, and so on.

Secondly, feminists have been keen to emphasize that morality and politics, as well as personal experience, are very much part of the research process. Some feminists would argue that this is even the case in the natural sciences, Sandra Harding being one example (see Harding, 1991). But there is almost a consensus amongst feminists that in social inquiry a researcher's moral values, political leanings and experiences have an influence on the research that they undertake. To pick just one example, Gail Letherby is a feminist researcher who states that:

> Feminist work highlights the fact that the researchers' choice of methods, of research topic and of study group population are always political acts.
>
> (2003: 4)

And although feminists are concerned with the moral and political commitments in their own research, they are also keen to highlight that even research which seems 'neutral' or 'un-committed' is still shaped by value commitments. One particular area of focus here has been the attempt to look at purportedly neutral research and expose the hidden masculine values shaping research questions, methods and findings. One classic example of this is Ann Oakley's (1981) critique of the advice given to interviewers by methodologists. Oakley argues that this advice encouraged interviewers to strongly constrain their engagement with interviewees, deflecting any questions directed at the interviewer and operating almost like a mechanical-recording machine. Oakley contends that this is not a 'neutral' way to conduct interviews but one which is shaped by a masculine ideal of the detached, unemotional, unresponsive self, this ideal being premised on a rejection of feminine emotionality, engagement, and so on.

Can we explain the similarities?

Having outlined a number of similarities between feminist constructionism and the Analysis school, I now want to address this as a puzzle: how is it that these similarities exist? This puzzle would be very easy to solve if it turned out that members of the Analysis school were an early influence on feminist constructionists or vice versa. But this simply does not seem to be the case. *On the Beginning of Social Inquiry* was not cited by feminist constructionist writers in the 1970s and 1980s, and has only occasionally been cited by them since (see e.g. Miller, 2000). And feminist views are not cited or discussed in *On the Beginning of Social Inquiry*, although they have occasionally been considered by later sympathizers with Analysis such as Bonner (2001). Given this apparent lack of mutual influence, how are we to explain the overlap?

One possibility would be to call on the kind of theoretical apparatus Foucault develops in *The Order of Things* (2002 [1970]). In this work Foucault argues that different domains of knowledge – those relating to life, language, and labour – share deep assumptions that give them a common underlying structure. These deep assumptions have been transformed at particular points in history, with the result that theories and concepts in the areas also transformed in character. Foucault called these deep assumptions 'epistemes', and he was particularly interested in assumptions about the appropriate way to order objects and those addressing the relationship between words and things. We have already seen that the question of the relation between words and things, or more broadly between words and their subject matter (thing-like or otherwise) is a concern of the Analysis school and feminist constructionism. Foucault's approach also seems relevant in that he is undoubtedly intending to provide an account of how different knowledge-producers can share assumptions when they have not influenced one another. However, in my view there are unsatisfactory elements to Foucault's analysis of epistemes. For one thing, Foucault implies that epistemes are not able to be grasped by knowledge-producers that operate within them (see for example Foucault, 2002: 307). It would be rather ironic if the shared presuppositions of schools that are committed to exploring their own assumptions were intrinsically unavailable to them. However, it seems to me that Foucault does not really offer an argument to support his claim. Secondly, Foucault's epistemes are somewhat mysterious in their operation. Foucault himself acknowledged that he does not give an explanation of what caused them to change (2002: xiii–xiv). As well as this, we can point out that he doesn't give an explanation of why some forms of knowledge are subject to a specific episteme and others are not.[2] Thus, even if we were take up the idea that feminist constructionism and the Analysis School share an episteme, it would be not clear why they fall within this episteme whilst, say, realists do not.

As a tentative alternative, I want to suggest that the solution to the puzzle lies in another factor: shared influences. This might seem an odd claim. After all, there is a case for seeing the three main influences on *On the Beginning of Social Inquiry* as Wittgenstein, Heidegger, and ethnomethodology. Although there is important feminist work in the ethnomethodological tradition (particularly West and Zimmerman, 1987) I think it would be inaccurate to see ethnomethodology as a major direct influence on feminist constructionism. Likewise, neither Wittgenstein nor Heidegger are direct sources of influence on feminist thought in any substantial way. Nevertheless, I think there is a case for seeing one of these writers as having had an important *indirect* influence on feminist thought: Heidegger. The key point here is that Heidegger had an influence on feminism, but mediated through the ideas of Foucault.

So how did Heidegger influence each approach? Starting with *On the Beginning of Social Inquiry*, we might infer the influence of Heidegger from the way that communicative acts are seen as necessarily based in a 'Being' that 'does not show itself in itself' (McHugh *et al.*, 1974: 16), although there are only brief references to Heidegger in the text (e.g. McHugh *et al.*, 1974: 110, 149). Broadly speaking, I would argue that the Analysis school follow Heidegger in seeing speech as 'grounded' in a contingent linguistic community. From a Heideggerian perspective this applies as much to scientific speech as other forms of utterance (Gadamer, 1981: 162–163), and this is developed in *OBSI* through an analysis of positivist practices in the social sciences.

Turning to feminist constructionism, it is fairly clear, as noted above, that proponents of this approach were influenced and inspired by various aspects of Foucault's analysis of language and subjectivity. One concern of Foucault was to challenge the idea of a trans-historical 'subject', that is, the idea that individual actors and knowers might have certain features that were the same no matter what socio-historical era they were located within. This was taken up by feminist constructionists who argued that subjects are crucially shaped by socio-historically located discourses, such that subjects' self-conceptions are (at least in part) a contingent feature of these discourses rather than tapping into some generalized form of rationality or indeed into direct empirical apprehension. Of course, there is a missing link in this attempt to connect feminism and Heidegger here, and that is the connection between Foucault and Heidegger. I admit that there are markedly different views about the character of this link (see for example Ijsseling, 1986; Sluga, 2006; Dreyfus, 1996). One likely reason for this is that although Foucault insisted in a late interview on the importance of Heidegger's writings to his development (reprinted in Foucault, 1988), he made very few explicit references to Heidegger's ideas in his work. The line of argument I want to put forward here is that there is a meaningful connection between Foucault and Heidegger in that both are concerned with the contingent and historical character of subjects, and in the important role of language in producing this (Ijsseling, 1986). In this respect their views are in marked contrast to those of Hegel, who saw the subject as historical but importantly as non-contingent, as travelling through necessary phases of development on the way to the culmination of spirit. Thus, I accept Foucault's remarks about the importance of Heidegger to the development of his thought and see this influence as being taken up and developed by feminist constructionists.[3]

I don't want to overstate my confidence in the explanation that I have provided, but nevertheless I do think it is worth taking seriously the view that the overlap between the Analysis school and feminist constructionism derives, at least in part, from the shared (though in one case mediated) influence of Heidegger. Of course, to *situate* these approaches in terms of their influences is not to *reduce* their ideas to those of predecessors, and both feminist constructionism and the Analysis school push forward our understanding of the situated character of language and subject-hood. In particular, both are concerned not with these ideas as broad philosophical assertions, but with developing ways of conducting and reflecting on social inquiry that take seriously the situated character of the social researcher, and make this a matter for exploration.

Feminist constructionism and *On the Beginning of Social Inquiry*: an issue

Having explored the similarities in the commitments of Analysis and feminist constructionist positions, I would now like to consider one problematic issue with these approaches. This relates to the question of what a reflexive orientation can hope to achieve. As we have seen, both feminist constructionists and members of the Analysis school place a great deal of attention on exploring the situated character of their own knowledge production, and see the value of locating the grounds on which social inquiry is based. The issue I want to explore here is the question of what the ideal form of reflexive knowledge is understood to be. What I want to argue is that there is potentially a tension in the work of the Analysis school and in some feminist constructionist accounts between a recognition of the situated character of knowledge and the ideal of knowledge being upheld. The particular problem here is the way in which both approaches seem to, at least sometimes, uphold transparency as an ideal.

Let me start to develop this with a quote from *On the Beginning of Social Inquiry*:

> ...analysis brings to light the contradiction which every speech re-presents by treating the speech as an appearance of that which grounds it. The problem for analysis is always the difference ... the success of the solution to a problem does not reside in its elimination of a difference – but in making the difference between speech and language transparent.
>
> (McHugh *et al.*, 1974: 18)

Here, one of the contributions of Analysis is held to be the way that it reveals that concrete speech is not identical to its grounds. This is presented as a matter of making this difference 'transparent'. A similar invocation of transparency emerges in the later discussion of the question of positivism and its ideas of bias. McHugh *et al.* state:

> We do not reject bias, but we make its claim transparent by showing how it rests upon a particular version of knowledge and how this version of knowledge formulates adequate speech as speech which accurately describes things.
>
> (1974: 66)

The idea of transparency is invoked in this case as a way of characterizing how the grounds of positivist conceptions of bias have been revealed in the process of Analysis.

The idea of 'transparency' is also invoked at times by feminist constructionists. As an example, let us consider the widely cited feminist methodologists Mauthner and Doucet. In their article 'Reflexive Accounts and Accounts of Reflexivity in Qualitative Data Analysis' (2003) they argue that researchers need to be aware of the various epistemological and ontological conceptions that shape their work: Mauthner and Doucet state:

> We suggest that the particular conceptions employed are less important than the *epistemological accountability* involved in making these conceptions as transparent as possible for the readers of our research accounts...
>
> (2003: 424)

I should acknowledge that these writers don't say that background conceptions can be fully transparent. Nevertheless, the idea that they should be as transparent as possible, that transparency is an ideal, is clearly advocated here.

Moving into a critical mode, what strikes me about the idea of transparency is that it seems to invoke an idea of representation that is actually being rejected by both approaches. It seems to imply a merging of the representation into the represented. This is because when we think of transparency, we think of a layer that is see-through, that allows what is behind it to come through undistorted and unaltered. But both the Analysis approach and feminist constructionists argue in their core accounts that this is not how representation works. They argue that representation is not direct, that concepts and utterances are not 'see-through', but that they necessarily have a thickness, a contribution of their own.

If this point stands, then perhaps what is needed is a different concept or metaphor to deal with what is being advocated. It is interesting to ponder such an alternative, as many potential candidates seem 'realist' in their presuppositions, in a way that is out of keeping with the non-realist presuppositions of these approaches. So talk about 'revealing' the background concepts, or 'revealing' the relation between speech and its grounds, would seem to involve a commitment to unmasking appearances and showing the reality behind. 'Displaying' is perhaps a bit more neutral, and does not have the same connotation of unmasking. But arguably it is still realist, in that it implies that those who are displaying are 'showing' what really is there. Once again, we see that the lingering realism within many such concepts and metaphors makes them unsuitable to replace the notion of transparency.

Of course, there is not space in the remainder of this chapter to develop a substantial alternative. But let me float, if only briefly, a possible conceptualization that does not have an obviously realist orientation. This is the idea that analysts might be seen as 'accounting for' something, taken to mean 'giving a satisfactory account of' that subject matter. So, in the feminist case, what we might say is that it is important to 'account for' the presuppositions of the research. And in the Analysis case the goal would be to give a satisfactory account of, say, the relation between some form of speech and the language that underlies it. The advantage of this formulation is that there is no implication that the analysis in question needs to disappear (become transparent) to be successful. Rather, success is translated into a matter of giving a satisfactory account. Of course, there is a degree of vagueness in the idea of a 'satisfactory account'. However, this vagueness may be analytically advantageous insofar as it does not require that inquirers set up foundational criteria from which to judge the adequacy of their accounts, or identify a state of perfect knowledge as an ideal.

Nevertheless, it is reasonable to ask of this idea of a 'satisfactory account': 'satisfactory for whom?' and 'satisfactory on what basis?' Social constructionists have often linked these questions together, arguing that different social groups frequently have different criteria for judging beliefs, such that what is a satisfactory account for one group of inquirers may not be satisfactory for another. I would follow constructionists on this point. However, those who are inclined towards relativism are likely to add that there is no reasonable way of deciding between criteria, and thus there is no way for a group of inquirers to justify its reliance on one set of criteria rather than another. This being so, the relativist would argue, satisfaction with an account, as it is derived from an arbitrarily accepted set of criteria, is arbitrary itself.

I want to resist this argument. I agree with relativists that there is no meta-criterion which inquirers can use to decide which criteria are justified and which are unjustified. And I likewise accept that there is no algorithmic procedure that inquirers can use to decide between criteria. However, this does not mean that inquirers cannot use contingent reasoning and argumentation to give a reasonable defence (in the sense of giving reasons) for adopting the criteria that they use. We see debates of this kind in philosophy frequently, such as debates about the merits of criteria such as predictive power and parsimony as means to assess natural scientific theories (e.g. Leplin, 1997; Baker, 2003). And in defending their criteria, inquirers are giving reasons for accepting an account as satisfactory, in the context of those criteria.

A relativist might respond to this by arguing that in giving reasons for criteria, inquirers must in turn be invoking some criteria which makes those reasons good ones. And if different groups have different views about which of these higher-level criteria are justified then the debate will go in circles rather than moving forward. I admit this is a possibility. But debates often don't seem to go that way. They frequently seem to involve not disagreements that we can see no way to resolve, but ones that we feel that discussion and perhaps the collection of evidence can have a positive bearing on.[4] This process may not be simple; it may be very drawn out and extended. Nevertheless it does involve inquirers in making reasoned arguments in defence of their approach. And, this being the case, until such debates lead inquirers to change the criteria that they use they can reasonably defend judgements based on those criteria as satisfactory. Thus, my (sketchy) answers to the questions posed before are as follows. For whom is the account satisfactory? For the group of inquirers who uphold the criteria on which its satisfactory character is judged. On what basis is the account judged satisfactory? On the basis of consistency with the criteria upheld by the group of inquirers, criteria that they can give a contingently reasonable defence of using when debating with proponents of alternative criteria.

To note one further point, an emphasis on 'accounting for' some phenomenon rather than rendering it 'transparent' has the advantage for both the Analysis school and feminist constructionism that it emphasizes the work that it is done by the analyst. Whether attempting to give an account of one's own presuppositions or the presuppositions of another approach, the analyst is still engaging in work, and it is exactly this kind of work that feminist constructionists and the Analysis school are interested in exploring. This seems to make 'accounting for' an appropriate concept for the theories of inquiry promoted by feminist constructionism and Analysis.

Conclusion: the future of reflexivity?

Up until this point in the chapter I have been focusing on the perhaps surprising set of overlaps between the work of the Analysis school and feminist constructionism. To conclude the discussion I would like to argue that each approach has something that it could offer the other that would help further develop how each approach deals with questions of sociality and reflexivity.

Beginning with the potential contribution of Analysis to feminist constructionism, this relates to the possibility that feminist reflexive analysis can have atomizing or fragmenting effects. We saw above that feminist constructionists are concerned to situate knowers, but it is relevant to emphasize that this is frequently done by encouraging knowers to locate themselves within intersecting social inequalities. That is to say, feminist constructionists believe that knowers should locate themselves within social constructed patterns of gender inequality, ethnic inequality, class inequality, and so on because of the potential impact of these on the values and assumptions of the knower. The issue that has been raised by some feminist thinkers, however, is the potential for this approach to hermetically seal each intersectionally-formed group of knowers off from the others, e.g. fundamentally separating the views of black lesbian feminists from white heterosexual feminists. That is to say, treating the understandings of knowers in that way seems to assume that members of each group are trapped in their perspective such that interactions with others simply result in each side retaining their pre-existing viewpoint. Useful moves have been made by thinkers such as Susan Strickland (1994) and Sylvia Walby (2001) to challenge the idea of 'epistemological chasms' (to use Walby's phrase). Strickland and Walby argue, in different ways, for the importance of engagement between perspectively-shaped sets of understandings because that will help these to develop. My proposal here is that these conceptual moves could be further advanced by interaction with the Analysis-based idea of collaboration.

As outlined in *OBSI*, collaboration is seen as crucial to Analysis because it allows inquirers to formulate the auspices, the grounds, of their understandings. The model is not simply of 'ego' speaking but a collaboration between 'ego' and 'alter' to help formulate the auspices of the other and develop their understandings further (see particularly Chapter 1 of McHugh *et al.*, 1974). Such an orientation has the reflexive character that feminist constructionists wish to incorporate within their work. But it is also explicitly oriented to engagement with the other and to the development of a perspective, rather than to stasis. This understanding of the productive nature of dialogical collaboration can be further augmented by reference to the work of Charles Taylor, whose ideas have strong affinities with those of the Analysis school. In particular, it is possible to draw on Taylor's idea that the process of engagement should not be treated as one that necessarily leaves one or both sets of understandings intact, but instead should generate a 'language of perspicuous contrast' (Taylor, 1985: 125). By relating sets of understandings through this language of contrast it may become apparent that one or both is in need of revision, thus introducing a dynamic of development. Proponents of Analysis would surely add that this new language of contrast will need to have its own auspices formulated through collaborative Analysis, and this is a further legitimate part of the ongoing work of developing understanding. Although only briefly characterized here, these conceptual resources may help feminist thinkers who are critical of the atomisation of different viewpoints to conceptualize alternative ways of relating.

Is there something that feminist constructionism can contribute to Analysis in order to reciprocate? I would argue that there is. When members of the Analysis school are undertaking a reflexive analysis, their tendency is to focus on features like shared 'forms of life' (or later, the 'lifeworld'), the auspices of which have to be located through Analysis. It seems to me that feminist constructionism can help to take this forward through its concern with the way in which those who share a form of life may, nevertheless, be positioned in different ways within that form of life due to social inequalities. In *OBSI*, McHugh *et al.* reject an approach which argues that 'thinking is "caused" by "things" like society, groups, classes, and world views' (McHugh *et al.*, 1974: 17). In my view this critique of a reductionist approach to the sociology of knowledge is justified. Nevertheless, if one treats inequalities not as 'things' but as meaning-based features of a form of life, their relevance should be acknowledged insofar as positions of advantage and disadvantage are not shared by all, but differentiate members. As well as raising moral issues, these inequalities impact on what can be thought and said by different members, their 'possibilities', and this is something that deserves further investigation.

It would be fair to acknowledge that at least one proponent of the Analysis school has explored some of the issues around the complexity of the community in relation to inequality. McHugh (2005) addresses the inequalities brought about in the USA by slavery and considers the on-going relevance of such inequalities in relation to debates about affirmative action. Although this is undoubtedly an insightful analysis, McHugh's focus is on the justification for affirmative action rather than on the way that inequality impacts on the auspices of different members of the community. It is a concern with the latter that I would suggest feminist constructionism can help Analysis to develop.[5]

Of course, it would be inconsistent of me to argue that in adopting a concern with the stratification of a form of life and the impact of this on the perspectives of members, Analysis should resort to the idea that differently-located individuals have distinct, sealed-off perspectives on the world, each sub-group having its own bounded set of understandings or indeed auspices. This would be to recommend the adoption of an approach that I have just questioned in relation to feminist constructionism. What seems more plausible is that there is some degree of shared understanding and some degree of differentiated understanding between different members of a form of life, and these different understandings are not self-validating and self-sustaining but can be challenged and developed through interaction with others, including collaboration.

I have argued in this chapter that both feminist constructionism and Analysis already share a range of presuppositions. What I have suggested in this concluding section is that both feminist constructionism and Analysis can nevertheless benefit from taking into account aspects of the other's approach.

Notes

1 In making a separation between realist and constructionist approaches to feminism I am setting aside a tantalizing issue about the possible convergence of the two. It might be argued that in seeing social influences as shaping the understandings of inquirers, constructionists are adopting a 'realist' attitude, i.e. seeing these social influences as something that can be represented in their own discourse (cf. Latour, 1992). It is this kind of point that leads Gillian Rose to argue for the uncertainty of self-representation as well as alter-representation when exploring the appropriate approach to reflexivity (Rose, 1997).

2 Gary Gutting notes that Foucault is unclear even on this point, sometimes characterizing his approach as one that does deal with specific regions of knowledge and at other points characterizing his approach as one that applies to Western thought in general (Gutting, 1989: 178).

3 It is perhaps also worth considering here that feminists have also drawn on Derrida's thought (see for example the aforementioned Jackson, 2003) and that Heidegger was also an influence on Derrida (Dews, 1987: 5).

4 My suspicion is that this is because such debates rarely involve two groups whose sets of criteria are such that they share no criteria at all. What is much more common is that groups agree on and use some criteria but disagree about others. The points of agreement can then be drawn on as part of resolving disagreements.

5 I should note that there are hints of how these issues might be conceptualized from the perspective of Analysis in the paper on snubs (see particularly p. 133 of McHugh *et al.*, 1974). These are another resource for developing an understanding of inequality and difference within the community.

Bibliography

Archer, M. (1995) *Realist Social Theory: The Morphogenetic Approach*, Cambridge: Cambridge UP.

Baker, A. (2003) 'Quantitative Parsimony and Explanatory Power', *British Journal for the Philosophy of Science*, 54(2): 245–259.

Bhaskar, R. (1975) *A Realist Theory of Science*, Leeds: Leeds Books.

Blum, A. and McHugh, P. (1984) *Self-Reflection in the Arts and Sciences*, New Jersey: Humanities Press.

Bonner, K.M. (2001) 'Reflexivity and Interpretive Sociology: The Case of Analysis and the Problem of Nihilism', *Human Studies*, 24(4): 267–292.

Bryant, C.G. (1985) *Positivism in Social Theory and Research*, London: Macmillan.

Cameron, D. (1998). 'Gender, Language, and Discourse: A Review Essay', *Signs*, 23(4): 945–973.

Davies, B. (2003) *Frogs and Snails and Feminist Tales: Preschool Children and Gender*, New Jersey: Hampton Press.

Derrida, J. (1976) *Of Grammatology*, Baltimore: John Hopkins University Press.

Dews, P. (1987) *Logics of Disintegration: Post-Structuralist Thought and the Claims of Critical Theory*, London: Verso.

Dreyfus, H. (1996) 'Being and Power: Heidegger and Foucault', *International Journal of Philosophical Studies*, 4(1): 1–16.

Foucault, M. (1972) *The Archaeology of Knowledge*, London: Tavistock.

Foucault, M. (1988) *Michel Foucault: Politics, Philosophy, Culture*, Lawrence Kritzman (ed.), London: Routledge.

Foucault, M. (2002) *The Order of Things: An Archaeology of the Human Sciences*, London: Routledge.

Gadamer, H.G. (1981) *Reason in the Age of Science*, Cambridge: MIT Press.

Gutting, G. (1989) *Michel Foucault's Archaeology of Scientific Reason*, Cambridge: Cambridge University Press.

Hanfling, O. (1981) *Logical Positivism*, Oxford: Blackwell.

Harding, S. (1983) 'Common Causes: Toward a Reflexive Feminist Theory', *Women & Politics*, 3(4), 27–42.

Harding, S. (1991) *Whose Science? Whose Knowledge? Thinking from Women's Lives*, Milton Keynes: Open University Press.

Haraway, D. (1988) 'Situated Knowledges: The Science Question in Feminism and the Privilege of Partial Perspective', *Feminist Studies*, 14(3): 575–599.

Haraway, D. (1990) 'A Manifesto for Cyborgs: Science, Technology, and Socialist Feminism in the 1980s' in L. Nicholson (ed.) *Feminism/Postmodernism*, London: Routledge.

Haraway, D. (2003) *The Companion Species Manifesto: Dogs, Species and Significant Otherness*, Chicago: Prickly Paradigm Press.

Hayles, N.K. (1990) *Chaos Bound: Orderly Disorder in Contemporary Literature and Science*. Ithaca, NY: Cornell University Press.

Ijsseling, S. (1986) 'Foucault with Heidegger', *Man and World*, 19(4): 413–424.

Jackson, A. (2003) 'Rhizovocality', *Qualitative Studies in Education*, 16(5): 693–710.

Latour, B. (1992) 'One More Turn After the Social Turn' in E. McMullin (ed.) *The Social Dimensions of Science*, Notre Dame, IN: Notre Dame University Press.

Leplin, J. (1997) *A Novel Defense of Scientific Realism*, Oxford: Oxford University Press.

Letherby, G. (2003) *Feminist Research in Theory and Practice*, Buckingham: Open University Press.

Mauthner, N. and Doucet, A. (2003) 'Reflexive Accounts and Accounts of Reflexivity in Qualitative Data Analysis' *Sociology*, 37(3): 413–431.

McHugh, P. (2005) 'Shared Being, Old Promises, and the Just Necessity of Affirmative Action', *Human Studies*, 28(2): 129–156.

McHugh, P., Raffel, S., Foss, D., and Blum, A. (1974) *On the Beginning of Social Inquiry*, London: Routledge and Kegan Paul.

Miller, L. (2000) 'The Poverty of Truth Seeking: Postmodernism, Discourse Analysis and Critical Feminism', *Theory & Psychology*, 10(3): 313–352.

Oakley, A. (1981) 'Interviewing Women: A Contradiction in Terms' in H. Roberts (ed.) *Doing Feminist Research*, London: Routledge and Kegan Paul.

Pateman, C. (1983) 'Feminist Critiques of the Public/Private Dichotomy' in S.I. Benn and G.F. Gaus (eds.) *Public and Private in Social Life*, London: Croom Helm.

Psillos, S. (1999) *Scientific Realism: How Science Tracks Truth*, London: Routledge.

Raffel, S. (2013) *The Method of Metaphor*, Bristol: Intellect.

Rose, G. (1997) 'Situating Knowledges: Positionality, Reflexivities and Other Tactics', *Progress in Human Geography*, 21(3): 305–320.

Sluga, H. (2006) 'Foucault's Encounter with Heidegger and Nietzsche' in G. Gutting (ed.) *The Cambridge Companion to Foucault*, Cambridge: Cambridge University Press.

Strickland, S. (1994) 'Feminism, Postmodernism and Difference', in K. Lennon and M. Whitford (eds.) *Knowing the Difference: Feminist Perspectives on Epistemology*, pp. 265–274, London: Routledge.

Taylor, C. (1985) *Philosophy and the Human Sciences: Philosophical Papers 2*, Cambridge: Cambridge University Press.

Walby, S. (2001) 'Against Epistemological Chasms: The Science Question in Feminism Revisited' *Signs*, 26(2): 485–509.

Weedon, C. (1997) *Feminist Practice and Poststructuralist Theory*, Oxford: Basil Blackwell.

West, C. and Zimmerman, D.H. (1987) 'Doing Gender', *Gender & Society*, 1(2): 125–151.

10 Collaboration and the birth of comedy

From the symbolic to the real in the development of analysis

Patrick Colfer

Tragedy, comedy, and the real

This chapter will try to develop tragedy and comedy in relation to the (non)place of the real in life, primarily by focusing on certain key motifs of the book whose 40th year we are enjoying (that is, celebrating and reflecting on) here: *On the Beginning of Social Inquiry* (McHugh *et al.*, 1974).

Zupančič (2008) summarizes Hegel's analysis of the development of the subject universality and the singular through the forms of Greek epic, tragedy, and comedy. In tragedy, via the actors, the universal starts to speak (25). It is not just narrated, as in epic. With the help of the mask, the actor represents the essence. 'This means, however, that here also the essence ultimately exists only as the universal moment, separated by the mask from the concrete and actual self, and that as such this essence is still not actual' (25). In tragedy, 'the actor … has to make us forget his actual self, and see only the sublime character as essence' (25–26). The intrusion of anything contingently related to the actor, bodily functions, and so on, is bad performance.

The universal, that is, remains separated by a mask or a screen. This is related to tragedy's sublimity: in Kant's sublime, 'the Real is situated beyond the realm of the sensible (nature), but can be seen, or "read", in the *resistance* of the sensible or of matter, its inflections, its suffering' (Zupančič, 2003: 170). Drawing on Badiou, and the notion of two lives, life in the biological sense and life as 'the subject's capacity to be a support of some process of truth' (171), if we think for example of Antigone, this other life, the 'unconditional or real life' (171), hence the (tragic) 'truth' of life, 'becomes visible on the scene of death as that something of life that death cannot reach or get at, that it cannot abolish' (171). That is, 'death' names the limit between the two lives, that is, 'the fact that they do not coincide, that one of the two lives can suffer, or even cease to exist, because of the other' (171). The truth of tragedy is thus a deadly truth, or the truth of death, or death as the (ultimate) truth, death as master not only sovereign but true.

The other life, the real life, is visible in the sublime splendour of the tragic image. In tragedy, 'the Real is identified with the Thing' (171), and thus in tragedy, there is 'an *incorporation* of the Real, which makes the latter both immanent and inaccessible (or more precisely, accessible only to the hero who is supposed to "enter the Real" and who therefore plays the role of the screen that separates us, the spectators, from the Real)' (171).

A common response is to contrast comedy with tragedy by seeing it as the human side of representation, 'the physical remainder of the symbolic representation of essence (Zupančič, 2008: 26). Zupančič argues the insufficiency of this conception, and that Hegel goes much further: 'the comic character ... is the very essence as physical' (26). Where tragedy is the duality of abstract universality and Fate on one side and self-consciousness on the other, in comedy, the 'universal powers, gods, Fate, essence' lose 'the form of representation (that is, the form of being separated from the actual self)' (26). That is, 'absolute powers lose the form of things represented by appearing themselves as subjects or as concrete beings' (27).

Zupančič sums up comedy in a Hegelian slogan: '*comedy is the universal at work*' (27). This takes the form of the negative power of the individual self that 'preserves itself in this very nothingness, abides with itself and is the sole actuality' (26–27, quoting Hegel (1977)). The movement develops as follows: 'in epic, the subject narrates the universal, the essential, the absolute; in tragedy, the subject enacts or stages the universal, the essential, the absolute; in comedy, the subject is (or becomes) the universal, the essential, the absolute. Which is also to say that the universal, the essential, the absolute become the subject' (27–28). Comedy, in short, is quintessentially Hegelian in that it accomplishes the key movement of spirit from abstraction to the concrete, and the key movement to the birth of the singular subject as 'the free artist of himself'. Comedy, as the 'universal at work', is the movement of spirit itself.

In comparison with the notion of tragedy as an incorporation of the Real, comedy deploys the paradigm of *montage* in which 'the Real is, at one and the same time, *transcendent* and *accessible*' (Zupančič, 2003: 171), a combination that seems as strange as its reverse (the tragic incorporation of the Real as immanent and inaccessible). Let's draw on an example of comedy from James Sherman (used by permission), and quoted and discussed by Zupančič (2008: 137–147), before we explicate this further.

Hu's on First

By James Sherman

(We take you now to the Oval Office.)

GEORGE: Condi! Nice to see you. What's happening?
CONDI: Sir, I have the report here about the new leader of China.
GEORGE: Great! Lay it on me.
CONDI: Hu is the new leader of China.
GEORGE: That's what I want to know.
CONDI: That's what I'm telling you.

GEORGE: That's what I'm asking you. Who is the new leader of China?
CONDI: Yes.
GEORGE: I mean the fellow's name.
CONDI: Hu.
GEORGE: The guy in China.
CONDI: Hu.
GEORGE: The new leader of China.
CONDI: Hu.
GEORGE: The Chinaman!
CONDI: Hu is leading China.
GEORGE: Now whadd'ya asking me for?
CONDI: I'm telling you Hu is leading China.
GEORGE: Well I'm asking you. Who is leading China?
CONDI: That's the man's name.
GEORGE: That's whose name?
CONDI: Yes.
GEORGE: Will you or will you not tell me the name of the new leader in China?
CONDI: Yes, sir.
GEORGE: Yassir? Yassir Arafat in China? I thought he was in the Middle East.

The conversation proceeds at further length, eventually introducing Kofi Annan, coffee, Rice, and egg rolls, with George directing Condi along the way to 'stay out of China, and stay out of the Middle East'.

Zupančič contrasts the joke, where 'the sparkle (of surprise and satisfaction) is produced at the end', with comedy, where 'there is first an unexpected sparkle (a kind of inaugural joke), and the unexpected surplus it produces is not conclusive, but functions as the motor of the subsequent comic sequence' (139). The 'quilting points' of the comic sequence, e.g. the homonymy of Hu and who, are treated as comic objects that in turn produce further quilting points (Yes sir/ Yassir, Kofi/coffee, and Rice/rice). We see here an example of the 'montage' paradigm at work in comedy, with its 'bouncing ball' or 'ping-pong' back and forth in the comic space (147). 'In this exchange we can observe how a Master-Signifier that pops up in comic sequences is immediately transformed into a comic object that both protagonists try to appropriate for themselves' (147). Zupančič concludes that the comic object becomes 'a compound of enjoyment and sense (Lacan would say jouis-sense, which was translated into English as enjoy-meant)' (147).

Returning now to the notion of comedy's transcendent but accessible Real, Zupančič depicts the transcendence of the Real, that is, the inexplicability, or the 'miracle', of its real effects, as 'the motor of comedy' (2003: 172). As we have just seen in our example, it is the unexpected surplus of the montage or juxtaposition of two semblances that make the Real's transcendence accessible. Comedy is thus the movement, in relation to tragedy, from desire to the drive. Yet this movement is not simple, teleological, it does not abolish what it leaves or arrive at a final point of terminus.

The inaccessibility of the real in *On the Beginning of Social Inquiry*

Let's turn now to the book itself, *On the Beginning of Social Inquiry* (McHugh *et al.*, 1974) where we will see that the centrality of collaboration is closely tied, in that book, to the very problem of the (in)accessibility of the Real.

Analysis makes collaboration necessary. The second sentence of the Introduction informs us that the book is 'also a collaboration' (McHugh *et al.*, 1974: 1). This is not an accidental feature: 'Just as it is our conception of sociological analysis that has produced these topics [e.g. positivism, art, common sense], so also does our conception of analysis make collaboration a necessity and not a happenstance' (1). Various flawed versions of collaboration, such as united fronts, which 'never last', or division-of-labour-based 'teamwork' models (where the individual contributions remain distinguishable), or simple effectivity, are rejected, since they all fail to emerge of necessity in relation to the work.

What then is this necessity? It arises from the nature of the work, which consists in 'the concern not with anything said or written but with the grounds of whatever is said – the foundations that make whatever is said possible, sensible, conceivable' (2). 'An interest in analysis is an interest in [grounds or] auspices' (3), not only in those of the phenomenon (bias, snubs, etc.), but also in 'what makes it possible for us to have produced these descriptions in the first place, i.e. to our auspices, and therefore to what, as it were, makes us possible as well' (3).

The need for collaboration reflects the problematic relation of writing and auspices: 'collaboration is necessary because to write is to lose one's grasp of auspices by attempting to formulate them: to write is to forget why you write; to be caught up in the activity of formulation is to face away from one's own fundamental grounds through which those formulations come about' (34).

Here is the tragic actor whose writing or speech acts as the mask that as such separates the universal (language) from the actual. The separation is experienced not only by the other (the concrete alter), but also in the split between the heroic ego whose passion for auspices is a passion for 'that something of life that death cannot reach or get at', and the speaking/writing, empirical, or concrete ego. In this formulation, the 'essence is still not actual', but remains separated by the screen or mask of inaccessibility. The author/hero does not die, but rather forgets. Forgetting is thus the book's name for the limit between the two lives, the empirical/concrete speaker and the analytic hero, the name of 'the fact that they do not coincide, that one of the two lives can suffer', although he or she does not literally die. Forgetting is thus our protection against destruction by the Thing, though in an analytic sense, it is our destruction by the sublime Thing (language), namely our amnesia. Collaboration is thus the use of the mask (of speech/writing) as a protection against the immanence of the Thing (language), as well as a counter to the analytic death suffered by the (heroic, analytic) ego (by having an alter to remind her of her auspices). The speaking ego, in collaboration with alter, lives to speak and to write another day. Thus collaboration is articulated in *On the Beginning of Social Inquiry* as both necessitated by the (tragic) inaccessibility of the Real and as a kind of antidote that prevents the analytic death (forgetting) from degenerating into chatter, speech indistinguishable from silence, nihilism.

Although we proceed at this point by drawing a sheer contrast between the notion of collaboration as it is articulated in *On the Beginning of Social Inquiry* (as a tragic notion) and the move to a comedic relation of speech to language in *Self-Reflection in the Arts and Sciences* (1984), later in this paper it will emerge that the practice of collaboration provides the vehicle that enacts the movement from one to the other. This in fact illustrates the Hegelian movement of consciousness or development of the notion beginning from the very failure or inadequacy of the initial articulation of collaboration to its notion.

The move to comedy in *Self-Reflection in the Arts and Sciences*

If the issue of tragedy and comedy centres on the problem of the (in)accessibility of the real, this difference can be developed by examining first the difference between *On the Beginning of Social Inquiry* and, published ten years later, *Self-Reflection in the Arts and Sciences* (1984). Later, we will develop the notion of collaboration as the practice (or in Zupančič's terms, the motor) that enables a connection or movement to take place between the two.

The problem that *Self-Reflection* develops throughout its course is that of convention, that is, the symbolic order, the big Other, the level of the signifier. The problem the *Self-Reflection* takes up is whether we are or have to be limited to the self-reproduction of convention, either on the part of members of society, and/or on the part of sociologists themselves.

The book develops the problem of rules and principles as a way of illuminating different possible relations to convention. Where rules orient to the competent actor, the actor who fits into and 'replicates' the symbolic order, the principled (or self-reflective) actor speaks out of a need for a stronger relation than this. For example, 'a spirited relation to [an] injunction requires that we appreciate its point or purpose' (124). And: 'the deep sense of any order depends for its support upon an ascription of necessity without which the order is sheer *techne*' (124). The symbolic order is not self-sufficient or self-sustaining, it depends on the real of spirit. Enjoyment itself is a matter of principle (because enjoyment is more than another convention) rather than something mechanical (enjoyment as merely another convention).

So there is a need to answer the challenge: if principle and enjoyment are other than (more than) convention, is it possible to grasp a sense of the symbolic order that allows us to see it as invested, or as having the potentiality of being invested, with necessity? Here is where the turn to Hegel comes to the fore, precisely as the turn to comedy. Blum and McHugh invoke Hegel's example of Antigone, 'a social being expressing a universal order' (143). 'We conceive of the principled actor as personifying a social necessity' (143). Here, however, we seem close again to the field of tragedy. We must ask, what is it in the self-reflective actor that differentiates this from the tragic-heroic personification of the actor separated by the mask from what is personified?

This is pointed to in the question that comes next. 'Our problem now is to demonstrate how we can develop a positive and enjoyable version of discourse as an ironic relation to language' (143). Or as we might summarize this and make it more pointed for our own inquiry: what would a non-tragic Antigone, an Antigone for whom the Thing is not the Real, look like?

'Everything depends [Hegel wrote] upon grasping and expressing the ultimate truth ... as subject' (143). Here Blum and McHugh make a decisive move: 'the ultimate truth has to be grasped and expressed, and so, in this respect it is subject to the need to grasp and express, i.e. to discourse' (143). Discourse as an ironic relation to language is discourse pervaded by the sense of how the 'majesty [of the ultimate truth] must be adapted to human needs of grasping and expressing' (143). That is, it does not remain inaccessible and destructively immanent, as in the tragic mode, but becomes accessible as comically mediated in the multiplicity of speeches. The movement is from tragedy to comedy, from being crushed by the majestic to the enjoyment of its mediation in the ways it is grasped and expressed. This enjoyment is expressed in and through our participation in the life-world of grasping and expressing the ultimate truth. Through the development of a principled relation to convention, there is a move from alienation in the symbolic (the symptom) to the enjoyment of the symbolic (the sinthome). In our terms, the irony of the ultimate truth's being subject to discourse is what provides for the possibility of comedy, for it is this 'subjection to discourse' that provides for the possibility that the universal can 'work', be active, be alive, that the subject can do more than just represent the universal (like the conventional actor), but can walk and talk as the universal. So the principled actor of *Self-Reflection in the Arts and Sciences* is the comic actor, the 'universal at work'.

From the symbolic to the real in analysis: the Lacanian parallel

In considering the analogous movement as it develops in Lacan's work, Žižek (in Wright and Wright, 1999) provides a useful orientation: 'In the earlier stages [of Lacan's work], the accent fell on the boundary separating the Imaginary from the Symbolic; the aim here was to penetrate through the imaginary fascination to its symbolic cause – to the symbolic overdetermination regulating imaginary effects. In the last stage, the emphasis shifts to the barrier separating the Real from symbolically structured reality: to those leftovers or remnants of the Real that escape symbolic "mediation"' (18). We have to remember that 'symbolically structured reality' here means convention, or the notion of the conventional actor as one who subscribes to the view that there is nothing beyond convention. In this sense of the symbolic-as-merely-conventional, the real, as Žižek puts it, 'escapes symbolic mediation'. The Real intrudes into this order in ways analogous to how principle intrudes into the world of rules: it is troublesome and disruptive to the smooth functioning of this (or any) orderly world.

To illustrate the intrusion of the Real into the symbolic order (or what Žižek calls 'ordinary reality'), let's look at the use he makes of a science fiction novel, Robert Heinlein's *The Unpleasant Profession of Jonathan Hoag*. Private investigator Teddy Randall and his wife are driving into New York, with instructions from Hoag, who is involved in putting right a 'minor blemish' in the cosmos, not to under any circumstances roll down the car windows. They witness an accident and subsequently roll down the window to report it to a patrolman. 'Outside the open windows was no sunlight, no cops, no kids – nothing. Nothing but a grey and formless mist, pulsing slowly as if with inchoate life.... It merged with the frame of the window and began to drift inside' (Heinlein, quoted in Wright and Wright, 1999: 19).

'What is this "grey and formless mist" [Žižek asks] if not the Lacanian Real – the pulsing of the pre-symbolic substance in all its abhorrent vitality?' (19). Žižek notes the place where the Real interferes: 'it irrupts on the very boundary separating the "inside" from the "outside", materialized in this case by the car window'. The jouissance of the intrusion of the Real is disturbing and disorienting as well as exciting and liberating. Without this 'answer of the Real' we remain caught in the web of the symbolic, unable to engage the Real.

This raises the issue of madness, since if madness is in Hegelian terms a loss of the world, 'the closing of the soul into itself' (36), or in Lacanese, being overwhelmed or flooded by the Real, then what differentiates comedy from madness? Does comedy in some sense pass through madness? Is comedy the pharmakon, the little piece of madness that saves us from madness? Can there be such a thing as a little piece of madness? Plato's wager, Hegel's, Lacan's, Žižek's also, is that there can. Can collaboration be one figure for the little piece of madness that is also the way out of madness?

Antigone in the defiles of the tragic signifier

Recall in this regard that we have asked what a non-tragic Antigone would look like. To put it differently, what is it that is 'tragic' about the *Antigone* (the drama rather than the character of the same name), and can we see in Antigone herself something that resists the tragic, despite, in terms of our argument, her inscription in the representational field (representing the Essence) that, following Zupančič, we have designated 'the tragic'?

In our initial response, we pointed to Blum and McHugh's use of Hegel, and the notion of the ultimate truth as 'subject to ... discourse' (1984: 143). The majestic, or ultimate, or the Essence, is 'adapted to human needs of grasping and expressing' (143). In terms of our earlier discussion, this is nothing else than the move from tragedy to comedy, the move from the mere representation of the truth to *being* (that is, grasping, expressing) the truth. That is, the grasping or expressing are not mere representations, they enable the enjoyment (jouissance) of truth to occur by bringing truth to being in speech. In short, the Hegelian movement of the spirit (from abstraction to the concrete) accomplishes the move from tragedy to comedy. Can we now develop this more fully by asking how it plays out in the case of Antigone?

We are asking (and are far from being the first to do so) how it would be possible to read Antigone as resisting the tragic rather than merely representing it? If there is a move from the tragic to the comic (which we will seek to delineate with respect to *On the Beginning of Social Inquiry* in terms of the notion of collaboration), can we read the figure of Antigone, within the dramatic universe set out by Sophocles in the drama, as presaging this movement beyond the tragic? If the drama itself does not present a fully developed 'resolution' beyond the tragic, is there a way in which, as one who has also asked similar questions puts it, Antigone 'enters the discourse of intelligibility' (Butler, 2000: 82) that would open up a future?

Let us return to the relations of tragedy and comedy to the signifier as articulated by Zupančič. As we have seen, in the tragic, the universal (the symbolic order) is 'separated by the mask from the concrete and actual self': tragic consciousness, we could say, consists in taking this separation as definitive. Definitive separation is alienation in Lacanian terms. In terms of Žižek's portrayal of Lacan's development 'from the Symbolic to the Real', we could say that the 'early' Lacan is a tragic thinker in that he defines the subject entirely in terms of this alienation. The symbolic order masks the concrete and actual self, leading to the phenomenon of the 'two lives'. In a case of conflict within the symbolic order (law of the family, law of the state), if this materializes or polarizes as a clash of two mutually exclusive master signifiers (family, state), the Real crushes the one who loses the conflict and thus the protection of the tragic mask. The tragic mask is thus a figure of that which gives us a kind of nobility but does not ultimately protect any of us from the Real of the concrete and actual self, the immanent life that suffers and dies. The lesson of tragedy is thus the inevitability of death, or better, the defeat of the signifier-as-master by death. Thus, for Hegel, both Creon and Antigone are guilty, in the sense that their respective master-signifiers (like all master signifiers) are one-sided. The early Lacan disagrees with this impartiality and rescues Antigone's 'immortalization of the family Ate' as an instance of not giving up on one's desire. Desire and the signifier are thus in an essentially tragic relation. The nobility or 'truth' of tragedy consists in its willingness to sacrifice even its biological life for its 'true' life.

The experience of comedy is a breaking free of this through comedy's discarding of the mask, its experience of the negative power of the individual self that 'preserves itself in this very nothingness, abides with itself and is the sole actuality' (Zupančič, 2008: 26–27, quoting Hegel). Drawing on Žižek, we have portrayed this above as Lacan's movement 'from the Symbolic to the Real', and we have drawn a parallel to the development in analysis from, in Lacanian terms, the 'alienation' of speech and language in *On the Beginning of Social Inquiry*, to the later 'positive and enjoyable version of discourse as an ironic relation to language' (Blum and McHugh, 1984: 143).

Tragic alienation from the signifier is no longer definitive. Without the mask, the Real becomes accessible (to the concrete and actual self), but no longer in its (destructive) immanence but rather as transcendent. What can this mean?

If the Real is what 'escapes symbolic mediation' (Žižek, in Wright and Wright, 1999: 18), how is it possible to avoid what Lacan calls the 'defiles of the symbolic', the defiles of a tragic relation to the Real? Precisely through a revolutionized notion of the symbolic order as that to which we can have a 'positive and enjoyable' relation. Taking this further: it is through the development of an enjoyable relation to the symbolic order that we effect the shift from the tragic to the comedic relation to the Real. In Lacan, this occurs in articulating or analytically working through the four discourses, those of the master, the university, the hysteric, and the analytic. If the master's discourse is the discourse that imposes the master's signifier on the other, while the discourse of the university does the master's bidding for the 'service of goods', and the hysteric always wants to know what the symbolic order wants, the discourse of the analyst is the one that adopts the comedic relation to the Big Other: the symbolic order is itself incomplete and inconsistent. In this regard, the symbolic order is in fact grounded in the Real. Žižek reads Hegel and Schelling as the great predecessors of Lacan in this discovery, and in his major works on each of them (1996 and 1997 on Schelling, 2012 and 2014 on Hegel), sets out an ontology of what this aboriginal 'incompleteness and inconsistency' consists in and what it implies for our relations to the symbolic order. 'There is no Other to the Big Other' (there is no meta-language) does not mean we should simply ignore or reject the symbolic order (the psychotic position). There is a movement, Žižek says, from 'alienation to separation'. In the terms of this paper's argument, this is the movement to comedy.

The event and the real

The contemporary effort in philosophy to articulate the event is resonant with this problematic: how can the Real, that which 'exceeds', be theorized? How should we live in relation to the 'constitutive excess' that insinuates itself into the heart of our being? *Self-Reflection in the Arts and Sciences* is a 'philosophy of the event' in the sense that the book's problematic is the principled actor beyond rule-governed convention. That is, it presents the principled or 'self-reflective' actor as an 'event' in relation to convention. Indeed, *On the Beginning of Social Inquiry* was and is considered by readers to be, an event. It was, and remains, memorable as the book that first *declared* analysis as an event within sociology, and its status as an event seems to hinge around or rely on the fact that it declared its own eventfulness in this way.

What is the significance of this self-declarative feature of *On the Beginning of Social Inquiry*? Zupančič (2003) in fact identifies the same tension of declaration and event in relation to the work of Nietzsche, and if we examine this it will enable us again to retroactively, as it were, bring out a certain strange, and comedic, temporal structure in *On the Beginning of Social Inquiry*. The issue turns around the relation of the declaration and the Real. Thus for Badiou,

Nietzsche's declaration of the event of his philosophy, his 'ecce homo' so to speak, remains tragic in that 'the declaration lacks the Real' (9), causing Nietzsche to 'have to make himself appear on this point of the Real' (9, quoting Badiou). For Badiou, 'this is precisely what will be called Nietzsche's madness' (10). In other words, Nietzsche becomes an Antigone-like figure, being tragically consumed by the real as sublime Thing. It is Zupančič's contesting of this that can provide us with some suggestive beginnings for both a comedic Nietzsche, and an *On the Beginning of Social Inquiry* that opens through collaboration towards comedy.

For Zupančič, in Nietzsche, 'the event is not external to the declaration'. She compares Nietzsche's declaration to an avant-garde manifesto. The manifesto does not lack the Real, but has the structure: 'I, the event, am speaking'. That is, it speaks from inside rather than outside the event, because 'the point is that the declaration is itself part of the Real it declares' (11). Zupančič uses the example of a declaration of love: it stands on the ground of the Real. It is a 'precipitated statement' that creates 'the conditions of [its] own enunciation' (12).

Collaboration and the comedy of the edge

Zupančič positions herself at the duality that is not a mere opposition but a Mobius 'topology of the edge', where the edge is the thing 'whose sole substantiality consists in its simultaneously separating and linking two surfaces' (12). This edge 'makes [the Real] take place through the very split that gives structure to this duality' (12). The truth takes on the paradoxical structure of only *becoming what it is*, or as Lacan put it, the truth is that which runs after truth.

Zupančič's formulation of truth has the most direct bearing for my purposes: 'The temporal mode of truth is that of existing *as its own antecedent*' (13, emphasis added). In *On the Beginning of Social Inquiry*, analysis exists as its own antecedent, precisely in this sense.

There is an economics of the event involved here: Nietzsche says 'I live on my own credit'. This is 'to pawn something which one does not yet have and will only become what it is' (Zupančič, 2003: 19). In terms of *On the Beginning of Social Inquiry*, which this brings to mind, collaboration is the living on the edge (in this instance between ego and alter) that honours the temporal transition from the earlier to the later. Collaboration, as long as this is rightly grasped, is thus the name of the work that redeems the credit required by the event. Here we must understand work as the universal at work, the movement of spirit itself.

As *On the Beginning of Social Inquiry* itself puts it, alter and ego, in 'collaborat[ing] to generate analysis' (McHugh *et al.*, 1974: 4), help each other to remember, since 'to write is to forget why you write' (3). Yet collaboration does not redeem credit in the same way that bankers do, for this would be collaboration in the tragic mode (the split between the two lives, the sublime creator and the concrete, empirical, indebted worker). Collaborators give each other what they do not have to give, they live on their own *and each other's* credit – and this is the necessary edginess and riskiness of collaboration. Collaboration occurs in the knowledge that the debts can never be called in, that the credit is not that of finance capitalism. As *On the Beginning of Social Inquiry* already says in effect, collaboration must be principled, not instrumental. It is driven by its own declaration of the event that it is. 'I, the event, am speaking'.

The edge does not merely separate, it also connects. Comedy enables us to inhabit the edge by giving us delight in what in life would otherwise be merely banal, empty or disgusting. Collaboration, as evidenced in the unfolding of the event of analysis subsequent to *On the Beginning of Social Inquiry*, has the capacity to enact a movement from the temporality of the tragic (destruction by the sublime, or endless deferral of that destruction) to that of the comic (credit, surplus, and becoming what one is). In this way, the practice of collaboration does not render *On the Beginning of Social Inquiry* comedic-in-itself, but leads the collaborators to the (comic) enjoyment of discourse that is subsequently announced in *Self-Reflection in the Arts and Sciences*.

The charges against the comedic

Given that the comedic is in a certain sense more 'cavalier' than tragedy towards life, it provokes the hostility of non-comedic discourses. Whereas tragedy pays due respect to death (by studying the failed attempts of the mask to protect the 'concrete and actual self' from the Real), the comedic promotes a transcendence through the Real that unapologetically celebrates the 'indestructibility' of the concrete and actual self, or better, her drives – akin to the indestructibility of the cat in the cartoon, who always returns in full health in the next scene no matter if he has been steamrollered flat, or diced and shredded, just moments before.

One way to open up a conception of a 'non-tragic' Antigone is to remind ourselves of the charges made against the comedic. Because comedy is principled in its enjoyment of the symbolic order, the pleasures of the text, the charge against it are invariably, of course, a lack of due reverence towards the symbolic order, but in addition, and tellingly, a 'cerebralism' or over-intellectuality in its enjoyment. We may discern this critique of comedy in the trial and condemnation of Socrates by his contemporaries, the citizens of Athens, as well as by so many in the tradition since. Thus Socrates was charged with not respecting the gods, and thus corrupting the youth – and with being a gadfly, an endless questioner, engaged in something akin to Garfinkel's (1967) experiments in disruption, and with similar results. That is to say, not respecting the 'seriousness' of the daily business of the citizens. Among contemporary responses, Socrates' critique of tragedy is seen as a refusal to acknowledge the 'fragility of goodness' rooted in the dualism of the Idea, that is, excessive distance towards life (Nussbaum). Again, Henry Staten in *Eros in Mourning* (1995) critiques Lacan by likening him to Plato (Chapter 8: 'The Bride Stripped Bare, or Lacan *avec* Plato') as one who engages, through psychoanalysis in Lacan's case, in a distancing from everyday life and its losses that is punitive in particular towards the feminine. Many others, including Hegel and Nietzsche themselves, might be added to this list of accusers.

Conclusion: comic distance and the economy of the real

In terms of the argument of this paper, comedy is a shift from the tragic representation of the universal to the declaration of the event, a declaration that announces the engagement of the Real in the enjoyment of discourse. We have seen how there is a parallel between the movement from the symbolic to the Real in Lacanian psychoanalysis, and in sociology the movement from the tragic to the comedic in analysis.

We have said that analysis, like Nietzsche, declares the event of itself, or lives on its own credit, or is its own antecedent. What do such images betoken? Is this a matter of Zeus giving birth to Athena from out of his own head, without the aid of a mother? Or as Lacan puts it at the end of Seminar XI (1981: 276): 'Any shelter in which may be established a viable, temperate relation of one sex to the other necessitates the intervention – this is what psycho-analysis teaches us – of that medium known as the paternal metaphor'. Or what of the old motif of Socratic midwifery? Is this too a kind of sublimation that only works by devaluing (in the Naming of the Father or the Idea, that is, in the name of the idea, by the Son Plato) the transient, the changing, life itself?

The challenge of comedy is to redeem such gestures from the charge of sterility or asceticism by taking its place in everyday life as the drive's enjoyment of the partial object that enables us to place our mourning of our 'lost objects' as an immanent condition rather than a sign of a more truthful but inaccessible (and hence tragic) transcendence.

Comedy's claim is that our topoi are not those of finitude and death, but rather excess and sex. This it declares through exuberant explosions of energy that motor themselves through the force of the unexpected letters of the symbolic itself.

Comedy (at its best, in its fidelity to its notion) seeks collaboration as the risky or edgy, principled, evental, engagement with the real through the symbolic. This collaboration, besides being risky, is also essentially and unavoidably selective. In declaring itself as an event (visible in the ways comedy signals its difference from the non-comedic, indeed accentuates its self-contained and artificial character), comedy challenges the interlocutor to enter into a collaborative relation. All declarations, the Nietzschean, the avant-gardist, or the analytic, are challenges to the other (but also, as is often forgotten, to the self). Think here of Oscar Wilde to the customs official: 'I have nothing to declare except my own genius'. I, the event, am speaking. In the case of a stand-up comedian, for example, the collaboration is with the enjoyment of the audience ('of' in both the transitive and intransitive senses) – that is, an audience that 'gets the joke'. The enjoyment requires the good delivery and timing of the comedian and the audience's alertness and responsiveness to the quality and the pleasure of the jokes: it is the combination that brings about a 'good night at the show'. Hence we tend to see an explicit display of challenge or edge on the part of the comedian towards the audience members as a key element in such a show. This is essential for all true collaboration. So the distance or separation is there, in that the comedian, far from becoming indistinguishable from the audience, or the members of the audience from each other, rather creates an edgy (non)world that invites and provokes us, for a time, to take up the challenge it throws down, to collaborate.

Bibliography

Blum, Alan and Peter McHugh. (1984). *Self-Reflection in the Arts and Sciences*. Atlantic Highlands: Humanities Press.

Butler, Judith. (2000). *Antigone's Claim*. New York: Columbia University Press.

Garfinkel, Harold. (1984 [1967]). *Studies in Ethnomethodology*. Cambridge: Polity Press.

Hegel, G.W.F. (1977). *Phenomenology of Spirit*. Oxford: Oxford University Press.

Lacan, J. (2005). *The Seminar of Jacques Lacan Book XI: The Fundamental Concepts of Psychoanalysis*. New York: W.W. Norton & Company, Inc.

McHugh, Peter, Stanley Raffel, Daniel E. Foss, and Alan F. Blum. (1974). *On the Beginning of Social Inquiry*. London: Routledge and Kegan Paul.

Nussbaum, Martha. (2001). *The Fragility of Goodness*. Cambridge: Cambridge University Press.

Sophocles. (1984). *The Three Theban Plays*. Translated by Robert Fagles. New York: Penguin Books.

Staten, Henry. (1995). *Eros in Mourning*. Baltimore: The Johns Hopkins University Press.

Wright, Elizabeth and Edmond Wright. (1999). *The Žižek Reader*. Malden: Blackwell Publishing.

Žižek, Slavoj. (1996). *The Indivisible Remainder*. London: Verso.

Žižek, Slavoj. (2012). *Less Than Nothing*. London: Verso.

Žižek, Slavoj. (2014). *Absolute Recoil*. London: Verso.

Žižek, Slavoj and F.W.J. von Schelling. (1997). *The Abyss of Freedom/Ages of the World*. Ann Arbor: The University of Michigan Press.

Zupančič, Alenka. (2003). *The Shortest Shadow*. Cambridge: MIT Press.

Zupančič, Alenka. (2008). *The Odd One In*. Cambridge: MIT Press.

11 Resistance in collective and collaborative problem solving

Andriani Papadopoulou

The exemplification of Analysis in *On the Beginning of Social Inquiry* as collective-collaborative problem solving provides the opportunity to re-think the notion of resistance This is so because theorizing, in the form of collective-collaborative problem solving, stands as the purportedly rational discourse between an 'ego' and an 'alter' through which the auspices of any behaviour or social action may be constructed or revealed. Theorizing in this sense includes attending to the incompleteness of the actor's actions, such as what 'ego' and 'alter' do, or leave behind or unsaid, in order to construct the rationality of their action.

This conceptualization of collaboration generates a feeling of uneasiness: it seems that for better or worse we must suffer our incompleteness. The theorist is never alone and whatever he/she considers depends on or presupposes others. Consequently the theorist is unable to provide answers or solutions to inquired matters despite being driven and tempted to do so. The 'other' would always make sure to disclose the theorist's impotence. Perhaps then this version of collaboration does not fully grasp the truth of the relations of 'ego' and 'alter', or of how interactional life is lived. Rather, it reveals an image of the battle carried on over the incompleteness of the actors as a reflection of some 'ultimate truth' – how things are – when this is the fact that is ultimately being challenged by the very act of attempting to collaborate.

The notion of resistance has been preoccupying me for a long time. In my dissertation I thought of it as it related to subversion.[1] More recently I began thinking about resistance when my work as an Ombudsman failed to bring about resolution, through collaboration, in situations where the lives of people were at stake. Having tried to comprehend the standpoint and interests of the players involved in these situations, having made every effort to satisfy different needs and demands, and fill in gaps, in the end, in certain situations crucial to the lives of those involved, there was failure. It could, of course, have gone the other way, though the game would have been the same. Attending to the standpoints of the players involved (including myself), trying to identify the auspices that made these standpoints and interests sensible, while simultaneously utilizing the possibilities or the pitfalls presented in these situations, and thus making every effort toward bringing about a desired resolution, is worthwhile even in view of the fact that in the end, what may remain from this endeavour is a sense of the struggle and a conflicting feeling about its impact.

Roma: the threat of otherness

To comprehend the situation where a collaborative effort in an actual social setting could be called for and to highlight the role resistance plays in its various forms, let us consider the following example.

At the very centre of Athens there is an illegal settlement of a large community, composed of approximately a thousand people, adults and their children, foreign citizens, of Roma descent. This totally spatially and socially excluded community (hidden from the main road by the remnants of old factories) has resided in this land for more than a decade. A makeshift camp, established on mostly private lands, and composed of huts made of collected wood and plastic materials, is this community's home. Of course life here is unacceptable for human dignity and the conditions of human health. None of the large number of children of different ages attends school, no adult has stable employment or is part of the typical labour market work, and the subsistence of the population is attained by gathering and selling metal and other scrap, or by begging and/or by engaging in non-lawful activities. These activities (for example, the burning of tyres or of electrical wires to extract the metal they contain) are not only in discord with the law but also extremely dangerous and toxic. Due to these subsistence activities serious social discord, with racist manifestations, is generated between the local non-Roma and the Roma residents, with the former demanding the removal of the latter from the area. The different aspects of the problem, practical and philosophic-political, multiply as one examines them vis-à-vis the interests of each of the parties involved. The situation created brought together diverse groups and interests (the local residents, the Roma themselves, the local and central authorities, police authorities and other control agencies, international human rights organizations, activists for the protection of the environment, and perhaps cells of international illegal trafficking).

Manifestations

What is at play in a situation such as this that will be of interest from the point of view of the notions of collaboration and resistance? The usage available in this situation is the stirring, in opposing directions, of compartmentalized interests of distinct people and of diverse activities, which takes the form of an unstable formation.

On the surface, all the involved players agree on the goal: namely, to have the situation resolved in a fair and just manner (i.e. in respect of the rights of all involved and in addressing the needs generated in an appropriate way). To this end, the relocation of the camp and the integration of this population into wider society was the way to go. However, how this was to be implemented was the point of disagreement, as every time a particular procedure or measure was proposed, it was felt that it was again like holding and unfolding Ariadne's thread. Understanding all the aspects of this complex social problem, unveiling and understanding its causes in order to determine the proper and just solution to it, was the challenge presented. There is no need, for the purposes of this paper, to refer to all actions that were thought/initiated in order to resolve this issue. Suffice it to say that the initiative to bring the players together to collaboratively find ways to adopt the policies and measures required to accomplish the desired aim failed. In the meetings that took place it was really interesting to observe the specific issues, concerns, obstacles that each of the players, due to their areas of competence, expertise, and interest, brought to the forefront. On the surface, most of the players engaged displayed interest and willingness to work so that a resolution could be found. However, they were reluctant to accept the responsibility to do what was required. For this reason, the most serious and structural measures, which had to be adopted, were postponed with various justifications. During this intermediary period of contacts and back and forth discussion in the decision making of actions to be undertaken, we learned, by chance, by reading newspapers, that on a fine August day in the year 2010, the Roma camp had been demolished to the ground. The whereabouts of the members of the community are unknown and it is assumed that some of them, after they were taken to the police for identification, were deported, while others perhaps were scattered in other areas of the country, creating new makeshift camps. For the time being, the acute problem disappeared from the centre of Athens, while the State has been slow in dealing with new camps in areas where they have appeared.

The aim and the process

Reflecting on this particular effort and on the inability to produce an instance of real agreement and convergence of the actions of different actors to resolve a serious and complex social issue in order to achieve a common goal – namely, the real integration of a community – I wonder what went wrong and how things could have gone otherwise if the process of collaboration had been accomplished differently.

The image of people stirring with different interests, being in danger from one moment to the next, being swallowed by an undifferentiated marsh (pointlessness, nihilism), or by the difficulty and the tediousness of the process of distinguishing what is essential to preserve/avoid and then developing a path out of it (social contract, understanding), is still very powerful. Armed with the ideas of justice, fairness, and general will, which abstractly neutralize or supersede differences, one feels obliged to try to bring to life a better balance between people and things. But in so doing, one rejects or negates the existing divisions or differences, perhaps by considering that they are inessential, the result of accident or egotistical interests. On this basis, there occurs the procession towards a resolution defined as the 'common interest' or a 'better life'. The goal could of course be something else.

Acting in this manner, the situation is deemed unacceptable. Forgetting what its content is (the existence of deep differences) the doer embarks on a process of establishing a new situation, which, in fact, presupposes that which is rejected. Putting aside the knowledge that the motivation in doing this betrays a stance of godly superiority, of know-how, and of the power of denial and of creation (overcoming a sense of shame), the doer embarks on their path towards achieving their goal like Don Quixote attacking his windmills, superseding both their own vanity and the resistance of reality. Vanity is hidden under the intention of carrying out a humanistic duty while reality is taxonomized: at one level, there is the realization that there are communities which, by their very nature, are distinct and separated from other communities. At another, there is the recognition of the particularity of their distinctiveness (e.g. being an oral travelling community). At still another level stand the challenges this authenticity represents for others. Priorities are set and the consequences that these challenges present to the prevailing order of things are measured. Solutions are selected and ways to implement them are adopted. Some of the consequences of their materialization (i.e. preserving the order, altering it in some form or other, letting things unfold as they may) may be thought of, but always under the frame of the set goal.

Accepting that external conditions, such as the hidden agendas of 'non-involved' decision makers who made the decision for the demolition while this whole process was on-going, the players who were not sincere in their 'collaboration', and the inability to foresee and to take into account unpredictable consequences, cannot be controlled, how can the initiative to collaborate bear fruit? In other words, is this an example of a failure to collaborate?

To judge whether this was a failure, we must ask what was the product or the expectation of collaboration. Also, how are we to comprehend failure? Is it meant as the inability to arrive at a resolution or as destroying the ambiguity that is the ground of it? Is this a technical failure, that of forgetting to attend to a factor, or is it an essential failure, of unsurpassable resistance? If so, what is the source of this? What goes wrong when you try to apply in reality the principles, processes and goals that may work in theory? Was it *naiveté* to embark on such an initiative believing that the different players could be motivated into courses of action and decision making towards a desired goal? Is the in-itself of collaboration therefore encapsulated in its success or failure, or in its doing? And what is that? Is it the bracketing differences (disregarding limits), in the attempt to be neutral (no trace, impersonal) or the initiation of a new path?

Furthermore, what is the role of resistance in all this? Is it the various forms of opposition of the disputing parties? Is it the unconscious, perhaps, perseverance of the type of life different players embody? Is it the vanity and stubbornness of the collaborators? Or, is it what Hegel calls, '*the rich and concrete abundance of real life*',[2] that is, that which is unsaid, the auspices which enable the doer to act and which always reveal the one-sidedness of their complete structure?

Different approaches

I realize that theorizing is not the same as dealing practically with reality. In the conference that generated *The Reflexive Initiative*, we have addressed this issue in many different ways: One such way (presented by David Lynes[3]) was by addressing the distinction between the concrete and the analytic. In that view the concrete was linked to the failure to theorize. Applying Lynes' approach to our problem, the players in our case could not attend to another's standpoint or authentically seek convergence or resolution due to being too concrete in the sense that their singular, egotistical interests led to indifference or blindness to the theoretic ground which makes these interests sensible.

Also, in the analysis (presented by Chamathka Devasiri[4]) of Crito's friendship with Socrates, the same issue was addressed and there the character of Crito was constructed as the one who couldn't comprehend and essentially could not take part in theorizing, despite Socrates' maieutical effort to bring him to that path. However, who is Crito in our example? The public servants, the Roma who did not succumb to or comply with the demands of the order, the State/society that does not see the problem represented by the Roma? Crito perhaps is any character who does not search for the reasons which make the 'other's' action or stand meaningful, sensible, or just.

There was also the intervention (of Patrick Colfer[5]) which raised the question of who really is the 'other' in Analysis and how the 'other' may be addressed as the real other in Derrida's terms. This last standpoint helps to make the connection which I am trying to point out: *The 'other'* (the 'concrete', 'Crito', citizens/public servants, Roma) *is not an inessential, bothersome detail that we could do away with. What we arrive at in theoretical terms, through Analysis, since it derives from reality, should have a practical impact in ordinary life.* This is not meant in the sense of transporting conclusions and theories in everyday practice which, as we very well know, may lead to authoritarianism or totalitarianism and thus to the death of theorizing. It is not in finding an ideal type forcing disputants to agree. That would be imprisonment, a denial of life. It is also not a collection of points of view which are all seen as equally valid.[6] That would be creating a life in the form of Babel. It is rather meant in the sense *of applying the method of Analysis so as to resolve tensions, gaps, bring down walls and create an environment where new things may flourish.* That is, to make choices in and through life so as to unleash possibilities for a better life. This is where the unity of the two (the concrete and theorizing, necessity and freedom) is exemplified.[7]

Discovering why people act the way they do, trying to comprehend how what they say and do is possible, rational, and sensible could enable us to identify the common ground upon which collaboration may unfold and the resolution of the problems that occur. With regard to our example this would mean to think about the challenge the Roma community presents to our bureaucratically organized society: what is the place of an orally sustained culture, of a community whose poverty undermines our prevailing system of fairness and justice? In a system which values achievement only in the form of success within the system, as an outcome of the individual's interest, compliance and effort, what role is played by a way of life which contravenes its established rationalistic, hierarchical organization?

The analytic point of view

In *On the Beginning of Social Inquiry* collective-collaborative problem solving does not occur naturally and it is not simply the result of happenstance.[8] It is a necessary relation because of the nature of the 'doer', 'the ego', and the 'alter'. The 'alter' attends to the ground left behind by the 'doer' who, in order to act, must necessarily negate the basis that makes his/her act possible. In other words, by acting (deciding, writing, doing anything) the 'doer' changes form, and what he/she wanted to accomplish or strove for, stands as incomplete, less than what it could have been. The 'alter' reveals this – intentionally, as in comedy, or unintentionally, as in not being able to control ahead of time all the consequences of one's doing. In other words, in *On The Beginning of Social Inquiry* both the 'doer' and the 'alter' are conceived as existentially, necessarily I would say, incomplete. This is not meant in the sense of needing a supplement. 'Alter' is not thought of as a crutch for 'ego'. Nevertheless, their doing is conceived as something negative, and collaboration is the way of overcoming or surpassing this negativity.

However, if, instead of attending to this incompleteness, attention is placed on the force that encapsulates the doing of 'ego' and 'alter' then we may comprehend the meaning of resistance. Collaborative problem solving is necessary because actors always, consciously (and this is what interests us) or unconsciously, resist. How are we to think of the 'alterity' represented by the Roma and of the relations this generates?

In terms of usage, we know that there are different forms of resistance: in order to be born, for example, you need to fight all that may negate you. To preserve your way of life, as an individual and/or as a group (irrespective of whether it is worth preserving or not), you will have to confront what might annihilate you.[9] A writer or an artist's existence is captured by what distinguishes him/her, by their mark, which essentially means that they have opened up a new path amongst the chaos of so many others. As it is shown in the photo[10] below of the 'children playing tag', the outcome of resistance is not something separate from the game, and despite the pulls and pushes it is unquestionable that through resisting we exist and create new forms of life.

In the photo of the children playing tag, the meaning of resistance takes physical form. It is opposition but also togetherness; it is pull and takeover; it is being: laughter, sunny faces of success, but also of effort, of anger, and disappointment. In this game there is always a loser and a winner – more or less. The photo also captures that beyond the bodies there is the shadow that unites them, as a force beyond them (i.e. tradition, what we start with, our predecessors). There is also the ground, solid, unmovable (principles) in which they stand and which makes it possible for them to play. Is problem solving a game in which all

Figure 11.1 Children playing tag.

the aforementioned are some of its manifestations and is collaboration a way of preventing the dissolution of the game?

There could be no need to consider 'collective or collaborative problem solving' if there was no *resistance*. Resistance I consider to be at the heart of Analysis. The engagement of 'ego' and 'alter' would not even make sense unless we attend to the force that encapsulates 'their doing': resistance as being, as prevention, as negation, as criticism, as conflict and simultaneously as bonding, hands tied together while the players are pulling apart to win. But what lies beyond the dualism of opposition and togetherness?

Derrida would tell us that there is nothing else and that just the disclosure of the necessary binding by these opposites unleashes possibilities which, if 'ego' or 'alter' would not take advantage of, others will. Thus resolution is not necessary. The possibilities unleashed through disclosure lead to different paths, some of them already known (such as armed struggle), others to be created utilizing imaginative linkages (as in art and in theory). But then what about the question of justice or fairness as opposed to enslavement and impoverishment? How does being the medium of unleashing possibilities serve the interest of fairness and justice in communal living? Does understanding the motives or interests of the actors suffice as an answer to the problem of building a community/ society on the basis of justice and fairness (irrespective of the content these notions acquire at different historical times)? In other words, is it sufficient for the theorist to always reflect on this process, which may be produced as a response to different kind of motives, and remain detached without seeking its real life materialization? In fact is the temptation to see it materialized a desire to concretize it and thus destroy it? How can the theorist, as a simple 'doer' who takes into account the 'other', participate in exemplifying the interest in justice in his/her everyday living without bringing an end to theorizing?

Socrates, and Plato, for that matter, would not leave things to chance. Having already set a goal or having identified a new one through the process of disclosure, through reasoning, they will outline a path that will lead to a resolution. Not a final one of course, and not unchallenged, but nevertheless a resolution. Their effort is directed in reaching it and finding pleasure in the effort of overcoming resistances. In this manner, theorizing actualizes as a form of life of combating ignorance and striving to achieve a positive end. However, this resolution is achieved by having the 'other' comprehend their flaws or failures. As such it can be considered as not being respectful to life and as having actual consequences in it and that is why, according to Aristophanes, this process remains in the realm of the *'thinkery'* and foreign to everyday life.

Aristophanes then haunts Plato and Socrates and by revealing the one-sidedness of their achievement (that form of philosophy) laughs at how handicapped, incomplete, they seem. With regard to our example, Aristophanes would say it is not enough to comprehend the challenge the Roma present but to create the conditions so that their life will not be on the outside of the parameters of society, i.e. outside conditions of justice, as this notion is comprehended by the society in which they live.

The risk of collaboration

In view of the above, it seems that we have organized, as it were, with the help of Aristophanes, a new Symposium: Life is lived, marks are left behind. We do not care about the marks that were not materialized, due to blindness or incompleteness, but for those which took form because they were willed.

The danger in collaboration is that it might become fossilized through typification or bureaucratization.[11] Here the temptation is to secure, to assimilate, to find and exhaust all possible courses of action relevant to the problem, all arguments that may be raised about it so that, victorious, we may safely arrive at the conclusion that nothing was left outside this structure, nothing was left unsaid, nothing left to the imagination or accident. However, this temptation means the end of collaboration since in essence it seeks to eliminate the real 'other'.

Furthermore, resistance could be negated if it becomes a goal in and for itself. The figure of the subcomandante Marcos portrayed in the photo below[12] constitutes such a representation since it denotes resistance as entrapped in a process of continuing opposition, a battle to overthrow the system that keeps the people of Chiapas permanently in poverty and servitude.

Of course this version of resistance may be due to the negating reaction of the State vis-à-vis the revolt of the people of Chiapas, which is very different from that exercised by the Roma in Europe. Nevertheless, despite the just cause, one cannot avoid seeing this transformation of resistance as a constant battle for survival, which does not change course and form depending on the circumstances. This happens when we lose ourselves in the nostalgia of what we wanted to achieve and carry on a battle that has no relevance to reality any more but is an abstract adherence to principles or ideas and as such may be characterized as violence, in more ways than physical force. Resistance in this case is overcome by time since its occurrence is always in the present.

Figure 11.2 Subcomandante Marcos, Chiapas.

Beyond the aforementioned, for me the absence of resistance represents a vastly greater danger, that of homogeneity and slavery. Imagine if everything that was said, created or proposed was accepted without critical thinking, without resistance. What would life be like? It will be a life in uniformity, in similitude, a life without colour. That is the image that comes to mind when I think about life without resistance. In this type of life there will be no need for collaboration since agreement and compliance would be automatic, already imposed, without any hint of the temptation to think that it could be otherwise. Is this kind of life unknown to us? What about Nazism, globalization, or the attempt of authorities, political and intellectual, to govern what we do by putting first the need to 'sustain order'? Do we not need to ask which order? The terror that this image of the absence of resistance generates is something that should stay with us so that we may always stand against it.

The photo below[13] shows some Roma individuals together with their German captors before they are led to the death camps.

To the reader the absence of resistance is unveiled here: the Roma, whose very existence embodies a different way of life and culture and was considered a threat to the Nazis, stand together with their captors unaware that they were about to be led to the death camps. Their presence, their existence, their (unconscious perhaps) perseverance to 'remain' different in view of the prevailing culture, was conceived as 'resistance', as the threat that had to be eradicated. Unaware that their very particularity was the cause of their predicament, they were peacefully following their German guards. The German officers themselves carrying out orders to take people to the death camps do not stop to think what that meant and if they should do it. For different reasons, both parties fail their human nature by failing to think, i.e. to question and to resist. And we all know what the result of this was.

Figure 11.3 Roma under German guard.

What then should we learn from this today? What is that we should do when we are encountering a way of life that challenges the one we are immersed in, which frightens or bothers us or which may enchant us by its call and by the fact that despite every opposite effort is not going to disappear or eliminated? This call resembles the call of the sirens: what would happen if we give in to it?

I don't know if resisting is different from simply being. But it seems to me that it is a positive way of being. It is willed, it is followed through; it is having a direction and attending with certainty to a goal. It is living instead of worrying about what is missing. This is the innocence and the blindness of resistance. Resistance to oneself, to the other, to forms of life that might negate us, may itself appear as backwardness or stubbornness. Still this is better than playing dead or letting oneself be taken over.

The positivity of resistance, as I see it, is battling with death, with obscurity, with indifference. Through this battle the ground of collaboration is made possible. This is not to deny that resistance involves a number of different and possibly contradictory senses. It manifests itself as strength when persons' control is challenged; as demand when facing opposition; as attack when battling domination; as endurance when withstanding hardships.

The presence both of danger and desire seem unavoidable as the strength of resistance is usually manifested as an exercise of a dialectic of internal versus external control. Very often resistance is pictorially represented as a raised fist or as brandishing a weapon, which entails battle. As such, it appears as polemical and does not show the internal impetus for doing so, or any obvious connection to the idea of collaboration as necessarily involving the 'other'. Less common is the representation of resistance as an invitation not to openly engage in battle but to simply be, that is, to sustain a way of life in the face of opposition, irrespective of the negative stand against it. Roma have sustained their culture and way of life in the face of extreme opposition to without polemically fighting for the preservation of it but by enduring, surviving.

Resistance in this sense should be considered as perseverance. The presence of the Roma as defiantly distinct, culturally and ethnically, accounts for their treatment as a threat that had to be eradicated or subjugated by the representatives of the hegemonic culture. This rarer way of comprehending resistance is, we argue, more closely related to its essence and to the need for collaboration that stems from the existence of alterity, an alterity which may not be obliterated.

The forms which resistance takes in life disclose their essence as a 'political' stand in life: it is an assertion of strength/power when established power or rule is challenged. The one who resists treats the order[14] which is confronting her/him as foible, not as sacred or as 'off-limits' or unbeatable. In this way resistance speaks 'truth to power', to the power it combats and the one it brings to life. It does so by simultaneously obliterating limitations and demarcating new ones, by unmasking the fallibility of 'ultimate truths' and 'ultimate solutions' while revealing its own. Through the excess it produces in this process resistance rejuvenates life.

Epilogue

Recently, going out to dinner late one night, I met a group of very young Roma children selling flowers to passers-by. I asked them where their parents were (selling flowers at another location, they told me), what they do with the money they earn (besides contributing to the family income they are allowed to buy shoes and whatever else they want), if they were going to school (none of them was), how they avoid the dangers of the night (being in a group helps) and finally if the police ever bothered them or showed concern about them being out this late working. The disarming reply of an eight year old girl was, 'Oh yes, one of them actually gave me a fine of two hundred euro'. 'They gave *you* a fine?' I asked. 'Yes', she said with a giggle. 'In what name?' I asked, knowing that such a young girl could not have an identity card. She said: 'Oh, I made up a name and an address and told him and he wrote the fine', still giggling.

The absurdity of the whole situation, irrespective of its seriousness, led me to laugh as well. The eight year old knew how to resist, how to contravene the system, while the action of the police showed the indifference towards the real issue as well as what it means to bureaucratically carry out your duty. Perhaps the policeman presumed that in acting this way he was giving a warning. However, the fine, since it was written and issued, will still be sought and some other public servant will be preoccupied with collecting a fine from a non-existent person. The absurdity of the system and the co-existence of two totally foreign worlds were facing me, generating innumerable issues that could be of interest in this situation.

Analysis, as exemplified in *On The Beginning of Social Inquiry*, provides a path that enables consideration of collective-collaborative problem solving from the standpoint of resistance. That is, from the standpoint of attending to the 'other' as an 'alter' who returns to us the fertile ground to both criticize and combat but also to reflect on what our actions are all about. Today the conditions of life we encounter, without eliminating any of the dangers facing humanity of the past, have added a plethora of issues to consider, at a single moment, in order to make a decision or to choose a stand. In order not to be lost in either the multiplicity of possibilities available, thus forgetting what is essential, or in the obliteration of differences, thus eliminating alterity out of fear or expediency, we should always attend to the auspices that make our stand possible and rational, so that we are guided by a view of what is of value for humans and of the life we truly desire to live. Certainly this will be revealed by our stand toward the foreigners in our mist, to the most vulnerable of our compatriots and, perhaps, to our 'enemies'.

Theoretically the relations of 'ego' and 'alter' have many ways to be constructed through their collaboration. There are, however, only rare illustrations of this construction in everyday life. The example of the Roma in this paper tells us that in real life differences are not easily accepted or overcome and that the creation of a community as envisioned in theory is as difficult to build in reality as in theorizing. The same passions, flaws, mistakes and obstacles occur in both. Resistance is showing us this. It is also shows us that when guided by an interest in justice we will embark on collaboration by not treating the difference between the concrete and the theoretical as belonging to completely different realms but as feeding each other.

Therefore, what is shown through our exploration of resistance in the setting of collaboration is that, however humble or grand our motives are, when we embark on problem solving, the 'others' who would meet in this process will object, challenge us and reveal our limitations and flaws whether by choice or force. This should not lead us to despair, by making us feel that we after all are not gods or heroes strong enough to transport our ideas to reality. Facing the opposition, or acknowledging limitations and obstacles, may mean that we need to follow another path and to accept that we may not have the answer we were looking for at the beginning of our endeavour. Instead of treating this condition as a failure, we should attend to what it has made possible. Embarking on a process to create, as the example of the Roma allowed us to do, a formulation of the problem of establishing a just society, where the other remains an 'other' and where what is thought of as best, just, and fair, stands opposed to that which constitutes hubris for human life.

Notes

1 Andriani Papadopoulou, *The Place of Comedy In Social Life*, (Doctoral Dissertation) Toronto: York University Press, 1994, pp. 223–280.
2 As Alan Blum pointedly reminded me.
3 David Lynes, 'On The Beginning of Social Inquiry – The Movie: "Analytic Wit" and Everyday Life', Edinburgh Conference presentation July 2014.
4 Chamathka Devasiri, 'A Case Study in the Application of the Dialectical Analysis on Friendship and Shared Understandings in Plato's Crito', Edinburgh Conference presentation, July 2014.
5 Patrick Colfer, 'From The Symbolic To The Real In The Development Of Analysis' Edinburgh Conference presentation, July 2014.
6 We are reminded here of Jose Ortega y Gasset's, *The Revolt of the Masses*. New York: W.W. Norton & Company Inc., 1957.
7 Is this standpoint itself a form of instrumentalism? Is it cheating and/or a barbaric turn to avoid facing the real struggle of theorizing? I do not believe so, as we shall see.
8 We see the difference here from practical problem solving.
9 The common reaction to the Roma is that they do not want to be integrated; that they do not want to become like all others; that not taking part in the education system indicates battling assimilation on their part; that even if they built houses they would still have a tent next to them. However, it is the Roma whose way of life and culture represents a genuine challenge to prevailing, bureaucratic culture.
10 *The Photographer Voula Papaioannou: From the Photography Archive of the Museum Benaki*: Publisher Agra, Benaki Museum, Athens 2007, p. 375 [293. 'Play in a camp', Karpenisi (?) 1945–1946].
11 With regard to our example, it could not have helped if the whole process of discussions were organized better, if the questions were more specific, if an action plan was demanded of all. Beyond all these possible additions are the interest and the will of the players to collaborate. This interest may not be replaced by a mechanical procedure or ethic of how to carry it out more efficiently.

12 http://upload.wikimedia.org/wikipedia/commons/7/71/SubMarcosHorseFromAfar.jpg
citation: Jose Villa. Subcomandante Marcos, the spokesman of the Ejército Zapatista
de Liberación Nacional in Chiapas, Mexico. Distributed under a CC BY-SA 3.0
license. Extracted 20.1.2015.

13 http://upload.wikimedia.org/wikipedia/commons/3/36/Bundesarchiv_R_165_Bild-
244–47,_Asperg,_Deportation_von_Sinti_und_Roma.jpg. Photographer Unknown.
Sinti and Roma about to be deported from the German town of Asperg, 22 May 1940.
Provided by the German Federal Archive (Deutsches Bundesarchiv). Distributed
under a CC BY-SA 3.0 de license. Extracted 20.1.2015.

14 Whatever that may be, i.e. the existing political system, the status quo, common
sense, etc.

12 Analytic desire and everyday life

The practice of theory in *On the Beginning of Social Inquiry*

David A. Lynes

Part I The theory of practice

The 40th anniversary of the book *On the Beginning of Social Inquiry* (1974) serves as an opportunity to reflect upon one of the most enduring and compelling aspects of the work, something that might best be described as a perplexing problem as well as a mandate. It is the problem of the need to live in the everyday world with the knowledge of what this book offers and exemplifies in the form of a commitment to what is referred to in the book as analytic desire. Insofar as appreciating the need for this desire engenders a will to pursue the social inquiry named in the title, the problem the book presents is how to live up to or do justice to whatever it is you know after reading the book that you did not know before. What does the practice of the pursuit of the theory the book proffers, consist of or look like?

An important assumption underlying this question, an assumption not incidentally integral to the theory the book both is about and enacts, is that the pursuit of a theory that would call itself social, needs to and will make a difference in one's life. It is a difference that extends to how one lives life, including everyday life, a difference which is integral to a life that could be called socially/ theoretically responsible. While questions about the relations between theory and practice are never simple or straightforward, what makes them particularly challenging in this instance is that the book is about the grounds of speech. In light of the fact that the grounds of speech are what makes speech possible and so are always and necessarily presupposed by any speech, they are, as the authors emphasize in the book's introduction, 'hidden'. In light of the concealed nature of these grounds, however, the only way of uncovering them and revealing the essential role they play in the origin and production of speech, is through discourse itself. Since any discourse conceals by taking for granted its own grounds, its own grounding in communal visions of meaning, value, and purpose, the challenge as well as the promise of *On the Beginning Of Social Inquiry* is that it envisions the possibility of engaging discourse in ways that are responsive to the question of its own and others' grounds. In fact, differentiating between such talk, talk animated by what is referred to as analytic desire and all other kinds of talk, turns out to be the work of analytic theorizing itself. It is the nature of this work, or rather the nature of the commitment to the need and value of this work that we assume can and will manifest itself not just in the life of social theory, but in the life of the social theorist as well.

An important consequence of analytic discourse itself being but an instance of speech, is that what discourse uncovers (when directed to the goal of uncovering the grounds and origins of speech), is not something that can be finally or concretely fixed in the appearance of discourse itself. This necessarily elusive character of the grounds of speech has consequential implications for the status of everyday life within the context of the effort to reveal these grounds that this paper will explore, by paying particular attention to the book's introductory chapter. From page 10 of the 'Introduction' where the authors introduce the idea of everyday life, McHugh *et al.* (1974) write:

> As we use it, the notion of everyday life has the analytic status of an example. Rather than refer to everyday life as the 'rockbottom' certainty to which our descriptions purport to correspond, such a notion of everyday life is itself a construction.

> In a way then, our analyses are directed to the history of everyday life, if by that it is understood that examples serve to alert us to the ways in which the conventions of ordinary thought have become segregated from their grammatical grounds. Whereas 'history' suggests for us the character of such grounds, 'everyday life' typifies any and all of the occasions of thought and action which we decide to take as a point of departure for historical analysis.

> Everyday life is then not a phenomenon but an impetus; it provides the practical and concrete incentive for reflexive inquiry.

> (10–11)

These quotes emphasize that everyday life has the analytic status of an example and that such a notion of it is a construction so that, within the analytic purview, everyday life is not a phenomena. And yet, it still provides the *'practical and concrete* incentive for reflexive inquiry' (emphasis added). The quote also says that everyday life 'typifies any and all occasions of thought and actions which are taken as points of departure...'. So, while everyday life here merely establishes the points of departure for the work of investigating the history of the thoughts and actions they typify, the problem is that the practical, concrete circumstances of everyday life never completely disappear.

Referring to the persistence of the concrete circumstances of everyday life as problematic requires some explanation, however. Not least because the idea of inquiry the book is about and undertakes to portray, relies upon – and as such, we could even say is indebted to – these everyday circumstances for the work of inquiry to begin. So in what sense is everyday life problematic? The problem emerges within the above quote where it emphasizes the need to treat everyday life as a construction (in the service of the beginning of social inquiry) by suggesting a danger associated with the failure to treat it in this way. To repeat, 'Rather than refer to everyday life as the "rockbottom" certainty to which our descriptions purport to correspond, such a notion of everyday life is a construction'. In other words, if we do not treat everyday life as an analytic construction, our ability to describe it and otherwise respond to it can produce in us a false sense of security, a security born of the impression that with our ability to take stock of and to continuously respond to the everyday circumstances that confront us, we have accomplished all that needs to be done. We are on 'rockbottom' secure footing insofar as we are able to maintain our social, interactional, and practical balance, enough at least to move us on to meet the next challenging circumstance.

What is false about this security is that it does not secure or attend to less pressing and less contingent questions about the direction and purpose of life in general and our own lives in particular. This point will be taken up in more detail shortly, but for now what is being emphasized is that even though everyday life needs to be thought of as typifying any and all occasions of thought and action, and therefore in the service of social inquiry, it does not, as mentioned earlier, disappear or cease to exist. What this means is not just that the everyday circumstances which need to be constantly attended to do not disappear (which they do not, of course), but that the lure of the sense of security and accomplishment born of our ability to so competently deal with these circumstances also does not disappear.

Again from the book's Introduction:

> Thus everyday life as an example typifies the concerted tendency of analysis to begin with some 'matter' securely in hand. Our analysis then seeks to dissolve what is in hand by treating the security of the example as covering over and concealing its history.
>
> (McHugh *et al.*, 1974: 11)

To repeat the point of the above in slightly different terms then, just as the physical circumstances of everyday life never disappear, so too does the false sense of security surrounding and attached to the accomplishment of negotiating the physical realm also never completely dissipate. In other words, even knowing that the sense of security so provided is false, does not entirely falsify or ever completely and finally dissolve the potential attachment to the illusion of solidity and finality. The fact of this very illusion, that the work of social inquiry works to destabilize in order to reveal the grounds upon which speech relies and takes for granted, has implications for understanding and appreciating the necessarily practical nature of the work of social inquiry itself, within and as a necessary part of the everyday life of the social theorist.

In the interest of expanding the import of these implications, it will be helpful to look in more detail at the distinction emphasized in the Introduction between concrete and analytic speech, a distinction recognized, as suggested earlier, to be essential to the work of theorizing the book envisions:

Theorizing makes necessary a distinction between the concrete and the analytic. Insofar and whenever a theorist fails to formulate a distinction between the concrete and the analytic – between concrete and analytic speech – he loses his ability to account for his own activity: for theorizing. Without a distinction between the concrete and the analytic we necessarily formulate theorizing as a reproduction or reporting what appears.

(Ibid.: 16)

Concrete speech is presented here as the failure to theorize. The idea of this type of speech is further reinforced by the description of analytic writing as the attempt

...to preserve in its very organization the Socratic methods of *aporia* (the disillusion of the security of the hypothesis), the *elenchus* (the sense of Socratic irony which in attempting to differentiate between chatter and meaning treats words as icons of language), and *anamnesis* (the effort to reconstruct and reorganize resonances which have become alienated from the idea).

(Ibid.: 19)

Concrete speech is presented here, therefore, as speech that labours under the illusion of the security of the hypothesis, constitutes meaningless chatter, and is alienated from the idea. Furthermore, it is analytic theory that rescues talk from this fate.

It is tempting at this point to imagine the analytic theorist as inhabiting a world populated by concrete speakers. However, as the introduction emphasizes: 'The idea of theorizing makes a necessary distinction between the concrete and the analytic' (ibid.: 16). The very idea of the distinction, in other words, is made necessary by the theoretic desire and responsibility of the analyst. Since the very idea of the distinction is a feature of analytic work, concrete speech appears to be an artefact of this work and so not a concrete 'thing out there' in the world. It seems to be, we could say, 'a figure of speech' created and necessitated by the need of theorizing to distinguish itself from other kinds of talk or ways of speaking. Nevertheless, however much it may appear this way at this point, the Introduction also says:

The distinction is necessary for our own activity of theorizing because to deny the distinction would be to affirm ourselves as mere imitators or reporters of appearance.

(Ibid.: 16)

Here, on the other hand, concrete speech is not just a 'figure of speech' but an actual (concrete) way of speaking made possible by the denial of the distinction between itself and analytic speech. However, if we can presume that anyone truly committed to what is referred to earlier as 'analytic desire' would not and could not deny the distinction between concrete and analytic speech, and even knowing, as the Introduction says '...that the concrete/analytic distinction ... is a necessary condition of [the theorist's] existence' (ibid.: 16) just as it is a necessary condition of the realization of the book's theoretic endeavour, the possibility of reporting or of being imitative on occasion remains ever present. In other words, the necessity of making this distinction notwithstanding, it seems we could never completely rule out the possibility of writing that is imitative or that reports on appearances, not as a denial of the concrete/analytic distinction and not as a rejection of the commitment to and necessity of uncovering the grounds of speech, but as part of the on-going struggle to come to terms with the conditions of speech in the process of making this effort.

There is a passage in Alan Blum's book *Socrates: The Original and its Images* (1978) where everyday life and the life of the theorist are brought together in ways that are especially relevant and revealing within the context of our current discussion. Linking the distinction between essential and inessential speech to the multiplicity of everyday life, Blum writes:

'No one will deny that lives are different, that the differences between lives are many. The multitude is concerned with these kinds of differences and that is how the multitude acquires its name, from its concern with multis, manyness, and plurality.

The theorist faces the opposition and enmity of multis, of the idea that inessential differences are essential. The theorist must respect these differences because he cannot sustain conversation into the idea of life without the occasioning of different lives as precedents and examples...

The theorist himself makes a difference only because he shows the difference between what is essential and inessential. What is essential is that all speeches are sheltered by language, even speeches that deny such sheltering; what is inessential are the concrete differences among speeches. And yet, *the essentiality of language can only be spoken, i.e., it needs and requires as essential the inessential differences which it originates.*

(3, emphasis added)

To say that the essentiality of language can only be spoken and that it needs and, requires as essential, inessential differences, suggests that theorists are tempted to dismiss the multitude, to see themselves as above it, or to forget it is needed. But alongside this, an important part of respecting inessential differences includes respecting the inevitable involvement with and attractions to the many differences as part and parcel of the effort to appreciate how they are inessential. The problem is it would be a mistake to value the inessential as essential *and yet* the essentiality of language requires *as* essential the inessential differences. In other words, this requirement, the requirement of the need to respect inessential differences as essential, is also the requirement to respect the physical limitations of both speech and life. The fact that social theory has to be done as part of life and that doing so in ways which are respectful of the inessential means being respectful of what will emerge as inessential in the ongoing effort to uncover and express what is truly essential, namely, the origins of speech.

This helps to clarify something very paradoxical about the Introduction of this book. Where the Introduction talks about the failure to distinguish between concrete and analytical speech 'as affirming ourselves as imitators and reporters of appearance', it appears to be setting itself the seemingly impossible task of reporting on the idea of analytic inquiry while speaking in ways which can be recognized as different from reporting. Additionally, it attempts to reproduce the work of analytic inquiry, to make it apparent or appear to those unfamiliar with it in ways which are inimical to the idea that the work is imitative of analyses already accomplished by others or, presumably, even by the authors themselves.

While the Introduction poses this difficult task for itself, it poses an equally difficult task for its readers in that it suggests that any aspirations towards participation in the social inquiry exemplified in the book, should similarly eschew imitation or reportage. However, we now know that being respectful of theory's reliance on the inessential, also means being patient with the need to be imitative at times and to report on appearances as well, not as the denial of what is truly essential but as part of the ongoing struggle to reveal what is truly essential.

This takes us back to the very beginning of the Introduction where the authors talk about the method they used to create the papers included and the process of actually writing. While explaining how the potentially superficial first draft of any paper proposed as a candidate for inclusion in the book (likened to an 'ego') 'makes possible its own deepening' (McHugh *et al.* 1974: 6) in the form of subsequent drafts (which are comparable to 'alter'), the authors explain:

> An original paper is never a concretely perfect ego. Some originals cannot be responded to. Others formulate themselves to some extent, which is to say they do the work of both ego and alter. Similarly, some responses seem irrelevant to the original. Other responses are more useful egos than alters. Sometimes we have to throw away material. Often we give up on some material in midstream. Our procedures, in spite of their theoretical grounding, are ad hoc rather than invariant.
>
> (6 Ibid.)

We can see now that the difficulty of creating this book parallels the difficulty of doing theoretical work. Where the necessarily ad hoc procedures described above can be understood as the necessity of learning to live with and respect our own epigonic and descriptive tendencies as part of the continual effort to transcend them.

Part II The practice of theory

As might well be anticipated from what has been developed to this point, the difficulty of transcending the temptation to describe and imitate is closely related to the problem of distinguishing between what is essential and what inessential not just among the multitude of social issues and concerns that surround us, but also with respect to how these concerns are understood, presented, and responded to. Respecting these understandings and presentations requires that they be taken seriously, where doing so within the context of the commitment to uncover and examine the grounds of speech, means recognizing that the assumed authority of what is written or spoken must be revealed and examined.

One useful example of the need for such a commitment and of the consequences of its absence can be found within many discussions about how to deal with and overcome the marginalization within Canadian society of its Aboriginal population. As chronicled by Dickason and Newbegging (2010), the result of a long history of repressive colonial policies developed and implemented first by the British and French, and since 1867, by the Canadian government itself, Canada's First Nations, Inuit, and Métis Peoples have found themselves in an on-going struggle to regain their political, economic, cultural, and judicial sovereignty and autonomy. The devastating consequences of this country's colonial past in terms of indigenous rates of unemployment, levels of health, and over-all cultural identity and affirmation, is well documented and understood.[1] What is much less well understood is just how to deal with this situation in ways that are just, equitable, and respectful of both Aboriginal and non-Aboriginal aspirations. Focusing on one, not atypical, attempt to do so serves as a useful example of how inattention to the authoritative grounds of both how the problem is described and suggested ways to respond, can effectively undermine, if not altogether scuttle, the possibility of collective justice regardless of how well-meaning and sincere the attempt may be to achieve this.

In his book *The Rights Revolution* (2000), the well-known Canadian author and academic, Michael Ignatieff, addresses the concerns surrounding the Aboriginal population in Canada within the context of human rights. Notwithstanding the fact that such rights are conceived as something all are deserving of, Ignatieff well recognizes that the need for their identification and articulation stems from the reality that no matter how many people apparently enjoy such rights, certain groups within the collective do not. Aboriginal peoples in Canada have, in fact, suffered grievously from these rights being overridden or systemically denied (see Aboriginal Affairs and Northern Development Canada, 1996). The recognition of these different groups leads to Ignatieff's contention that 'The purpose of human rights is not to make those in danger the wards of conscience of those in zones of safety, but to protect, defend, and restore the agency of the defenseless so they can defend themselves' (Ignatieff, 2000: 43).

One interesting aspect of Ignatieff's statement is its reference to the idea of human rights as something which exists in 'zones'. But what is also problematic is what follows from this division, namely the assumption of the legitimacy of the responsibility that accrues to those purportedly in 'zones of safety' toward those perceived to be in more dangerous precincts. In this instance, uncovering the grounds of Ignateiff's speech will be aided by deconstructing and reconstructing the nature of the zones being referred to, because embedded in this distinction is the justification for the implied moral obligation which forms the basis of Ignatieff's broader understanding of social responsibility.

As the Office of the High Commissioner of Human Rights for the United Nations (2015) states: 'Human rights are rights inherent to all human beings, whatever our nationality, place of residence, sex, national or ethnic origin, colour, religion, language, or any other status. We are all equally entitled to our human rights without discrimination. These rights are all interrelated, interdependent and indivisible' (no page numbers). As this statement also affirms, 'The principle of universality of human rights is the cornerstone of international human rights law' (no page numbers). Despite the principle of universality, then, as the statement appears to recognize, discrimination in one form or another can and does restrict the entitlement. The significant difference, therefore, between Ignatieff's 'zones' is that some identifiable groups within the larger collective or state are discriminated against while the rest consider themselves 'safe' from this experience. More specifically, the 'safety' being referred to by Ignatieff, indicates not only that those who inhabit such zones understand themselves to be in possession of such rights, but that this possession also frees people from the need to protect, defend, or restore these rights for themselves. Secure in the knowledge of their own rights therefore, people are then free to turn their attention to the protection, defence, and restoration of the rights of others – people unfortunate enough to inhabit the apparently less secure zones.

However, the fact that the zones being referred to are not geographical designations but rather are interactional and organizational constructs, achieved by way of more or less discrimination, has significant implications which are easily overlooked. Presenting himself as someone in a position to recognize these different zones, as well as to undertake the work of restoring human rights to those discriminated against, Ignatieff invites us to share in his ostensibly moral commitment. What this invitation also does, however, is effectively divert attention away from the historical achievement of the security of Ignatieff's own 'zone', one enjoyed by those free from discrimination or free enough at least to be able to treat the absence of human rights as a problem belonging to others, and its potential remedy as a legitimate responsibility.

Within the terms of our earlier discussion, uncovering the grounds of Ignatieff's speech involves resisting the avowedly humanitarian impulse to attend to the absence of human rights as something which can and should take precedence over the need to first uncover the theoretic foundations of the language used to describe and frame such an inducement. In the process we can begin to see how doing so is not just an exercise in theory, but has very practical implications. In order to appreciate these implications, however, it is necessary first to note some important historical considerations related to the formation of states in general and Canada in particular.

When the first Europeans landed and began colonizing the land which was to eventually become Canada, it was, of course, not uninhabited. One important consideration with respect to the formation and perpetuation of modern states which is relevant here, is found in Max Weber's (1974) famous essay entitled

'Politics as a Vocation'. He points out that the modern state can be defined sociologically 'only in terms of the specific means peculiar to it, as in every political association, namely, the use of physical force' (77–78). Weber continues:

> Of course, force is certainly not the normal or only means of the state – nobody says that – but force is a means specific to the state.... Today, however, we have to say that the state is a human community that (successfully) claims the monopoly of the legitimate use of physical force within a given territory.... Like the political institutions historically preceding it, the state is a relation of men dominating men, a relation supported by means of legitimate (i.e. considered to be legitimate) violence. If the state is to exist, the dominated must obey the authority claimed by the powers that be.
>
> (78)

The broader collective within which Ignatieff's different zones exist is the Canadian state, with the largest 'zone' consisting of the non-Aboriginal population.[2] In Weber's terms then, not just the existence, but the creation of Canada is predicated upon the monopoly of force, used specifically in support of the claim to sovereignty over territory to which there existed no 'right' save that afforded by this monopoly. While much of the conflict which occurred prior to confederation was between the colonial powers themselves, with Aboriginal Peoples forming shifting alliances with the British, French and later the Americans, the Canadian policies and laws introduced after confederation were aggressively and determinedly assimilative.[3]

Against the background of the acknowledgement of this history, it is difficult not to see that Ignatieff's 'zone of safety' is no more and no less than that segment of the population whose existence is safeguarded by a monopoly of force on the part of its 'legal' political representatives. But what is also clear is that in this case, the exercise of this monopoly effectively creates not only what Ignatieff refers to as a 'zone of safety' with respect to rights that appear to be so secure as to be taken for granted, but also what can now be recognized as 'collateral zones' whose less than secure status is the result not only of discrete or even more organized expressions of overt discrimination, but which are a feature of the monopoly Weber refers to as essential to the very existence of the state. Against the background of this understanding, Ignatieff's idea of the responsibility of those whose rights appear secure towards those whose rights are threatened, assumes the contradictory form wherein those responsible for the absence of the rights of others are nevertheless assigned the task of remedying this situation.

For the purposes of our more general discussion, however, what is particularly interesting is the way the more practical interconnections between these groups can be heard to reverberate in the more theoretical grounds of Ignatieff's discussion. In particular in the form of his proposed outline towards a just resolution to the many outstanding areas of discord and disagreement which continue to exist as the country's historical foundations are finally being more fully understood from the perspectives of, in Weber's terms, the dominant as well as the dominated.

As part of the process of addressing the differences between the rights secured by the Canadian majority, and the establishment of the rights sought by First Nations communities, Ignatieff sees the need for mutual sharing:

> Either we must share power, land, resources, and sovereignty among the nations of this country, or we will founder in civil strife. But the sharing has to go both ways. The majority's recognition of aboriginal peoples must be followed by aboriginal recognition of the legitimacy of our equal claim to the land.... What is required is a process that builds a mutual and equal recognition, each side publicly acknowledging the other's right to govern and live in peace.
>
> (2000: 84)

The problem, of course, is that the plea for the recognition of the majority's claim to a legitimate right to the land is in fact a plea to legitimate the monopoly of physical force upon which the original claim was based. To the extent, therefore, that the majority's claim is challenged, what is being questioned is not just the right to land inhabited by Aboriginal peoples for thousands of years prior to first contact. What is being resisted is any claim that stakes its legitimacy upon the threat of force. On a more subtle level, what is also being rejected is the implicit invitation to accept the monopoly on violence as the standard against which fair and just dealings between people ought to be measured. The mutual and equal recognition Ignatieff calls for, therefore, is actually the recognition that the monopoly on force not only is but ought to be the standard against which people measure the justice of their relations. And finally, as a consequence, to the extent that a higher standard is insisted upon and pursued, the more 'troublesome' and 'uncooperative' Aboriginal resistance will seem from the perspective of a dominate majority.

Interestingly, however, and much to his credit, Ignatieff himself is not altogether blind to the paradoxical nature of his proposed way forward for Aboriginal–non-Aboriginal relations in Canada, as evidenced by the following quote from the same book:

> At the moment, might lies with the majority and right with the minority. Mutual recognition must rebalance the relationship, with both power and legitimacy finding a new equilibrium. Then, and only then, will we be able to live together in peace in two countries at once, a community of rights-bearing equals and a community of self-governing nations.
>
> (Ibid.: 84)

Ignatieff recognizes that might, in and of itself, is not and cannot be all there is to what is right. So what the minority has a right to, certainly, is to challenge the legitimacy of might, or rather, the legitimacy of any authority that rests exclusively on might. The problem is that this, in and of itself, does not mean that the minority (or those subject to the 'might' referred to) is necessarily 'right'. This is because the much more fundamental challenge only obliquely glimpsed in the preceding quote is to conceive of and strive towards a community whose legitimacy rests upon an idea of the creative engagement of differences between people – a community, in other words, that recognizes the value of concerning itself with something more meaningful and fulfilling than the distribution of, and access to, the levers of violence.

Discussion

The conception of social theory which animates *On the Beginning of Social Inquiry* itself envisions a community, or rather an idea of communal coexistence; one which anticipates an essential connection between how we use language and how we live our lives. Given this, the commitment to investigating and uncovering the grounds of speech is no less than a commitment to understanding the grounds of our actions, and of the destinations of the lives our actions (and our speech) are bound to take us. It is, therefore, an essentially self-reflexive commitment, but one that resists the temptation to be self-absorbed by beginning with and depending upon the speech of others. The above examination of Ignatieff's understanding of the relations between Canada's First Nations and the Canadian state is such a beginning and as such, the development of the limitations of the community Ignatieff's writing presages is not unrelated to the limitations of the social theorists' concerns and priorities with respect to the society we live in, but also aspire to. However, the meaningful potential of the lives of the communities we are part of can only really be imagined insofar as social theory includes a relentless offensive against the limitations of the words we all speak and with this, the lives we can imagine living.

Notes

1 One of most thorough and respected overviews of connections between the past and the present situation of Aboriginal Peoples in Canada is contained in 'The Royal Commission Report on Aboriginal Peoples' published by Aboriginal Affairs and Northern Development Canada (1996).

2 According to the latest statistics available from Employment and Social Development Canada website, Aboriginal Peoples constitute 4.3 per cent of the Canadian population as of 2011. (Accessed from: http://well-being.esdc.gc.ca/misme-iowb/indicator.jsp?indicatorid=36#NAP).

3 Laws were introduced and treaties signed which restricted the territories and movements of Aboriginal People, their participation in scared ceremonies, the selection and operation of traditional band leadership, as well as the introduction of a residential schooling system which lasted for generations and which is responsible for what has recently been referred to as cultural genocide (see Wilson, 1999, Tasker, 2015).

Bibliography

Aboriginal Affairs and Northern Development Canada. 'The Royal Commission Report on Aboriginal Peoples' www.aadnc-aadnc.gc.ca, 1996.

Blum, Alan F. *Socrates: The Original and its Images.* London: Routledge & Kegan Paul, 1978.

Dickason, Olive Patricia, with William Newbigging. *A Concise History of Canada's First Nations.* Toronto: Oxford University Press, 2010.

Employment and Social Development Canada. http://well-being.esdc.gc.ca, 2015.

Ignatieff, Michael. *The Rights Revolution.* Toronto: Anansi, 2000.

McHugh, Peter, Stanley Raffel, Daniel C. Foss, and Alan F. Blum. *On the Beginning of Social Inquiry.* London: Routledge & Kegan Paul, 1974.

Office of the High Commissioner of Human Rights for the United Nations. www.ohchr.org, 2015.

Tasker, John, Paul. 'Residential School Findings Point to "Cultural Genocide", Commission Chair Says'. Canadian Broadcasting Corporation News. www.cbc.ca/news/politics/residential-schools-findings-point-to-cultural-genocide-commission-chair-says-1.3093580. 30 May, 2015.

Weber, Max. 'Politics as a Vocation'. *From Max Weber: Essays in Sociology.* Ed. H.H. Gerth and C. Wright Mills. New York: Oxford University Press, 1946. pp. 77–128.

Wilson, James. *The Earth Shall Weep: A History of Native America.* New York: Atlantic Monthly Press, 1999.

13 Dialectic, reflexivity, and good troublesome company

Kieran Bonner

In *On the Beginning of Social Inquiry*, McHugh *et al.* developed the reflexivity that ethnomethodology showed to be foundational for social life into research as a collaboration inspired by Socratic dialectic, especially as described in the 'Introduction'. This chapter revisits this dialectic by analysing the relation between the method of collaboration, its mode of production, and the product of that collaboration. While their topic is collaboration, the chapter shows that the taken for granted resource is good troublesome company, a resource developed as a way to respond to the impossible problem of reflexive integrity. Through this resource, the chapter argues that what was begun was a way of showing how responding to impossible questions has an authentic relationship to contingent beginnings, when the inquirer takes seriously the concern with reflexive integrity.

An introduction to an introduction

> This book is a treatment of certain important ideas in sociology and social science, among them positivism, art, and common sense. But it is also collaboration, and it would be best to introduce our work with this fact because, although it is not to be found in the table of contents, our collaboration is as much responsible for this book as any of the topics which appear there. Just as it is our conception of sociological analysis that has produced these topics so also does our conception of analysis make collaboration a necessity and not a happenstance.
>
> (McHugh *et al.*, 1974: 1)

With these sentences, *On the Beginning of Social Inquiry* is launched. We have authors who seek to provocatively and ambitiously begin social inquiry. There is brashness in this title. The words 'social inquiry' are not new but the title proposes that this book begins social inquiry or perhaps begins anew. And how do these authors begin? They begin by talking about their way of working together, the form of their working relationship, a form they call collaboration. They introduce their 'treatment of certain important ideas in sociology and social science' by saying that the best way to introduce this treatment is, through a description of their working methods.

Let's reflect on this some more. An introduction to what McHugh *et al.* are doing takes the form of an introduction to how they work together as the best way to understand what they are doing. We meet the work of McHugh, Raffel, Foss, and Blum and they introduce themselves as workers who invented a way of working together. Though they did not invent the important topics in sociology and social science, whether art, travel, motive, bias, etc., they did invent a way of analysing art, motive, travel, etc. And, they say, they need to begin with what they invented because their 'conception of analysis makes the particular way they work together, collaboration, necessary'.

In these first three sentences, McHugh *et al.* have asserted a dialectic between what they talk about and how they talk about what they talk about. And while the objects of their analysis – motive, snubs, bias, art, etc. – make up the content of their book, they assert it is *the way* they talk these topics that is important.[1] They begin with the interrelation between what they say and how they say what they say. For example, to illustrate the complexity of this interrelation, their analysis of snubs (109–136) is an outcome of their collaborative process and their conception of analysis makes such a process necessary. And, to add to this interrelation of method and object, their analysis of snubs is an analysis of the virtues of collaboration versus criticism, and thus through their analysis of snubs they make a topic out of their way of working together.

Though McHugh *et al.* begin by asserting the dialectic between what they talk about, and how they talk about what they talk about, it is not a dialogue as Gadamer developed it in his hermeneutics. Gadamer's hermeneutics (1975) privileges the question and answer process (the model of Platonic dialogue), the importance of the communicative context (effective history) of the participants, as they attempt to come to an agreement about the object of the dialogue, in the context of the horizons which subject participants (fusion of horizons). McHugh *et al.*, on the other hand, reflexively relate their collaboration to what they have produced. Their collaboration is embodied in the outcome of the collaboration, their analyses of motive, bias, snubs, art, etc. To this extent and initially speaking, their dialectic is closer to an orientation inherited from Marx's mode of production than Plato's dialogical encounter, and this despite the fact that for both Analysis and philosophical hermeneutics Socratic dialogue is exemplary.

Because, dialectically speaking, their mode of production is intimately tied to what they produce, they feel it is best to begin by addressing their mode of production. Thus, to the question of what these social inquirers begin, they have answered that they are beginning a mode of production. There is a dialectical relationship between what they talk about and how they talk, a dialectical relation between what they produce and how they produce, and a reflexive attending to this way of producing, as if a particular instantiation of the Marx and Engels formulation: 'what they are, therefore, coincides with their production, both with *what* they produce and *how* they produce' (Marx and Engels, 1947: 7). Blum (1974) is more direct about this Marxian analogy in his *Theorizing* published in the same year.

Marx says that [humans] relate through their products, but their products are produced through their labor.... Labor is a metaphor for the re-thinking that is theorizing and so, to say that [humans] relate through their labor is to say that they relate through their re-thinking. But, [humans] who relate through their re-thinking are [humans] who relate through their commitments to speech and thought.

$$(262)^2$$

The collaboration of these four sociologists points to inquirers 'who relate through their commitments to speech and thought' and I note at this stage of the chapter a possible tension between the 'what' and the 'who'.

The dialectic of theory and practice

To provide a biographical context for this chapter, I have studied under Blum, McHugh, Raffel, and another colleague who haunts these pages (in their invocation to Socrates and Plato), Stephen Karatheodoris. I have taught this material in my classes and I have written about their work (e.g. 2001, 2010); I have interviewed Raffel, McHugh, and Blum about the historical beginning of this work. But I am going to bracket that 'data' and 'experience' in order to take up the 'Introduction' as my 'data'. My experiential and theoretical knowledge, for the most part, will be treated as a resource, in order to privilege, hermeneutically speaking, the text of the 'Introduction'. This 'Introduction' begins decisively with the dialectical relation between what the authors analyse and how they analyse, and privileges a focus on method as the best way of understanding what they produce. In this case, dialectic is both the method and object of analysis. I propose to re-visit the 'Introduction' in light of their relation to dialectic.

Dialectic has several meanings, all of which, according to Gadamer, belong to the theory and practice of Platonic dialectic. 'On one level it simply means the back and forth discussion. In its more technical senses it can either mean the sophistic rhetorical skill of reducing a position or an assertion to an absurdity or the philosophical skill of collecting and differentiating according to essence' (Smith, 1986: 1). Dialectic, then, is both a method of analysis and an object of analysis: it means the ordinary back and forth of dialogue, the rhetorical skill of exposing contradictions, and the philosophic skill of collecting and differentiating according the essence of the object being discussed. 'There is also the Hegelian element in Plato's dialectic in the sense that dialectical refutation of a position is not always merely negative but often points to a higher truth', (Smith, 1986: 1) the *aufheben* or sublation, where a term or concept is both preserved and transformed through its dialectical interplay with another term or concept, what Fichte calls the synthesis of the thesis/antithesis conflict. (Gadamer, 1976).

One other sense of dialectic emerging out of all of the above but which also stands alone is the relation between theory and practice. True dialecticians hold on to what they know to be true and, because they know it to be true, they live by it. What dialecticians discover makes a difference; it is not just an added piece of information or knowledge: it contributes or develops self-understanding in such a way that it is integrated into life. As both Plato and Aristotle state, the real difference between the sophist and the dialectician is the life they choose to live. Dialecticians practice what they know to be true (Gadamer, 1986: 100). In some ways, it is this latter element, practising one's theory, which this bold Introduction points to and which ultimately points to Plato over both Marx and Hegel.

If we look at the tone of these first three sentences, it suggests the authors hit upon the collaborative process during the process of undertaking to analyse ideas. That is, as they practically accomplished their analyses they hit upon a method or mode of production that became as important as their products. In fact, it is so important that they decided to introduce themselves with this method. Here we have a direct theory and practice relation. Their theory or their analysis made the practice of collaboration necessary. 'Just as it is our conception of sociological analysis that has produced these topics', they say, 'so also does our conception of analysis make collaboration a necessity and not a happenstance' (1). If their theory makes a particular method or practice necessary, we need to understand their 'conception of sociological analysis' in order to understand their mode of production. What, then, is their conception of analysis?

'Analysis is the concern not with anything said or written but with the grounds of what is said or written – the foundations that make what is said possible, sensible, conceivable. For any speech, including, of course, speech about speech, our interest is reflexive' (2). In analysing snubs, bias, or art, analysis seeks to recover the 'possibility of *any* finding, puzzle, resolution, answer, interest, location, phenomenon, etcetera, etcetera' (2). Their interest in social inquiry involves reflectively recovering the grounds that made the object of being investigated possible and so is fundamentally a reflexive interest. Forty years later, and as affirmed by many of the contributions in this book, we now know that this interest speaks to intellectual movements in the 1960s and early 1970s, and, in particular, to the authors' beginnings in phenomenology and ethnomethodology.

This reflexive interest was announced in Blum and McHugh's (1971) first collaboration together, reproduced in *OBSI*, 'The Social Ascription of Motive'. If 'the analytic status of social action resides in its character as behavior which is normatively oriented to the very same environment it constitutes, then motive can function as an observer's rule for deciding the normatively ordered character of behavior' (1974: 23–24). Anyone familiar with the work of Garfinkel would recognize here ethnomethodology's demonstration of the way members' methods constitute the environment to which they are oriented, 'the "uninteresting" essential reflexivity of accounts' (Garfinkel, 1967: 7). As Garfinkel describes it: 'members treat as the most passing matter of fact that members accounts, of every sort, in all their logical modes, with all of their uses, and for every method for their assembly are constituent features of the settings they make observable. Members know, require, count on, and make use of this reflexivity to produce, accomplish, recognize, or demonstrate rational adequacy for all practical purposes of their procedures and findings' (8–9).

McHugh *et al.*'s interest in reflexivity is social and methodological (as against introspective and intentionalist) in this sense. And while their research into the topics they analyse does not, like ethnomethodology, issue in an empirical program of research (again as demonstrated in the Motive paper), by itself the reflexive interest does not make collaboration necessary. It may make collaboration inviting, enjoyable but not yet necessary. What, therefore, have they begun that would make collaboration necessary? And what is the relation between the dialectical approach they begin with and their stated reflexive interest?

Here they are very direct. Though analysis for them involves locating the grounds or 'origins' of the 'world of bias, art, snubs, evaluation, motive', this does not exhaust their interest; rather, such analysis points 'to what makes it possible for [them] to have produced those descriptions in the first place, i.e., to [their] auspices'. In showing how social life is constituted in and through the taken for granted reflexivity of accounts, they ask the question about the reflexivity that makes *their* description of social life possible. In other words, if the essential reflexivity of accounts is uninteresting to members, it is of interest to the one who is interested in inquiring into that reflexivity. The ethnomethodologists, Sharrock and Anderson (1986: 110), have described this conceptual move on the part of Blum, McHugh, and colleagues as 'one more step' regarding the implications of recognizing the 'essential reflexivity of accounts'. Analysis is responsive to the question of the 'rational adequacy' of inquiry into the reflexive grounds of social life, but they treat their election to do social inquiry in this way as itself open to the same focus. For them, to take up the study of the essential reflexivity of accounts, invites a query about the essential reflexivity of that undertaking.

As we know, there is a committed strand in ethnomethodology, a strand most clearly represented by Michael Lynch (2000), which sees the invitation to be reflexively accountable for the reflexivity of accounts as beside the point, or as pointless and unproductive, a position I have addressed in another paper (2013). Here I want to highlight the way the implied invitation to be reflexive about the interest in reflexivity is taken seriously by the *OBSI* authors. If through their analyses of motive, snubs, art, etc., they locate the taken for granted grounds or the seen but unnoticed background expectancies that make the phenomenon possible, they are reflexively sensitive to the query about the ground of their analysis. They take up the challenge to be accountable to the same demand in their own work that ethnomethodology demands of strong social inquiry, but does not reflexively demand of itself. This suggests a concern with some sort of reflexive integrity, a sensitivity to the concern of practising what is preached. This, perhaps, is one of the first glimpses of the relation of reflexivity to dialectic.

Reflexive integrity

What is the relation between taking the claim about the essential reflexivity of action and accounts seriously and seeing that self-same concern as a claim on one's own undertaking? Is there a relation between being consistent with one's investigations and having reflexive integrity? Here their analysis is concerned with practising what is preached, practising a relation to reflexivity that their inquiry seeks to investigate. The 'essential reflexivity of accounts' is now doubly reflexive, and doubly reflexive because there is an interest in application of what they say to their own work. Is this a way to see that the 'one more step' Analysis takes with regard to the reflexivity of accounts actually opens up a moral or ethical concern? In beginning social inquiry are they beginning to explore the relation between what is called the cognitive and the normative, theory and practice, knowledge and integrity? Are we now glimpsing a reason for why they begin by pointing to the dialectical relation between what they produce and how they produce, in such a way that their method starts to take on prominence?

McHugh, Blum, Foss, and Raffel point to a realization of a dialectical moment in the relation between theory and practice; they see the need to hold their own analysis accountable in the way breaching experiments show social life to be accountable in a 'profoundly normative, and morally sanctionable' way (Heritage, 1984: 101). This is the 'analytic nerve' that distinguishes Analysis and ethnomethodology (McHugh *et al.*, 1974: 23), the courage to apply to one's own practices the implications of the insights into social life that one's research and analysis develop. And we see a continuity with Blum and McHugh's later collaboration, *Self-Reflection in the Arts and Sciences* (1984: 17) where Marx is directly invoked: 'Marx felt that we arrive at the truth of a matter when our thinking penetrates and illuminates the character of our conduct'.[3]

As their product does not stand as independent of their mode of production, their reflexive method does not stand apart from the analysis of the topics. From this perspective, to treat method, theory and the analysis of social life as separate activities or areas is to reproduce the alienation and commodity fetishism that critical theory (e.g. Fromm, Marcuse, Habermas) so articulately identifies as a feature of modern capitalist society. Rather, for them, reflexivity raises the problem of how it can be practiced in ways that do not contradict the insights developed through its practice. Is this the real radical step that they begin? If so, it is the development of a line of thought that led Hannah Arendt in her later work to Socratic self-questioning as she sought to understand the intrinsic connection between thinking and morality (Arendt, 2003).

The problem of being reflexive about being reflexive

The problem of being reflexive about being reflexive, a problem that for many social theorists is impossible, dangerous, or unproductive, is ambitiously and confidently faced by Analysis, though McHugh *et al.* do acknowledge that resolving this problem 'is no easy matter' (3). Why? 'To be caught up in the activity of formulation is to face away from one's own fundamental grounds through which those formulations come about'. They recognize that complete speech, speech that is self-sufficient, speech that formulates a topic and self-sufficiently articulates the grounds of its formulation, is impossible. To this extent they acknowledge that the problem, avoided by others, is a very deep one.

Yet, they do not use that to give up on the problem. They choose to speak (do inquiry) and to be reflexively accountable for speaking. Their beginning is both to speak strongly about the reflexive ground of the social but also be responsive to the question of the reflexive ground of their own speaking as another social activity. Every analysis, they say, 'in being done ... always makes available for analysis a new problem, how *it* is possible' (3). They accept that there can be no last word, no final solution, no ultimate analysis as each analysis invites the reflexive question, what grounds does it rest on.

To ask this (to use the language of Blum and McHugh's 1984 work) is to address and respond to a 'deep need' or as Blum (2003) more recently put it, an impossible question. And while the relation and response to the possibility of the impossible question developed over the years of the work, the 'deep need and desire' to respond to impossible issues – birth, death, shared being, identity, culture, the city, power, health and illness, circulation, etc. – began with *On the Beginning of Social Inquiry*. McHugh (1992: 108–109) in *A Letter of Resignation* called these 'first questions' pointing to 'fundamental scholarly inquiry' concerned with 'what are we and how should we live'. In 1974 the *OBSI* authors began by confidently making a place for engaging such impossible first questions, in this particular case, seeking the truth about reflexivity by allowing their 'thinking to penetrate and illuminate the character of [their] conduct' (Blum and McHugh, 1984: 17). The Pandora's box that reflexivity opens up, the problem of being reflexive about being reflexive, that seems to invite the charge of navel gazing or 'helpless swirling' (Giddens, 1976: 166) is courageously faced in *OBSI* as inviting a fundamental question: why we speak at all, or even more fundamentally, why we do what we do? With this we hear shades of Heidegger and the interest in foundations (*What is a Thing?*; *What is Called Thinking?*) as a fundamental human matter and are beginning to glimpse why they might say: 'in our respective attitudes toward ordinary language and the everyday world, we have as much in common with ethnomethodology as Heidegger shares with Austin' (1974: 23).

This relation to Heidegger and to foundations is more directly articulated in one of their following published collaborations, another 'Introduction', in this case to *Friends, Enemies, and Strangers: Theorizing in Art, Science, and Everyday Life* (1979). Drawing on Heidegger's reflection of Heraclitus' fragment 50, 'When you have listened not to me but to the logos it is wise to say: All is One' (1979: 3), Blum and McHugh address the issue of the problem of hearing the 'unsayable' in the context of the teacher–student relationship.[4] The 'unsayable' can only be heard through what is said (Heraclitus' speech), in this case through a speech that reflexively acknowledges its own inadequacy ('listen not to me'). If members' accomplishments (e.g., the housemaid in the story of Thales) rest on grounds that are unformulated, so too are accounts that make the reflexivity of accounts observable. Every reflexive analysis is a speech, an accomplishment, and in this very specific way is subject in the same way to the essential reflexivity of accounts as everyday members' accounts. This is the equality of speech announced in *OBSI*, an equality shown through beginning with the phenomenon to be examined rather than (like Aristotle) on the opinions and scholarship regarding that phenomenon, an equality explicitly affirmed in Blum and McHugh's 1979 'Introduction'.

Yet, to begin inquiry, especially to begin inquiry into the reflexive and incarnate grounds of social life, grounds that everyday members in their everydayness are uninterested in, is already to make a difference; it is already to propose that this speaking makes a difference. Ten years after *OBSI*, Blum and McHugh (1984: 89) affirm the commitment to take one more step with regard to this problem: 'Ethnomethodology's own self-reflection upon its place in loose common sense does not establish the necessity of [its] speaking, because in [its own] reflection, speech follows in the trail of convention, and it is always unnecessary and could always be otherwise'. The question of why one needs to speak, especially why one needs to speak in the form of social inquiry haunts *OBSI*; it is the ghost of the contingency of conventionalism (nihilism) that they refuse to ignore or deny.

The problem of being reflexive about one's interest in reflexivity is for these authors a problem of reflexive integrity, and yet this problem of the deep integrity of social inquiry is impossible, in the sense that it can never be solved once and for all. Given its impossibility, one response is to ignore it. 'Common sense, according to Schutz, exists to solve the problem of reflexivity by ignoring it' they say (1974: 162) in their Art paper. In Garfinkel's terminology, the reflexivity of accounts is essential but uninteresting to common sense members. Analysis, like ethnomethodology, does not choose to ignore it, but unlike ethnomethodology, it does not choose to sidestep this problem. An alternative response to the problematic nature of reflexive integrity would be to refuse to speak; if speaking cannot provide for its own grounds, if it cannot completely account for the need to speak, why speak? In response, they say: 'Yet, we speak. In speaking we are denying that we are doing an inadequate activity. Otherwise our speech would be no different than chatter, than silence, than what Rosen calls nihilism' (1974: 3).

The resolution of collaboration

OBSI begins with the problem of the deep significance of beginning to speak, whether that beginning is a greeting, a motive account, an evaluation, or, in this case, an analysis of such beginnings. How can inquiry into the reflexive ground of social life grasp its own difference, its own beginning to inquire, given that self-sufficient analysis is impossible? 'This' they say, 'is where collaborators come in. They serve to formulate for us the inadequacy of our speech.... By formulating our speech they allow us to be committed to speaking *and* to the reflexive character of analysis' (italics in original, 4). These authors found a strong response to the impossible problem of reflexive integrity by developing a way of working together, a collaboration that allows them to steer between the Scylla of chatter or contingent conventionalism and the Charybdis of silence or resignation. Both are possibilities that *OBSI* resists but both are possibilities that it recognizes and is responsive to. If chatter is thoughtless everyday talk, perhaps one way of thinking of the dilemma of sensitivity to the limitations of thoughtful speech is a Samuel Beckett kind of silence. 'Every word is like an unnecessary stain on silence and nothingness' Beckett once said (1969: 210). If being reflexive about being reflexive points to the 'unsayable', why not be silent. As with Beckett, *OBSI* is sensitive to this inadequacy of speech, and to the irony of saying that speech is inadequate, an irony that Blum and McHugh posited as the way of life of the principled actor in their 1984 work.

As I have noted in another paper (Bonner, 2001), Gadamer (1975: xxiv) in *Truth and Method* recognized the challenges of a reflexive self-grounding inquiry. As he said of his own hermeneutics, 'the demand for a reflexive self grounding ... is unfulfilled'. Where Gadamer reconciled his inquiry to this limit in the presupposition that the tradition of speaking, in which he and his interlocutors stand, does not automatically need justification, and so stands in the confidence of the inheritance of language, *OBSI* find the confidence to go on speaking in finding collaborators, first in McHugh and Blum finding each other, and then finding students who could hear that need. As they were to develop in a 1984 paper, the teacher–student relationship or pedagogy invigorated their collaboration. The call in the 'Introduction' for readers to respond as collaborators to what they have produced is a call rooted in pedagogy and perhaps accounts for the stronger influence this work has on students than readers. *OBSI* begins with their method of production as it provided the opportunity to engage the inadequacy of speech with full acknowledgement of how fundamental and irreparable this limit is but also how, with collaborators, they can engage the limit with ambition.

The authors of *OBSI* came to the realization that strong inquiry, inquiry that responded to the essential reflexivity of accounts, had to deal with a contradiction. Everyday members do not so much solve this problem as ignore it. To ignore this problem is to speak as if it does not exist, a speech that is analytically indistinguishable from contingent conventionalism. The beginning that is Analysis seeks to make a strong difference by speaking in a way that shows its difference from contingency. Analysis is inquiry concerned with the grounds of any phenomenon but in recovering such grounds, it inevitably has to forget its own grounds. They engage this impossible problem by resisting the temptation to ignore it (conventional speech) but recognize that this strong beginning remains inadequate vis-à-vis the unavoidable reflexivity of accounts. Silence is one way of acknowledging this inadequacy, but insofar as it aims to be precisely such an acknowledgement (and not accidental), it too speaks, even if such speech, in Beckett's terms, is a 'stain on nothingness'.

In what way can Analysis speak without denying the inadequacy of such speaking or be silent without that being indistinguishable from chatter? For these authors, collaboration is their dialectical resolution of this contradiction. They show inventiveness about a way to be true to both sides of this contradiction. The dialectic between what they produce and how they produce is now represented as a resolution to the contradiction between the dependency of intelligible speech on the essential if contingently local reflexivity of accounts and the need to respond strongly to that dependency, to speak in the face of the inadequacy of speaking. The synthesis of collaboration overcomes the opposition between chatter and silence while preserving both the adequacy of inquiry and the inescapability of the reflexivity of accounts. While they resist everyday members who resolve the reflexivity of accounts through ignoring it, they also resist ethnomethodologists who are satisfied with a description of how members accomplish this ignorance as a practical matter. On the other hand, they acknowledge the possibility that silence is a response to the fundamental inadequacy of speaking, perhaps a response that has a fragment of integrity,[5] but one that gives up on the ambition to tackle the problem of a commitment to the reflexive character of speech.

To resolve the tension between inquiry and the fundamental inadequacy of inquiry they introduce the language commitment, the promise that the impossible problem of grounding social inquiry will not be given up or ignored. Here we see that the contingent and conventional beginning that is the fate of all inquiry and all speaking is simultaneously acknowledged and resisted, a possibility that depends on the promise they make to themselves and to their reader. Though 'we tribal members can only begin such an enterprise by speaking through the mouth of a tribe ... analysis seeks to dissolve what is in hand by treating the security of the example as covering over and concealing its history' (11).

What is particularly noteworthy is that their synthesis is the outcome of a very practical inventiveness. It is not a logical synthesis but rather a practical and inventive one. It is a sublation that developed through the experience of their conversation with each other as they sought to be true to the reflexive character of analysis. It is not a resolution that points to a universal law or even, as we will see, to a method requiring imitation; it is a resolution that they happen upon as they reflexively recognize the implications of their own analysis. It shows that reflexive integrity is necessary for inquiry but that reflective human inventiveness is capable of responding to this impossible problem.

The topic of collaboration and the resource of good troublesome company

OBSI goes on to describe and to formulate the process of collaboration through the terms of ego and alter. As they describe it, ego provides an analysis that makes reference to his or her grounds in order that alter may formulate them. That is, in different and ad hoc ways, ego analysed the grounds of the idea of snubs in order to make the grounds of this analysis available for alter to formulate. Being moderns, and so more like Hegel than Plato in being reflexively self conscious, they recognize that the analysis of bias, snubs, art, motive, etc. that issue from their collaboration now must be treated as ego, with the reader of *OBSI* being invited to be alter to their essentially unfinished analysis. The reflexive integrity that they applied to themselves in the practice of their analysis is now offered as an invitation to the reader to collaborate with them.

Let's tease out some more what is involved in the collaboration in order to see another element of what was begun here. The kind of collaborative work that they describe through the process of first and second speakers assumes a shared commitment and good will. It requires actors who willingly give themselves to the process of analysing the grounds of the important ideas of motive, snubs, evaluation, art, etc., through analysing papers that analyse the grounds of such, accepting that the perfect analysis, the last speech, saying the *logos*, is impossible. This requires setting aside the temptation to despair, setting aside a suspicion or charge of wasting time, setting aside the urgency of demands of life regarding careers, financial solvency, being absorbed by practical and technical problems, taking care of the necessities of life (in Arendt's terms), in order to fully give oneself over to speaking and analysing these matters. It also requires developing openness to responses that address the limitations of one's contribution. Collaboration is not about affirming speakers in their speaking but rather reminding speakers what they (even if necessarily) forget in their speaking. This points to another tension in the synthesis that is collaboration, the tension between confidence (to tackle an impossible problem) and reserve (with regard to the inadequacy of one's response).

The book is a demonstration of the way reserve on both everyday urgencies and on the inadequacy of one's own speech allows for the examination of important ideas as a way to address first questions. As such, it shows that collaboration, while not unlike Arendt's (1958) public realm, is more like the conversation of friendship and good company.[6] Collaboration shows what the conversation of friendship and good company can make possible; it enables the confidence or spirit to tackle impossible problems and the reserve or reason to acknowledge the limitations of that accomplishment. Like the conversation of friendship, this kind of collaboration creates a world within which the undertaking to inquire or theorize is divined as first (Bonner, 2014). The world of good, if troublesome, company, company that pushes one to think through the implications of one's own talk, makes possible a focus on working out the commitment to adequate speaking in the face of its fundamental inadequacy. Collaborating with those who are reasonable with regard to being open to the inadequacy of their own talk but who are spirited to find inventive solutions to such inadequacy, enables the dialectical integration of what are logically opposite and contradictory: ambition and reserve, spirit and reason. The goodwill, the willingness to give oneself over to the intractability of impossible questions, the discipline to dedicate oneself to the work of theorizing 'deep needs', the shared commitment to a common project, and so on, are all resources that the collaboration announced in *OBSI* draws on. If this is not the topic of *OBSI* it is the resource. Parenthetically, I note with Arendt that implied in this ground is 'a point where all objective standards yield precedence to the "subjective" criterion of the kind of person I wish to be and live together with' (Arendt, 2003, 111). Good company necessarily takes into account 'who' is speaking as well as 'what' is being spoken.

If through one's writing one seeks to offer the strongest possible analysis of a topic, through collaboration one also has to be open to responses which address the inadequacy of that offering, as part of the process of developing the strongest possible analysis of the topic – in light of the fundamental inadequacy of speech. If the pathos of writing requires a sense of confidence in the worth of one's offering, collaboration requires recognizing that such confidence not be fragile. Insofar as alter addresses the inadequacy of the strongest offering of ego, ego and alter both need to be open to the trouble-making character of this process, a trouble making exemplified by Socrates the gadfly (who, incidentally, has more references in *OBSI*'s index than any other name). The world of good company where ego and alter push each other more and more to think through their talk is a world where good company and the untimeliness of conversational trouble making are in friendship.

Goodwill, discipline, passion, commitment, having a shared sense of what is worthwhile, and so on, are all features of the kind of friendship and good company that Socrates, Plato, and Aristotle articulated as necessary and essential for inquiry. It is the absence of this in the teaching situation that led Peter McHugh to resign his position at York (1992, 108), where, as he experienced it, fundamental scholarly inquiry 'is pre-empted in consumerism by an image of life as endless and unreflective movement and accommodation – from place to place and thing to thing – and of education as a merely technical means for achieving these'. He did not give up on his commitment to theorizing but through his actions showed that the absence of good company made his commitment to collaborate difficult if not impossible to realize. In their very modern way, McHugh *et al.* re-discovered the value of this ancient virtue as they sought to respond strongly to the problem of the 'unformulability of grounds' a friendship that can recognize that while the difference between the part and the whole, beings and Being, speech and language is not a thing, that does not make it nothing (1974: 20).

Where Gadamer found confidence in the inheritance of language, McHugh and Blum found it in their working together and in working with their students. Where Gadamer (1976: 116) finds confidence in language because 'however far language might slip into a technical function, as language it holds the invariable things in our nature fast, those things which come to be spoken of in language again and again', the inquiry begun by *OBSI* 'that the need to work out and develop [to examine, to speak, to analyze]' is grounded in 'the need to defer in a way that we must accept with confidence rather than with suspicion' (1984: 151) as they conclude in their later work. It is the contention of this article that the *OBSI* authors can give themselves to the analysis of impossible first questions, because of respect for the problem of reflexive integrity in the context of an enjoyable working through the questions. They enjoy working out their relation to the content in a way that was articulated more directly in the *Self-Reflection* book. The core work of Analysis means developing the object of one's talk (the notion) in relation to the impossible possibility of fully adequate speaking (the absolute, the *logos*) and along the way develop the self of the inquirer. This is the Analysis way of separating and re-joining self with the world, and self with the self.

This tells us something about the nature of those who would or could hear this work and hear it in such a way as to take it up. A first requirement would involve an interest in a strong intellectual challenge. The integrity of the problem of being reflexive about being reflexive is an impossible intellectual challenge; this work invites those who have the ambition, intelligence and aptitude to take on such a challenge. But it also requires sensitivity, being sensitive to the charge of not practising what one preaches or of addressing the necessary inadequacy of one's own response to this problem. Thus we are at a contradiction again, this time between the intellectual confidence to tackle puzzles and problems and the humility to be open to the critique of the inadequacy of one's solution to the puzzle.

This tension is addressed more directly in Blum and McHugh's 1979 'Introduction'. Teachers invite students to compose themselves to hear the unsayable (the logos) in what is said (listening to the teacher), an invitation to the stranger that may be indifferently ignored, heard (friend), or actively resisted (enemy). As such, teaching 'needs to moderate impulses towards humanism [affirming] and criticism [rejecting] without disregarding what is critical to the human' (1979: 12). It is tempting to speculate that the excesses of responding to the call to collaborate would be the temptations to arrogance on the one hand, or to impotent perfectionism on the other, to the tension between intellectual snobbery and/or an intimidating sense of inadequacy. This issue is precisely spoken to at the end of this 'Introduction'. Speaking to the conference that preceded their 1979 publication, they say (17):

> One consequence of this encounter was a reassessment of the notions of familiarity and difference, a reappraisal of how we stood and of what we meant to one another, a recollecting of the relevant strengths of our common necessities and multitudinous purposes. The conference permitted many to see that they had wanted familiarity [good company] at the price of criticalness [troublesomeness] and often these many left disappointed. It also permitted others to appreciate how criticism [troublesomeness] could turn to contempt unless it respected its unity [good company] with those whom it sought to engage and some of these others left a little wiser.

While *OBSI* is a confident synthesis of these contradictory extremes, in retrospect, is it possible to glimpse what is now a more experiential contradiction?

Good troublesome company and the difference of dialectical theorizing

At the end of the 'Introduction' McHugh *et al.* formulate the nature and virtue of the method of collaboration as explicitly dialectical (1974: 14).

> While we produced this collection by transforming our collaboration into a kind of conversation that is interaction, our primordial notion of collaboration makes reference to the conversation within language and in this sense

the 'relation' between ego and alter can be re-presented as the dialectical engagement between the speaker and his tradition which is exemplified in his course of thought.

In developing this idea, they draw on the example of the relation of Socrates and his dialogue with interlocutors, where 'Socrates and his interlocutors ... [make] reference to the theoretical life, to the soul of the ideal theorist'. In this case, 'each interlocutor' is seen as an 'objection which the theorist ought to generate for him/[her] self' where every dialogue becomes

> the trace of an inward exchange reflected in the theorists struggle to speak faithfully by freeing himself from the dispersed mouthings of his self-centered interests and the Desire for truthful speaking.... The interlocutors personify the theorist's own self-interest, and the conversation within the soul that Plato speaks of as theorizing is a contest between self-interest and truth that makes the theorist apart because of all men he knows the difference.
>
> (McHugh *et al.*, 1974: 14)

With this formulation of dialectic as thesis and objection, of self-interest in struggle with the Desire for truthful speaking, a formulation that explicitly refers to Plato's formulation and exemplification of dialectic, I note a tension in their relation between dialogue, dialectic and good company. Here we have a distinction between interlocutors and collaborators. Interlocutors are not so much good company working within the limit of inadequacy of speech in the way described above, as temptations to self-centredness and self-interest. Here what they say about dialectic, on the surface seems to contradict the description and exemplification of the practice of collaboration, the practice of goodwill, enjoyable conversation, and recovering the good (desire) the collaborator speaks to. Rather, with this formulation, the claims of interlocutors need to be approached with suspicion, as if expressions of false consciousness in Marx's sense, the kind of suspicion (as I have noted) Blum and McHugh reject in their later work. And yet, as they describe their working practices of collaboration we get as sense of a collaborative relationship, exemplifying the strongest possible solution to the impossibility of self-grounding inquiry. Does the desire for differentiation, for seeing the theorist as 'apart from all men,' help make sense of the way they formulate many of the topics in the book?

Throughout many of the important ideas they analyse, they show their difference between the world sustained by bias, snubs, motive, travel, and even art (the phenomenon they are most respectful of) and the work of analysis. In the ideas analysed, though they are strongly and decisively engaged, in working to show their world they show their difference. Motive talk is treated as a deep interest in searching for cause and so in a misplaced version of origin (43–46), bias as a commitment to a method and, in explicit contrast to analysis, to a community that hides its own commitment (47–75), snubs as a world that is

dominated by the concerns of membership (109–134), art as different from analysis by virtue of the latter's commitment to formulating grounds and form of
life (154–182). All are strong analyses of important ideas, but also a form that
shows the difference between the analysis and what is analysed, as if regarding
the distinction between the speaker and language, Being and beings, analysts,
'apart from all men know the difference' (14–15).

Is this a contradiction that is at the heart of this exciting book, a contradiction
that they came to recognize and in ways resolve in their later work, *Self-
Reflection in the Arts and Sciences*? And is this contradiction built into the vocation of theorizing, the tempting conceit that theorists need to think of themselves
as apart from all men? The sense of intellectual pre-eminence and moral judgment that exudes from their analysis of travel, snubs, motive talk, is perhaps
necessary for the ambition needed to confidently begin an inquiry into ideas that
cannot be reduced to measurable things but are not nothing either.

Again, I have written on the way Blum and McHugh's later work responds to
the limits of *OBSI*. *Self-Reflection* takes a more conversational sociality with its
interlocutors. While maintaining their focus on the modern self-grounding
project, Blum and McHugh develop a dialectic that responds by treating all theorizing, regardless of difference, as recommending principles for acceptance
(1984). Their conversation with their interlocutors – whether Husserl, Marx,
Simmel, Garfinkel, Habermas, Barthes, and so on – is now how they work out
themselves and their relation to the principle of inquiry.[7]

But here I want to dwell on, as I see it, this contradiction in *OBSI* as providing the basis to grasp how theorizing and speaking goes forward. Their collaboration, it seems, is now seen here in terms of a contradiction between their mode
of production (good troublesome company) and the products of that mode (differentiated practices). To return to the Marx and Engel's formulation, what they
produce is now in tension with how they produce, if the latter requires virtues
that can sustain good troublesome company while the former requires the virtues
that sustain theoretic differentiation. The objects of analysis and the collaboration by which those objects were produced seem to operate on a different ethos,
showing the Real that has broken into the reality of the symbolic.

What is the nature of dialectic that sustains itself through its work of separating itself from what it is not? Clearly a theorizing is sustained, by virtue of 'the
Desire for truthful speaking' (1974: 14), a theorizing that continued to issue in
work that develops. They analyse snubs as a contradiction in the following way:
a snub, in its refusal to collaborate on a greeting, actually collaborates on the
offer of the greeting and so collaborates in way that denies the collaboration;
snubs, therefore, are deeply a contradictory practice. They go on to show, in contrast, that analysis embraces the principle of collaboration, in contrast to critical
theorizing. Their concluding section on snubs is interesting in this regard:

> We cannot snub anyone if we are to do our analytic work. Snub means
> affirming a difference.... It is our view that analysis requires ... collecting
> ... and consequently the sheer affirming of difference alone is not to do

analysis…. The same world (here: the concrete world) in which a snub can cause pain (although not too much pain because basically snubs protect) is one in which snubbing, i.e., being concrete, is a possibly proper action. The form of life that is bothered by snubs allows them to happen.

(1974: 135)

Here, the *OBSI* authors have thought through the reflexive implications of their analysis fully. They recognize that analysis and collaboration are essential features of the commitment to undertake inquiry. And while this analysis belittles the everyday world where snubs have a life, as if this were a world in which theorists did not also live, they affirm (through their analysis of greeting as deeply an offer to collaborate and suspend difference in order to collect) the invitation to collaborate built into the fabric of the offer to speak. That is, the possibility of communality that is the accomplishment of good troublesome company is built into the desire that a greeting hints at, the possibility of conversation. Good troublesome company is the remainder of the collaboration that issues in an analysis of snubs that claims not to be bothered by a snub.

Though the difference of this work is decisively demonstrated, and asserted in ways that posit the conversation of analysis as different from the worlds of positivism, common sense, university life, and even art, there are moments where they speak more to the principle of good troublesome company than the principle of analytic differentiation. Here, I want to select two. In the Art paper, they affirm the principle of 'mixed company' in recognition of the co-existence of the otherness of art and the identity of analysis. In this affirmation of 'mixed company', they resist interlocutors who would reduce art to a weak sister in the pursuit of truth (e.g. science) or reduce the otherness of art to an expression of self (e.g. sociology of art). They affirm the difference of analysis in their recognition of the otherness of art, a difference that needs neither to be belittled nor denied. In affirming the principle of mixed company, they show the ground for their openness to the anti-philosophical theorist they later embraced, Hannah Arendt, and her notion of plurality, especially in relation to the *polis* (1956). This helps articulate good troublesome company as both same and other, same in relation to showing one's commitment, and other in relation to making the meaning of that commitment subject to dialogue and conversation and so needing the otherness of plurality as intrinsic to dialectic.

I remember Peter McHugh once saying to me that he recognized Arendt's vivid description of the ancient *polis* in *The Human Condition*, as analogous to his experience of the annual conference in Perugia, Italy. Good company in this sense is organized around the actualization of diverse voices and actors who speak and act under the auspices of being with each other, neither for nor against, as a way of actualizing the diversity in the always unfinished conversation. In *OBSI* their recognition of the difference of art and their notion of mixed company are suggestive of a notion of the taste that good company cultivates and, again in contrast to ethnomethodological work, the recognition of the importance of the humanities as a friendly interlocutor.

Another moment of the affirmation of good company despite their differentiation of themselves from the subjects of analysis is their trusting call to the reader to collaborate on their work, to be alter to their ego.

> Because participation by the reader is differentiated in our case according to the differentiated relation between ego and alter, we can anticipate and hope that we are 'only' providing a way of seeing these concrete affairs such that you [the reader] could see those affairs in some grounded way, not necessarily in just the way we do. These are papers which seek a conversation, as it were.
>
> (8)

Here, in this very open and emancipating invitation, an invitation that after re-reading this book, while working in Alaska in a construction camp 300 miles north of the Arctic circle, I decided to take up by applying to York in Toronto, *OBSI* shows its openness to the world, an openness that the reader can find in this conversation the enjoyment of theorizing first or impossible questions, as both a way to develop a strong response and to develop self in relation to such responses. And yet, the actual experience of being a student in the community (good troublesome company) of analysis, an experience the book had not prepared me for, I learned the significance of the difference between the experience of being a reader and the experience of being a student, an issue Blum and McHugh began to come to terms with in their 1979 'Introduction'. Here they end with a formulation of the relation between theorizing, impossible first questions and pedagogy, a formulation that could be read as pointing to the insight of the necessary awkwardness of good troublesome company: 'The awkwardness of being humane with strangers (but not familiar) and of being critical with familiars (but not exegetical) will be seen for the necessity that they are' (17). The praxis of the teacher–student relation is truer to the experience of good troublesome company than the reader–writer relation, pointing to the tension between writing and dialogue Socrates highlighted in the *Phaedrus*.

The claim I make here is that this conversation both nurtures and is sustained by a continued development of a relation to good troublesome company whether as an internal dialogue between me and myself (Arendt, 1978), as interlocutors in theorizing, or as an interaction among colleagues. It is the dialectical relation between conversation and good troublesome company, a dialectic *OBSI* instantiates, that makes the dissatisfying quest to respond strongly and productively to impossible first questions enjoyable. If the difference between sophists and dialecticians is not necessarily in what either say but rather in the way they live what they say, the conversation that friendship and good troublesome company nurture through their collaboration is what *OBSI* began.

Ironically, and despite their own beginning, the significance of their beginning was not a new mode of production, a method of collaboration that was replicated in other works, but rather a commitment to conversation that takes seriously the promise to take responsibility for one's speech. Good troublesome company made it possible for Blum, McHugh, and colleagues to recognize that the inadequacy of all beginning (to speak, inquire) can be transformed by a commitment to conversation, a commitment that makes it possible to address impossible first questions. Taking seriously the question of reflexive integrity did not have to mean a denial of the inadequacy of speaking. What was begun was a way of making 'fundamental scholarly inquiry, such as "what are we and how should we live?"' (McHugh, 1992: 108), an ever-present, local and necessary aspect of inquiry. All beginnings are contingent, yet the good troublesome company that issues in analytic conversation means that the beginning can become the occasion 'to ask after the foundation of the human. To ask after the human is to exemplify the human is part of the whole'. The beginning that is social inquiry 'is the way in which the human exists as such a part by asking after the relationship of part to whole' (Blum and McHugh, 1984: 141).

Taking the question of reflexive integrity seriously, the inventive solution of collaboration means that that one neither has to be intimidated (Beckett) nor idealistically abstract (Heidegger) about asking after 'the foundation of the human'. The contingency of the beginning of social inquiry in the essential reflexivity of accounts does not need to resign to contingency nor, in totalitarian fashion, seek to eliminate contingency through abstracted theorizing. Good troublesome company allows for the recognition that through a collaborative analysis of an always-contingent beginning, humans can exemplify their humanity, and so point to the possibility of the universal and unconditional, but ironically in ways that are particular and conditional. What was begun was a way of showing that responding to impossible questions has an authentic relationship to contingent beginnings, when the speaker takes seriously the concern with reflexive integrity.

Notes

1 This is in contrast to Arendt, for example, who begins her *Life of the Mind* by addressing contingent facts from her past to explain why she takes up an area to inquire into that normally belongs to 'professional thinkers'.
2 As we will see, collaboration refers not just to intellectual relationships but also to social relationships. 'This product is the work of a dialectical relationship begun at Columbia University with Peter McHugh and some of our students' (Blum, 1974: ix). 'Therefore, Marx's notion recommends deeply that the idea of relationship is exemplified in the notion of [humans] relating through their commitments ... and is shown in the speaking with displays its Desire to be a hearing' (Blum, 1974: 262).
3 They explicitly read Marx's 'material conditions' as referencing 'what Husserl called the "life-world"' (16) and so are more semiological than Arendt in relation to Marx.
4 I thank Stanley Raffel for drawing my attention to the relevance of this to my paper here.
5 Think here of the silence that finds a practice in the religious traditions of meditation, or the silence that marks a tragic event or the commemoration of such. I thank Barry Sandywell for motivating me to think some more on the manifold temptations of silence.
6 'For the Greeks the essence of friendship consisted in discourse.... However much we are affected by the things of the world, however much they may stir and stimulate us, they become human for s only when we discuss them with our fellows. Whatever

cannot become the object of discourse – the truly sublime, the truly horrible or the uncanny – may find a human voice through which to sound into the world, but it is not exactly human. We humanize what is going on in the world and in ourselves only by speaking of it, and in the course of speaking of it we learnt to be human' (Arendt, On Men in Dark Times, 24–25).

7 As well and separately, both Raffel (e.g. 2006) and Bonner (e.g. 2010), draw on this later development in Analysis to take up Socrates' interlocutors in order to show that there is more going on, for example, with either Crito or Alcibiades than 'dispersed mouthings'.

Bibliography

Arendt, H. (1958). *The human condition.* Chicago: University of Chicago Press.

Arendt, H. (1961) *Between past and future: Eight exercises in political thought.* New York: Viking Press.

Arendt, H. (1965). *Eichmann in Jerusalem: A report on the banality of evil.* Middlesex, England: Penguin Books.

Arendt, H. (1978). *The Life of the mind.* New York: Harcourt Brace Jovanovich.

Arendt, H. (2003). *Responsibility and judgment.* Ed. with Intro by Jerome Kohn. New York: Schocken Books.

Beckett, S. (1969). 'Samuel Beckett talks about Beckett', interview with John Gruen, *Vogue* (December 1969): 210.

Blum, A. (1974). *Theorizing.* London: Heinemann.

Blum, A. (1978). *Socrates: The original and its images.* London: Routledge and Kegan Paul.

Blum, A. (2003). *The imaginative structure of the city.* Montreal: McGill-Queens University Press.

Blum, A. and McHugh, P. (1971). 'The social ascription of motives'. *American Sociological Review,* 36, 98–109.

Blum, A. and McHugh, P. (1979). *Friends, enemies, and strangers: Theorizing in art, science, and everyday life.* New Jersey: Ablex Publishing Corporation.

Blum, A. and McHugh, P. (1984). *Self-reflection in the arts and sciences.* New Jersey: Humanities Press.

Bonner, K. (1997). *A great place to raise kids: Interpretation, science and the urban–rural debate.* Montreal and Kingston: McGill-Queen's University Press.

Bonner, K. (1998). *Power and parenting: A hermeneutic of the human condition.* London: Macmillan/New York: St. Martin's Press.

Bonner, K. (2001). 'Reflexivity and interpretive sociology: The case of analysis and the problem of nihilism'. *Human Studies,* 24, 267–292.

Bonner, K. (2010). 'Peter McHugh and analysis: The one and the many, the universal and the particular, the whole and the part'. *Human Studies.* 33, 253–269.

Bonner, K. (2013). '*Mundane and radical referential reflexivity: The Pollner/Lynch debate and the hermeneutic circle of topic and resource'.* Paper presentation at 11th International Institute for Ethnomethodology and Conversational Analysis, Waterloo, Ontario.

Bonner, K. (2014). 'Principles, dialectic, and the common world of friendship: Socrates and Crito in conversation'. *History of the Human Sciences* 27: 2, 157–179.

Brown, M. (1988). 'A radical re-collection of sociology: Self-reflection in the arts and sciences'. In M. Van Manen (ed.), *Self-reflection in the human sciences* (24–40). Edmonton: Lifeworld Editions.

Dallmayr, F. (1988). 'Praxis and reflection'. In M. Van Manen (ed.), *Self-reflection in the human sciences* (1–15). Edmonton: Lifeworld Editions.

Gadamer, H.G. (1975). *Truth and method.* London: Sheed and Ward.

Gadamer, H.G. (1976). *Hegel's dialectic.* (Translated with an Introduction. P.C. Smith). New Haven: Yale University Press.

Gadamer, H.G. (1985). *Philosophical apprenticeships.* Cambridge: MIT Press.

Gadamer, H.G. (1986). *The idea of the good in Platonic-Aristotelian philosophy.* (Translated with an Introduction. P.C. Smith). New Haven: Yale University Press.

Garfinkel, H. (1967). *Studies in ethnomethodology.* Cambridge: Polity Press.

Giddens, Anthony. (1976). *New rules of sociological method: A positive critique of interpretive Sociologies.* New York: Basic Books.

Heritage, J. (1984). *Garfinkel and ethnomethodology.* Cambridge: Harvard University Press.

Lynch, M. (2000). 'Against reflexivity as an academic virtue and source of privileged knowledge'. *Theory, Culture and Society*, 17, 26–54.

Marx, K. and Engels, F. (1947). *The German ideology,* New York: International Publishers.

McHugh, P. (1992). 'A letter of resignation'. *Dianoia*, 22, 106–111.

McHugh, P. (1996). 'Insomnia and the (t)error of lost foundationalism in postmodernism'. *Human Studies*, 19, 17–42.

McHugh, P. (2005). 'Shared being, old promises, and the just necessity of affirmative action'. *Human Studies*, 28, 129–156.

McHugh, P., Raffel, S., Foss, D., and Blum, A. (1974). *On the beginning of social inquiry.* London: Routledge and Kegan Paul.

Plato (1945). *The republic* (F.M. Cornford, Trans.). New York: Oxford University Press.

Raffel, S. (2006) 'Parasites, principles and the problem of attachment to place', *History of the Human Sciences* 19(3): 83–108.

Sharrock, W. and Anderson, B. (1986) *The ethnomethodologists.* New York: Tavistock Publications.

Smith, P.C. (1986). 'Translator's Introduction' in Hans-Georg Gadamer. *The idea of the good in Platonic-Aristotelian philosophy.* (Trans. P.C. Smith). New Haven: Yale University Press.

Wittgenstein, L. (1958). *Philosophical investigations.* Oxford: Basil Blackwell.

Part V
Origins and prospects

14 On the unending beginning of social inquiry

Alan Blum

Preamble

The problem of approaching a book such as *OBSI*, a landmark from the past for some of us, lies in determining the kind of influence it was for us and whether it reflects a spell we fell under temporarily, and so, a historical moment that marked our intellectual immaturity, or the nucleus of something larger that might continue to live for us after its time has passed. On the lowest step of Plato's Divided Line, this concern leads us to ask of what is this book an image.

At the next step imagined as we ascend to the level of opinion, debate, and the war of beliefs, we might suggest that the book on the one hand reflects a historical moment that has passed, and, like antiquated paradigms in a positivist history, was fated to be surpassed in the name of progress. On the other hand we can ask if that moment in our history was more than this, something that we might still use to learn from. Here, our original question asking what we can imagine for the book materializes in an argument over whether the book is once and no more, or an influence that we can still affirm, and in so doing translate the question about its value today and whether it can redeem both itself as a book and us, or remain as part of a past that our worldly experience has separated us from. Extremist responses here could say that the book and its time are over, a vestige of intellectual adolescence, or that it is untouchable much like a fundamentalist text and law.

This argument forces us to another level where we can begin to realize our desire to think through this opposition in order to recover the common problem that it discloses, even in such a specification, through contested beliefs. Here, the Real challenges us to overcome this opposition while preserving their differences as expressions of a fundamental situation of perplexity regarding the unstable and ambiguous status of the past, memory, and its embodiment in the book, the enigmatic question concerning the meaning of what is past. That is, if we distrust the extremes as I do as unconversational abstractions, that can deny the past on the one hand and/or absolutize the past on the other hand, we must begin to engage the relationship between this book of our past and our present by trying to ground its relevance for us today and the continuity this must assume, by disclosing how the landmark works for us now, how the ambiguity of the problem it invites us to engage requires an art that connects this book of the past to us now. This is what I try, to bring the past to bear upon our present and to make our present indispensable for recovering the value of this past. The book still lives and I cannot either treat it as a ghostly vestige or allow it to remain a symbol of perfection, but must provide for how it has become contemporary not because of or in spite of the changes and influences it has absorbed but through the very action of engaging and remaking them as conditions for us today.

A model of amplification derived from Erasmus' rhetoric provides for how we analyse the recurrence of the same in the otherness of circumstances varying over time by identifying a situation of action concealed by the appearance of the change as different in kind rather than degree (Hegel: cancelling the opposition and preserving the difference). The analysis then works to make transparent the problem raised by the situation and the discourse surrounding its intended solutions as an ethical collision needing to be playfully reinvented in practice as a relationship to clarify.

Amplification

In *On Copia*, Erasmus ([1512] 1963) identifies *techné* as the capacity to vary (which he calls 'amplification'), the form of inventiveness distinctive to the human. This is important because originality is detached from any sense of creation *ex nihilo* by virtue of its affiliation with the figure of variation or of varying what, in some sense, already exists. True originality then always operates within limits that it inherits by varying what is received and secure, expressing or amplifying what in some sense is in need of being diversified. True originality does not aspire to imitate divine creation (say, making something out of nothing) but to vary what is known and accepted. Amplification always resists the temptation to equate inventiveness with genesis.

In this sense the recovery of the past in the present exemplifies amplification as the model of our view of history as something other than sterile repetition but as an interest in constantly reworking the orientation of the position to intervene in contemporary circumstances that always seem to change. Here, the notion of amplification, borrowed from Erasmus' rhetoric, captures for us the fertile relation of the Same to the Other as diversification where the creativity of the work resides in its capacity to maintain its voice in new circumstances and to grasp such changes as different expressions of the same. For example, the apparent changing world of data collection and management today does not stand as a difference in kind but as a difference of degree, something not opposed to analysis but an opportune occasion to specify and develop its positioning. Thus, amplification describes the relation of a hypothetical origin to its diversification in changing circumstances much in the way a problem is expressed in different shapes and forms. The 'origin' is then hypothesized as a problematic situation of action dramatized in a collision over the best path(s) to take. The problem is then never solved as in an algorithmic model of a finite and determinate outcome but clarified as a site of ambiguity that can be engaged in ways that might produce jouissance for all participants in disclosing the situation as a common project that remains irresolute.

Language provides the material for variation in its abundance: 'the rich *copia* of thoughts and words' of which Erasmus speaks is made possible by the fertility of language. It is this abundance that makes possible both speech that is 'admirable and splendid', and those excesses of brevity and loquacity that 'befall a few mortals' and leave them to 'burden the ears of their wretched hearers'.

Erasmus' image of language as abundance, as a source of variation and differentiation, as anything but a situation of scarcity, makes possible both historical and contemporary diversity. As the capacity to express verities through diversification and amplification, language offers us a continuous opportunity to develop what appears closed. Both society and individual can always find a place in language, by virtue of their ability to vary what appeared secure, by opening up what appeared to be closed.

If, then, there is always the opportunity for particularity, so too is there always an opportunity for the community to show itself by varying or amplifying what is handed down. If the Renaissance of Italy, for example, was supposedly paralyzed by the magnificent and apparent finality of the achievement of the ancient world, it was also stimulated to discover its own means of amplifying such achievements as its way of being in the world. Amplification reformulates rather than dismisses originality so as to preserve the status of individuality as something not absolute but social.

In his *On Copia*, Erasmus pictures the relation of the origin to its inscription in terms of the image of variation, of the varying problem. It is not as if the origin has some sort of antecedent and discrete authority or privileged priority in relation to its various inscriptions, because the empowering and inspiring character of the origin can only be discerned in what it inspires. This is to say that the problem and its expression go hand-in-hand. Such an origin is then the problem imagined and hypothesized as the ethical collision animating the speech.

As a phenomenon, the origin functions much like a question that elicits intended answers or solutions to the question it implies. It is in this sense that the origin is nothing other than a representation of the question that initiates a discourse and in whose name the discourse moves. In our sense the origin posits an opening for dialogue into the framework or paradigm that organizes classification and conditions of action. All usage in this way is fertilized by a question that is posed of the matters that the usage is intended to clarify. For example, at the time of our book the question or general conception it addressed was the usage on positive thinking. The usage then reflects the ways in which any present amplifies the question that it conceals and by which it is animated. Thus, concerns today for so-called 'big data' or algorithmic problem-solving are different usages that invite specification of certain recurrent problems or questions that they assume and mask. In this specific sense there are no mistakes in usage, no errors, since all usage amplifies a problem. Yet amplification, though always true to its question in the way an answer 'belongs' to its problem as one method of intending a solution, can be distorted in its way (say, in the ways algorithmic formulations exclude the ambiguity of the actions they identify, or 'big data' must mask the complexity of the subject in a format that externalizes action in terms of variables).

At this point, we can begin to appreciate how the ambiguity of theorizing occurs in relation to the way language itself empowers diversification and, in that empowerment, covers over what is varied. That is, the material that is varied, the question to which the usage is a response, always risks being masked or concealed by the spectacle of diversity itself since our immediate attachment to an inscription often tempts us to forget what is varied; that is, the original speech, or question that has inspired what we apprehend.

If abundance makes possible both diversification and variation, and its shape as individuation and the concealment of the problem that is masked by variation, it is *in that masking*, also expressed by variation itself. Thus, Erasmus' model of amplification stresses the character of ambiguity as it exists in amplification itself insofar as what is expressed needs the distortion offered by expression to show itself as a phenomenon and to stimulate the seductive entrapment that is always promised by the loss or absence of what is shown.

What Erasmus' conception of amplification suggests is the inescapable continuity of human inventiveness as an opportunity of the species insofar as the fertility of language is a continuous occasion for development that includes all of the risks that this implies. It is this *copia* which makes possible human inventiveness in a way that includes both its realization and its distortion, that is, in a way that provides both for its enjoyment and for the anxiety of freedom and/or influence. Amplification improvises with inherited usage by making transparent assumptions and conditions held in abeyance in order to negate the sense of security that protects distinctions from exposure.

In this way, beginning the book with the chapter on motive expressed our desire to intervene in a line of thought and action that we felt to be exhausted as it stood, in which what we called positivism, as an implicit doctrinal orientation, seemed to rule the university. Positivism shaped its subject (that had to include us as 'victims' of its influence) in at least three ways: by disciplining us to strive for an ideal of neutrality in ways that required us to hold in abeyance personal inclinations; following this, by teaching us that the difference between good and bad work is given by standards that are justifiable in terms of criteria that are best left untouched because anything else would disturb the neutrality that is coveted; and in stipulating that guidelines follow from these assumptions that need to be accepted in practice at the cost of inquiry being praised or discredited. As Foucault was later to make crystal clear to the widest possible academic audience, and as the phenomenological tradition and specifically Schutz ([1953] 1973), Merleau-Ponty (2005), Sartre (1963), and, for us, Garfinkel (1967) had long reiterated, such a subject was shaped, regulated, and turned into a puppet of the normative order and *yet*, at the same time, endowed with capacities that make some degree of resistance possible. This is also a special contribution of our work, to dwell upon Plato's final cause as the relation of theorizing to life and the particular connection that I make and hope to continue developing between education and rehabilitation, a connection originating with Plato, modernized by Marx and Freud in their respective ways and continued in our research and in the works of a few others as the conception of jouissance as a 'solution' to the problem of life that identifies it in the enjoyable bearing of ambiguity. We have learned from Simmel's notion of self-transcendence that the drive called jouissance is both a normal feature of human desire and a source of ambiguity by virtue of its capacity to sustain both positive and negative outcomes but always as an engagement and drive towards excess as self-empowering. In his conception of self-transcendence Simmel supplied the definitive version of social affectivity that was to become a staple in sociological views of action as performance that was later developed in Goffman, Garfinkel, and ordinary language philosophy and is of currency in many contemporary derivatives.

> Certainly the category I call here 'the reaching out of life beyond itself' is thus meant only symbolically, only with an inclination that it can probably be improved. Taken in its essence, I hold it at all events to be a primary one.... Insofar as life's essence goes, transcendence is immanent to it (it is not something that must be added to its being, but instead is constitutive of its being). The simplest and most fundamental instance of what is meant here is self-awareness, which is also the original phenomenon of the living human spirit.
>
> (Simmel, [1918] 2010: 9)

Beginnings

It has to be appreciated that the book was produced as part of the spirit of the 1960s when the mood of the time influenced the most precocious of its generation to stage a coup d'état against its older predecessors and more cautious or sluggish peers and to express this resistance in challenges to various conventions relating to popular culture, so-called life style, political arrangements, and dogmatic formulae that appeared to govern relationships to race, gender, and age, and various disputes between types of student and faculty regarding the policies and structure of the university. What Lacan was to call two of the four discourses, of the university and the hysteric, were pitted against each other (Lacan, [1969–1970] 2007: 11–29). We could say that this was the scene for the emergence of the book within the context of an environment that included contentious views of the university typified in methods and procedures in circulation that seemed to objectify both faculty and students, and selected administrators and faculty in an acrimonious exchange in the name of a kind of spiritual regeneration that seemed to be in the air.

Moreover, within this context, in New York City and on the campus of Columbia University and its environs, the book was the outgrowth of a friendship and collaboration between two young professors, McHugh and myself, bonding to survive and overcome such objectification that we viewed as inflicted upon us by the university and its pedantic ethos of professionalism, while yet also benefitting from that persecution to create alliances with students who were to become friends such as Stanley Raffel, Stephen Karatheodoris, Daniel Foss, and many others, and to work together in a creative collaboration destined to bear the fruit of its materialization in the book. So the book was overdetermined, by the spirit of the times, by the dialectic between persecutors and victims, by the friendship of two vulnerable faculty, and by their appetite for convivial relations with their own students. Finally, the book was created in the great city of New York where friendship could be stimulated and translated into collaboration in an environment conducive to the marriage of pleasure and work.

Motive for inquiry: intervention

We inherited the distinction of culture and its resonances as a cliché that emphasizes the artifice of custom or convention that emerges in response to formlessness and its threat of discord, as for example when culture is used as a figure for the pacification of violence (unruliness, self-interest, the jungle, war of all against all, etc.). In this sense, informed by the accent of political theory and the social order problem, culture was typically treated as an antidote to violence. If models of law supported such a version, then it was also conceded over time that law exercised its own violence in ways that made it difficult to distinguish the violence of legal interdiction or of classification from any other kind of violence. Thus, the violence of dogmatic classification was recognized as political at its core. The turmoil of the 1960s – Berkeley, Haight-Ashbury, the Black Panthers, the music of The Doors, the conflict between old left and new left, the march on Washington, Dylan, the Democratic convention in Chicago, the plays of Pinter, Vietnam, the French New Wave in cinema, the strikes at Columbia and in European cities – all tended to make views of violence transparent and even facilitated the easy transfer of this interpretive machinery to the domestic infrastructure and to the suburban mentality, to conceptions of mealy-mouthed other-directedness as the forerunner of today's corporate-driven glad-handed positive thinking, to the tepid organization man, to the manipulative hidden persuaders and such images as marks of a new understanding of oppression eventually habituated in the figure of pacific authoritarianism anticipated by Gramsci, the dissemination of the work of Foucault, and the migration of critical theory in the aftermath of fascism. So with the distinction we also inherited the desire to intervene in the discourse in its name. But as Derrida (1994) says of any inheritance, using Marx as his signpost, it is basically heterogeneous, diverse and usable in many ways.

We discovered in the resources of classical sociology, joined to the Greeks and those such as Heidegger and Wittgenstein, the promise of an alternative conception of culture as a version of ontology, or what is today called limit thinking. Here the influence of Freud's conception of the frustration and aggression that so-called civilization perpetuates on nature through mechanisms such as repression could only enable us to see the origins of civilization in (symbolic) violence. Thus, eventually, in our retrospective reflection on this beginning, we note now how many inquirers at the time and after us came to dramatize the figure of the violent origins of the symbolic order in the system of classification that has to silence the ambiguity or connotative excess haunting of any act of signification. For us at the time, in a trajectory that was seen through our lens as developing in works of Karl Marx, Max Weber, Émile Durkheim, Georg Simmel, eventually George Herbert Mead, Kenneth Burke, and now many up to and through Erving Goffman and beyond, we came to recognize how any social order has to distribute evaluations and support a hierarchic organization of right and wrong that is grounded only in its own conception of legitimacy and that creates scapegoats and victims simply by virtue of its own justification. This idea of the legitimate order inherited from Weber, who analysed its pretense of neutrality, its scapegoats and victims determined normatively, and the questionable appearance or visibility of the impact of such an order, made our eventual topics of Bias, Evaluation, and Snubs provocative openers for analysis.

Yet this inheritance included for us more than the affirmation of the rule of social construction and artifice in life, of role, custom, convention, performance, and the rest of that machinery that opened itself to the universality of interpretation, but correlative with this, a recognition of the space in Being that was vacated by what metaphysics called the transcendental and that we treated as a kind of otherness within, an alterity that was both external and internal, a space of fundamental ambiguity at the heart of action that rendered it inevitably as the remainder that always remains, and so, that always demands of us some accountability in taking its measure and/or disposing of it. The idea of a remainder captured for us this space not as a deprivation or loss but as a parameter of the human condition, whether the hole in Being or das Ding, as Lacan called it, or the site of fundamental ambiguity or Grey Zone as we came to understand. Yet in contrast to our compatriots in ontology, under the influence of our American pragmatism, we saw this space as a problem-solving situation that was two-sided in the spirit of Durkheim's ([1895] 1938) social fact, external as a constraint, and liberating as an incentive for action. This innovation seems to mark us over time as exercised in a unique way by a conception of fundamental ambiguity as a problem to solve, and so, as a site for research into the convoluted problem-solving of social actors under various conditions. In this way we reconnected sociology to the Greeks and to many dialectical influences we borrowed and translated from Hegel, Heidegger, Wittgenstein, and to their followers who were ready to take risks with their works rather than repeating them exegetically. For example, even the supposedly conservative Talcott Parsons' (1966) focus on social life as a set of solutions to functional problems made implicit and undeveloped reference to 'ultimate meaning' as the bedrock and inescapable ground of representation, which though unspoken in his work, was a stunning intervention for a sociologist, and allowed us to appreciate the social order as a collection of methods and procedures for solving the problem of such ambiguity. The problem is not 'solved' in any determinate sense but only as the creation of a representation that imitates the gaze of logos in its reflective practice, exhibiting a capacity to take pleasure in bearing finality as libidinal and inconclusive.

Garfinkel saw this, of course, but in his work it took shape in a fantasy of description, and it could not be made palatable because discussions of Parsons were limited by 'official' disputes about functionalism and conflict theory that externalized his work, and our accidental positioning in sociology made other kinds of approaches appear 'unsociological' or philosophical. In the American university of this time, sociology tended to be peopled by those who treated areas of specialty such as deviance and criminology and ethnicity as major avenues of intellectual advance and challenge, always seeing what they called 'theory' as if a separate field or domain, or as marked by a capacity to identify themes or make typologies of this-and-that into final judgments rather than playful provocative beginnings. This would invariably make sociology a comedy for us unless we could restore its strongest voice against the majority interest.

Yet it was typical that we could make no headway in such an environment, seeking as we did in our approach that imitated the nomenclature of Heidegger, to relay grounds of texts as a method that was only just beginning to titillate some few in the humanities under the name of deconstruction. When I brought a new translated copy of *On Grammatology* to Peter who was living in an apartment in Paris for the year, we examined this text together with pleasure for happening upon one who appeared as a soulmate, though different from us in substantial ways. Yet we continued to plough on, finding jewels here and there, coming to understand ultimate meaning not as a metaphysical fantasy or objective for philosophy but as the intimation of a problem-solving situation in which fundamental ambiguity comes to view in myriad mundane events of everyday life, as a recurrent perplexity both vivid and forceful. Thus, in accord with Freud's mantra that large matters betray themselves in very small or slight indications, our reading of the sociological classics in conjunction with the works of the Greeks stimulated by Heidegger and my student Stephen Karatheodoris, and the work of Wittgenstein stimulated by our encounter with ordinary language philosophy through Garfinkel's texts, permitted us to take up matters as researchable phenomena through case studies of what seem to be innocuous actions. This territory, mined particularly by Goffman (1967) and by Baudrillard (1991), reverses the concrete, hierarchical division of macro–micro by viewing the interdependence of large- and small-scale not in the events represented, but in the nature of representation itself, and in contrast to symbolic interaction and ethnomethodology, it can see the value-laden nature of all conduct in what Simmel ([1918] 2010) called the Ought as a pervasive feature of mundane life that is both indefinite and observable.

Variations on a theme: the eternal problem of positive thinking

We saw positivism as rooted in the ideal of positive thinking (Blum, 'Positive Thinking,' *Theory and Society* 1 [3]) as an emphasis on forward progress and an advance, measurable as progress through definite criteria or milestones. In this sense it emerges as a call to action, requiring commitment to such movement and, consequently, demanding a kind of self-organization that is capable of renouncing 'incidentals' or distractions that could impede this campaign. In a real sense, all life requires a positive embrace of the present situation as having consequences and so as making a difference. To imagine an interlocutor to this position, a kind of anti-life gesture of arrested dedication, we should read Miriam Toews' novel (*All My Puny Sorrows* (2014)) that represents a character's attempt to seduce her prodigy sister to desire life and renounce her drive for suicide. Yet, being positive in this sense or embracing life as consequential still needs to make a place for the activity of negation – not as such melancholic resignation or even negativism – but as a kind of forceful and playful engagement within life itself. This is because negation as the desire to question and modify our inheritance is every bit as necessary for progress as loyalty to the convention required to speak of it since an untouchable inheritance will stagnate and dissolve as circumstances change. Positive thinking that resonates with an ideal of productivity then has to make a place for negation in its practice. Negation as a gesture that questions and intervenes in the legacy of any present is the means for beginning to invest the inheritance with vitality and of saving it from becoming petrified. The direction of our work was and remains to resist the tendency to expel life because of its absurdity but to work on discovering a place within life for a positive affirmation of negation itself. There is a tendency within positive thinking to fear ambiguity and the irresolution that it brings to the surface as endangering its drive for rootedness and stability. Thus, a primary focus of our work has been on how positive thinking sanctions a jouissance of administration, that is, a version of authoritative ways and means of self-composition under conditions of its demand for movement and undiluted concentration. In the idiom of sociology, the march forward demands of the subject a particular shape of motivated compliance that Durkheim and Weber exposed in bringing to view the instabilities besetting such a subject and that Foucault has modernized under contemporary conditions. Yet, Descartes remains the figure celebrated for bringing such an imaginary to view and the question we can always raise asks how we might inject into such a subject and its situation of action a degree of playfulness towards its inheritance that can interrupt its concentration in order to rebuild it in any present. We needed to show how the motivated compliance to the jouissance of administration that the ideal of positive thinking seemed to imply (its ideal of self-composure) was an affective commitment that needed to be challenged by a drive for more than this, a drive towards self-transcendence that could risk bearing the irresolution as its remains without guilt.

We can treat Descartes as a mouthpiece for the imaginary of positivist thinking in his conception of progress as dependent upon the expurgation of ambiguity as a purification of our procedure by starting with basic agreements that promise to create an algorithmic series of steps leading to a determinate outcome. He imagines the possibility of evaluation proceeding from such agreement in which all extraneous 'subjective' influences are expelled so that people can concentrate without distraction on 'essentials'. Basically, the imaginary desires to exclude what cannot be rationalized, and so, what might 'infect' any procedure. In this way the element of aesthetic and affective engagement in the action (what praxiology called the values and ethics of the procedure) is excluded on the basis of assumptions (the same sense of values and ethics) that are seen to be excluded). If it is reputed that Descartes inaugurated the drive of positive thinking, this formula still uses him as a scapegoat for the collective imaginary, even in Girard's sense, needing to find a source responsible for the sacrificial crisis of positivist dispute and the anxiety over its irresolution. Descartes exemplifies the collective desire for exactitude, for certainty, for consistency, and total transparency, for a unity between wish and fulfilment that is always at risk and always dreamt as an obstacle to be overcome. In this sense Descartes is also used as the scapegoat for an idealization of unity between word and action that is forever anticipated and unattainable. Positive thinking when criticized is seen as a plague inflicted on a community for its inability to be self-governing and is reflected in three ways: first, in views of discussion as a war between different doctrines that makes it impossible for agreement to be achieved, permitting evaluation to proceed without adversarial wrangling and self-justification; second, in attributions of the absence of a method as due to the lack of the will to compose oneself and eliminate self-aggrandizing inclinations that lead to persistent bias; and finally, in the fear that even when an agreement is established between reasonable speakers about self-composition, an area of ambiguity always persists (as between Descartes and Hobbes, Gassendi, and the others) that cannot guarantee unity. In contrast to polemical critique of such positive thinking we want to analyse the pleasure that such thought can be seen as giving its practitioners. This is a task that we inherit as part of our need to struggle with our tendency to act out against positivism by seeking to overcome this temptation by focusing upon the ways such an intellectual regime imagines it and enjoys engineering and administering a forward march.

Our method then connects to Hegel's comments (1955) in his preface to the *Phenomenology*, where he both shows and tells what it is to set up a problem for consideration in ways that make analysis begin necessarily with a negative gesture that is positive in its status as a beginning, and so is negative not in the sense of being sceptical about the content but desirous of bringing out what seems latent in the notion, *negating* this general conception neither by 'counter assertions or random thoughts from the outside' but by developing the conception through analysis of the action of distinguishing that is meant to demonstrate the specificity of the general conception by systematic reference to what he calls 'the rich and concrete abundance of real life'.

And our intention was to develop an exposition that could negate the general conception of positive thinking by developing it through reference to the rich abundance of real life. In this sense we sought to make a place for the gesture of negation within positive thinking (see Herbert Marcuse, *Reason and Revolution* for a classical and still timely formulation of this intellectual territory, and many other of his works such as *One-Dimensional Man*).

The architecture of the book

What we sought to negate was not any one particular conclusion or 'finding' but the resistance to positing that lay at the core of positive thinking in its belief that positing only equivocates and hesitates rather than progresses with strength of will. Thus negation negates the settlement of meaning in sanctified and unexamined declarations that should be continuous opportunities for revisiting usage rather than final judgments. We suggest that the relation to positing must accept the need to continue and develop in the absence of dogmatic assurance, that is, in the absence of certainty about beginnings and endings. In this way we tried to resurrect the latent ambivalence towards what is seen as the indecisive character of positing that lay covered over in dogmatic positive thinking. Our work suggested that what positing must posit is the limit of any conclusion and the necessity to embrace and develop what can only be hypothesized. Positing must posit the value of life in the present in the absence of conclusive reassurance signified by the fact (as Lacan says) that Other does not answer.

The two papers beginning and ending the volume are appropriately matched to the topics or commonplace relationships of motive and art because motive focuses on beginnings, that is, motive addresses sources or grounds of thought and action, on how the action and thought of inquiry might be said to result from other beginnings while reopening paths of inquiry as new avenues for exploration. In ways similar but different, art focuses on ends, that is, on how the action of inquiry might be said to engage the excess or surfeit of inquiry, and so, how inquiry must begin where words and their determination end.

If in this sense art might provoke us to see all discourse as unending, and so, as always having the capacity to begin anew as both end and beginning, motive always provokes us to see any beginning as the end of a line of thought and action that must begin again. Both motive and art teach us if we are alert, to appreciate how life needs the mix of ends that begin again and beginnings that reopen endings as features of both motive and art, because we need to see results as the offer of new beginnings and to see new beginnings as indebted to precedents. Further, both motive and art purport to deal with what cannot be known, in one case the inscrutable past that birth can only leave unspoken, and in the other case, the unforeseen future that death can only leave unknown. Both motive and art require us to invent stories that will try to solve such problems speculatively in the shape of fictions that are necessary and desirable, stories serving as our equipment for living. This helps us place the book, too, recognizing that its beginning occurred in response to the need for revitalization and that its end was always an invitation to renew what was started there and continues today and hopefully hereafter.

In *On the Beginning of Social Inquiry* (McHugh *et al.*, 1974), we tried to develop this locus of tension around the ambiguity of violence and its two-sided character as a research programme that was not fully appreciated at that time. We could only accomplish our project by reformulating violence as the methodical system of classification and exclusion on which any social order was based.

Yet violence seemed a hyperbolic figure for describing the methods and proced-ures entering into the constitution of social life described eloquently by Goffman and by Garfinkel, making culture transparent not only in routines and ritual for doing activities but for undoing as well, for example in excluding matters of concern and relevance. In that work we took up the surreptitious violence perpet-rated by a normative order in our inquiries into positivism, objectification, bias, acceptance, and rejection of research and the problematic criteria on which such evaluation had to be based. Yet the violence of our approach seemed to recipro-cate the violence of the social order in a transference relationship that appeared to offer no escape through analysis, no respite from what Girard called a sacrifi-cial crisis.

The sacrificial crisis and the hysterical exchange: reciprocal caricature

The book begins with a paper on 'Motive' that we had already published in the *American Sociological Review* and ends with a paper on 'Art'. Positive thinking, always uneasy with motive and art, typically and at its best rationalizes and externalizes these notions or, today, converts them into neurological or chemical factors. An analysis of the symbolic order of positivism seems to be sandwiched between these two pillars but this is a ruse that makes reference to positivism in order to display a method and means of making reference, a method and mode of dialectic that we named Analysis and was intended as our alternative to posit-ivism. Thus, at first glance the book appears to be both a debate between posit-ivism and Analysis, and a showcase for the display of the method of Analysis: this can invariably raise both the question of which of the two it is, *and* the rejec-tion of this either/or alternative that argues instead for its use of the debate to reveal the method, or to poach from Benjamin's ([1928] 1977) description of the Baroque, its use of the debate as content serving as a stage prop for the display of the method.

If in psychoanalytic lingo, say Laplanche (1999), the message is the voice of the unconscious, this fits well because when the content is the work of con-sciousness, this can reaffirm the helpful platitude that speaking discloses the unconscious as medium and message. So we could say that the book sets out to explore the unconscious of positivism as it had never been done and shows in part in such an enterprise, a glimpse of *its* unconscious, the unconscious of so-called Analysis that needed to be exercised and dangerously exposed by such an undertaking as we shall see today. Thus, if positive thinking is unsettled by the conception of libido, we show this by disclosing the libidinal character of the positive imaginary.

Yet it seemed as if our analysis of positivism, even as a symbolic order rooted in an unconscious regime, risked reciprocating the violence by virtue only of the difference between us, and just as positivism expected us to be similar to it and its orthodoxy, we seemed to expect positivism to be like us. We claimed in the book that positivism protected its speech, made gratuitous and ungrounded accusations and evaluations, but we could be seen to do the same, creating a spectacle of two different approaches to inquiry, each claiming superiority to the other in terms of criteria that were specific to each. This mutual objectification was joined to our inability (and certainly the positivists') to provide a sense of how our difference made a difference. For example, our claim that we differ by virtue of our capacity to analyse positivism in contrast to their inclination or inability to analyse us according to *their* criteria, simply reiterates our differences without showing how what we do and what they do not do is good, that this difference between us makes a difference. Without this little something extra, this mere trifle, we are simply acting out our differences in an adversarial exchange.

The conditions of hysteria are here insofar as we each can claim that the other sees us as we are not and that we see the other as they are not, that we objectify one another; we each can claim that we cannot say who we are, that each and the other cannot put into words what is being missed, can only note the fact that the kernel is not seen for its quality. We are fated to be condemned to an exchange of furious mutuality because we are each, both and together, tongue-tied about the attack on self that we view the other as inflicting upon us, driving us to imitate one another's aggression. The hysteria begins with the experience of presumption conveyed by the other's imposition of a classification upon us that can appear to us as motivated by the desire for an advantage. If positivism snubs us by accusing us of bias and by rejecting our work and its influence, we can show very well how they *must* do this according to their standards, policies, and laws, and so, how their representations of us and of anything else are ways and means of doing self-disclosure. We say that they do not recognize this and protect their work from such an acknowledgment. Yet, we are in this same position of doing self-reference in snubbing, accusing, and rejecting them. It is in this spirit that we search for a common problem that will enable us to position ourselves in ways that can make such differences conversational. If Christianity calls this the desire to will the common good, Hegel has identified its spirit in the *aufheben* that seeks to cancel the opposition and preserve the difference.

The symbolic order 1: bias as normal trouble

Inescapable self reference leads to the infection imagined as bias where the subject is helpless to prevent the insistence of subjectivity into each and any every word and deed; it leads to the interminable pollution of argumentation seen as ruled by competition over who should have the last word; and it leads to the haze of inconclusiveness imagined as always concealing and/or compromising the meaning behind the word and action. The nightmare of positive thinking, that the Real is capable of annulling self aggrandizement, at its worst fantasizes a subject incapable of being positive towards the present and its promise of fertility. Bias, evaluation, and snubs originated as usages and examples to analyse and in the process reveal implications relating to the fear harboured by positive thinking at its core for the remains of ambiguity.

Therefore, in the sandwich between beginning and end we sought to analyse the symbolic order of positivism using as data the three essays of Bias, Evaluation, and Snubs. Each of these three when brought to view by us was seen to reveal the regime of positivism in a different but related light. Bias accepted the value of protected speech but treated disregard of this value as grounds for accusation and we stressed the way accusatory moves such as this always make implicit reference to criteria regarded as unassailable (for all practical purposes). That a regime can be 'read' through its accusations is interesting but led us to focus upon a limited case of bias instead of the notion per se. Though agreeing that bias testifies to a belief in anonymous speech, a fear of commitment, the value of neutrality, and the like, we still needed to extract ourselves from a cycle of retribution in order to see the total picture. In later work we identified the common problem of bias to be a reflection of the inevitable partisanship of any speaker, what the Greeks called the stigma, as the particularity or 'angle' the speech showed as its inflection or specific signature (see the discussion in Blum, 2007: 40–41, 46).

Beyond the negative implications of bias as an accusation in the paper, we needed to escape from the adversarial exchange in order to appreciate the problem as one of managing and moderating the excess of partisanship that is stirred up in any strong speech as a 'normal trouble' and that invites not neutrality but the kind of distance Simmel identifies in the figure of the stranger, or in the best sense of impersonality and objectivity that is required to orient to the universality of our partisanship as a typical constraint and condition faced by a subject. Indeed, the inevitability of bias, of a particular identifying mark or signature, seems to make reference to the inescapability of the unconscious as a force in speech and to the need to develop a relation to its caprice and unruliness. The paper on bias inspired then by the impulse to display the distortion of positivism is capable now of recovering it as one particular expression of ways and means for solving the problem of the place of the unconscious in social action, and so, as an intended solution to a fundamental ethical collision.

Thus, we seemed driven by the contagiousness of mimetic violence released by the speech of positivism and its hyperbole, to miss the total picture of bias as a notion and not as a limiting case, as a path that could have moved us to overcome the transference that forced our contentiousness to imitate the single-mindedness of the other. This would have led us to recognize the play of neutrality to be more than protective but a dialogical move designed to enhance a relationship and to overcome its reciprocal violence. On one level then, bias seemed to reveal to us the distortion of positivism, but our capacity to see it as a relationship in itself allows us to overcome the temptation to fixate upon this by asking how the speaker's governance of particularity in any situation can become either or both positive or negative, a resource for creativity as in poetry or the best political action, or a fetter or constraint worthy of accusation and condemnation. This suppressed conversation that the paper on bias leaves unspoken seems to be what Hegel would call the 'real' object of inquiry.

A reflection on bias as a social form does show the capacity of any speaker in pursuit of objectives to impose a framework upon the other that organizes the relevance of all conduct for the framework in the way Goffman (1961: 20) discussed rules of irrelevance or structures of inattention or holding at bay, in everyday life. As a social form, bias permits us to enter into the extensive discourse that makes reference to how abeyances are negotiated in relation to the management and framing of the personal and particular in many areas. In this sense, positivism exemplifies the attempt to master such methods by officially legitimating as necessary for inquiry the need for being inattentive to the personal and particular, but in ways that are necessarily attentive by virtue of their methodical character. Perhaps then, from this distance, what positive speaking begins to disclose is a worldly view that treats argument, based upon what it considers proper evidence, to be a way of reconciling differences and coming to a consensus because it fears dialogue to be unending and unenjoyable compared to the ambition to conquer an opponent in argument. We could say that positivism denigrates conversation as superfluous foreplay in contrast to the phallic consummation it anticipates in the triumph of a clinching 'proof'. This permits us to use the formula of bias as one way of addressing the administration of attention and inattention, of relevance and irrelevance in speech, as a way of measuring how positivism might allocate its involvement in speech to the jouissance of administering its organization of affect, perhaps reflected in the jouissance of being consistent as reflected in the syllogism that Stanley Raffel (2013) discusses as an algorithmic vision of proof through demonstrating entailment in contrast to metaphoric play. Here, we begin to engage the question of how consistency in speech models for a subject the being of consistency in life and how such consistency is intended to reveal the mastery of regularity, reliability, and self-composure in ways that are admirable. In this way, the jouissance of administration in positivism might be understood as linked to the production of an administrative style that is capable of fusing dependability and the excitement of argument inherited from conventions of agonistic confrontation in order to affirm and sustain a positive face for its enterprise.

The symbolic order 2: evaluation as self-reference

The paper on Evaluation claims that any appraisal is a way of doing self-reference, but to say that evaluating the other is in its way a disclosure of one's own values was never news for us (think of grading, ranking, voting, choosing, and preferring of all sorts), but was an operational definition of Parmenides' maxim that All is One, in other words, that all (no matter how diverse and varied their abilities, opinions, and the like) are unified as subject to language and bearers of criteria that they enact and implement in many ways.

Instead, we suggested in the paper that the inevitable character of speaking as oriented in terms of standards that are not necessarily shared means that the attribution of deficiency to any other that assumes their imperfection to lie in failing to meet our standards can only reveal how any attribution of mistake or contradiction to them must depend upon this assumption. Again, this ignores the common problem of ambiguity as a situation of problem-solving faced by all speakers as noted in differences between speaking and saying, statement and enunciation, and the like as reflections of a collective problem of social action that is oriented to in many ways.

In our paper we pointed out the failure of positivism to concede this zone of ambiguity as a problem to address because they seemed to us to assume that it could be settled by unequivocal appeals to criteria of reasoning, evidence, and the like (as we noted in the discussion of bias). Positivism seemed to us to both accept what is called relativism *and* its insolubility through conversational means because of the remainder or infinite regress that it feared such differences to produce as they imagined the unruly darkened horizon of subjectivity. The best illustrations of this quandary are Berger and Luckmann's (1966) contrast of the Tibetan monk and the North American businessman, or MacIntyre's (1981) tiresome talk on 'alternative traditions'.

The conditions of any discourse ruled by criteria as constraints, and so, as external in some sense always invite inquiry to develop a position in relation to such criteria and the common speaking habits and clichés by which they are governed. My colleague Kieran Bonner (1998) has been trying for years to develop a conception of phronesis that overcomes such views of relativistic impasse by reimagining the strength of inconclusive conversation if reflectively attuned to the common problem our differences might reflect and that we share despite their diverse manifestations for us as a contentious landscape. The Evaluation paper confirmed that the art of inquiry always positions it between the finite and the infinite, in the middle of things, and so, while never free from such conditions, was yet always capable of acting upon them in ways that might be innovative.

In this way the Evaluation paper was capable of bringing to view a sense of the need to relate to the condition of in medias res, of intermediacy, as a beginning both topical *and* constraining. In contrast to the roadblock of relativism seen in views of social construction, we considered that our unity as speaking beings subject to fundamental ambiguity that manifests itself differently to different people must not be used as an opening for trying to convince the other to accept our idea as if we both want to reach a consensus, but as a common condition to navigate as part of our All being One. If what appears to separate us is really shared, the differences that we certainly can be said to have and also to share (according to Heraclitus' maxim that we are forever changing) need to be developed as a way of searching for the common problem that seems to inspire the discord. This common problem is an opening for conversation and not a final judgment, much in the way Freud ([1937] 1964) formulated it as an opener in his discussion of constructions or interpretations offered to the patient in the process of analysis.

Towards this end I have suggested that the usages of bias and of evaluation separately and together reflect normal and universal troubles that we can formulate in different ways as discursive masks and mirrors of collective anxiety. So it is not the trouble that is crucial, as if one of the speakers has it as a disease and the other not, but the problem of shared being that the usage displays as our common problem-solving situation (McHugh, 2005). As we say in the book at many points, the imperfection of language is the environment in which we must operate and that we now recognize not as imperfect at all but as the fundamental ambiguity of the Grey Zone in terms of which we must develop (in Kenneth Burke's (1957) sense) equipment for living (Blum, 2014/2015). Part of such equipment is the discernment for reading between the lines of speech, action, and texts of all sorts, even in hallucination and corruption, recognizing neither perpetrator nor victim but a situation of the action of problem-solving. Yet to find our voice in relation to such a search we need some sense of a resting place for doing the analysis. This requires overcoming the either/or position of critique and of complaints of bias and relativism where we might each be tempted to say what the other lacks but cannot say with respect to this what we have and what we are. This search makes reference to the method of dialogue that we engage provisionally in order to develop an analysis of the symbolic order, always trying to overcome a ruling sense of ambiguity as lack, say as Oedipal, rather than as a hole in Being. This opened the door for the paper on the snub that demonstrates how any action can and does at least two things at once.

The symbolic order 3: snubs and recognition

Even as a snub denies recognition, we said that the denial as an action *does* recognize what it denies. The word can affirm what it denies and deny what it affirms and this is due not to a deficiency of the word but to its status as an opener that is oriented to, making problematic meaning, deceit, and any sense of finality. This interpretive link between word and deed discloses the ambiguity resident in any notion of convention. In another idiom we say exclusion must include what it excludes by positing it just as inclusion must exclude what it includes by leaving many matters unspoken. This idea builds from the notion of the social fact as the phenomenon that must be oriented to even if denied, leading to quandaries that seem contradictory. It is the spine for the liar's paradox and for the age-old attacks on scepticism or atheism for having to accept what they reject in representing any content, that it exists as a social fact by virtue of being spoken and oriented to. The snub reiterates for us the maxim of Parmenides that All is One, that recognition cannot be escaped, *and* Heraclitus' notion that we cannot hide from the logos. The snub tears apart the cliché of the seen-but-unnoticed by intimating that anything must be seen to be unnoticed (the absent presence), or that we must be noticed to be unseen (the present absence). Thus, the ghost is present though absent as a stand-in for the past and its haunting memories, making the absent dead possibly present, just as the child of the present as a presence is absent in the way its promise or potential can only foretell what a future might hold (Agamben, 2010). The snub shows, unlike what positivism is said in the paper to take for granted, that recognition does not depend upon physicality, that we can be included and excluded, that is, included in ways that exclude us (think of second-class citizens, bad relationships, or not belonging at a table, as Nietzsche says), or excluded in ways that include us (think of the terrorist threat, or being remembered, or being tolerated but not liked). Even better, just as we can be present though absent as forceful influences, so can we be present but really absent if treated as a non-entity.

Yet, we approached a literal version of snub as if it displayed the positivist conception of convention. Instead of taking up this opener as an opportunity to engage the common problem, we showed again how it seemed to make positivism appear foolish compared to us. What we did not do was begin to analyse the necessity of having to begin any analysis with a caricature of the convention in the shape of a cliché (as we were doing too with positivism), a necessity that characterizes any beginning as momentum for its need to assume as generic, undeveloped, or empty the speech act that it will explore.

This tension between the word and the deed that the snub makes clear discloses meaning as an ever-present source of ambiguity that is registered in the gesture and the open-ended character of expression. If we could be denied and accepted in the same gesture, we need to reflect upon our different relationships to that problem, and as a problem for us all. For we could both accept and deny ourselves at once in ways that not only make the relation of speaking to doing problematic but the relationship of any one to the self, and of one to eternal life, death, or whatever. Could we pose the universal problem that asks the question, how might we speak about what we do, that is, put it into words, or how might we do as we say and say as we do, or do as we want or want to do as we say? The snub reveals how we must work-through anything and everything, needing and desiring to question what counts as being conclusive and inconclusive on any occasion.

In reviewing these three papers as a unit I need to ask how they each separately and together point to the form of positivism or the grounds of the jouissance that it produces and that we tended to gloss by seeing it as an adversary. In the book we spoke of a community of similar members who function as messengers for disseminating the interests of nature. This invites us to identify the jouissance of such an enterprise as the style of eroticizing the administration of law itself as a process of making that discloses its commitment to cooperation and to the progress it anticipates in an image of paradigmatic succession towards a destination marked by increments in the enlightened advance of knowledge governed by a timetable of specified milestones, accountability, transparency, and governance. The jouissance of administering a present march towards a future, this drive to engineer in such a way, revels in the making or organization directed towards very specific goals or outcomes. Such a speaker desires to excel as an administrative virtuoso, a paragon of an efficient grasp of real life, which touches us all as a skill required in order to master our sanity.

The real: people and travel

In *OBSI*, we analysed travel and art as two non-violent attempts to subvert the oppressive regime of expectations governing any social order regarding gains and losses. Further, the limits of escapist travel and even of the best of art led us to appreciate the dialogical method of our book as an alternative means for restraining violence and as a possible way of arresting or mediating the ideological exchange between normative and transgressive extremism.

At this point, people seem an unexamined issue.

(173)

This curious reminder invites us to face 'people' and the Real as a missing element as if our absorption in the transference relationship elicited by the apparatus of the symbolic order and its 'imperfect' standardization is more or less unsettled by its porous normative character as a convention that can be oriented to in many ways. 'People' seems to complicate the calculus by introducing ambiguity in a concrete rather than abstract way, forcing us to note it and to take it into account. To escape rancorous diversity positivism is said to encourage us to move about in search of respite as if looking for the relief of rest and rehabilitation or the surcease of sorrow that many pine for in retirement. Rescue is counselled not only in criteria of objectivity, but in Weberian conceptions of value relevance, in religious doctrine and many solutions. Positivism invites us to travel in search of some relief. Though we rejected such advice as escapist, we seemed to accept what we reject as we are discomforted enough to claim in a footnote (140) that 'each of us travels and likes it in certain concrete ways'. So we are decidedly nervous about having to do something of which we disapprove, nervous enough to say that we do not disapprove, nervous enough to divide ourselves into two parts as if one does while the other admonishes. As Spinoza says, humans typically know the best and pursue the worst.

In our *Introduction* to the book we formulated the process of composing a paper as the travel of such an ideal speaker through a narrative passage modelled, after conversation, as writing and revising in contrast implicitly to the conception of positive travel as movement for relief. Here, we developed a view of such a dialectic as in part the imaginary relation of a speaker to a beginning and end, first stimulated by the goal of pain relief as in positivism and then needing and desiring to engage the different sites of usage as cases that promise, if taken as such, to become occasions for challenging distinctions. The revisions we noted in each of these cases produce a glimpse of qualities required for enhancing the passage: the impersonality demanded to correct the intensity of partisanship, the discernment of a common problem for moderating the contentiousness of disagreements, and the patience coveted for inhabiting the living space of ambiguity, all reflecting together the narrative as a passage and method. The method improvises with the usage posited by relaying its grounds through an *aufheben* that overcomes the oppositions and preserves the differences, creating in this way a situation of action for a subject confronting ambiguity as if a fork in the road. In the present chapter, I revise the usage by seeing it through the eyes of an ideal speaker, that is, a speaker made to personify the collective self-understanding, the collective speech about the usage at its best, as one imagined as encountering conditions laid down by the conventions of representing the usage as if external constraints, and as so one animated by the desire to over-come their force not through flight but by reworking them or working-through their repetitions. There are three parts here: this ideal speaker is an artist, and so, by virtue of me and my art, making the two of us into a relationship. But my art that empowers me to imagine this artist is mediated by a collision of values in which the impasse created by our different orientations to the problem comes to view.

Our traveller, unlike the one imagined as governed by the positivist appetite for movement, is guided by a concern for place as a position from which to exer-cise one's voice in relation to exigencies and conditions that cannot be deter-mined with finality, a figure we called the ideal speaker. Again our traveller's passage is conceived as oriented in ways akin to Cavell's description of the destination as a place free of the 'dispersal of empty assertions' (1995: 30). Yet the Real intervenes here inflicting upon us a sense that we might not be true to ourselves, the division evoking the possibility that we could risk confusing our search for meaning (and self-knowledge) with its limited case as movement as an end itself. We note that the division is caused by the implicit and unspoken pleasure that we must get from travel, the pleasure that makes us both do it (and presumably like it) while being reserved about its good. Do we do it and like it or not and what does this mean for and to us? The Real provokes us to question (as we claim positivism does not) the relation of our words to deeds, of language to jouissance. Basic ambiguity is here, for throughout we say that ambiguity is everywhere and anywhere while our saying it is unambiguous. Travel discloses the Real as the concern for the relationship between freedom and its constraint, enjoyment and its limitation, the perpetual problem of the human subject who must come to terms with the tension between what Simmel calls sacrifice and gain, the problem prosaically of value or of the Ought. Because we cannot solve this problem, our destination must lead to finding the place for the exercise of an art that will allow us to freely cultivate our creative relation to irresolution and to do this in a way that is neither guilty for losing something or shameful for not living up to what we never had. Is this not the scene of our primary ethical colli-sion, as witness to our existence in time as the fundamental ambiguity enunci-ated by fate as mortal beings?

Again, though we might still be seen as limited by a positivist view of travel as movement inspired by a search for difference and nothing more, we pose in contrast a version of the search that we do in our very writing as a journey guided by an anticipation of recovering a settlement offering repose and intensity in a mix that might secure a new beginning in the posit of a method to frame our present. This seems to show how our search is not sheer movement but a working-through of the passage that takes on the usage in an examination much like a dialogical narrative. Travel then is made to identify our method, formu-lated in the *Introduction* and carried out in the book in the analysis of an unstated ethical collision in the symbolic order of Positivism that displays its traumatic engagement with ambiguity that has different symptoms in the three cases. Our version of the positivist relation to travel is different from the figure of the nomad conceived by Deleuze whose journey is described more strongly. Our travel through the usage and the cases revealed as a contrast to us the unconscious of positivism to be animated by an Oedipal dream of overcoming placelessness through movement towards a final essentialist destination. I cite in support of our contrasting approach Cavell (1995: 30), who says of this destination: 'the better world we think and know not to exist, is not a world that is gone … but one to be born, witnessed'.

The real: people and art

Our paper on art, designed to finish the volume, extended and applied the method of dialogue we described in the *Introduction* that was modelled after the process of writing and revision. Travel leads to art because the narrative passage leads to the place where inquiry is exercised as an art in its practice of travelling, through usage that it accepts as inviting a continuous revision of its developing formulation, created through a series of encounters for a subject imagined investing making with jouissance. The end is a place for recovering the common problem that these encounters assume and leave unspoken much like a recovery of the place as the site of an enigmatic situation that demands resolution but must remain indefinite. As an end the book returned to that beginning and in its way offered to describe our method in contrast to the enterprise we called positivism. So the method for doing this guided the travel of an ideal speaker destined to find the place of art: as suggested, the method itself was inspired by routines modelling writing and revision, improvisational theatre, and the *aufheben*. Most dramatically, we claimed to stand for art as a practice, to be bringing out inquiry as an art, and we proceeded by analysing a practice (such as positivism or any speech) as if it was a conflicted trajectory imagined for an ideal speaker conceived as struggling with conditions faced in travelling through such a passage.

I have tried to show that the hyperbolic rejection of externals described in the Art paper should be read as pointing to a conception of the imaginary of theorizing embodied in the figure of a speaker desiring to work-through speeches by translating usage into opportunities for the articulation of a style, seeing the usage as opportune in this way. The style of such work or inquiry refers not to an idiosyncratic manner of an individual, but to an inflection of the collective speech about the object. The inquirer asks – how can I find my voice in this speech, in these representations? – and puts an answer into practice by making this usage into an embodiment of collective perplexity as a problem to solve. The representations are external in the way of an inheritance. They were handed down to us imperceptibly, perhaps by chance, accident, or whatever. As art, inquiry does not deny an inheritance as psychosis might, but in seeking to find its voice in representations, must negate or rethink absolutistic gestures to disclose the 'real object'. So the analysis of usage, as we did in the book, was formulated as if the passage of an ideal speaker oriented to the art of inquiry, travelling through such an interpretive landscape to a destination marked by settling upon a resting place for the analysis of the usage. At this resting place, inquiry (we) begins to see the art in the usage by making the usage over as an expression of the singular style of the inquirer.

To produce the style in the usage (to see it as a style) is to design it as a situation that embodies the tension between its finite word(s) and the infinite perplexity it creates as a collective problem. This is exactly what I have been doing in renovating the usages of the book by translating them into relationships intended to reflect diverse and specific mirrors of a fundamental impasse in the relation of speech to action. In the Art paper we said that style was the grammar that permits us to see intention in the concrete, intelligence in the accident, orientation in the convention. In other words, to see the method of production as style permits us to identify making as meaningful (as eroticization of genesis) rather than as a causal account. To see art as producing style in this way is to see the narrative as travelling to a place where this struggle and its tensions, instabilities, and contortions becomes a site that mirrors ethical collisions.

I developed the notion of ethical collision from Hegel's theorizing of art where he speaks of art's dramatization of such tensions, but this can be misrecognized as other examples of what sociology called conflict theory or of disagreements. I connected the notion to Plato's discussion in the *Sophist* of the tension intrinsic to Being, and to Heidegger's conception of the relation of Being to becoming, appearance, and the Real in *Introduction to Metaphysics* ([1935] 2000). Yet I wanted to differ from metaphysics or even ontology by making what Heidegger called Being and the relation of the ontological to the ontic into a problem-solving situation similar to what ethnomethodology calls a member's problem that is recurrent and enigmatic in every sphere of life. Heidegger did this in part in *Being and Time* ([1927] 1962). Thus, the ethical collision, not a conflict or disagreement, is a parameter that manifests itself when its absolutistic grip upon the subject is relaxed on any occasion. Again, Cavell gives it a Wittgensteinian slant.

> Ethics is not a separate field of philosophical study, but every word that comes from us, the address of each thought, is a moral act, a taking of sides, but not in argument … but … thinking that formulates a way … in leading words back home.
>
> (1995: 28)

Our book tries to produce its style, the style of Analysis, in remaking commonplace usage and I am suggesting that in taking this risk the book tempts the extreme of limiting itself by discrediting the usage it analyses as in a zero-sum exchange. So in trying to reproduce this style of Analysis by revisiting the usage in analysing the book, I am trying to rethink this style of Analysis. For me, appreciating this style involves in part seeing its struggle to transform polemic into eloquence, its aspiration to develop its way as an art that can reinvent the taking of sides as play, as a healing touch that administers jouissance, which it does in practice by seeing in its cases their jouissance of administration.

The play of art

Each example of usage such as bias, snub, evaluation is seen as a course of action that is made, and so, as an instance of making that exhibits its freedom from externals as an undoing that does *this* and nothing else, that does the undoing of its characterization(s) in ways that accept it (say, as a cliché or formula), and modifies it in the same gesture (say, by seeing it as an expression of desire). The jouissance of such an art resides in its seeing action as being in between making and unmaking, being on the border of the security of the finite and the indefiniteness of the infinite, between what is said of and in the usage (all of the external whatnots) and what such a finite corpus might/could lead us to say of it. On art as the production of style we must read de Certeau on Lacan from a paper in 1983.

> If we were to follow Lacanian speech from its theatrical conclusion back to its psychiatric beginnings, we would find that speech traces the history of a 'style.' In fact, this theory ... develops an aesthetics, if we understand this to mean that the signifiers 'operate' by doing without the things which they seem to signify.... The analyst's ear ... makes itself attentive to the poetics which is present in every discourse: those hidden voices forgotten in the name of pragmatic and ideological interests, introduce into every statement of meaning the 'difference' of the act which utters it. The signifiers dance within the text. Loosened from the signified, they multiply, in the gaps of meaning, the rites of inquiry or response – but to which Other are they directed?
>
> (26)

Where we said that art's form of life is parasitic we meant that it dramatizes its freedom from externals by treating the conventional usage as such an external and by analysing those conventions in ways that demonstrate the togetherness and apartness of inquiry from the externals' usage. Again, '[t]he analyst's ear practices precisely on hearing the murmurs and games of these other languages' (de Certeau, 1983: 26). The freedom from externals we described in our paper is exactly this 'doing without the things which they seem to signify' that de Certeau calls loosening from the signified. Art can imagine 'doing without the things which the signifiers seem to imagine' as a way of 'loosening the hold' of the sig-nified in the way we boldly identified art's freedom from externals. The usage is both a topic and a resource for our analysis in ways that operationalize the Greek conception of *in medias res*, or being in the middle of things. The usage as the relationship between signifier and signified is inherited, and so, is both shared and open to experimentation, for it is the signifiers that are both present and absent, allowing us to intervene with them to 'do without' them *while* hearing the voices of the discourse and to recover these very same signifiers (bias, evaluation, snub, travel, art, positivism) and to 'make them dance within the text'. To see the practice as the eroticization of genesis, as a method of making in this way, is to negate the aura of necessity that the usage seems to require in order to appreciate how it is or can be designed. This is how we could say that negation is the beauty of art, that is, by seeing the production of style and the remaking of the practice as beauty in itself, such beauty begins to appear in hearing the murmurs and games of discourses and in putting such a capacity into practice. We are not science and have happily chosen the path that could lead to our development of an art of inquiry for making signifiers dance within any text and we claim to do this work by even making the signifiers of positivism do their dance. In this way, theorizing shows its style or art through analysis of the style of a practice.

Therefore, art enjoys not freedom from externals in the way of the ascetic but its articulation of freedom in this very disengagement and its play (the play of such hearing), making the externals both necessary and insufficient in the way usage and its representation is necessary as a starting point and a place for resettlement but not more, and so, making art both dependent upon such beginning and ending, and free to experiment in between. The struggle of art with externality (depicted in the usage analysed) is then its play form and is practised in the thinking that seems to revel in being in between even as it accepts and experiments with the authority by which it seems enclosed. The struggle of art resides in making this tension visible, the tension of inhabiting this space between finitude and infinite perplexity and to distinguish the way art makes from other kinds of making (see Lotringer and Virilio, 2005 on accident and interruption).

For example, in each register of the trajectory of theorizing as a passage, jouissance takes different shape as desire for consistency, and is provoked by a different contradiction or hole. Ultimately, the stigma first marking the unconscious is translated into style, or what Lacan calls a sinthome or equipment for living in the way the interpretation of usage that manages and exposes the limits of the symbolic order must be converted into the art of representing the ethical collisions that it holds in abeyance, revealing in this gesture the irresolution of art itself, that its erotic finality still needs to be tested in the present life. In this sense, the final cause is equivalent to what Lacan calls the fourth knot as the drive to deal with ambiguity by representing it as the collision around the Nothing. Here, we might imagine a world without bias, evaluation, snub, travel, art, positivism, and we make this a story by representing it in a scene ruled by infractions as aporia, and so, into cases that can disclose the necessity of ambiguity.

Conclusion

I suggest that the relation of inquiry to art problematizes making as mastery by raising the question of what Plato called the final cause in relation to the object that is made (an object unlike a painting, a sonata, a commodity, or a book such as ours), an object of jouissance and its influence. I suggest that what an art of inquiry such as ours makes is jouissance, guiding the ideal speaker to live in and through the present by inhabiting the ambiguity of the usage as both topic *and* resource. The jouissance of Analysis resides in the art of hearing what de Certeau calls the murmurs and games of any speech and of applying and remaking what is heard in representations and action. I propose that our focus on inquiry as an art of negation rather than positive speaking is meant to drive theorizing to constantly and playfully make-over commonplace speech and habits into scenes of action that we are together with and apart from, imitating the impersonality of the Simmelian stranger and not neutrality or detachment, and that can direct and engage us to do the best we can with whatever we have and hold dear. In its making, the book seeks to objectify spirit itself, risking to name the unnamable in commonplaces that are fated to be reworked and revised. Now, I have tried to do this with bias, evaluation, snub, travel, and art: I have both accepted their constraints as reflected in their commonplace discriminations and have tried to challenge these habits in order to articulate an analytic style. Further, I have taken this book itself and tried to continue it as an object of value, a bearer of style that might be remade over and again as a locus of collectivization.

I eroticize the (re)making of these usages as follows: bias discloses the unstable ambiguity of the unconscious and the need to address it rather than simply regulate it; evaluation reveals the border between conversational improvisation and the deadly intensification of resentment in argumentative acting out; the snub discloses the minor and major registers of the irresolute border between presence and absence both for the world outside and for me, myself, and I; travel depicts the trajectory of reading, writing, revising, improvisation and their overcoming and sublation. Art of course can only display the tension aroused by the motive to live with intensity and some integrity if possible, between the spirit of the book and of a book such as this, and the book of spirit that it is both fantasizing and trying impossibly to imitate, as an irreparable problem for those such as us, and those before us and to follow.

Bibliography

Agamben, Giorgio. 2010. *Nudities*. Translated by David Kishik and Stefan Pedatella. Stanford: Stanford University Press.

Baudillard, Jean. 1991. *The System of Objects*. London: Verso.

Benjamin, Walter. [1928] 1977. *The Origin of German Tragic Drama*. Translated by John Osborne. London: NLB.

Berger, Peter L. and Thomas Luckmann. 1966. *The Social Construction of Reality: A Treatise in the Sociology of Knowledge*. Garden City, NY: Anchor Books.

Blum, Alan. 1974. 'Positive Thinking'. *Theory and Society* 1 (3): 245–269.

Blum, Alan. 2007. 'Comparing Cities: On the Mutual Honouring of Peculiarities'. In *Urban Enigmas: Montreal, Toronto, and the Problem of Comparing Cities*, edited by Johanne Sloan, 15–51. Montreal: McGill-Queen's University Press.

Blum, Alan. 2014/2015. 'Guide(s) for the Perplexed: Science and Literature as Equipment for Living'. *Philosophy and Rhetoric* 48: 54–72.

Bonner, Kieran. 1998. *Power and Parenting: A Hermeneutic of the Human Condition*. New York: St. Martin's Press.

Burke, Kenneth. 1957. *The Philosophy of Literary Form*. Berkeley: University of California Press.

Cavell, Stanley. 1995. *Philosophical Passages: Wittgenstein, Emerson, Austin, Derrida*. Oxford: Blackwell's.

de Certeau, Michel. 1984. *The Practice of Everyday Life*. Berkeley: University of California Press.

Derrida, Jacques. 1994. *Specters of Marx*. New York: Routledge.

Durkheim, Émile. [1895] 1938. *The Rules of Sociological Method*. Edited by George E.G. Catlin. Translated by Sarah A. Solovay and John H. Mueller. Glencoe, IL: The Free Press.

Erasmus, Desiderius. [1512] 1963. *On Copia of Words and Ideas*. Translated by Donald B. King and H. David Rix. Milwaukee: Marquette University Press.

Freud, Sigmund. [1937] 1964. 'Constructions in Analysis'. In *The Standard Edition of the Complete Psychological Works of Sigmund Freud*, translated and edited by James Strachey, 255–269. London: Hogarth.

Garfinkel, Harold. 1967. *Studies in Ethnomethodology*. Englewood Cliffs, NJ: Prentice Hall.

Goffman, Erving. 1961. *Encounters: Two Studies in the Sociology of Interaction – Fun in Games & Role Distance*. Indianapolis, Bobbs-Merrill.

Goffman, Erving. 1967. *Behavior in Public Places*. Glencoe, IL: The Free Press.

Hegel, G.W.F. 1955. *The Phenomenology of Mind, Second Edition*. Translated by J.B. Baillie. London: Allen & Unwin.

Heidegger, Martin. [1927] 1962. *Being and Time*. Translated by John Macquarrie and Edward Robinson. Oxford: Blackwell.

Heidegger, Martin. [1935] 2000. *Introduction to Metaphysics*. Translated by Gregory Fried and Richard Polt. New Haven: Yale University Press.

Lacan, Jacques. [1969–1970] 2007. *The Seminar of Jacques Lacan Book XVII: The Other Side of Psychoanalysis: The Seminar of Jacques Lacan*. New York: W.W. Norton.

Laplanche, Jean. 1999. *Essays on Otherness*. New York: Routledge.

Lotringer, Sylvère and Paul Virilio. 2005. *The Accident of Art*. Translated by Mike Taormina. Cambridge, MA: MIT Press.

MacIntyre, Alasdair. 1981. *After Virtue: A Study in Moral Theory*. Notre Dame, IN: University of Notre Dame Press.

McHugh, Peter. 2005. 'Shared Being, Old Promises, and the Just Necessity of Affirmative Action'. *Human Studies* 28 (2): 129–156.

McHugh, Peter, Alan Blum, Stanley Raffel, and Daniel C. Foss. 1974. *On the Beginning of Social Inquiry*. London: Routledge and Kegan Paul.

Merleau-Ponty, Maurice. 2005. *Phenomenology of Perception*. Translated by Colin Smith. London: Routledge.

Parsons, Talcott. 1966. *Societies: Evolutionary and Comparative Perspectives*. Englewood Cliffs, NJ: Prentice Hall.

Raffel, Stanley. 2013. *The Method of Metaphor*. Bristol: Intellect Press.

Sartre, Jean-Paul. 1963. *Search for a Method*. Translated by Hazel E. Barnes. New York: Random House.

Schutz, Alfred. [1953] 1973. 'Common Sense and Scientific Interpretation'. In *Collected Papers, Volume 1: The Problem of Social Reality*, edited by Maurice A. Natanson, 7–34. The Hague: Martinus Nijhoff.

Simmel, Georg. [1918] 2010. *The View of Life: Four Metaphysical Essays with Journal Aphorisms*. Translated by John A.Y. Andrews and Donald N. Levine. Chicago: University of Chicago Press.

Toews, Miriam. 2014. *All My Puny Sorrows*. Toronto: Knopf Canada.

Index of names

www.ingramcontent.com/pod-product-compliance
ngram Content Group UK Ltd.
field, Milton Keynes, MK11 3LW, UK
HW020359010325
577UK00021B/534